Technology and Gender

D1603251

A

Philip E. Lilienthal

B   O   O   K

---

*The Philip E. Lilienthal imprint honors
special books in commemoration of a
man whose work at the University of
California Press from 1954 to 1979 was
marked by dedication to young authors,
and to high standards in the field of
Asian Studies. Friends, family, authors,
and foundations have together endowed
the Lilienthal Fund, which enables the
Press to publish under this imprint
selected books in a way that reflects the
taste and judgment of a great and
beloved editor.*

Technology and Gender

*Fabrics of Power in
Late Imperial China*

FRANCESCA BRAY

University of California Press

BERKELEY   LOS ANGELES   LONDON

University of California Press
Berkeley and Los Angeles, California

University of California Press, Ltd.
London, England

© 1997 by
The Regents of the University of California
Library of Congress Cataloging-in-Publication Data

Bray, Francesca.
    Technology and gender : fabrics of power in late imperial China /
Francesca Bray.
        p.   cm.
    "A Philip E. Lilienthal book."
    Includes bibliographical references and index.
    ISBN 0-520-20685-1 (alk. paper). — ISBN 0-520-20861-7
(pbk. : alk. paper)
        1. Sex roles—China—History. 2. Women—China—Social condi-
tions. 3. Technology—Social aspects—China—History. 4. China—
Social conditions—960–1644. 5. China—Social conditions—1644–1912.
I. Title.
HQ1768.B72   1997
305.3'0951—dc20   96-28828
                                                                        CIP

Printed in the United States of America
9 8 7 6 5 4 3 2 1

The paper used in this publication meets the minimum requirements of
American National Standard for Information Sciences—Permanence of
Paper for Printed Library Materials, ANSI Z39.48-1984.

The following chapters are revised versions of materials published elsewhere: chapter 5: "Le travail féminin dans la Chine impériale: sur
l'élaboration de nouveaux motifs dans le tissu social," *Annales, Histoire, Sciences Sociales* 49, 4 (July–Aug. 1994): 783–816; chapter 6:
"Textile production and gender roles in China, 1000–1700," *Chinese Science* 12 (1995): 113–35; and chapter 7: "A deathly disorder: understanding women's health in late imperial China," in *Knowledge and the
scholarly medical traditions*, ed. Donald Bates (Cambridge: Cambridge
University Press, 1995). These revised versions are reprinted here by
permission.

Seal used as text ornament by Wu Jinyang.

For Joseph

Map 1. Central provinces of modern China

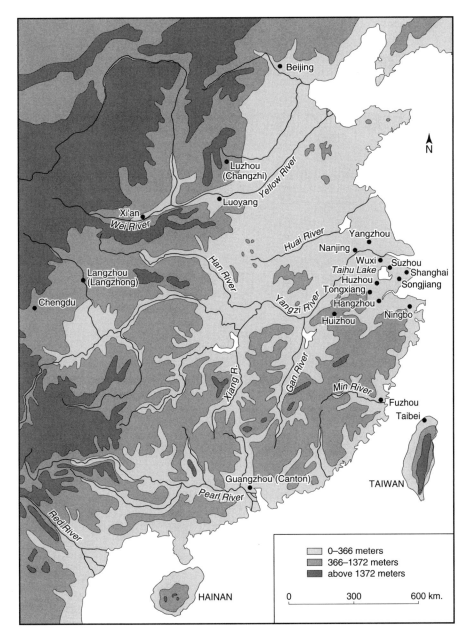

Map 2. Relief map of China

Contents

Illustrations and Table

Maps

Figures

Table

Chinese Dynasties

Zhou	1066–221 B.C.
Spring and Autumn period	722–481 B.C.
Warring States	c. 403–221 B.C.
Qin	221–206 B.C.
Han	206 B.C.–A.D. 220
Three Kingdoms	220–80
Six Dynasties	222–589
Northern and Southern Dynasties	317–589
Sui	581–618
Tang	618–907
Five Dynasties	907–60
Northern Song	960–1127
Southern Song	1127–1279
Yuan	1279–1368
Ming	1368–1644
Qing	1644–1911
Republic of China	1911–49

Acknowledgments

Several institutions have provided generous financial support for the research that went into this project. I would like to thank the National Science Foundation Program for the History of Technology for funding a year of research leave; Ronald Overmann of the NSF and Norton Wise of the Center for the History of Science at the University of California at Los Angeles helped me formulate my project in terms acceptable to scientists. The Center for Chinese Studies and the Center for Pacific Rim Studies of the University of California at Los Angeles provided funds for research assistance, and I also received research support funds from the UCLA Academic Senate and from the University of California at Santa Barbara. The Departments of Anthropology at UCLA and UCSB kindly allowed me to take research leave. I spent three months as a visiting fellow at the Sinologische Institut of the University of Würzburg working on the project, and a little later a month as a visiting fellow at the Ecole des Hautes Etudes en Sciences Sociales in Paris presenting my ideas as a seminar series; for arranging these two delightful and stimulating episodes I would like to thank Dieter Kuhn and Viviane Alleton. And thanks to the kind support of John Pickstone and of the Wellcome Trust for the History of Medicine I was able to spend almost two years at the Centre for the History of Science, Technology and Medicine at the University of Manchester, during which time I completed the section of the book on reproductive technologies.

The University of California Board of Pacific Rim Studies funded the international conference "Gender and Sexuality in East and Southeast Asia." Coorganizing this conference and presenting a paper on reproduction in China provided a crash education in feminist discourses and their pretensions; I am very grateful to Sue Fan and especially to Emily Ooms for support and instruction. In a more relaxed vein, I organized two work-shops on technology and culture under the auspices of the Maison des Sciences de l'Homme in Paris, one concentrating on China, the second expanding our comparative scope to the Andes. Both were extremely stimulating and productive, and I would like to thank the Director of the MSH, Maurice Aymard, for making them possible.

This book is the outcome of many years of border crossings, between disciplines and between countries. I think of it as a piece of California cuisine: Chinese ingredients cooked in an American kitchen with French sauce. No doubt several of the people I thank here will wonder what they have contributed, and inevitably I have not included everyone I should. My main intellectual debts are to Joseph Needham and the international group of scholars connected with his project *Science and Civilisation in China;* to André-Georges Haudricourt, Lucien Bernot, and the scholars of technology and culture who worked with them at the Centre National de la Recherche Scientifique in Paris; and to the American feminist scholars whom I met when I arrived in California. For help, criticism and sugges-tions I would like to thank Viviane Alleton, Barbara Bray, Carole Browner, Craig Clunas, Sophie Desrosiers, Roger Friedland, Ramón Guardans, Jack Goody, Suzanne Gottschang, Richard Gunde, Elvin Hatch, Dorothy Ko, Dieter Kuhn, James Lee, Sheila Levine, Harvey Molotch, Ellen Pader, Frank Perlin, Saito Osamu, François Sigaut, Nathan Sivin, Donald Wagner, Ellen Widmer, Pierre-Etienne Will, two anonymous reviewers for the University of California Press, and most particularly Susan Mann, who also acted as reader for the press and gave me most generous advice as well as showing me her own work in progress. Most generous of all was Charlotte Furth, who introduced me to the Chinese gynecological tradition and freely shared not only her ideas but also her research materi-als, including medical case studies; over the years we have explored so many themes that sometimes I forget who thought of what, so I hope she will forgive me if I sometimes lay claim to one of her ideas by mistake. I was also fortunate in having excellent research assistants who entered into the spirit of my project with enthusiasm and imagination: thanks to Yuan-ling Chao, Chu Pingyi, Hsiao Lien-hui, Mayumi Yamamoto, Alison Sau-chu Yeung and Zhang Da for their creative contributions. And above all thanks to Sandy Robertson, for the sternest criticisms and the most fertile ideas.

Introduction

The Framework of Everyday Life: Technology, Women and Cultural History

It must I think be perfectly clear that to understand lives, the ordinary activities of human beings in ages other than our own, it is indispensable to consider the technologies that served them, for they formed in many respects the very framework of those lives themselves.

Jack Simmons, *History of Technology*

Among the most popular exhibits in local and national museums are the displays of everyday objects, the sets of craftsmen's tools and the reconstructions of kitchens or workshops that allow the visitor not just to view each step in the making of a cheese, a cart or a bolt of cloth, but to envision a world.[1] The glass cases, the roped-off spaces and "Do not touch" notices are far more frustrating here than the enforced separation between viewer and painting in an art gallery, for in the case of artifacts we feel strongly that the key to deciphering these tokens of the past is physical: if we can actually pick these ordinary objects up, weigh them in our hands, try them out (if only on the air), the physical experience will translate us back into the world in which they belonged, an everyday world of working, making and consuming that made up the lives of ordinary people. Enlightened museum curators recognize the urgency of this need for physical communion and provide some working machines where visitors can take turns with the trained and costumed personnel, fumbling for a few minutes at a loom or potter's wheel, then compensating for their incapacity by purchasing the "authentic" artifact in the museum shop.

For ordinary people the fascination of old technologies is that they seem to convey the core experiences of past lives. But conventional history of technology is rigid and reductive in its dealings with this rich world of

---

1. Throughout this book, I almost invariably use the masculine form of terms such as *craftsmen, kinsmen, man,* and so on, because in the Chinese context they refer to males.

meaning. It focuses on the production of commodities and the development of scientific knowledge, and relies on categories of analysis like "relations of production," "stock of knowledge" or input-output ratios. Nor is *technology* in the crude material sense a word to conjure with in social or cultural history, in fact it is quite out of fashion. We decode the sexual body and the gendered body as cultural artifacts, but despite routine allusions to Michel Foucault's "technologies of power" or to Pierre Bourdieu's concept of habitus, only a few historians pay serious heed to another fundamental level at which epistemes and relations of power are embodied: the everyday technologies that shape material worlds.

Every human society constructs for itself a world of food, shelter, clothing and other goods, a domain of material experience that is often richly and diversely documented in words, in numbers, in pictures and in artifacts. From these sources we can piece together a historical text that records the changing patterns and textures of a social fabric. We can tease out the strands that wove rulers and subjects, artisans and merchants, peasants and landlords, wives and husbands into interlocking patterns of hierarchy. We can try to retrieve the messages conveyed by technical practices and products, to see how social roles were naturalized through that most powerful form of indoctrination, the bodily habit. We can set these systems of material practice and experience against written formulations of metaphysics and ethics to explore the mutual penetration of ideology and popular belief. To read this immensely rich text creatively, to recover the meanings of the shifts, negotiations and ruptures that it records, we must go beyond the terms of conventional history of technology to analyze a society's technologies as part of a web of political and cultural practices.

This book explores the role of technology in shaping and transmitting ideological traditions, focusing on the contribution of technology to the construction of gender. The case I take as my illustration is late imperial China from the Song to the Qing, a society for whose material culture we possess an extraordinarily rich legacy of documentation.

Despite wars and invasions, natural disasters, dramatic population changes and economic growth, the social system in China between A.D. 1000 and 1800 displayed remarkable continuity.[2] From the Song to the

---

2. I have chosen to conclude my study before the nineteenth century, when China suffered the massive impact of Western economic and political demands and of exposure to Western ideas. Despite its weakness during the nineteenth century, however, the Qing dynasty survived until 1911, when the imperial era ended.

Qing the vision and indeed the practice of the basic political order remained essentially unchanged: the emperor ruled the common people through a bureaucracy staffed by scholars; as the economy became increasingly commercialized merchants grew in number and wealth, but they never gained political influence as a class, largely because their ambition was to join the ranks of the scholar gentry. This long period of continuity, which historians of the economy and of technology have tended to view as stagnation, is regarded by political, cultural and intellectual historians as something of a miracle. Given China's huge size, its social complexity and regional diversity, the effects of population growth and the violent shocks of war and invasion to which it was repeatedly subjected, not to mention the differences between the elite and the uneducated, how can we account for the fact that the culture of late imperial China became so well integrated and durable, and that people at every level of society had so much in common?

True, the political structure and modes of production in late imperial China were not dramatically transformed in the way that the social structures of early modern Europe were by the emergence of capitalism and the industrial revolution. But given the enormous shocks and challenges that the Chinese social order managed to absorb and contain over the centuries, the continuities that have often been labeled inertia or stagnation are better understood as resilience: they represent complex processes of cultural negotiation, incorporation and adaptation, the forging of symbols, identities and roles that eventually came to be accepted at all levels of society throughout a vast and heterogeneous empire. In recent years historians and anthropologists have worked hard to unravel and interpret these processes of cultural reproduction. I suggest that the study of technology can significantly enrich our understanding of such processes.

I am particularly interested in how technologies contribute to producing people and relations between people, which in turn requires me to look at technology as a form of communication. Taken overall, a society's technology gives out as many mixed messages as any other aspect of its culture: a study of a country's coal-mining industry will provide very different insights into the social formation from a study of cookery. Here I work on the premise that it is possible to identify within a particular society significant *sets* of technologies that constitute *systems*, providing overlapping messages about a particular kind of person. These messages are not necessarily identical even within one technological domain, and certainly not within the set. They operate at different levels, they present variations and contradictions; their power lies in the flexibility this permits, the rich scope for "practice," for accommodating or expressing both synchronic differences and historical change.

This book looks at a set of technologies that one might call, in the spirit of Lewis Mumford, a *gynotechnics:* a technical system that produces ideas about women, and therefore about a gender system and about hierarchical relations in general. In this Chinese example of gynotechnics I include three technological domains that were particularly important in giving shape and meaning to the lives of women in late imperial China: the building of houses, the weaving of cloth, and the producing of children.[3] The relations between women and technology have usually been ignored in Chinese history, as elsewhere, and when I started to search for original sources I was surprised to find just how much there was. In concentrating on technologies that directly affected women's lives and identities, I have been able to explore not only what they can tell us about ideas and experiences of women and femininity, but also what we can infer about constructions of masculinity and of difference, and therefore about the changing organization of Chinese society as a whole.

Part 1 of the book looks at the material shell of family life. It analyzes the building of houses and the complex structuring of domestic space that embodied in microcosm the hierarchies of gender, generation and rank inherent to the Chinese social order, tying all its occupants into the macrocosm of the polity. Although women did not build the houses in which they lived in the sense of assembling bricks and mortar, they played an active role in the production of domestic space, which they experienced in ways very different from their menfolk. The evolution of domestic spatial practices during the later imperial period can be seen as the production of a text with multiple grammars, female as well as male, that could simultaneously accommodate popular visions of cosmos and society and the secular orthodoxy of the educated elite. Increasing numbers of women lived in strict physical seclusion, but orthodox ideology continued to insist on the importance of their contributions to the world outside and to the social order. The nature and readings of women's moral, human and material contributions altered in the course of the late imperial period, however, as

---

3. No doubt food preparation and cookery should also have been included, but I was not sure I would be able to find enough solid information, particularly about the roles of men and women in cooking. Françoise Sabban, a historian of Chinese dietetics and food preparation, informs me that she has found very few sources for any period that provide unequivocal information about the sexual division of labor in cooking.

the balance between what we would consider productive roles (part 2) and reproductive roles (part 3) shifted.

Part 2 penetrates inside the walls of the house to examine the meanings of the productive work that took place there. It focuses on historical changes in the production of cloth, traditionally a female domain construed in terms of complementarity to the male domain of farming.[4] Up to the Song the social contract between state and people was embodied in a fiscal regime based on the working couple, in which husband and wife contributed equally—he in grain and she in cloth—to the upkeep of the state. All women, even noblewomen, worked in the production of textiles. In the course of the late imperial period, however, the textile sector became increasingly commercialized and specialized; new forms of organization of production meant that commoner women's work in textiles was marginalized, while upper-class women abandoned spinning and weaving for embroidery. In classic Engelsian terms, one would expect the reduction in the recognized value of women's productive labor to bolster patriarchal control by allowing women to be represented primarily as reproducers dependent on men and living separate from the male, public world. In certain respects Engels's hypothesis holds for late imperial China; however, we must also take into account the fact that many elite men of the later Ming and Qing tried strenuously to reverse the trend by bringing women back into textile production. By now ordinary working families saw work, whether by men or by women, chiefly in economic terms, but for statesmen and philosophers "womanly work" in textiles was an indispensable moral contribution to the social order; its practical importance was that it protected families from destitution and allowed them to pay their taxes. We see an interesting divergence between popular forms of

4. Farm work in China was represented as a male activity (fig. 2). Women's real involvement in work in the fields was extremely limited compared with most of sub-Saharan Africa, where farming is women's work, and also with neighboring regions such as Southeast Asia or Japan, where tasks like transplanting rice or harvesting were often construed as mainly female. When a member of the male elite in imperial China noticed women working in the fields he saw it as unnatural, a symbol of profound social and moral disorder. So although women did in reality participate in all kinds of field work, from picking cotton (fig. 16) to plucking tea to harvesting grain, written and visual representations of farming generally masked this role. It is often asserted that Chinese women were physically unable to work outside the house because of their bound feet, but in fact foot binding restricted mobility much less than we imagine and did not prevent women from participating at least occasionally in almost every kind of field work except wet-rice cultivation.

patriarchy, in which women's childbearing role became increasingly prominent, and an elite orthodoxy that continued to represent an ideal world as one in which women (or at least wives) contributed actively to the maintenance of the polity.

Part 3 focuses on the women's quarters and the marital chamber. It looks at conceptions of the body and at the repertory of medical and social techniques that were available to women of different rank and class in pursuit of maternal status. I argue that fertility, far from determining the fate of every woman in "traditional China," must be understood in the context of a wider ideology of "nature" versus "culture" that defined male as well as female ideals and expressed differences in class even more clearly than it did those in sex. Once again we see a divergence between elite and popular ideals of femininity and forms of patriarchy. In poor households that could not afford the luxury of polygyny, all the burdens of the wifely role fell on a single woman, whose performance was likely to be judged by her natural fertility. For many elite women, however, social motherhood was more important than giving birth, since they were legally entitled to appropriate any children fathered by their husband on concubines or maids. I argue further that if we combine all the reproductive responsibilities of women in late imperial China, we see that the role of mother was subordinate to the overarching feminine role of wife. According to elite orthodoxy, both as a wife and as a mother a woman made active and indispensable contributions to the social order beyond the walls of the inner chambers. A wife's role was still represented as "the fitting *partner*" [5] of her husband. But although almost all women were attached to men, by no means all of them were legal wives. The ideals of reproduction thus reinforced class differences and exploitation not just of women by men, but of women by women, and of class by class.

Bringing together the spaces Chinese women of different class, rank and age inhabited, the work they did or did not do, and the ways in which they struggled to fulfill demanding reproductive roles while protecting their own health and life gives a new density and definition to the complex historical negotiations of gender and other social hierarchies that underpinned the political continuities of late imperial China. As a set they help us understand how historical redefinitions of domesticity, of gender roles, of the meanings of concepts like "wife" and "mother," of differences among classes, and of the relations between orthodoxy and popular custom took on the powerful shape of material practices.

5. *Book of Rites*, tr. Kuhn 1988: 20.

In two senses this book is an attempt to recover a history for a people without history. First, historians of technology treat non-Western societies as having not histories, but an absence of history. And second, women are invisible in most history of technology. In the case of China, historians who have studied Chinese technology agree that after an initial flowering up to about 1400, during which time it surpassed Europe in productive capacity and inventiveness, China fell into a period of stagnation and decline—a failure to generate the significant qualitative change that constitutes real history. Furthermore, today's conventional representations of "traditional" Chinese gender roles characterize women primarily as biological *reproducers* and as passive consumers or victims of patriarchal ideology. Their roles as *producers*, whether of commodities, of knowledge, or of ideology, have been marginalized and neglected. Since conventional history of technology focuses primarily on the production of commodities and the development of scientific knowledge, it follows that histories of technology in China pay almost no attention to women or to gender, whereas histories of Chinese women seldom even mention technology.

As conventionally defined and studied—that is, as a system of knowledge and equipment that allows more or less efficient production of material goods and control over the environment—technology is a central element in the discourse of Western superiority. More perhaps than any other branch of history, the history of technology retains a colonialist mentality. "For historians of technology, the 'master narrative' is the whig reading of Western technological evolution as inevitable and autonomous," writes John Staudenmaier, referring to Joan Wallach Scott's definition of master narrative, or historical received opinion, as an account of the past "based on the forcible exclusion of others' stories." In this epistemological framework, Western technology becomes a symbol in a structured hierarchy that opposes modern to traditional, active to passive, progress to stagnation, science to ignorance, West to rest, and male to female. Just as female is not-male, a looking glass that sets off the male image to advantage, so other societies and their technologies are not-West, a flattering mirror in which the West can contemplate its virtues.[6] By definition negatives of the original, the features of such mirror images can by and large be deduced: there is no need to accord them the same painstaking attention that the history of Western technology commands.

6. Staudenmaier 1990: 725; Scott 1989: 690; for an analysis of how technology is used as a symbol of Western preeminence and a justification for imperialism, see Adas 1989.

There have, of course, been serious historical studies of indigenous technology in non-Western societies. Joseph Needham's project on China, the first volume of which appeared in 1954, was the pioneering work that set the stage for a radical venture. Rather than cobbling material from different periods together to assemble patchwork images of a timeless, undifferentiated Chinese past, Needham used the wealth of sources he had collected to show how things changed with time. This was the first serious historical study by a scientist of non-Western science and technology,[7] and it has been absolutely fundamental in challenging ahistorical representations of non-Western societies. Still, it constitutes a first step rather than a critical revolution.

Needham's explicit purpose in devising the multivolume series *Science and Civilisation in China* was to demonstrate that real science and technology were not the unique products of European minds—that the history of modern science and technology was in fact a world history. His strategy was to divide Chinese knowledge into the disciplinary branches of modern Western science, pure and applied. Technologies were among the applied sciences. Thus astronomy was classified as applied mathematics, engineering as applied physics, alchemy as applied chemistry, and agriculture (the technical domain entrusted to me for the *Science and Civilisation* series) was classified as applied botany.[8] Himself a distinguished scientist, Needham was able to argue convincingly that China preceded Europe in a number of important discoveries and inventions—including documenting the three Chinese inventions that Francis Bacon associated with the birth of the modern world: printing, the magnetic compass, and gunpowder.[9]

7. Encyclopedic studies like those by Singer et al. (1954–78) or by Gille (1978b) either provide largely ahistorical glimpses of technology in non-Western societies or take it for granted that they were essentially static and argue why that should be.

8. For astronomy as applied mathematics see Needham and Wang Ling 1959; engineering as applied physics, Needham and Wang Ling 1966; alchemy as applied chemistry (a view strongly criticized by Nathan Sivin), Needham, Ho Ping-Yü and Lu Gwei-Djen 1976; and agriculture as applied botany, Bray 1984. I worked at Needham's East Asian History of Science Library in Cambridge (now called the Needham Research Institute) between 1973 and 1984 and have remained involved in the *Science and Civilisation in China* project ever since. I share with many of my colleagues there a strong commitment to carrying the project on to a further stage.

9. In fact Needham's claim that the magnetic compass was introduced from China to Europe is only circumstantial. Nor is it clear that Chinese woodblock printing was the direct inspiration for Gutenberg's movable type. But even if the precision of these claims has subsequently been called into question, there is no doubt that it was a brilliant move to invoke Bacon in this way.

Furthermore, Needham was able to construct convincing historical narratives of intellectual progress in all the scientific and technological categories covered in *Science and Civilisation in China,* although he felt that the extraordinary creativity and inventiveness of the Song dynasty (960–1279) died away in succeeding centuries, to be followed by a long period (from about 1400 or 1500 up to the nineteenth-century confrontations with the Western powers) during which China contributed little or nothing to the growth of world scientific knowledge.

Needham's project and its methods have been extremely influential both within and beyond the profession of history of science and technology. His work was warmly welcomed in China, and also in India, as a means of restoring national self-respect; both countries have now established institutions to study the history of indigenous science and technology. And in the West children now learn from their high school textbooks that the Chinese invented gunpowder and fireworks. Nevertheless, the teleology inherent in Needham's project raises two serious problems. First, accepting the evolutionary model of a family tree of knowledge whose branches correspond to the disciplines of modern science allows Needham to identify Chinese forebears or precursors of modern science and technology, but at the price of disembedding them from their cultural and historical context. One could caricature this as a Jack Horner approach to history, picking out the plums and ignoring the rest of the pie. It emphasizes "discoveries" and "innovations" in a way that is likely to distort understanding of the broader context of skills and knowledge of the period. It distracts attention from other elements that may now seem dead-end, irrational, less effective or less intellectually exciting but may have been more important, more widely disseminated or more influential at the time.[10]

Second, taking the scientific and industrial revolution as a natural outcome of human progress leads us to judge all historical systems of skills and knowledge by criteria derived from this specifically European experience. The rise of capitalism, the birth of modern science and the industrial revolution are so closely intertwined in our intellects that we find it difficult to separate the concept of technology from science,[11] or to think

10. See, for example, Pinch and Bijker 1987 on "closure" and on the interest of studying trails that came to a dead end.

11. Historians, sociologists and philosophers of science and technology nowadays recognize that it is best to consider the two domains as representing different kinds of knowledge, reasoning and skills; however, a more popular view of the relationship between the two is still that technology is applied science.

imaginatively about trajectories of technical development that emphasize other criteria than engineering sophistication, scale economies or increased output. Any deviation from this narrow path then has to be explained in terms of failure, of history grinding to a halt. Societies that produced undeniably sophisticated technical repertoires but failed to follow the European path to the same conclusion—such as the medieval Islamic world, the Inca empire, or imperial China—are then subjected to the so-called Needham question and its correlates: Why did they not go on to generate indigenous forms of modernity? What went wrong? What was missing? What were the intellectual or character failings of that culture?[12]

After six multipart volumes (altogether about twenty separate books) detailing what the various branches of Chinese scientific and technical knowledge achieved, the three parts of the final and as yet unfinished seventh volume of *Science and Civilisation in China* are devoted to addressing the "Needham question," offering a constellation of linguistic, epistemological, social and political explanations for China's failure to build on its impressive medieval achievements and generate a modern society. Taking the Needham position a step further, Mark Elvin argued in *The Pattern of the Chinese Past* that exogenous forces were necessary (in the form of the impact of Western imperialism) to open China to a phase of true progress.

Needham's arguments, and Elvin's, have been widely if selectively drawn on by economic historians, comparative sociologists and historians of Western science and technology not as the essential first step to open up a critical world history of science and technology, but to confirm versions of the master narrative. Paradoxically, historians of science and technology can continue to ignore what happened in other societies precisely because of pioneering work by scholars like Needham—because the questions they set out to answer about China, or India, or Islam were framed in the terms set by the master narrative. In a sense, this absolutely foun-

---

12. Gille (1978b) lists China, the Muslim world and pre-Columbian America under his heading of "blocked systems." The Muslim world has perhaps suffered most explicitly from Orientalist gendered contrasts. It is commonly depicted as a *passive* repository of Greek learning rather than a realm with many outstanding centers of learning that actively advanced scholarship. The reconquest of Moorish Spain is represented in more than one study as the natural outcome of a confrontation between the passive, luxurious and effeminate worldview of the Muslims, congenitally unable to reap the full benefits of the rich heritage of Greece and Rome, and the virile, aggressive, questing culture of Christian Europe (e.g., Crow 1985; Mokyr 1990).

dational work has been sadly underexploited; in another sense, it has been sadly exploited. Within the discipline of history of technology, the differences between Europe and China or other non-Western societies are taken not as a challenge to recover other cultures of knowledge and power with different goals and values, but simply as confirmation that only the West is truly dynamic and therefore worthy of study.

As an indication of how serious the neglect of non-Western societies remains within the discipline, Staudenmaier pointed to the official journal of the Society for the History of Technology, *Technology and Culture*. Of the articles published between 1958 (when it was founded) and 1980, only 6 percent dealt with non-Western societies; after 1980 the figure dropped to 3 percent.[13] As another example, reading the program for a four-day international conference entitled "Technological Change" (held in Oxford in 1994), I noticed that of about a hundred papers, two or three dealt with some form of West-to-East technology transfer, and there was a theoretical session on evolutionary models of technological development; otherwise there were no papers dealing with non-Western technologies.

James Clifford has noted how ethnographic museums put together exhibits by selecting artifacts according to categories that fulfill Western expectations of a "primitive" or "traditional" society, thus creating the illusion of adequate representation.[14] Until one questions the underlying master narrative, the conventional history of technology—and the economic history and comparative sociology that draw on it for material grounding—succeed in creating this illusion of adequate representation. The technological histories of non-Western societies are depicted as faltering steps along a natural path of progress that only the West has trodden boldly to the end. Sometimes these alien technological systems are shown as coming up against insuperable cultural obstacles to further development, sometimes they are treated as inherently inert. The focus is always on what they failed to do, rather than on whether and how they met the goals, values and purposes of the society that generated them.

A critical history of technology should explore the local meanings of technological systems not in order to construct comparative hierarchies (and perpetuate ethnocentric judgments), but seriously to study alternative constructions of the world. The criteria in general use for evaluating technological success are seldom treated as culturally relative, but in fact, as Marx long ago made clear, they are an ideological product of our own

13. Staudenmaier 1990: 724.
14. Clifford 1988: 220.

history. If we assume that real technology is inseparable from experimental science, if we judge technical efficiency by mechanical sophistication, by the productivity of labor and of capital, by the scale of operation and the reduced number of human agents on the assembly line or in the field, if we think growth and change are more advanced than stability or continuity, it is because that is how our modern Western world was made.

But other worlds were made in other ways. How did past societies see their worlds and their place in them, what were their needs and desires, what role did technology play in creating and fulfilling those desires, in maintaining and reshaping the social fabric?[15] Such questions should provide the framework for exploring the technologies of non-Western societies. How else can we dispel the illusion of adequate representation and look at people in other worlds as something more (and more interesting) than benighted fools?

> There is a story, repeated by a number of Roman writers, that a man—characteristically unnamed—invented unbreakable glass and demonstrated it to Tiberius in anticipation of a great reward. The emperor asked the inventor whether anyone shared his secret and was promptly assured that there was no one else; whereupon his head was promptly removed, lest, said Tiberius, gold be reduced to the value of mud.

To a Roman mind, M. I. Finley says, this did not mean that Tiberius was an idiot blind to new ideas, still less did it mean that he or the Roman ruling class despised wealth. What did this tale signify then? "We must remind ourselves time and time again," writes Finley, "that the European experience since the late Middle Ages in technology, in the economy, *and in the value systems that accompanied them,* was unique in human history until the recent export trend began. Technical progress, economic growth, productivity, even efficiency have not been significant goals since the beginning of time . . . other values held the stage."[16] How then can we reconstruct those other values?

It is not surprising that some of the most fruitful approaches to the interpretation of technology have come from anthropologists, since anthropology is a discipline committed to investigating other systems of meaning. What is surprising, however, is how marginal this domain of experience remains in mainstream anthropology, especially in the English-speaking world. As Pierre Lemonnier remarks, "It has been some

---

15. In the contemporary world, the Greens offer one example of an attempt to construct a world around noncapitalist values and desires.

16. Finley 1973: 147, emphasis added.

decades since the interest in what was, in the 1930s, rightly called 'material *culture'* declined, and for years France has been alone in developing institutionalized research in the anthropology of techniques."[17] The French tradition grew out of a Durkheimian interest in *mentalités*. Marcel Mauss, a student of Durkheim, founded the tradition with a study of an aspect of technological experience that might surprise conventional historians of technology, namely "techniques of the body." Reflecting a deep concern among French social scientists to connect language, psychology and social norms, Mauss discussed bodily deportment and gestures as learned cultural practices and as a form of communication.[18] In the French ethnological tradition, technology has continued to be studied as a form of symbolic communication and cultural reproduction.[19] But even within French ethnology, technology remains a specialist domain rather than an integral part of cultural interpretation.[20]

The *Annales* school of history has also, in its many avatars, shown a consistent concern with exploring how material production and material culture relate to social, psychological and symbolic dimensions of meaning.[21] The preeminent example is Fernand Braudel's *Civilisation matérielle, économie et capitalisme*, which treats eating habits as well as the

17. Lemonnier 1993a: 7.

18. Mauss [1935] 1979. This approach to integrating nonverbal and verbal communication fed into the work of the ethnomethodologists and into current work in linguistic anthropology on contextuality.

19. Leroi-Gourhan entitled his two-volume study of communication *Gesture and Speech*; the first part being *Technology and Language*, the second *Memory and Rhythms* (1964–65). In the work of scholars like Haudricourt, Bernot, Barrau and Cresswell, and of the younger generation of ethnologists connected to the "techniques et culture" research team of the Centre National de la Recherche Scientifique, the study of techniques is always linked to linguistic and to symbolic practice (e.g., Haudricourt 1987; Koechlin et al. 1987; the journal *Techniques et culture*; Lemonnier 1992, 1993b). I myself was a member of the French research team for several years, although unfortunately I never acquired any competence in linguistic analysis.

20. Lemonnier believes a trend toward integrating technology and material culture into cultural analysis has begun beyond France. He draws attention to the work of ethno-archaeologists and postprocessual archaeologists, and also of a few anglophone ethnologists working independent of the French tradition (e.g., Ingold 1988; Reynolds and Scott 1987; Sillitoe 1988).

21. Perhaps because so many scholarly institutions are oriented primarily toward research rather than teaching, French scholars have less often been bounded by the disciplinary segregation typical of English-speaking universities, where the objects and methods of history, anthropology, sociology and other human sciences are often defined as distinct. But the role of Marc Bloch and Lucien Febvre in establishing the interdisciplinary journal *Annales* was extremely important in fostering this ambiance.

production of daily bread, furnishing styles as well as architectural techniques, as keys to explaining a civilization and its history. "Our investigation takes us . . . not simply into the realm of material 'things,' but into a world of 'things and words'—interpreting the last term in a wider sense than usual, to mean *languages* with everything that man contributes or insinuates into them, as in the course of his everyday life he makes himself their unconscious prisoner, in front of his bowl of rice or slice of bread."[22] But Braudel is no Norbert Elias; he places the economy firmly in the driving seat of history. In the section devoted to "technologies" it becomes clear that Braudel (not surprisingly, since his interest is in explaining the rise of capitalism in Europe) fully accepts both the boundaries and the master narrative of conventional history of technology:

> First the accelerator, then the brake: the history of technology seems to consist of both processes, sometimes in quick succession: it propels human life onward, gradually reaches new forms of equilibrium on higher levels than in the past, only to remain there for a long time, since technology often stagnates, or advances only imperceptibly between one "revolution" or innovation and another. It often seems as if the brakes are on all the time, and *it is the force of the brakes that I had hoped to describe more successfully than I perhaps have.* . . . [The role of technology] was a vital one. As long as daily life proceeded without too much difficulty in its appointed pathway, within the framework of its inherited structures, as long as society was content with its material surroundings and felt at ease, *there was no economic motive for change.* . . . It was only when things went wrong, when society came up against the ceiling of the possible that people turned of necessity to technology.[23]

As Braudel himself acknowledges, he does not succeed in conveying the nature of the "force of the brakes," not least because in his view the brakes are not so much active mechanisms as an absence of acceleration. Despite Braudel's privileging of economic production, he insists on incorporating the full experience of material life into his analysis of history. My study has been greatly influenced by Braudel's insistence on the need to link production and consumption, and to embed local technologies in the broader geographical and social context. But unlike Braudel's work, the heart of my study is precisely the interplay between accelerator and brakes, or rather, the various ways in which a social system can channel or absorb the potentially disruptive energies generated by disequilibria. Most materialist theories of human evolution or history, Marxist or not,

---

22. Braudel 1992: 1: 333.
23. Ibid.: 430, 435, emphases added.

are basically interested in the instability of modes of production; they highlight the role of technology as a vehicle for precipitating change. Historians have generally paid less attention to the fact that at another level, technologies, like kinship or gender, can also serve to reproduce the social system, channeling and absorbing the very energies that they generate.

This brings me back to gynotechnics. To understand the part technology plays in supporting a social formation, one must go beyond looking at a single technology or domain of technology (for example, the technologies of economic production), to consider the interplay of *sets* of technologies, or technological *systems*. In *Technology, Tradition and the State in Africa*, Jack Goody correlates African forms of political organization with kinship practices and agricultural technology on the one hand ("polity and the means of production") and with the technologies of warfare on the other ("polity and the means of destruction"). Analyzed as a system, the technologies reveal not just the material dimensions of a mode of production, but the social and ideological world it underpins.[24] The technologies I have brought together here also constitute a set or system: they were technologies for producing women. Each gave material form to different fundamental components of the overarching ideology of gender and hierarchy in late imperial China—gendered and hierarchical space, gendered and ranked work, and gendered reproduction tied to rank and status. Considered historically, each technology reveals changes that illuminate different dimensions of the overall historical process by which gender roles and social hierarchies were redefined, allowing the social order to adjust to the pressures of changing circumstance.

There are even more definitions of technology in circulation than there are of science—some sixteen hundred according to François Sigaut.[25] Many studies treat technology primarily as the rational application of knowledge to meet material challenges. While I recognize the importance of this aspect of human technical endeavors throughout history, here I am most interested in the social worlds that technology builds. Like Braudel, I am therefore interested in the language of technology and of things. For my purposes a *technique* can be defined as an action performed on some form of inanimate or animate matter (including oneself, as in the case of movement through domestic space, or of various practices of fertility

24. Goody's explorations of literacy as a technology of control also suggest helpful ways to explore the intellectual dimensions of technologies and the mindsets they make possible, as well as their role in producing certain forms of social stratification or political organization (J. Goody 1986, 1987).

25. Sigaut 1985.

control), designed to produce an object with human meaning. A *technology* is the technique exercised in its social context, and it is this social context that imparts meaning, both to the objects produced and to the persons producing them.[26] Technologies in this definition are specific to a society, embodiments of its visions of the world and of its struggles over social order. In this sense the most important work that technologies do is to produce people: the makers are shaped by the making, and the users shaped by the using.

Following Mauss and Goody, I have included in my Chinese gynotechnics some social and material practices that are not conventionally accepted as technology, for instance the tangle of medical theories, kinship rules, cosmological ideas and legal definitions that together shaped practices of fertility control. But at the core of each technology, even by my broad definition, there is a material core. This is important not least because of the key role that the Chinese accorded to material experience in shaping identity, morality and the understanding of the world.

My arguments about gender and technology in China depend on translating between material practices and forms of subjectivity. To what extent can we use material technologies as a guide to how people think about nature, about society, about meanings? Social studies of modern Western technology have been enormously creative in developing new, critical ways to analyze technology as ideology, as culture, as process. Feminist scholars have been especially innovative in analyzing the relations between technology, ideology and subjectivity, exploring the ways in which technological systems in the industrial world have given material form to social identities and inequalities and naturalized them in daily, embodied experience. They have been at the forefront of the critical approach to the technological history of the industrial West, questioning the selections and exclusions, redefining categories, pushing back the borders of what can legitimately be considered technology. I would like to mention just a few works that I have found especially stimulating in formulating

---

26. Marcel Mauss described a technique as "an action which is *effective* and *traditional* (and in this it is no different from a magical, religious, or symbolic action) felt by the [actor] to be mechanical, physical, or physico-chemical . . . and pursued with this aim in view" ([1935] 1979: 104). Lemonnier prefers to distinguish the technological from the magical or religious by confining techniques to processes that "lead to a real transformation of matter, in terms of current scientific laws of the physical world" (1992: 5)—but that drastically reduces both the scope of what constitutes technology and the criteria by which we judge its efficacity. For my purposes the emic understanding of what constitutes the material world and its transformations proposed by Mauss is more appropriate.

my own research on gender formation. Two outstanding works on the constitution of American domesticity are Ruth Schwartz Cowan's study of household technologies and the changing role of the "homemaker" and Dolores Hayden's analysis of postwar American house design, lifestyle and family values.[27] Aihwa Ong's study of the cruel pressures on Malay factory girls, inside and outside the workplace, is a feminist analysis of industrial alienation in a transnational framework; Ong extends her exploration of the meanings of women's work far beyond economic considerations, illustrating how a society whose values are under stress from rapid change may project its insecurities onto gender constructions. And Marilyn Strathern's recent work dissects the ethnocentric formulations of "nature and culture," gender relations and kinship goals that underlie public reaction to the New Reproductive Technologies, suggesting new ways to think about reproductive practices and beliefs in other cultures.[28]

For studies of technology and ideology in the contemporary world we can draw on a vast range of resources. Since the industrial revolution we have become acutely conscious of technology's place in our lives and anxious to record our feelings about it. We are as preoccupied with technology as Reformation scholars were with religion, or neo-Confucians with morality. Anyone wishing to study modern technology as ideology, from the perspective of reception as well as production, has ample resources to draw on. But is it possible to pursue cultural studies of technology in the past? Without factory studies, advertisements, statistics, personal interviews, novels and films, how feasible is it to unlock the past through its technologies, to make the jump from material form to social or mental world? An anthropologist assigns social or symbolic meanings to an artifact or process on the basis of detailed ethnographic, contextual observation. But for cultures of the past, systematic fieldwork is impossible and the retrieval of context may be at best partial or distorted. The interpretation of artifacts disembedded from or only partly situated in context is a challenge that defines the discipline of prehistoric archaeology, and it is naturally of interest to historians too. The richer the contextual remains, the greater

27. Cowan 1983; Hayden 1986. Staudenmaier remarks what a surprise it was that the Society for the History of Technology was willing to award the 1984 Dexter Prize to Cowan, for a book that dealt not with factory systems or military inventions but with the technologies of the "domestic sphere." But since then the impact of gender studies on the professional flag carrier, *Technology and Culture*, has remained limited: seven articles between 1984 and 1990 (Staudenmaier 1990: 723).

28. Ong 1987; Strathern 1992.

the claims one can make for interpretation—as in Georges Duby's *The Age of the Cathedrals,* or the series edited by Philippe Ariès and Duby entitled *The History of Private Life.* Where the context is more meager, how far can interpretation justifiably go? Let me give here one particularly interesting example of cultural analysis as applied to early Chinese technology.

David Keightley, a historian of early Chinese civilization, has sought to trace the intellectual roots of the earliest dynasties back to the prehistoric period by looking in the archaeological record for material expressions of certain concepts and values that are prominent in China's earliest written texts. During the neolithic period two distinct cultural complexes flourished in the Chinese heartlands. Both were well established during the sixth and fifth millennia B.C., one along the eastern coast and the other in the northwestern loess lands of the interior; in the central plains the two cultures coexisted. By the fourth and early third millennia eastern traits began to intrude in northwestern sites in the central plains, and by the late third millennium distinctively northwestern sites had vanished from the central regions and survived only on the far northwestern margins. Keightley asks whether ceramic styles offer any clues to explain the increasing dominance of the eastern cultural complex, and how they might relate to the worldview of the early Chinese state, which inherited many of the material characteristics of eastern culture.

Keightley analyzes the differences between potting techniques and ceramic styles in the two neolithic cultures. The northwestern ceramics have generous, softly rounded silhouettes and are painted with free-flowing naturalistic motifs. They are coiled pots, relatively unspecialized in form, each one made straight off at one go ("holistic construction"). The eastern styles are much more complex and angular in form and specialized in function. The potting wheel was in common use, and many of the eastern pot forms include elements that were separately molded and then assembled ("prescriptive construction"[29]), for instance pouring jugs with spouts and hollow legs, or tripod steamers (fig. 1).

Keightley hypothesizes the following social and cognitive differences between northwestern and eastern culture. First, the componential construction typical of the eastern style certainly required planning and careful measurement, thus presumably a greater level of abstract thought. It also most probably required a specialized division of labor and the capacity to communicate verbally about the construction process. Moreover, he

29. Keightley adopts these terms from Franklin 1990.

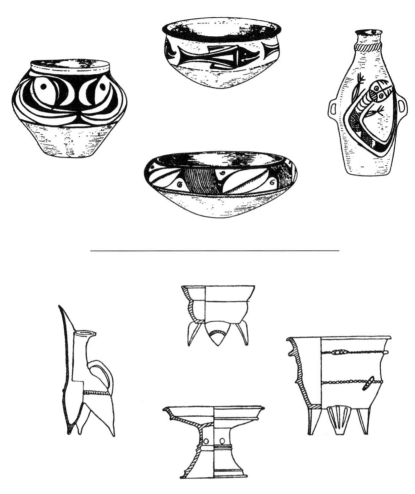

Figure 1. Ceramics from the northwestern (Banpo) culture (above) and from the eastern (Longshan) culture (below) (after Feng Xianming 1982: 10–11, and Weixian Museum 1984: 678–79). Note that the Longshan pots consist of several separately made components.

suggests that the eastern use of cores for forming components "is of significance socially and conceptually, since it implies a vision of creation as one of molding, of conformation to a model, of standardization—of 'engineering' in short."[30] Keightley concludes by connecting the use of molds in ceramics, and later in bronze casting, to the importance of moral exem-

30. Keightley 1987: 102; see also Keightley 1989.

plars as models for emulation in later moral and political thought. The crafts of potting, carpentry and jade carving provided the most frequent metaphors for statecraft in early Chinese philosophical texts; the potter forcing clay into a mold and the carpenter steaming timber to bend it into shape were central metaphors for the shaping of moral character.

There is no scientific method for making such jumps from the material to the conceptual, for linking artifacts to mentality or aesthetics to morals. Keightley is able to set his interpretation of the meanings inherent in neolithic potting styles in the context of later historical documents and philosophical texts concerning the world order of the early Chinese state. But there are no confirming statements by neolithic potters or their customers, telling us what different styles of potting represented in their eyes. Even if to a social or cultural historian such interpretations seem to fit nicely into broader cultural patterns, interpretations of this nature often arouse hostility and suspicion among archaeologists or historians of technology, many of whom believe that responsible scholarship should stick to functionalist explanations of the visible facts.

Yet if we accept that people in past societies probably had different intentions and values from our own, we are also obliged to be critical even of straightforward functional interpretations. Naturally in the search for meaning and power we must not neglect the problem-solving dimension of technology. The stylistic choices made by Chinese neolithic potters were not completely free. Clay pots were used as containers for storing, cooking or serving food and drink. The potter had to fashion and fire the clay in such a way that the contents would not leak or drop out—there were technical requirements and constraints that had to be met. But potting techniques were not predetermined by problem, resources and knowledge. Neither shape, nor size, nor pattern was inevitable, nor was the choice of clay or the method of forming the pot. In an important sense, the characteristics of a particular technology have to be accounted for in terms of choices: what are a society's tastes, its current needs and desires, and what technologies best fulfill them? We need to consider how to think about choices.[31]

To consider more realistically the meaning of technical choices, rather

31. See van der Leeuw 1993 on the choices exercised in neolithic ceramics. On technological choice as a heuristic concept, see Wagner 1995 and Lemonnier 1993b. The papers in Lemonnier 1993b study the interplay between material problem-solving and cultural meaning as manifested in a range of technological choices, from neolithic potting to plans for a revolutionary subway system—though in only a few cases do the choices consist of conscious group decisions (Latour 1993).

than reducing them to purely pragmatic considerations, we need to re-embed technologies in their social context to see what agendas they served. The northwestern neolithic cultures of China's central plains gradually merged with the eastern cultures, in the process adopting their potting techniques and styles along with other material features of the culture. Were the northwesterners of the plains impressed, seduced, or conquered? Probably a bit of each. When we consider the cultural conservatism of the last outposts of distinctive northwestern culture, driven far from the central plains to arid refuges on the edge of the desert, we may presume that these people were as familiar with the sophisticated techniques of the eastern culture as they were with the threat they posed to their cultural survival. Drawing a parallel with the experience of the non-Han minorities who were driven into the mountains as the Chinese empire expanded southward, or indeed with other cases of colonization, we might read the continued use of the traditional round red pots not as a pragmatic choice dictated by local clays, limited skills, or fuel shortages typical of the semidesert—but as a symbolic choice, an act of political resistance.

A good example of technical choice as political resistance is the case of the *swadeshi* movement in India, where nationalists advocated a boycott of imported British cottons and a return to the use of homespun cloth, *khadi*, produced in the household with simple handheld spinning wheels and traditional looms. This may have been a less economically efficient way of producing cloth than the British factory system, but it was certainly an efficient technique for producing Indian nationalism. For the Bengali nationalists of the early 1900s, the boycott of European cloth and the commitment to *swadeshi* techniques and the homespun cloth they produced symbolized a rejection of colonial dependence and the affirmation of Indian identity and tradition. But "Gandhi himself went beyond the use of homespun as a mere symbol to penetrate even deeper levels of meaning about the nature of weaving as a creative act, about the [low-caste] dhobi's cleansing as a token of redemption, and about the capacity of cloth to retain the luminosity of place and people." Gandhi played on the meanings of homespun to evoke the past, but in so doing portrayed a new future in which the Indian people would transcend the pernicious hierarchies of caste and gender: "The production of cloth in villages by spinning and weaving was to transform the moral fiber of the nation in a quite literal sense." "All Indians were to become spinners, weavers, and washermen," but in the process they would be redeemed from the impurity of craftsman status by the purity of the cloth they produced through the act of weaving. "Khadi in [Gandhi's] hands regained its transformative and magical qualities, while the spinning wheel took its place on the Congress flag."[32]

Here there can be no doubt of the conscious political symbolism of homespun in preindependence India: the public debate was vigorous and explicit, Gandhi and Rabindranath Tagore corresponded on the issue. But did homespun as a product, or the act of weaving, hold the same meanings for Indians who were consumers rather than producers of these political statements—did the ideology have grass roots? And did the *swadeshi* movement have any lasting effects on technological choices in the Indian textile industry or on the ideology of technology in India?

If Gandhi was able to forge a compelling national ideology around clothmaking, it was precisely because Indians at every level of society, Muslim as well as Hindu, responded powerfully to the notion of cloth as a political, religious and historical symbol.[33] Gandhi's vision of an independent India that would be spared the exploitation and degradation inherent in the relations of capitalist production perished with him. Nehru and the Indian industrialists who had supported Gandhi's campaigns were happy to ban foreign industrial imports, but "consciously or not, they enlisted the moral and political capital generated by the Mahatma's campaign for village weaving in support of their own push for Indian freedom and industrialization." Nevertheless, the industrial economy they developed was profoundly marked by Gandhian visions and commitments: "Bombay's mills . . . produced careful, machine-made copies of different sorts of homespun fabrics for distribution in the interior . . . [and] the Republic of India has spent large sums on the propagation of homespun through institutions such as the chain of Khadi Bhawans (homespun retail stores), which often function at a loss despite the government's strong commitment to competitive industry."[34] The official protection of the homespun industry symbolized a commitment by the state to protecting its citizens and communities from the effects of rapid commoditization. And the huge internal market for real or simulated homespun suggests an enduring popular belief in the social and personal moral values perpetuated by wearing this type of cloth.

In the modern world styles or items of costume have featured prominently in the formulation of many nationalist and political identities. One

32. Bayly 1986: 309, 312, 314.
33. Ibid.; Bean 1989.
34. Bayly 1986: 314.

thinks of the Phrygian cap and baggy pants of the sansculottes, the black fez or *songkok* that is the badge of Muslim political leaders in Malaya and Indonesia, the Sun Yat-sen jacket (well-tailored and pressed in the Kuomintang version, baggy and rumpled for Communist leaders), or of the invention and adoption of Scottish tartans. But perhaps only in India could such powerful political messages be attached not to a style of clothing, but to a *technology* of cloth production, understood as a symbol of a social and moral world. In many ways it parallels the symbolism of native rice in Japan. When a modern Japanese family sits round the supper table eating their bowls of Japanese-grown rice, they are not simply indulging a gastronomic preference for short-grain and slightly sticky Japonica rice over long-grain Indica rice from Thailand. They are eating and absorbing a tradition—in the sense of an invented and reinvented past. While the television beside the dining table pours out a stream of images of the here-and-now, of an urbanized, capitalist, and thoroughly internationalized Japan, each mouthful of rice offers communion with eternal and untainted Japanese values, with a rural world of simplicity and purity, inhabited by peasants tending tiny green farms in harmony with nature and ruled over by the emperor, descendant of the Sun Goddess, who plants and harvests rice himself each year in a special sacred plot. Simple peasant rice farmers are as marginal in contemporary Japan as hand-spinners are in India, but the small rice farm, like the *swadeshi* industry, lives on as a powerful symbol.[35]

Japanese agricultural methods and policies are much criticized for their inefficiency (and for their unfairness to foreign rice producers in a world of free-market competition). There is no doubt that by standard economic criteria the production of Japanese rice is highly inefficient in terms of production costs, labor productivity, overuse of chemicals, overinvestment in machinery, and consumer prices.[36] To this list one could also add

35. Most of Japan's remaining four million farm households work their farms part-time and derive the major part of their income from industrial or white-collar jobs. Moreover, rice plays an ever-diminishing part in the Japanese national diet as Western-style foods such as bread become popular. Despite strong opposition at home, at the final round of the Uruguay GATT negotiations in late 1993 Japan was obliged to open its doors, if only a crack, to rice imports. In March 1994 the Japanese government allowed foreign producers (from Australia, India, Thailand and the United States) to exhibit rice for the first time at the annual food show in Tokyo.

36. Almost all farmers own a full range of expensive machinery, and the average chemical use for rice is over 1 tonne per hectare, about ten times the U.S. average. Such methods are made possible by heavy government subsidies. In 1977 a Japanese economist calculated that energy inputs in rice production amounted

pollution of the rural environment. In political terms, however, the smallholder technology of Japanese rice farming has been efficient. The land reform measures promulgated under American guidance after the war eradicated landlordism and distributed land to former tenants; furthermore, selling and renting of farmland became subject to strict control. Farm support policies not only permitted farmers to modernize their methods and increase their incomes, but also supported the expansion of an internal market for Japan's manufacturing and service industries. Independent smallholder farming was firmly established as the basis of the rural economy. The average size of a rice farm in Japan today is less than one hectare, and many families continue to live on farms even though most of the members work in nearby cities. The proportion of the Japanese electorate registered as rural voters is especially high for an industrial economy, and the Liberal Democratic Party (LDP), the ruling party in Japan since the end of the war, has been kept in almost unbroken power largely thanks to a loyal rural vote.

The rice farmers and their families, the LDP, and the manufacturing and service sectors all benefit directly from this system of rice production. The benefits to the public at large are less obvious to outside eyes, but are nevertheless sufficiently appreciated within Japan for the rice protection lobby to be able to mobilize considerable popular support.[37] The modern parody of peasant rice farming provides the urban Japanese with a "tradition," an emotional and aesthetic refuge from rapid modernization and internationalization. Japanese rice is consumed not only as a food redolent

---

to three times the food energy of the rice itself. A 1987 comparison between the United States and Japan showed that yields per hectare were the same (just over 6 tonnes), but rice production costs in Japan were over eleven times those in the United States, farmgate rice prices were almost seven times as high, and as for labor productivity, while one American worker produced almost 2.5 tonnes of rice in an hour, in Japan the figure was a mere 106 kilograms (Bray 1986: 57, 1994; Tweeten et al. 1993).

37. "In questionnaires, more than seven out of 10 Japanese said they preferred domestic rice even at higher prices. But in blind tasting tests, six out of 10 could not tell the difference between Japanese and foreign Japonica" (*Guardian Weekly*, 13 March 1994). I visited Japan in October 1994 just after the rice harvest. In the foodhall basements of the big city department stores, which specialize in luxury foods (or at least the top end of the market), rice from up to a dozen well-known rice-producing localities was on sale at high prices. The only other products with comparable ranges of variety and provenance were tea, coffee and wine—the big notices announcing "the new rice is here!" reminded me of "le Beaujolais nouveau est arrivé!" campaigns. Meanwhile in less elegant streets the cheap takeout foodstalls were festooned with banners proclaiming that their dishes all used "100 percent Japanese rice."

of national essence, but also as a harmonious rural landscape, a weekend escape from the unnatural conditions of life in the modern city.[38] One could take the rosy-tinted public reading of this representation as what Michel de Certeau would call antidiscipline, a "reading in another key" whereby consumers of dominant representations subvert them and turn them to satisfying account. Yet at the same time it is the outcome of a highly successful political strategy of traditionalizing, of building modern national solidarity around an imagined past. The representation of Japan as a nation tied to its legendary roots by the labors of simple, thrifty and patriotic rice farmers has served Japanese nationalist causes well since before the turn of the century and still has immense popular appeal.[39]

The symbolic dimensions of farming are equally important in accounting for state policies toward agriculture in the premodern state of China. China was an agrarian society and the state continually intervened in the domain of agricultural production. All through the two millennia of the Chinese empire the state would undertake to open up new lands for cultivation; to loan tools, seed and animals to settlers on the lands; to develop irrigation projects; and to disseminate improved methods or equipment and encourage the cultivation of new crops. One of the responsibilities of local magistrates was to encourage agricultural improvement in the region under their jurisdiction, and many farming manuals were written with this form of transmission of knowledge in mind. But although the ubiquitous exhortation to "encourage agriculture" was taken seriously by almost everyone with official responsibilities, except possibly for a brief period during the Song dynasty, it would be a mistake to imagine that the Chinese state was trying to promote agricultural *development* in the sense that we use the word today.[40]

As conventionally used by economists, the term *development* implies continuous improvement in the productivity of a technical and economic system, resulting eventually in some kind of "qualitative" change, such

---

38. In a presentation of the arguments for preserving small-scale rice farming in Japan today, the economist Kenji Ozawa propounds the environmental importance of paddy fields in preventing floods and in maintaining a "traditional" Japanese landscape (1993). Yamaji and Ito also make much of the "cultural, emotional, and environmental factors" affecting whether or not Japan should open its rice markets (1993: 363). Ohnuki-Tierney discusses the role of rice in the construction of Japanese identity (1993).

39. See Bray 1986: 214–16 for a brief account of the literature on "agrarian fundamentalism" in Japan. On the importance of rural imagery in the construction of tradition in Japan, see Goto and Imamura 1993 and J. Robertson 1991.

40. Will 1994. On the Song dynasty, see note 49 of this introduction.

as a mechanical innovation that allows a quantum leap in labor productivity and thus produces a transformation of the relations of production. Economic historians of China, correctly noting the absence of this kind of change, speak of China in terms of stagnation, involution, or "growth without development."[41] It is true that the late imperial Chinese state was not favorably inclined to that kind of development. Growth of a kind that might transform the means and mode of production did occur at various points in the imperial period, in agriculture as in other sectors, but the state perceived the rapid generation of goods and wealth as a threat to social stability and inherently undesirable. It therefore countered this type of growth, directly or indirectly, to the best of its ability.

In England the technological advances of the agricultural revolution— and the consequent development of the labor-substituting machinery and methods that set the model for subsequent agricultural modernization worldwide—depended on the consolidation of land into large capitalist farms. The formation of large farms in England was facilitated by a state that represented the interests of the rural elite and so was willing to pass laws legalizing enclosures at the expense of the peasant class. But in China the state's commitment to the survival of peasant farmers was never questioned.[42] In one dynastic history after another we find legislation to limit landlordism, to redistribute land to the poor, to fix the ratio between the price of grain and other commodities, and to adjust levels of taxation where possible in favor of small farmers. The "stagnation" school quite rightly points to this political philosophy as an institutional obstacle to true conventional development.

Yet framing the issue in terms of the failure to develop seems to be asking the wrong questions of Chinese history. The evolution of farming systems in imperial China was profoundly shaped by the fiscal and agrarian policies of the state. The Chinese state controlled agriculture as part

41. E.g., Elvin 1973 on involution, P. Huang 1990 on growth without development.

42. The English parliamentary system allowed the members of the political (property-owning) elite to further the interests of their own class by representing them as beneficial to the country as a whole. In China, even though most of the literati who made up the civil service came from gentry families (that is to say, families whose primary source of income was rents from the land they owned), when they became officials they were expected to represent the interests not of their own group but of the state and its people. This frequently led to friction between magistrates and the local gentry, and was one reason why magistrates were not supposed to serve in their home region, or to stay too long in one place. The archetypal moral dilemma for a member of the Chinese elite was whether his first loyalty should be to his family or to the state.

of its strategy of maintaining a world order that acknowledged its authority to rule, and by this criterion it was clearly successful. My point is not that the long-term survival of the Chinese social order denotes a system that was in any moral way "better" than that of other, more dynamic (or less stable) societies. My interest is in the mechanisms by which this long-term continuity was achieved, and in particular the ways in which technical systems (such as farming) were contained or enlisted to maintain the social order.

When I speak of China as displaying long-term ideological or cultural continuity or stability, this certainly does not mean the absence of change. Between 1000 and 1800 China was three times conquered by foreign invaders; it also experienced numerous internal rebellions and civil wars.[43] There were territorial shifts,[44] population growth,[45] technical

43. The carnage and dislocation attendant on such upheavals were enormous. During the twelfth and thirteenth centuries the Mongols depopulated vast areas of the farming regions of North China, which they attempted—unsuccessfully—to convert to pastures. One of China's richest and most populous provinces, Sichuan, was reduced to a wasteland in the series of wars that brought the fall of the Ming in 1644 and the consolidation of the alien Qing (Manchu) dynasty. The consequences of such tribulations were not only material. The soul-searching and doubt among educated Chinese that followed the fall of the Ming and the Manchu conquest were especially profound and contributed to the formulation of a new critical scholarship that questioned the meaning of history and redefined the social uses of learning (Elman 1984).

44. Until about A.D. 800 the great northern plains were the heartland of the Chinese polity, economy and culture; for northerners the south was alien, a place of exile. By the mid-Tang the rich potential of the Yangzi rice lands had started to occupy a central place in state economic calculations (Li Bozhong 1990; Lamouroux 1995).

45. The population of China in the Tang-Song period may have been about 110 million (Hartwell 1982). During the Mongol invasions it dropped sharply, but it recovered again during the Ming and by 1700 had reached something like 150 million. Between 1700 and 1850 it grew to 430 million. This tripling represented a rather modest rate of growth at 0.7 percent (Ho 1959). But although long-term rates of population growth were low, the ratio of land to population fluctuated more rapidly, with invasions, wars, rebellions and natural disasters often drastically reducing the farming area, while the occupation or development of new territories or ecological niches counterbalanced population growth (e.g., Rawski 1972; Bray 1984; Perdue 1987). By the beginning of the eighteenth century, however, it seems that the problems of population pressure on land were no longer perceived as local or as soluble by internal migration or by innovations in the exploitation of local land. In the minds of the emperor and his civil servants population pressure had become an irreversible threat to food supply. The response of the state was not to suggest any limitation of family size, or to press for sustained innovation in agriculture. Instead it renewed the emphasis on "correct" farming methods, on frugality, and on stemming the flow of labor away from cereal farming into "parasitic" occupations (Will 1994).

advances[46] and a shift from subsistence to commercialization that marked a radical transformation of the national economy.[47] Whereas in medieval China most cities had been primarily administrative centers, from the Song era towns grew and flourished as centers of production and consumption. Subsistence farming was eventually limited to a few distant backwaters, as more and more of rural China was tied into a web of interregional commerce that encouraged local specialization. Sometimes entire rural districts were enmeshed in the urban economy and transformed from villages into suburbs. The prosperous urban middle classes that emerged included landowning gentry families as well as merchants and manufacturers; the boundaries between the old social categories of scholar, farmer, merchant and artisan became permeable. The marked medieval distinction between gentleman and commoner, between cultivated person and rustic, blurred with the spread of prosperity and literacy across classes.

Despite these significant changes and the new possibilities for government that they might have opened up, the late imperial state continued to

46. For example, considerable demands were made on southern agriculture following the loss of northern China to Jürchen invaders in 1126; in fact the withdrawal of the Song state and of numerous northern refugees to southern China led to extraordinary advances in southern agricultural yields and in silk production that seem to have increased per capita production as well as overall output (on the "Green Revolution" of the Southern Song, see Elvin 1973; Bray 1984: 597). Will (1994) states that in the present state of knowledge it is not possible to say definitively whether the economic growth that took place between the sixteenth and nineteenth centuries was only quantitative or had significant qualitative characteristics too. In the case of agriculture, Perkins (1969) argued that until about 1800 Chinese farm output kept pace with population growth, although the per capita output of farm workers did not expand, whereas Elvin (1973) saw the balance in more pessimistic terms, believing that as more labor was absorbed per capita output decreased. However, other scholars have pointed to instances where, even within the admittedly highly labor-intensive framework of Chinese farming systems, improvements were adopted that reduced labor demands or increased its productivity. For example, I have argued that late imperial improvements in water management, fertilizer use and plant breeding freed up time for rice farmers while tying them to the land, thus providing a natural basis for the development of rural petty commodity production (Bray 1986).

47. Until the Song dynasty the Chinese economy was predominantly noncommercial and characterized by local exchange, apart from the movement of tax goods. Given the highly regional and unintegrated nature of China's local economies right through the Qing, local cycles or variations cannot safely be taken as typical of the economy as a whole (Skinner 1985). But despite local and generalized hiccups and reverses, a secular trend toward commercialization characterizes the late imperial period. Interregional markets for commercial crops and products developed rapidly from Song times, as did international markets; see the treatment of the development of the cotton trade in chapter 5 for a good example of how interregional economic dependence developed.

define rural problems, even those of poverty and low levels of production, in terms that are better understood not as those of modern economics, but of political or even moral economy. The agricultural policies of the Chinese state all through the imperial period represented a continual and rather successful struggle to maintain a physiocratic political order in which the emperor and his administrators exercised direct rule over "the people" (*min*), that is, the peasantry. This political philosophy translated into a fiscal order that remained unchanged in its broad principles throughout the imperial period: the state was supported in large part by direct appropriations from peasant households.[48] The underlying assumption was that men worked in the fields to produce grain, and their wives produced the textiles that were used to clothe the servants of the state. Agriculture was defined as the fundamental occupation, crafts and trade were considered at best secondary, at worst pernicious; the rapid generation of wealth through commerce was seen by most statesmen and rulers throughout the imperial period as a source of dangerous social instability.[49] By the mid-Ming the real transformation of production was so profound that it had to be recognized in fiscal terms: in the late sixteenth century taxes in cash definitively replaced taxes in kind. But still peasant

48. I am grateful to Frank Perlin for directing my attention to the importance of modes of extraction in understanding social formations; my analysis of women and weaving in part 2 owes much to this perspective.

49. According to Paul J. Smith (1991), the early Song state was a unique exception. Because of the extreme military threats the government faced, statesmen of the period sought unprecedented methods to raise revenues. The Song state practiced economic activism at a level unknown before or later, at least until the late nineteenth century. It participated in a burgeoning commercial economy directly (through state enterprises and monopolies) and indirectly (through taxation of commercial activity). Song financial specialists were an elite within the bureaucracy. They elaborated a complex and powerful network of specialized fiscal institutions which regulated increasing proportions of the nation's activities. Commercial taxes provided an ever-growing proportion of state revenues and drain on the economy. The New Economic Policies, which operated from 1068 until 1085, "extend[ed] state control to new regions and industries and directly challenge[d] private commercial industries for the profits of foreign and domestic trade, in order to finance an aggressive new policy of territorial expansion and national defense" (Smith 1991: 9). As an example, the Sichuan tea industry was converted to a state monopoly in 1074 to finance the purchase of Tibetan warhorses. But these policies contained the seeds of their own destruction, leading to severe exploitation of the peasantry, an increasing state dependence on merchant middlemen or agents and, inevitably, corruption. The strategy of increasing state revenues through developing a commercial tax base was repealed in the mid-Song, after which it fell into permanent disrepute, particularly among orthodox neo-Confucians.

farmers were perceived as the state's authentic tax base—though at this point one might have expected a policy shift that would develop commerce and manufactures as the basis of taxation. Almost all late imperial legislation concerning agriculture was intended to keep a broad rural tax base by protecting peasant farmers: the ideology of a direct interdependence of state and peasantry remained unchanged. Qing policies were even more prosubsistence and anticommerce than those of the Ming; indeed one could say that the Manchu emperors fetishized peasant subsistence production. Numerous Qing imperial edicts demonstrated how central the valorization of what Pierre-Etienne Will calls "correct agriculture" was to their very traditional concept of social order.[50]

At this point a technological historian might wish to root the conservatism of Chinese rulers in the material realities of what Mark Elvin describes as a "high-level equilibrium trap": Chinese agricultural and manufacturing output was brought to high levels not by the development of labor-saving devices but by continually increasing labor inputs (a trajectory often labeled "involution"). Such a mode of production both supported and required population growth. Industrial capitalism did not develop indigenously in China because there was no incentive to invest capital in centralized and more labor-efficient production.[51] From there one might argue that since there was no radical transformation of productive relations, one would not expect a radical transformation in the ideology of state and subject. Conversely one could argue, as Needham has been inclined to do, that ideological conservatism was not the effect but the inhibiting factor, translating into policy that hampered any radical breaks.[52]

50. Will 1994. When serving officials tried to change agriculture in the locality under their jurisdiction, they were usually obliged to temper principle with pragmatism. Plans to implement ideal models of the rural economy, such as cultivation systems attributed to the Zhou dynasty that were supposed to give immensely high yields, fell by the wayside when a magistrate found that the climate was too harsh, the land too hilly and barren, the local landowners uncooperative, and the local peasants could demonstrate convincingly that their own system worked better. Perdue 1987 gives an excellent account of this.

51. Elvin 1973.

52. Needham blames China's lack of industrial or scientific revolution on what he calls "bureaucratic feudalism." In China itself until recently, marxist orthodoxy required scholars to cast the complexities and contradictions of late imperial economic history in terms of indigenous "capitalist sprouts" that withered away in the sterile soil of feudal China (see Brook, forthcoming); with the recent loosening of that dogmatic straitjacket exciting work has started to be published—Brook (forthcoming) and Wong (forthcoming) cite some examples. An interesting variant of the marxist approach, because it makes gender central to its analysis, has been

In the light of the growing body of recent work that documents the complexities and inconsistencies of Chinese economic history and the gaps between official discourse and real conditions,[53] perhaps it makes better sense to look at the ideological continuity embodied in economic and agrarian policy—and its undoubtedly significant influence on the persistence of social values and aspirations—not as directly related to material conditions, but as a fetish or a mantra. That is to say, the tradition of frugality, order and appropriate social roles and relations that was reiterated in successive economic and agrarian policies neither inhibited real change nor reflected its absence, but rather allowed the challenges it presented to be tamed, contained and addressed in manageable terms.

The Qing emperors were particularly assiduous in their pursuit of "correct agriculture." They issued a series of edicts condemning the lust for profit that drove farmers to abandon the cultivation of food staples for commercial crops or to leave the land to work as artisans or traders in the towns, edicts that attempted to persuade farmers all over China to concentrate on the production of staple cereals and to develop the necessary resources for local self-sufficiency. Imperial edicts and local magistrates' campaigns stressed that frugality and hard work were necessary so that peasants could support their families, survive lean periods—and pay their taxes. Imperial ceremonies were revived in which the emperor ploughed a ritual furrow in his sacred field each spring, while the empress and her ladies retreated into special apartments to raise silkworms. At one

---

advanced by Hill Gates (1989), who argues for a continuing dialectic in late imperial China between what she calls the tributary and the petty capitalist modes of production. Although the Chinese economy was indeed transformed in the course of these centuries, Gates argues, to the extent that small-scale, commercial household-based economic activities deserve to be thought of as a mode of production, the commercial sector was unable to dominate the economy because the state repeatedly acted to contain it. However, commercial imperatives intertwined in interesting ways to reinforce certain aspects of the state ideology of social organization, in particular kinship patterns and gender relations.

53. I have already referred to the Western-language publications of Skinner, Smith, Perdue and Will, but there are many others. Will (1994) offers a particularly fine critique of the relation between Qing imperial discourse on agriculture and its translation into real effects. He makes two important points in this regard. First, imperial edicts urging the improvement of agriculture did not translate into a coherent, centrally organized campaign; implementation depended on the individual efforts of local officials, and for that reason tended to be limited in both scope and duration. Second, in agriculture as in many other domains, Chinese rulers had traditionally ruled out compulsion or coercion, and tried to achieve their goals through education and persuasion; not surprisingly, persuasion often failed.

level the Qing ruling class's preoccupation with re-creating a hard-working and frugal peasantry stemmed from its fears that the population had begun to outstrip natural resources. At another level the edicts and campaigns were an attempt to forge anew the sacred Confucian social contract, the reciprocal bond of obligation between the rulers and the people (equated with the peasantry) that underpinned the ordered state.[54]

There were two reasons why the early Qing emperors, who in the eyes of many Chinese were barbarian upstarts, were so well served by such a strategy. The first was that the fall of the Ming was frequently blamed on a decline into luxurious living and consequent social promiscuity and moral decadence, and this ideological campaign was a means for the Qing rulers to distance themselves from Ming excess and commit themselves publicly to purity, moderation and order (yet without the inconvenience of having themselves to live in austerity). The second reason was that this strategy enabled the foreign Manchu emperors to declare their allegiance to the classic fundamentals of Confucianism by integrating themselves into the moral ruler-people dyad. They thus demonstrated their inherent worthiness to rule China here and now, while tying themselves into a native Chinese historical tradition. At the same time, for the Qing rulers "correct agriculture" was a fetish: if the people could be persuaded to practice it, then social order would be restored from below as well as from above.

The efforts of late imperial Chinese rulers to preserve a reasonably convincing and workable ideal of a "peasantry" might well have been in

54. This social contract was most directly expressed in the bimonthly lectures on the *Sacred Edict* that Qing local magistrates were expected to organize in all the villages under their control. The *Sacred Edict* was issued by the Kangxi emperor in 1670, when he was only sixteen years old and in the ninth year of his reign. It consisted of sixteen maxims, each seven characters in length, and "was recognized as the most concise and authoritative statement of Confucian ideology" from its promulgation to the end of the dynasty (Mair 1985: 325). Maxims 4, 5 and 14 related to "correct agriculture" and its social goals: "Recognize the importance of husbandry and the culture of the mulberry tree, in order to ensure a sufficiency of clothing and food"; "Show that you prize moderation and economy, in order to prevent the lavish waste of your means"; "Fully remit your taxes, in order to prevent being pressed for payment" (ibid.: 325–26). The *Edict* was elaborated for pedagogical purposes by numerous elite scholars and civil servants; pictures were added, poems and exegeses were composed either in classical language or in the vernacular, and thrilling tales of vice and virtue were appended to get the message across. Mair believes that although large numbers of the common people were familiarized with the messages conveyed in such lectures or readings, they listened when they had to but seldom read them on their own initiative, "whether out of duty, for pleasure, or for edification" (ibid.: 358).

vain were it not for the technical characteristics of wet-rice farming and the constraints they exercised on the development of the means and relations of production. The structures of power and the nature of the social contract might have been transformed if the economic center of China had not shifted in medieval times from the millet-growing plains of the north to the southern rice regions.

The history of farming technology in medieval North China offers an interesting case study of state efforts to control potentially disruptive development in the relations of production, made possible by technological development. During the first thousand years of imperial rule (from about 200 B.C. to about A.D. 850), the northern plains were the central economic region of China. This was a low rainfall area, and the main grain crops were millets, wheat and barley. Farming techniques in the north developed moisture conservation to a fine art. Crop rotation, the use of animal and green manures, drilling the seed in rows, repeated shallow plowings, harrowing, raking and weeding were all known by the first century B.C. and had been brought to a high degree of perfection by the sixth century.[55] They were only viable, however, if the farmer had a fairly large farm, animals for draught and manure, and sufficient capital for animals and animal-powered equipment; that is to say, the technical system presented significant economies of scale. During these centuries landed aristocrats (and Buddhist temples) were able to increase their wealth by practicing estate farming, adding to their centrally managed domains the land of small peasants unable to survive alone. The proportion of land concentrated in these feudal estates varied over the period, but when uncontrolled it always increased rapidly.[56]

Such concentration of land management represented a serious threat to the power of the central state: small farms each paid an individual land tax, but even when aristocratic (or religious or warlord) holdings were not exempt from the land tax, such powerful figures were able to evade many of their obligations. As a result, there was a continual oscillation: when a new dynasty came to power it would institute radical land reforms, some variant of an "equal field system" by which big estates were broken up and individual peasant households were allotted an amount of land depending on the fertility of the soil and perhaps the number of household

---

55. These methods are mentioned in fragments of agricultural treatises surviving from the second century B.C. and described in great detail in the *Qimin yaoshu* (Essential techniques for the peasantry), written by Jia Sixie in A.D. 535.

56. Bray 1984: 587–97.

members. But small peasant farms were seldom able to survive profitably under this regime for long, since they lacked the capital resources to practice the best farming methods. Meanwhile the aristocracy, given lands in perpetuity by the ruler as a reward for support, or allotted estates in return for service in the bureaucracy, hastened to buy up land from bankrupt peasants, for the elites were well able to practice the best methods and could therefore add to their incomes by increasing their estates. As the dynasty wore on, the rivals of the state became richer as its own income from taxes declined. Had northern China remained the economic and political center of the Chinese polity, it seems quite likely that at some point the state would have definitively lost control to its rivals.

The cycle of power shifts was broken, however, when the rice-growing regions of the Yangzi region started to rival the northern plains in gross output, some time around the ninth century A.D.[57] Wet-rice cultivation allows almost infinite intensification of land use, as Clifford Geertz famously noted in his study *Agricultural Involution*. In modern Japan this has been achieved by an enormous increase in capital inputs in the form of specially designed farm machinery, fertilizers, herbicides and other chemicals. In late imperial China it was achieved largely through improvements that required little in the way of capital. They included refinements in irrigation methods and in cultivation techniques, selective plant breeding, multicropping and the use of small quantities of commercial fertilizers such as treated nightsoil or beancake.[58] Rice requires intensive inputs of labor at transplanting and harvesting (fig. 2), but in other periods household labor can be spared for other activities, and in many areas of South China peasant households grew rice almost as a sideline, investing most of their labor in commercial cropping or other forms of household commodity production.[59]

57. Li Bozhong 1990; Lamouroux 1995.
58. Elvin 1973; Bray 1984: 477–510. Beancake was the name for the large fibrous disks that were the byproduct of crushing soybeans for sauce or beancurd; the extraction of various vegetable oils also produced cakes that were sold as fertilizer. Lime was another form of fertilizer that was commonly purchased. One beancake was apparently sufficient to fertilize the rice seedlings for a whole family farm (Bray 1984: 289–98).
59. Bray 1986: 113. In parts of the Yangzi Delta a kind of self-sustaining ecosystem of rice, silk and fish was developed. Mulberry trees were grown on the banks between the rice fields and their leaves were used to feed silkworms, whose droppings were used as powerful fertilizers for the rice. Fish fry were put into the fields soon after the rice was transplanted; they were fed the silkworm moltings and they also protected the rice by eating the larvae of insect pests. The men tended the mulberry trees, grew the rice and caught the fish. The women tended

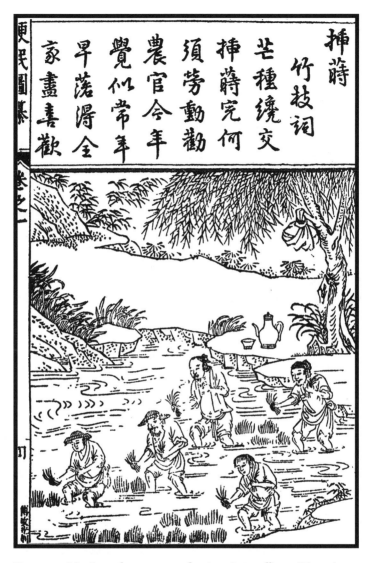

插蒔

竹枝詞

芒種繞交
插蒔完何
須勞動勸
農官令今年
覺似常年
早落淂全
家畫喜歡

Figure 2. Men's work: men transplanting rice seedlings (*Bianmin tu-zuan* 1/4a). The small field is typical of the intensive irrigated agriculture of southern China. Transplanting rice was women's work in Japan and throughout Southeast Asia, but in China women played little part in farming.

In medieval North China, the most productive and profitable farms were large ones that could afford expensive capital equipment; small farms that could not were economically vulnerable, though the state tried to protect them. In the wet-rice regions of China economies of scale did not operate, and little capital was needed to farm well. Although the ownership of land tended to concentrate in the hands of the gentry, the most efficient units of management were small and the countryside remained thickly populated by peasants working as independent or tenant farmers. The technological system of wet-rice farming was sufficiently productive to allow for a double level of extraction, so that in this case landlordism was not perceived by the state as a threat even though it often imposed severe levels of exploitation on peasant households. In conventional economic or technological terms, the estate agriculture of early North China had the potential for true development. But in the eyes of the state it was a threat both to the political ideal of relations between ruler and subject and to the fiscal regime.[60]

In fact what was at stake for the emperors of both medieval and late imperial China was not an economic but a symbolic order. The Chinese ruler was expected to strive for the welfare of his people, that is, the peasants. It was the duty of the state to provide help in times of hardship, and to take measures to prevent hardship arising in the first place. Such measures often resembled the technical packages of modern agricultural development policies. As well as distributing food and giving tax relief in famine regions, the Chinese state regularly opened up new farmland, invested in large-scale works for flood prevention or irrigation and encouraged improvements in peasant farming technology. The goal, however, was security and moderate prosperity rather than the uncontrolled (and unequal) generation of wealth.[61] The policies were intended not to develop the

---

the silkworms and produced silk thread for market. In other Yangzi regions summer crops of rice alternated in the fields with winter wheat. In the seventeenth century the semitropical regions of the far south grew two crops of rice a year, with a third crop of rape for oil, indigo for dyeing, barley or sweet potatoes. Their surplus rice was exported to Canton (Bray 1984: 509).

60. After the Song the north became something of an economic backwater, and peasant farming became the norm (Buck 1937) until the advent of capitalist industry to regional cities in the early twentieth century (P. Huang 1985). The introduction of the examination system in the late Tang marked the beginning of the downfall of the Chinese aristocracy. Moreover, the shift of the economic center to the Yangzi regions meant that control of land in the northern plains was no longer so profitable.

61. Official discourse on peasant prosperity frequently advocated the production of wealth *(shengcai)*. But Will opines that it is a mistake to interpret such an

economy, but to preserve (or in hard times to restore) well-being in a social order where the organization of agriculture symbolized proper relations between ruler and subject and defined the distinction between productive and parasitic occupations, toilers and thinkers, and also the proper tasks of men and women as male and female subjects of the state.

The examples I have given—of the symbolic roles of *swadeshi* in Indian politics, and of agricultural policy in contemporary Japan and imperial China—illustrate ways in which technological systems represent and diffuse dominant values. Basic productive technologies define the everyday work and material lives of large numbers of people; they are one important way in which ordinary members of society "live through" ideology and through which hegemonic values are transmitted. Technical knowledge and the hierarchies of working relations were passed down from generation to generation in the powerful form of bodily practices, naturalizing the values and beliefs they incorporated and inscribing them in social memory.[62]

Physical habits—deportment, etiquette, working practices—are powerful in two senses. First, they embody power relations. A Chinese son prostrating himself before his father embodied the respect and humility inherent in filial piety. A peasant woman working deep into the night at her loom, her eyes smarting and her fingers sore, struggling to finish the last bolt before the tax collector was due, embodied her family's subordinate position as peasants obliged to labor for the state. Second, physical habits

expression in the sense of quantitative, cumulative growth or growth in individual consumption. "What is meant is the production of the wealth indispensable for maintaining a general equilibrium, not the Faustian ambition of making each individual (or each family unit) ever richer" (1994: 881). Needless to say, the peasants did not usually see eye to eye with the state in such matters, nor did they draw such fine distinctions between the amount of surplus necessary to survive a lean period and the surplus that permitted a change in living style. Nor did they always draw the same line between "basic" and commercial production. Often specialization in commercial crops or household manufactures offered the best chance of economic survival or even enrichment. Commercial crops could be successfully cultivated as a sideline in most regions, but if it was cheaper to buy rice than to grow it, farmers often turned their land over exclusively to specialist crops (Bray 1986: 131). The state usually tried to discourage or at least control such trends in favor of self-sufficiency, fearing that regions which abandoned the cultivation of basic grains in favor of sugar, tea, oranges or cotton were paving the way to disaster. The Maoist policy of turning all available land, however unsuitable, over to grain would have been familiar to many earlier officials.

62. Connerton 1989: 72–104.

are powerful in the sense of being enormously forceful instruments of cultural reproduction. They are ingrained, unconscious, and therefore unquestioned.

While historians of technology still concentrate on the transformative aspects of material life, cultural historians or anthropologists are usually equally interested in its reproductive aspects as an embodiment of ideology. Today it is de rigueur, in any study attempting to integrate material experience and physical habit into the analysis of culture and power, to cite either Bourdieu or Foucault, or both. Bourdieu's concept of habitus includes deportment as well as the technologies of work and the use of space. Foucault's analysis of modernity decodes the "diffused power" inherent in the material experiences of everyday life, as shaped by techniques of observation, classification and containment ("technologies of power"). I find both Bourdieu and Foucault helpful when it comes to decoding the meanings and effects of technology within a limited timespan, but less so for historical analysis. Foucault's concept of immanent and thus anonymous power is unconcerned with personal agency or with the resolution of social tensions.[63] Bourdieu's socially rather self-contained concept of habitus does address the effects of time, especially cycles of diurnal and seasonal change; he also stresses the flexibility within habitus that allows for adaptation to circumstance. But I have been unable to fathom how Bourdieu's practice theory might be developed into a theory that could account for history.

Bourdieu (following Mauss) borrows the term *habitus* from medieval monastic discipline, a milieu we associate with tradition rather than transformation. Before its use by Bourdieu, however, the concept of habitus was developed for the purposes of social analysis by Norbert Elias, working with Karl Mannheim at the University of Frankfurt in the 1920s and 1930s. Elias was interested in the concept as a tool for dynamic, historical analysis—analysis that would account for processes of change (what he called socio- and psychogenesis) as well as reproduction. He defined habitus as the "psychic economy" characteristic of a specific social group or "figuration" and remodeled through shifts in the balance of tensions between figurations. Elias felt Marx was mistaken in believing that such dialectics were essentially dualistic, played out in the conflict between dominant and dominated class; he also held that the economic dimension is only one of several that fundamentally shape the relations between

---

63. Since Foucault in his early work explicitly stated that he did not deal in historical explanations, it would be tricky to reproach him on this count.

classes and the identities of persons belonging to them, so that "ideology" is not superstructural but far more central.[64]

Not all of Marx's work was published when Elias made these criticisms, and his main objections have since been met by the many marxist theorists who have developed more nuanced approaches to class conflict and to the role of ideology. But paradoxically, modern marxist scholars' interest in the material world is almost always abstract and narrow, devoid of significant detail. This I find disappointing and frustrating. The materialists are not interested in the material, Foucault and Bourdieu are not interested in history. Maybe that is why Elias's brilliant study of court society in France is so appealing, for it illuminates the importance both of material worlds and of the fine details of their meaning.

Elias believed that one of the most powerful forms of the expression and experience of ideology—as well as the most easily retrievable—was its concrete, material manifestations. For that reason he begins his study of ancien régime France, *Court Society*, with a chapter entitled "Structures and Significance of the Habitat," which describes and analyzes a new form of building characteristic of this period, the *hôtel* that was the Paris residence of the grand aristocratic family. He explores the values displayed and the social relations expressed by the spatial design of the *hôtel* and the meaning of the modifications that the bourgeoisie made to this style of dwelling, stressing that in a society where the political players fell into three groups—the absolute monarch himself, his courtiers, and the aspiring bourgeoisie—the aristocratic *hôtel* made sense only in relation to Versailles on the one hand, and to the bourgeois dwelling on the other.[65] In his treatment of habitat Elias decodes the *hôtel*, the stage that the French

64. This critique of marxian economic reductionism, in tandem with a critique of Freudian psychological reductionism, appears in Elias's *The Civilizing Process* ([1939] 1982).

65. For example, the lifestyle accommodated within the aristocratic *hôtel* depended on swarms of servants. These servants were invisible; they lived behind the façades of noble life, but even when they were in the same space as their masters they did not intrude. Aristocrats were concerned only with their own kind as audience; others were either too vulgar to count (the bourgeois), or not really human (the servants)—hence the absence of any concern with what we think of as privacy. Thus a noblewoman could undress without embarrassment in the presence of a male servant. However, this attitude reflected a code of ethics that was to the bourgeois mind immoral. Whereas the aristocrats justified an action in terms of its effects within their own group, the bourgeois extended their own morality and feelings to their social inferiors. This can be seen in the much more permeable boundaries—spatial as well as behavioral—that the bourgeois drew between themselves and their servants.

courtiers built for themselves to their own design. This was where they could give an uninhibited performance of what they saw as the role of their class, with its finely tuned aesthetics, relationships and forms of rationality.

Although my own work also begins with the structures and significance of a habitat, it is by coincidence (or perhaps force of logic), for I did not read Elias until my study was nearly complete. Interestingly, in the case of the Chinese habitat I am able to take my social analysis further than Elias in one important respect. Roger Chartier remarks in his preface to the French edition of *Court Society* that the work does not consider the diffusion of models of behavior beyond the court to other social strata. Elias does address this issue in the final section of *The Civilizing Process,* where he argues that cultural models do not simply diffuse or percolate downward: their transmission must be understood in terms of often conscious competition that obliges elites to develop new levels of civility. Interdependence is a crucial factor in this model.[66] In the case of *Court Society,* however, it is true that Elias omits the majority of the population—not least because at the time peasants and artisans were excluded from the domain of civility both by the prevailing political mentality and by their material condition. In late imperial China the contrary was true: the elite saw their task as drawing the lower orders firmly into the domain of civility, while maintaining the distinctions that justified their authority. The case of house design in China nicely illustrates reciprocal cultural influence of the kind that Elias hypothesized.

A concern with the power of material practice is not, of course, a modern invention, as the history of the term *habitus* shows. It is found in every religion and in much premodern political and social theory. Chinese Confucian philosophers argued over the relationship between ritual performance and moral orthodoxy for over two thousand years; they were also concerned with the symbolism and moral effects of different types of work and with the moral import of the most mundane details of their material world.[67]

Cultural historians and anthropologists have produced several key works in response to the question What held Chinese society together? Dis-

66. Chartier's critique appears in Elias [1933] 1985: xxiv. Elias looks at the question of diffusion in 1982: 2:229–336.
67. On the relation between orthodoxy and orthopraxy, see Ebrey 1991b and Watson and Rawski 1988; on the meanings of work see Cartier 1984.

cussing the various institutions and social processes that contributed to this cohesion, James L. Watson identifies one of the most obvious factors in the creation and maintenance of orthodoxy at popular levels as "control over the written word as expressed in literature and religious texts; equally important was the subtle manipulation of oral performing arts"; he then goes on to add death rituals, ceremonies of paramount importance in Chinese society since they converted dead relatives into ancestors. Others have added marriage rituals, kinship, and family organization and rules to the list of practices of cultural reproduction.[68] To this I add everyday technologies, seen at once as processes of cultural reproduction and as potential catalysts of social change.

At this point it becomes necessary to state the nature of my sources and to consider what kinds of reading they permit. Would the Chinese even recognize my organizing concepts of "technology" or "techniques"? I discuss my sources in greater detail in each section, but here I would like to give a general sketch of what sources are available, why, and what they can tell us.

Reflecting on why technology has never been incorporated into Indian studies, Marie-Claude Mahias notes that Indian thought shared with Western thought a predisposition to separate the spiritual and the material. Indian thought attributes high value to spiritual and low value to material activities, and the literate Brahmin elite tended to pass over technology in silence. Knowledge and skills of a practical kind were not considered to belong to the domain of true knowledge, and there is almost nothing written on technology in the historical record. If an outsider today (say a visiting ethnographer) wishes to enquire about a craft in an Indian village, even in the presence of the artisan it is the Brahmin who will reply to the questions, by virtue of his status as a person of knowledge—which in this case, of course, amounts to ignorance.[69]

Chinese intellectuals, on the contrary, paid meticulous attention to this practical domain, being acutely sensitive to the ways in which bodily action shaped identity, and to how the material world in which one lived produced a social and moral being. The Song dynasty saw the consolida-

68. Among the numerous works on neo-Confucianism and its penetration, see K. C. Liu 1990 on orthodoxy; Elman and Woodside 1994 on the examination system and its effects; Ebrey (1991b, 1991d) and Watson and Rawski 1988 on various kinds of ritual; Watson and Ebrey 1991 and Birge 1992 on marriage and female status; Johnson, Nathan and Rawski 1985 on the accommodation of orthodoxy with popular culture.
69. Mahias 1989: 5.

tion of a new political and cultural elite and of a new social philosophy in which bodily practices played a prominent role not just in the expression of identity but also in social incorporation. The aristocratic elite of pre-Song China had protected their status and maintained the social order through practices of exclusion: their status was transmitted through descent, and their marriage practices, family rituals, and other markers of status were forbidden to commoners. From the Song, however, the new political elite were meritocrats who worked through a strategy of inclusion. They strove to build an organic social order, ranked but open to all, that would bind the whole population into a shared culture of orthodox beliefs, values and practices. This strategy of inclusion was highly successful. It allowed the Chinese polity to absorb the populations of remote provinces and foreign invaders into its own culture, and gradually to incorporate the members of every level of Chinese society into a workable orthodoxy.

The social philosophy underlying classical learning in late imperial China is often referred to as neo-Confucianism. It was developed by a group of thinkers in the Song dynasty, the most famous of whom was Zhu Xi, as a response to the increasing popularity of Buddhist otherworldliness, on the one hand, and to the active interventionism of the early Song state, on the other. Neo-Confucianism elaborated the classical Confucian model of social order,[70] which depicted the family as the microcosm of civic virtues and skills: one learned to govern the state by managing one's own family. Perhaps in reaction to the relative power and independence of elite women of the Tang and early Song, neo-Confucianists during the Song strongly emphasized the segregation of the sexes, the seclusion of women and their subordination to men (to their fathers before marriage and to their husbands thereafter). But throughout the late imperial period we also find repeated expression, by men as well as women, of the classical view that wives were active partners rather than acquiescent subordinates. An important theme in this book is the interplay between these two views of gender and between different forms of patriarchy within Chinese society.

One way in which orthodox values were diffused in late imperial China was through the structures of education, which not only regulated access to political power but also were used to incorporate the population. The

---

70. Formulated by the fifth-century B.C. philosopher Confucius, elaborated by his adherents such as the fourth- and third-century thinkers Mencius and Xunzi, and accepted as state orthodoxy in the early Han dynasty, c. 100 B.C.

emperor ruled through a hierarchy of civil servants recruited through examinations that tested their classical learning. Many more people studied for the examinations than actually passed them and gained office. The examination system effectively transmitted dominant values to large sections of society through the system of classical education, and over time these values were disseminated to ever broader numbers of the general population, through such media as public lectures by local magistrates, sections on social morality and etiquette in popular encyclopedias and almanacs, and the increasing incorporation of neo-Confucian morality into the legal code.

Ideas and texts were fundamental elements in the Chinese concept of education, as they are in our own, but the material dimensions of education were far more prominent. Teaching appropriate bodily practices and the correct use of material objects was a way of reinforcing intellectual messages as well as an integral part of inculcating dimensions of morality and right thinking that could not always be completely encompassed in words. This aspect of education was the more powerful because it could be absorbed even by those untrained in literacy.

As I suggested earlier in my discussion of agrarian policies, late imperial intellectuals were concerned with the social and moral effects of different kinds of work, and "womanly work" became a prominent theme in statecraft and moral writings from the late Ming. The statement by the fourth-century B.C. Confucian philosopher Mencius—to the effect that those who work with their minds govern, while those who work with their bodies are governed—should not be taken to mean that laborers are naturally subordinate to thinkers, but rather as an expression of "the complementarity of human activities and the necessary solidarity of social groups." " 'Work' was highly valued as a productive activity synonymous with civilization," and the art of ruling over this civilization was explored through technical metaphors drawn from carpentry, building, spinning, weaving, potting and jade carving.[71]

At the same time work was ranked. The "basic" productive activity was agriculture, which like government was considered an essential form of labor. Other forms of labor than farming were considered of subsidiary dignity, even though houses, cloth, iron tools and other craft products were indispensable everyday items. Even the production of cloth, the work of farmers' wives and the source of half the state's revenues, did not have

71. Cartier 1984: 278, 304 on the ideology of work, and Keightley 1989 on political metaphors.

such high status as agriculture. The skills required for crafts like carpentry and metal working were popularly associated with magic. In medieval China craftsmen were classified as "mean" people; their status was hereditary, they were not supposed to intermarry with commoners, nor were they allowed to sit for the entry examinations to the civil service. Farming was not demeaning but an activity in which an educated man could engage with pride and pleasure when not serving the state. Giving people access to land was the best way to foster civic virtue, and we should not wonder that the reins of government were entrusted to landowners.[72] In China we would not find a philosopher who earned his living by grinding lenses.

Treatises on subjects that we would consider technological were a respected genre, dating back at least to the early Han dynasty (second century B.C.). The best-known works were transmitted over centuries, through new transcriptions and then through printed editions, often updated with commentaries or new sets of illustrations.[73] Most numerous were the agricultural treatises, written or compiled by members of the educated class. Most of them had personal experience as farmers, some had also served as administrators, and some authors tell us they interviewed "experienced peasants" to supplement their own knowledge.[74] The classic gender division of labor was expressed in the phrase "men till, women weave," and from Song times onward most farming treatises included sections on textile production (also treated in numerous separate works). Wang Zhen, who published his systematic *Agricultural Treatise* in 1313, decided to include diagrams and detailed descriptions of all the tools and machinery he described, so that people who wanted to try out new methods could do so.

The number of technical works on crafts (including building, carpentry, papermaking, ship building, metal casting and so on) is rather fewer. Most of them were originally put together not by literati but by artisans or other trained experts. Since the dexterity or skill (*qiao*) required for each craft was at least in part esoteric, the information supplied is often cryptic or incomplete—the written texts served the purpose not of descriptive

72. Cartier 1984: 304.
73. For example, the *Kao gong ji* (Artificer's record), a set of laconic, not to say cryptic, descriptions of crafts probably predating the Han, that was included in the canonical text *Zhou li* (Rituals of Zhou) around 140 B.C. Among its many recensions one might cite the explicated version produced by the Southern Song scholar Lin Xiyi in about 1235, and the critical illustrated edition produced by the famous classical scholar, mathematician and astronomer Dai Zhen in 1746.
74. Bray 1984: 47.

how-to books but rather of scriptures or even incantations. A complementary genre (this time the work of scholars, not craftsmen) is the information provided for consumers of crafts, in books of connoisseurship and popular encyclopedias. Again, such texts do not tell us "how to" make a lacquer box. The basic techniques are taken for granted; what is important is the different consistencies, textures and colors of lacquer, the methods of layering, carving or inlaying, that define a regional style or quality. We are dealing with techniques of taste rather than of production.[75] Technical books were often illustrated with woodcuts. The professional artists might sacrifice accuracy to artistic effect, but although this means that such pictures are not always entirely reliable as technical representations, they usually show the work taking place in reasonably characteristic surroundings, so that they are useful as social documents.[76]

Other sources of technical information include the economic sections of dynastic histories and local gazetteers, genre paintings, poetry and novels, archaeological excavations, and artifacts. To give some idea of just how rich the material is, Needham's series *Science and Civilisation in China* includes volume-length sections on architecture and civil engineering, ship building, paper and printing, textile production and dyeing, agriculture, food processing of various kinds, mining, ferrous and nonferrous metallurgy, weaponry and medicine.

When we consider how such material can be used in a study of technology and gender, we must bear in mind that of all the sources I have just listed, the written materials form by far the most important element. Apart from a few technical or magical works put together by artisans they were all written by educated men, even where they recorded knowledge passed on to them by working men or women. They therefore convey a male perspective and a privileged perspective. Some writers were sympathetic to the sufferings of the working classes or to the feelings of women, and even went so far as to question aspects of the social order that did such violence to certain kinds of people (the Tang poet Du Fu, who wrote movingly of the plight of farmers, weavers and other workers, is a notable

75. Ruitenbeek (1986, 1993) describes the mixture of esoteric and practical information conveyed in the carpenters' sacred text *Lu Ban jing* (one of my basic sources in part 1). Clunas (1991, forthcoming) discusses the late Ming literature of connoisseurship.

76. Of course there is a tendency to prettify. Work in these woodcuts always seems to be done by smiling people, neatly dressed and chatting pleasantly, their sweating brows cooled by the breeze wafting through a convenient bamboo-shaded lattice.

example of the former,[77] the seventeenth-century playwright and novelist Li Yu of the latter). But however deep their concern, they remained educated men, and their representations of class or gender roles and relations, as of different varieties of female experience, must be evaluated accordingly.

To some extent the sources written by elite males can be read "against the grain," examined for absences and contradictions. This is largely how I have used the sources on textiles, in order to reconstruct the emergence of new, unconventional gender divisions of labor and their impact on female status. Since all the female roles and experiences I am interested in were defined in relation to a corresponding male counterpart, what is said about men is often a good basis for speculation as to what might have been said about women, had it been thought necessary or interesting in this context, and vice versa. I should note that my sources provide considerable scope for investigating how forms of male power over women were exerted and experienced; they also allow me to suggest how women fashioned peculiarly female versions of orthodoxy and to throw some light on how inequalities among women were materially experienced. My sources reveal much less, however, on the fashionable matter of resistance.

Some of the most original feminist scholarship on late imperial China has now shifted away from viewing women predominantly as victims, to consider elite women at least as active—if relatively restricted—partners in the construction of the Chinese social order. While such women might have perceived some of the gendered restrictions on their actions as constraints to be resisted or subverted, their allegiance to the basic values of their world was seldom in doubt. Indeed, as Dorothy Ko demonstrates in *Teachers of the Inner Chambers,* elite women embraced their special and indispensable role as moral educators with enthusiasm. My materialist study does not contradict this view; rather, it tends to confirm it as far as the high-status women in elite families were concerned. But one can only have high status if somebody else has low status; power is exerted on people, it is not an intangible aura. My materialist sources also provide glimpses into how the dignity of high-status women was often achieved at the expense of women lower in the social hierarchy, whether under the same roof or in families of a lower class.

To return to whether we might take technology as a Chinese category: the notion of craft, cunning or skill, *qiao,* which I mentioned earlier in

---

77. Du Fu's proletarian sympathies made him the favorite classical poet of the early Communist regime.

relation to artisans, was an attribute that distinguished among men of different social status. *Qiao,* implying "cleverness in the practical skills of manipulating the environment,"[78] was not an attainment to which educated men or farmers aspired—it was characteristic of only one order of men, and they were of low status. *Qiao* enabled them to make objects that were classed as being of only secondary importance compared to the work of educated men or farmers (although paradoxically the instruments, vessels and dwellings that craftsmen produced were treated as central to the performance of Chinese culture). As a female attribute, however, *qiao* transcended class. It was associated with "womanly work," primarily textiles: all girls were expected to learn the skills of spinning, weaving and needlework. Textiles were classed as fundamental goods, indispensable to the maintenance of the world order. The other practical skills that women exercised to maintain the domestic order were equally integrated into the organic Chinese polity, in which a well-run household was the basis of a well-ruled state. *Qiao* was not at the top of the scale of human attainments—and its connection with cunning and magic made it a somewhat ambiguous category, like the word *craft* in English—but in its female manifestation it denoted a relation to the material through which women crafted a path to virtue and a cornerstone of the moral order. What I would call techniques or technology, therefore, strike me as an object that is particularly appropriate for investigating the female experience in China, not least because it provides unique possibilities, both for transcending class boundaries to identify commonalities in gender practices across classes and for exploring how inequalities among women as well as between men and women might be materially expressed.

78. Blake 1994: 680.

PART ONE

Building a Tradition

The Construction of Chinese Social Space

Before the coming of the legendary sages, the primitive Chinese sovereigns "had no palaces nor dwellings, but in winter they lived in artificial caverns, and during the summer in nests made of branches." The great sages devised the basic techniques for building palaces and humble dwellings, teaching their people how to "mould the metals and fashion clay, so as to rear towers with structures on them, and houses with windows and doors," "to pound earth and work wood to make dwellings, raising beams and laying roofs to protect themselves from the wind and rain, to escape the cold and heat."[1] These mythical dwellings represented far more than shelter from the elements. They were part of a set of civilizing inventions that included farming, weaving, cooking, music, written records and betrothal practices. Together these skills and practices defined an ancient culture that to the Chinese of imperial times was recognizable as the ancestor of their own, a culture in which the house was a central element.

Building a house is not a simple matter of providing shelter using the most appropriate materials and design. A house is a cultural template; living in it inculcates fundamental knowledge and skills specific to that culture. It is a learning device, a mechanism that converts ritual, political

1. The first passage quoted is De Groot's translation of a passage from the *Liji* (*Book of rites*) (1892–1910: 2: 372); his translation is more literal than that of Legge, which continues in the second quotation (1885: 1: 369). The *Rites* was a compilation of rituals attributed to Confucius himself; though the text took its present form in the first century A.D., parts of it may date back to the fifth century B.C., when Confucius was alive. These culture myths occur in a number of Han philosophical works such as the *Han Feizi* (Book of Han Fei), a work of political philosophy from the early third century B.C. and the *Huainanzi* (Book of the Prince of Huainan), a compendium of natural philosophy compiled c. 120 B.C. The third quotation is taken from the *Huainanzi* (quoted Robinet 1993: 161).

and cosmological relationships into spatial terms experienced daily and assimilated as natural. The encoded messages teach some lessons that are the same for all, and some that are different. As a child grows up and learns the practices of living in a house she learns her proper place within society; she internalizes the hierarchies of gender, generation and rank that are marked by walls and stairs and practiced in the rules and etiquette of receiving guests, performing rites of passage, and going about daily tasks.

The house is not the only locale where such knowledge is inculcated, but in some societies its role is more central, more continuous with the lessons taught by other domains. In the West we have experienced a series of separations between spheres of activity that has progressively reduced the dominance of the house in shaping people's lives. Classical Greece laid the foundations, marking a clear distinction between the concerns and actions appropriate to the domestic and to the political sphere, to the house and the city. In Christian Europe most important acts of worship and rites of passage came to be performed in the church. With industrialization came a separation of workplace from dwelling for large numbers of the population. The house became a home, a private domain that could serve as a refuge from the pressures of work and of political or religious ortho-doxy.[2]

Such demarcations were largely absent in imperial China. Rituals of birth, maturation, marriage and death were performed in the house; the liturgical rituals of the domestic ancestral cult paralleled the ceremonies of state orthodoxy; the family was the ethical and behavioral training ground for public life. Unlike in Europe, where nobody could possibly mistake even the grandest house for a church, in China ancestral temples, magistrates' courts and imperial palaces all shared the layout and architec-

2. In *The Human Condition* (1958), Hannah Arendt discusses the class and gender distinctions embodied in the spatial distinctions between the realms of *oikos* and *polis* in the city republics of classical Greece. She suggests that for a free man, a citizen, his own front door marked a passage between two modes of being; he left his political concerns behind when he entered his home, a domain where individuals interacted not as equals but within a strict patriarchal hierarchy. Women and slaves could not act in the public world. In a study of modern Costa Rica that parallels this spatial dichotomy, Richardson, looking at a place's smell, color, feel, etc., concludes that the experience of being-in-the-plaza is about the concept of "cultura," the appropriate and right behavior, that contrasts with "vivo," the experience of being-in-the-market, which denotes smart, quick, and clever behavior (1982). On the historical processes whereby European cultures came to demarcate the separation between workplace and home, and on the invention of privacy, see Ariès and Duby 1985–87.

tural features of the basic courtyard house, if on a larger scale. "The greatest palace hall has a look of being a glorified farm building, and between the painted pavilion on the marble terrace and the humblest thatched hut there was real harmony."[3]

One of the key roles performed by the Chinese house was the spatial marking of distinctions within the family, including the seclusion of women. One does not have to be a China expert to know that a Chinese man would commonly refer to his wife as "the person inside" *(neiren)*. But it would be wrong to infer that the seclusion of women marked a simple male-female binary pattern of dominance and control, or that it demarcated the same gendered separations of activity and identity as those of Greece or of industrializing Europe. As I argue throughout this book, the moral and political continuity between home, community and state in late imperial China requires us to revise many of our usual conceptual tools for the analysis of gender systems. Terms like *domesticity* or dualities like public and private may be more misleading than useful when applied to other societies than our own. This is hardly a novel argument, nor one that applies only to China. To cite one example, most of the essays in Shirley Ardener's pioneering feminist collection on space analyze gender relations in modern Mediterranean and Islamic societies where segregation is as important as it was in late imperial China, societies that we normally view as especially patriarchal and oppressive of women. They demonstrate how much we can enrich our understanding of the meanings of space if we abandon our preconceptions and look in detail at how people actually behave.[4]

The notion of gender segregation is repugnant to most modern Westerners, who presume that it is invariably the instrument of the most stringent patriarchal control and oppression. But as Lidia Sciama points out in her essay on Mediterranean anthropology, it is "an interesting contradiction that, while anthropologists are sometimes disturbed by lack of privacy in some simple societies, and their writings imply an understanding of privacy as freedom, some deprecate the existence of private feminine spheres, to which women are confined, and where privacy is interpreted

---

3. Boyd (1962: 48) attributed this to what he calls "directness and functional clarity," but in my opinion it is connected to the Chinese feeling of moral and behavioral continuity between spheres. In China even mosques and synagogues were built to the same indigenous and essentially domestic plan.

4. See the essays in Ardener 1981b, particularly those by Ardener, Hirschon, Khalib-Chahidi, Sciama and Wright, which I cite later. Moore 1986 is another good example of a feminist approach to spatial meanings.

as deprivation, robbing, bereavement."[5] As many Muslim feminists argue today, and as scholars such as Dorothy Ko argue for late imperial China,[6] a homosocial organization of society may offer women a degree of dignity, freedom and security that would often be impossible in mixed company. (Though I agree that this view applies to some extent to late imperial China, I argue throughout this book that the benefits that homosocial life might provide were generally dependent on rank.) Conversely, life in the world beyond the home, which to Westerners usually represents desirable freedom, may be experienced in other societies as a dangerous and hostile world; men who are denied access to the female domain of the house before nightfall (like the Iranian shepherds described by Susan Wright, and like men in late imperial China) may feel that this is a deprivation.

It is important not to think of the meanings and location of the spatial boundaries drawn by seclusion as fixed. In the Iranian villages studied by Wright, for example, while the men are off herding during the day women move freely around the public spaces of the village without wearing a chador; this scenario changes when the men return home at night. In the working-class section of Piraeus studied by Renée Hirschon, women go out on errands in the mornings, but although they enjoy the contact with others that these outings provide, they feel uneasy and operate in a mode of haste and righteousness; in the afternoons they stay dutifully at home, but this in fact consists of moving their living room chairs outside onto the sidewalk where they can talk freely (and this time uninhibitedly) to passers-by. In the case of late imperial China, the boundaries between "inner" and "outer" worlds were also relational and fluid. Furthermore, as I argue throughout, to understand how gender relations were conceived of in China, we must consider not just the physical boundaries that confined women's bodily movements, but also the passage across these boundaries of the material, social and moral goods women produced.

When teasing out the meanings of space, it is important to distinguish between representation and practice. Think of the working-class women of Piraeus, who mask their enjoyment of a chat at the baker's by putting on a preoccupied expression and running hastily out of the shop as soon as they have absorbed the latest piece of gossip. Or the Iranian shepherd community, where the precarious status negotiated by a man in his ostensibly sex-segregated power dealings cannot be achieved without the commensurate status and skills (necessarily exercised with modesty and

5. Sciama 1981: 93.
6. See Ko 1994 and Mann 1991.

discretion) in his wife. To add to the confusion, there will always be coexisting representations that contradict each other. In the case of urban Greece, Hirschon points out that the prevalent misogynistic representations by men of women as threats to the moral order directly contradict the view of the house as a sacred domain, a microcosm of the Christian orthodox sacred realm, guarded by the moral purity of women. Again, this is a rather common contradiction, for which late imperial China offers obvious parallels. It is particularly important to bear ambiguities of this type in mind should we be tempted to argue in simple dualistic terms that male is to female, as public is to private, as power is to dependence.

In neo-Confucian orthodoxy, the separation of spheres was a keystone of the social order. As I show both in my analysis of space and in the sections on textiles and on reproduction, however, this orthodoxy took different forms. One important school saw all humans, women as well as men, as educable and morally responsible individuals; this view attributed to women, or at least to legal wives, a dignified role as partners of their husbands. At the opposite end of the spectrum, it was held that women were morally inferior to men, their nature was evil, and their very existence was a threat to social order. Strict control through confinement offered the only solution. Depending on which philosophy the family subscribed to, identical material divisions of domestic space might be experienced by women as a prison or as a realm of independence. In the following chapters I show that at least in some cases we can find material as well as textual clues as to which brand of patriarchy most likely held sway among different groups at different periods.

The Chinese house provided the physical frame of women's lives and gave concrete form to the separation of men's and women's domains. It was the site for female production not only of material goods like food and cloth but also of social goods like offspring. It is the obvious place to begin a study of Chinese gynotechnics. The actual building of the house was the work of men, of bricklayers and carpenters, but women were essential participants in the creation of domestic space. A house could not be turned into a home without the participation of women in everyday activities such as cooking, weaving and child rearing, as well as in the liturgical practices where man and wife together renewed the social bond with their lineage.

The close connection between house and family in China has attracted several fine ethnographies,[7] but I do not know of any studies that look at

7. Hsu 1948; Cohen 1976; M. Wolf 1968.

the history of the Chinese house as a social space. It is perhaps not surprising that most historical studies of the Chinese house, written by art historians and architects, "pay hardly any attention to the non-technical aspects of architecture,"[8] for they are concerned with physical structures, and a structure does not necessarily reveal the processes that produced it, or the practices for which it forms a stage. Discussing the elaborate and indispensable geomantic calculations and rituals[9] involved in repairing or adding to a house in late imperial China, Klaas Ruitenbeek points out that sometimes the end effect is almost invisible, a matter of a beam placed a few inches higher or a gate an inch wider; at other times it is intangible: rituals are performed and timing manipulated, but the actual physical building ends up the same to our eyes as it would have been if no geomancy had been used. "One gets the impression that in China *an imaginary architecture existed which was superimposed on ordinary architecture, and which was the primary concern of the owner, geomancer and carpenter alike.*" Perhaps the reason why so little was written in China on the laws and principles of architecture, Ruitenbeek suggests, was that all effort and imagination were directed toward this imaginary architecture.[10]

In the chapters that follow I argue that Chinese houses embodied several "imaginary architectures," the combination of which made them distinctively Chinese. These architectures conveyed rather different moral messages and thus permitted flexibility of practice and interpretation. For instance, as I describe in chapters 1 and 2, almost all houses incorporated both neo-Confucian lineage- and community-oriented values, embodied in the family altar, and the selfish and competitive values embodied in a house design based on geomantic principles. I do not wish to imply that individuals would make conscious choices between one interpretation of space and another, rather that one meaning might modulate or replace another according to context. This polysemic quality applies particularly to interpretations of female seclusion.

In this section, then, I explore the phenomenology of Chinese domestic

8. Ruitenbeek 1993: 4.

9. *Geomancy* is the term most commonly used to translate the terms *fengshui* (wind and water) and *dili* (patterns of the earth), which in China denote the science of siting buildings or graves within a landscape. Some scholars like Bennett and Schipper prefer the term *siting* to *geomancy*, because in Europe the latter referred to a form of divination that used handfuls of soil to predict the future. I have followed Feuchtwang and Ruitenbeek in using *geomancy*.

10. Ruitenbeek 1993: 62, emphasis added.

space and try to explain how it exercised power over its occupants. One can picture the Chinese house as a kind of loom, weaving individual lives into a typically Chinese social pattern. I examine the relation between the structure of the house and the social and cultural fabrics that it wove, the processes by which this machine was modified and standardized in the course of the late imperial period, and the nature of its contribution to social reproduction.[11] To continue the metaphor of the loom, the Chinese house wove its occupants into a historical web of kinship: through the long warp threads of the descent line, stretching back through decades or even centuries, were woven the horizontal weft threads of present marriages and alliances. In many societies the house ties families into time in this fashion. But what is unusual in the case of China is the role of written texts about houses in forming a standard and self-aware cultural and historical tradition. During the centuries that followed the Song, different kinds of texts about the house were increasingly integrated in people's minds so that the house itself became a text, interweaving hegemonic Confucian social values with popular ideals into a strong and flexible fabric.[12] Bourdieu remarks that habitus is "embodied history, internalized as

11. Bourdieu identifies the house as a key mechanism in the inculcation of habitus, a site where symbolic relations are encoded in the everyday and naturalized as physical patterns of behavior (1977, 1990). The house teaches tacit knowledge, what Giddens calls practical as opposed to discursive consciousness (1984: 7). In this study of domestic spaces and spatial practices in China I have drawn on Foucault's analysis (1979) of how space reflects and imprints ideologies. Because (unlike Foucault) I am interested in historical process, I also draw on the marxist Lefebvre's study of the production of space (1974). For Lefebvre space is both a product and a producer of social relations that has to be understood as belonging at once to material base and to ideological superstructure. He is concerned with how perceptions and intellectual representations of space relate to power but also to historical change. Like Raymond Williams writing on the culture of technology, Lefebvre seeks to break open the concept of hegemony to clarify the interaction between residual, dominant and new representations within a particular society. The production of social space is treated as a historical *process*. In that vein, I try to illuminate a process of ideological reproduction and evolution in which divergent representations of space were gradually reconciled and integrated in a multivalent form acceptable to an increasingly broad social spectrum.

12. Clifford Geertz first developed the concept of culture as text, a multilayered document that can be read or interpreted by natives as well as outsiders in many different ways (see, e.g., Geertz 1973). In her study of the Marakwet of Kenya, Henrietta Moore analyzes household space as a "cultural text," focusing on its revision as gender roles shift with Marakwet incorporation into a national economy. As Moore points out, "Space considered as a text does not take as its object real social and economic conditions, but rather ideological representations of the real" (1986: 152).

second nature and so forgotten as history."[13] In the case of the Chinese house, however, an awareness of written texts suffused spatial practices, even among the illiterate, with a conscious sense of history. The house was as important as marriage practices and funeral rituals in producing and reproducing a Chinese tradition, and the hierarchies and relationships that underpinned it.

13. Bourdieu 1990: 56.

1 House Form and Meaning

Ruitenbeek directs our attention to an "imaginary architecture" built into the physical structure of the Chinese house, namely a magico-cosmological architecture. This concept can be extended to account for other considerations as well as geomancy. I suggest that a house in late imperial China is best understood as a material structure or shell incorporating the design principles of three "imaginary architectures," each conveying a different set of messages about the relations between its inhabitants, the cosmos and society at large.

First, the house was a space of decorum, an embodiment of neo-Confucian values. It was a family shrine, constructed around the ritual center of the ancestral tablets. This house sheltered a family line, the dead as well as the living, and tied it into a historical and geographic network of patrilineal kinship. Three of the Five Relationships basic to Confucian morality—those between generation, gender and age[1]—were played out within the walls of the family house. For Confucians, the ethics and principles of governing the state were those of governing the family; the family house was not a private world, a shelter from the state, but a state in microcosm. Its occupants were tied into a political network that stretched to the boundaries of the Chinese empire. The values of this neo-Confucian world were the eminently social, collaborative values of loyalty, respect and service. The inevitable antagonisms and conflicts that arose within a household were represented, spatially contained, and resolved in ways that conformed to these values.

---

1. The other two were the relations between ruler and subject, and between friends.

Second, the house was a cosmic, energetic space. The Chinese house
was designed as a magical shelter from wind or evil influences, a site that
could channel cosmic energies (*qi*) for the benefit of its occupants. The
science of geomancy, or *fengshui* (wind and water), was used both for the
siting of graves and for the siting and design of houses; the siting of
houses seems to have been the earlier development. "The *Site Classic* tells
us that 'All human dwellings are at sites [*zhai*]. . . . Sites are the foundations of human existence.' "[2] To summarize the principles of geomancy: a
house site was chosen at a favorable spot in the landscape, determined in
part by orientation but also by the configuration and form of hills and
streams, boulders and trees. As well as the site, the details of house construction (the arrangement of buildings within the compound, the height
of roofs and gates) were all designed to channel cosmic energy for the
benefit of the occupants and to exclude harmful influences. Since cosmic
energies were constantly shifting according to seasonal and astral cycles,
time was a factor that had also to be taken into account: a site was a locus
in time as well as space, and a configuration that was inauspicious at one
date might be auspicious at another. Principles of siting and orientation
were not necessarily incompatible with Confucian values; indeed Song
neo-Confucian philosophers developed cosmological systems that overlapped with geomancy in many respects. But as Stephen Feuchtwang remarks, the principles underlying geomancy were asocial, even amoral.
Geomantic techniques did not increase cosmic energy, they simply channeled it in new directions. Siting could therefore be a means of attracting
fortune for one's own house at the expense of others.[3]

Third, the house was a space of culture: it represented a Chinese view
of what it was to be human. It was the domestic domain, where raw things
were cooked and raw materials were treated to make them fit for human
use. It provided the spaces where infants were socialized and children became adults, the boundaries that separated family from outsiders, old from

2. Bennett 1978: 2. Ruitenbeek notes that house siting seems to have predated
grave siting (1993: 36).
3. Feuchtwang (1974: 16) discusses how geomancy was elaborated under the
influence of the Song neo-Confucian philosophers, many of whom wrote at length
about *qi*; see also Bennett 1978. Geomancy could be used to benefit the community, as for example in the siting of local temples or pagodas (Feuchtwang 1974: 2;
Schipper 1982: 35), but it was also commonly used competitively. "Let one man
in a village build a fraction too high; let him build a window or a door which can
be interpreted as a threat; and he has a struggle on his hands" (Freedman 1969:
14). Baker gives a detailed account of one case of fighting with *fengshui* (1979:
appendix II).

young, masters from servants, women from men. Moreover, houses provided a culturally specific experience of space, giving prominence to certain activities, providing certain vistas, certain aesthetics. The house marked a separation from the undomesticated world, and yet it maintained links with what we might call "Nature" in a distinctively Chinese way.[4] These nuances and textures were as important as the presence of one's family in defining a Chinese sense of home. A gender distinction has to be drawn here, however: a man would grow up, marry and likely die in the house in which he, his father and paternal grandfather had been born and in which his mother would live until her death. A woman would leave her natal home on marriage to become a stranger in a new house. So men and women experienced these familiar spaces with different expectations and emotions.

In the "text" that was the house in late imperial China, concrete and imaginary architectures, elite and popular visions, embodied and discursive knowledge overlapped. To reconstitute the house as cultural text, however, we have to draw together a variety of sources. There is no single genre in Chinese writing that intentionally and systematically connects all aspects of the Chinese house and domesticity. My study draws on four principle sets of textual sources, all of them illustrated (the fourth of them lavishly).

For the neo-Confucian house centered around the ancestral altar, the space of decorum, I draw on neo-Confucian writings on liturgy and household management. A key text is the *Zhuzi jiali*, the *Family Rituals*, composed sometime after 1169 by Zhu Xi and later circulated in numerous editions and versions.[5] Zhu Xi was a founder of the moral and metaphysical school of thought commonly called neo-Confucianism, and the most influential philosopher of imperial China. The *Family Rituals* was intended to provide a comfortable liturgical handbook for everyday use

4. See Dardess 1989, a study of literati perceptions of the different zones (habitations, fields, and wild areas) surrounding the small town of Taihe, Jiangxi province, in the sixteenth and seventeenth centuries. Although the perspective is necessarily restricted to male members of the gentry class, this is a rich and suggestive historical study of what French anthropologists like Condominas have studied ethnographically as *espace social*.

5. Patricia Ebrey's translation and studies of the *Family Rituals*, its circulation and influence, have been indispensable to me, particularly since she pays careful attention to the relation of the written text to actual practices. Her translations of Song neo-Confucian texts like the *Family Rituals* and Yuan Cai's household instructions are likely to become the standard (Ebrey 1991d, 1984), and I quote them rather than giving my own translations.

by ordinary people without a high level of education. It prescribed ideal forms of ritual practice that would replace heterodox or inadequate ritual and consolidate an orthodox morality based on the values of seniority, love and respect. Zhu Xi selected between ritual instructions for routine ancestor worship and for rites of passage, as prescribed in the works of other Song philosophers. The five chapters of the *Family Rituals* are on the general principles of ritual, on initiation rituals into adulthood (capping for boys, pinning for girls),[6] on weddings, on funerals, and on sacrifices. "One of the most important of [Z]hu [X]i's own ideas was to create a new first chapter to highlight the centrality of the offering hall and the more routine ceremonies held there, including daily 'looking in,' twice-monthly 'visits,' and more formal offerings on popular festivals like New Year"[7] (see fig. 5). The *Family Rituals* includes most of Sima Guang's *Miscellaneous Etiquette for Family Life* at the end of the first chapter; the etiquette Sima (1019–86) prescribes for domestic routines is a useful complement to the liturgies prescribed by Zhu: as with other normative neo-Confucian texts on deportment and management, the observance of spatial boundaries is a central theme.[8]

Magical and cosmological concerns, questions of orientation, proportion, and the timing and ordering of construction tasks as well as the accompanying rituals are all to be found in the *Lu Ban jing,* a carpenter's manual with some sections probably dating from the Song and others added later. Lu Ban was (and still is) the patron saint of carpenters.[9] This medieval carpenters' manual (which I hereafter refer to as the *Carpenter's Canon*) shows that what was being produced when a house was built was at once a technical, a cosmological and a magical construction (fig. 11). As

6. In many societies a change of hairstyle commonly marks the passage from immaturity to maturity. In China girls pinned their hair in a single coil or chignon instead of wearing it in two ribbon-tied knots on each side of the head; boys, instead of leaving their hair uncovered, started wearing a cap or hat. In each case, in gentle families, the change was marked by a ceremony in which the young person was sponsored by an older person of the same sex, from outside the immediate family group, who pledged to guide his or her charge in the ways of righteous behavior.

7. Ebrey 1991b: 105.

8. Western works on late Qing and early twentieth-century religion and ritual (e.g., De Groot 1892–1910) and ethnographic studies (e.g., Hsu 1948; Cohen 1976; M. Wolf 1968) are important complements to the study of orthodox texts and common ritual practices, and also to the magical architecture of the Chinese house.

9. See Ruitenbeek 1986 for the use made of the *Lu Ban jing* in contemporary Taiwan.

a manual, the *Carpenter's Canon* goes beyond building to provide instructions for making various common items of furniture.[10] The building instructions in the *Carpenter's Canon* show us the pillars, walls and roofs that defined the spaces of a Chinese home; the later sections help to furnish them. I have relied on the fine translation and explication of the *Carpenter's Canon* by Ruitenbeek. To make sense of the text, Ruitenbeek had to draw on additional sources to those used by historians of architecture, including interviews with living carpenters, treatises on geomancy, ethnographic accounts, and literary anecdotes. The result is a tour de force, a rich cultural history of the Chinese house in its own right that focuses on construction and the underlying beliefs, rituals and processes that produced the magico-cosmological structure and its material shell.

For insights into the aesthetics of the house I have drawn on the *Xianqing ouji* (Casual expressions of idle feeling), written by the playwright and erotic novelist Li Yu (1610–80) and published in 1671. Li Yu, as his biographer Patrick Hanan points out, was a lover of comic invention, who managed to put a new twist on everything. " 'Broadly speaking,' he once wrote to a friend, 'everything I have ever written was intended to make people laugh.' . . . His passion for invention carried over from literature to life. He was a designer and practical inventor as well as a writer, and his essays ring with the (slightly self-mocking) refrain: 'Is it not strange that the world had to wait for Li Yu to invent this?' " He was also a sensualist with far from orthodox views on what mattered in life. "For Li Yu, all pleasure is derived from an innate faculty which includes the primary instinctual pleasures or drives such as hunger or sex. The indulgence of one's nature . . . should not 'offend against human feeling,' that is to say against a decent regard for the feelings of others; but with this one reservation, the enjoyment of beauty and sex is mandatory."[11] Though unique in his talents, Li Yu was not alone in his views. In his rejection of puritanical Confucian values he was a typical example of what was called a "literary man" (*wenren*). Literary men had always existed, but the predisposition became a way of life for many educated men during the late Ming and early Qing, when there was a dearth of opportunities for conventional careers and therefore a moral justification for the rejection of

10. These instructions are probably Ming at the latest (Ruitenbeek 1993: 139–40).

11. The first quotation is from Hanan's introduction to his translation of Li Yu's erotic novel *The Carnal Prayer Mat* (1990: v, vi); the second from his biography of Li Yu (Hanan 1988: 59).

public service. Willard Peterson says of the *wenren* in the late Ming that they threw themselves into the arts as others might into moral philosophy or politics.[12]

Casual Expressions contains a cornucopia of musings on dilettante topics, including the composition and production of plays or opera, female beauty, gardening, eating and drinking, and maintaining health (including sections on dispelling melancholy and curbing excessive sexual desire). Books 8 and 9 of the sixteen-book work are devoted to houses, and they represent what Hanan calls the summation of a "lifelong passion for houses and gardens": Li Yu had designed numerous houses and gardens for patrons and friends, and for himself the famous Mustard Seed Garden in Nanjing, on a plot purchased in 1668.[13] Ruitenbeek remarks that, along with the *Zhangwu zhi* (Record of superfluous things) written by Wen Zhenheng (1585–1645) a few years earlier, *Casual Expressions* documents a development in which "architecture was for the first time added to the list of subjects which were seen as worthy of the attention of the literary man." Wen's book was a guide to connoisseurship that presumed a taste formed by superior education, but also the money to purchase.[14] Li Yu seldom had any money, but he came up with innumerable ingenious ways to live an aesthetically rich life for next to nothing. Here is one mischievous example, where he claims to bring beauty into his home by starving his wife: "I have been poor all my life and have moved constantly, without a place of my own. But although I borrow money to eat and have to rent my living-quarters, I never allow my place to become untidy or dirty. I love flowers and bamboos, but can't afford them. So I let my wife and servants go hungry for a few days or put up with cold through the winter, and by spending nothing on body and mouth we can indulge our eyes and ears. People laugh, but we are happy and satisfied."[15]

12. Peterson 1979: 32; see also Rawski 1985: 13 on the prevalence of *wenren* in the late Ming and early Qing.

13. Unfortunately this oeuvre vanished long ago (Hanan 1988: vii; Hanan refers to Li's passion for houses and gardens in a chapter in the same work, the quotation being from p. 29).

14. See Ruitenbeek 1993: 30 on the new attention to architecture; Clunas 1991 is a detailed study of the emergence and meanings of writings on connoisseurship in the late Ming, centered on the *Record of Superfluous Things*.

15. *Casual Expressions* 8.2a. Unless otherwise stated, the translations from *Casual Expressions* are the joint effort of myself and Alison Sau-chu Yeung, who kindly brought to my attention the relevance of this work for my study. Li Yu's poverty was relative. He failed to take an official post and depended largely on gifts or support from patrons; at the same time, he earned a considerable income by the standards of the time from his writing, and also ran a shop to sell books

Li's writings on the house are divided under five main headings, each with several subheadings. The first section, "Buildings," includes the following subsections: orientation, paths, height, depth of the eaves, ceilings, brick floors, sprinkling and sweeping, and disposing of dirt. The second section, "Windows and Verandahs," starts with a subsection on lattices and frames, followed by a fascinating essay on what Li calls "borrowing views" (*jiejing*). The third section, "Walls," has subsections on boundary walls, parapets, the walls of main rooms and of the study or library, the latter being the status symbol par excellence of the period. The fourth section is devoted to calligraphic scrolls and inscriptions, the fifth to garden decor ("Mountains and Stones"). Li is completely unconcerned with the ritual, magical or moral dimensions of a house. He is passionately absorbed in its aesthetics, in the fine grain of textures, in human proportions, in the relation between domestic and wild, house and landscape.

My fourth source is not Chinese but Japanese, the *Shinzoku kibun* (Recorded accounts of Qing customs [hereafter *Qing Customs*]), first published in 1800. It was compiled by a Nagasaki magistrate, Nakagawa Tadahide (d. 1830), to provide information about China to officers in the Nagasaki magistrature, who had to deal frequently with Chinese merchants using their port. The work also appealed to a broader audience of Japanese intellectuals, hungry for knowledge of the wider world.[16] Nakagawa gave the task of collecting information on China to two officers, one of them the head of the local education office, who spent a year working with seven Chinese merchants to put together a picture of the manners, customs and everyday life of "ordinary people" in China. The accounts were translated by naturalized Japanese of Chinese descent, and the illustrations were made according to the merchants' directions by two Japanese woodblock artists trained by Chinese masters. The seven merchants, like the translators who worked on their accounts, came from four cities in the Yangzi Delta (Hangzhou, Huzhou, Suzhou and Jiaxing), and they were also familiar with the port cities of Fujian. But as they told Nakagawa,

---

and elegant writing paper that he designed himself. His family was large, however, not least because in the course of the years he accepted two concubines as gifts from patrons (Hanan 1988: 8).

16. Japan under the Tokugawa shogunate was closed to foreigners and Japanese were forbidden to travel abroad. The port of Nagasaki was the only place where foreign traders were allowed to set foot on Japanese soil. The preface notes that whereas Japan had had close cultural links with China in the Tang dynasty, and had maintained contacts during the Song, Yuan and early Ming, since then the Japanese had been starved of information on China (*Shinzoku kibun* A: 8).

"China is a very large country whose customs are very different from province to province. We come from the Southeast, and can only describe the customs and scenery of that region."[17]

The book is in thirteen sections: yearly activities (including festivals); the house; clothes; food and drink; education; childbirth; the rituals of capping and pinning; marriage rituals; receiving guests; how to travel in China; funeral rituals; Confucian sacrifices and rituals; Buddhist and Daoist monks. The section on the house is by far the longest, seventy-five double pages in length,[18] and copiously illustrated (fig. 3). Although both Nakagawa and the merchants were anxious to show respect toward the venerable and sagely traditions of Chinese civilization, it is striking that Confucian ceremonies were left to the penultimate section.[19]

The accounts of domestic life in the *Qing Customs* are full of fascinating and intimate details of the kind that come up incidentally in Ming and Qing novels, but here are treated systematically. The merchants who provided the information seem to have been perfectly willing to discuss matters that members of the educated elite would have regarded as vulgar or improper. Prompted no doubt by the curiosity of their Japanese interlocutors, they take us beyond the reception rooms into their wives' sitting rooms and bedrooms, enumerating and describing the details of the furnishings. They tell us how visitors of differing degrees of familiarity are greeted. They describe the bathhouse and the latrine, the kitchen and its equipment, the maids' and the menservants' quarters and the conditions of their hire. They discuss the amount of ice a fishmonger uses on a summer day and the price of kindling. They show us the difference between a

17. *Shinzoku kibun* A: 13. I have used two editions of the *Shinzoku kibun*, which I refer to as A (a facsimile of the original) and B (an annotated and commented edition in modern Japanese; for details see list of references cited). In my translations I was greatly helped by Mayumi Matsumoto. The preface to the *Shinzoku kibun* discusses the various Chinese and Japanese persons whose expertise Nakagawa coordinated, and this information is supplemented in B 2: 156.

18. Books in China and Japan were made of lengths of paper folded concertina-style after printing and sewed together at one side; a double fold was counted as one page.

19. Nor did its contents represent the emphases of high Confucianism. Its eighteen double pages start with the ancestral cult at the lineage temple, at the grave and in the home, then go on to public cults of the city god, the god of the soil, Tianhou (the patron goddess of sailors), temple operas, and finally Guandi (the god of war). Tianhou and Guandi were both deities who had been tamed and claimed by the state over the centuries, much as the Christian church in the West tamed winter and spring festivals and turned them to its own purposes. See J. Watson 1985 on the state appropriation of Tianhou, and Brook 1993: 279, 288–93 on the cult of Guandi.

wealthy and a poor house. They tell us that the ladies of the house did not like to go out into the backyard to use the latrine, and show us the chamberpots they used instead. There is even a section on childbirth, the special clothes and equipment, the hiring of a midwife and a wet nurse, the special foods; this section contains a splendid illustration (unique as far as I know) of the newly delivered woman propped up by quilts on her bed (fig. 21).

Qing Customs also provides a lavishly illustrated inventory of the furniture that one might expect to find in a Jiangnan merchant's house of the period, arranged in groups after the description of the room or part of the house where that category of objects was most likely to be found. Furnishings are a key element in constructing domestic space and in defining an aesthetic or style, and they also constitute a highly visible marker of class and status. Unfortunately we know little about the furnishings of poor families in premodern China, only that they had very few. From Song times on, and most particularly from the Ming, it is possible to determine fairly fully the kinds of furniture that wealthy families were likely to use and how they were used, whether from written sources such as dictionaries and encyclopedias, or from paintings, from clay models included in burials, or from furniture that has survived in use to the present. Sometimes it is even possible to surmise how differences between men and women might have been expressed through furniture, for instance in pictures that show men occupying chairs while women sit on stools.[20]

These texts of different date and perspective are all imprinted with what is recognizably the same cultural template of domesticity. The *Family Rituals* and the *Carpenter's Canon* date from the beginning of the period of cultural formation in which I am interested, and they are particularly important because of their central contribution to forming the template and to composing the written "text" of the Chinese house. The *Casual Expressions* and the *Qing Customs* date from well into the late

20. It seems that most fine furniture was made of perishable lacquered softwoods until the Ming, when hardwood furniture, some of which has survived to the present day, became fashionable. The southern regions of China produced some excellent hardwoods, but the most appreciated timbers came from Southeast Asia; the open-door trading policy initiated in the Ming allowed the fashion for hardwood furniture to flower (see e.g., Wang Shixiang 1991: introduction). The Ming and early Qing are considered by most connoisseurs and historians to have been the golden age of Chinese furniture; by the later Qing a more ornate style became popular which many experts now consider degenerate, although demand for it was high in Western countries at the time. On Chinese furniture see Kates 1948; Ecke 1962; Clunas 1988; Wang Shixiang 1991; Xu Wen 1991.

Figure 3. Ordinary houses and shops (*Qing Customs* A: 72–73). "Ordinary" means that they do not belong to official families. The large house in the foreground probably belonged to a well-off merchant family. The hall at the front was for receiving guests. The plants and bamboos along the left wall of the inner courtyard probably face the sliding doors of a study. The women's quarters at the back of the inner courtyard are screened off by a wall with only one

small entrance door, as recommended by Sima Guang, but the upper story has an airy open verandah on which the ladies could enjoy the evening breeze. Behind the women's quarters, across the street, is a peasant's house, a simple thatched building with a stall for the ox at the front. On the other street we see the fronts of two shops: an apothecary's or physician's consulting room on the left and a cloth merchant's shop on the right.

imperial period. They were not widely distributed and did not contribute to the writing of the house-text. They are interesting, however, because they take the template for granted, and instead deal explicitly with concerns and aspects of spatial experience that are tacit in—not alien to—the earlier sources.

THE HOUSE IN LATE IMPERIAL CHINA: MATERIAL DESIGN

The family house has received only incidental attention from most historians of architecture and building technology. They usually concentrate on the more spectacular and elaborate forms of building—temples, palaces, the great Chinese gardens—treating domestic architecture as a minor application of a great art. Furthermore, most historical analyses have been centrally concerned with functional analysis, technical development and changing aesthetics rather than with buildings as social constructs.[21] Liu Dunzhen and Ronald Knapp between them have done more than anybody to rescue vernacular architecture from the shadow cast by more impressive buildings, treating it as a form in its own right. Both recognize the importance of the ordinary house in shaping the everyday experience of Chinese life. They are alert to the cultural and political dimensions of domestic space, even though that is not the central focus of their studies. Their works survey the variety of late imperial and twentieth-century Chinese domestic buildings as well as their common features, documenting adaptations of building technique and style to local environment and to wealth and poverty. It is to their surveys, supplemented by Needham's volume on architecture and Ruitenbeek's study of the *Carpenter's Canon*, that I principally refer in the following brief account of Chinese house structure.[22]

To what extent is it possible to reconstitute the material structures of the ordinary family house in late imperial China, to postulate a typical or ideal house, to account for variations in style? Almost no poor houses over a couple of centuries old survive in China today, but the well-built houses of the wealthy have lasted longer. In the 1950s architects documented several hundred fine Ming houses in the rural regions of southern Anhui province, mostly gentry or merchant houses, but also a few simple

21. Although several pay special attention to the dimensions of power inherent in elite constructions (e.g., Thilo 1977 and Johnston 1983), as well as works on architecture published in the People's Republic that always include allusions to extraction, exploitation and control.
22. Liu Dunzhen 1980; Knapp 1986; Needham et al. 1971; Ruitenbeek 1993.

cottages.[23] The pictorial record too favors the mansions of the wealthy, and technical treatises like the *Carpenter's Canon* and the *Yingzao fashi*[24] show separate elements of construction, not whole houses.[25] Nevertheless, sufficient information can be retrieved from texts and pictures to conclude that ordinary houses changed little through the late imperial period, so that "for the most part, one may look at a twentieth-century rural building and see one of an earlier time."[26]

The archetypal Chinese house occupied a walled enclosure in which buildings were arranged parallel or at right angles to the front façade, defining one or more courtyards. Layout was based on the principles of orientation, axiality and symmetry: all houses should face south; in large houses the successive courtyard units should be constructed along a vertical north-south axis; and the buildings on the left hand of the axis should be a mirror image of those on the right (fig. 4). Orientation was a cosmological requirement: south was the auspicious direction, and the ancestral tablets, placed in the main room of the house overlooking the open space of the main courtyard, should face that direction. Inside the compound, all the buildings would be arranged either north-south (vertical) or east-west (horizontal), with the most important rooms benefiting from the southern aspect of the horizontal structures. Public and ritual spaces (the room containing the ancestral tablets, reception rooms) were housed in the horizontal halls (*tang*, the back hall; *ting*, the front hall), while sleeping quarters or storerooms occupied the vertical wings (*fang* or *xiang*).

Most Chinese houses were surrounded by a wall several feet high, usually a bare façade pierced only by the gate. To guard against prying eyes and evil winds a somewhat lower screen stood a few feet inside the gate. The inner façades of the buildings were as open as the climate permitted,

23. Knapp 1986: 19 fig. 1.13; Zhang Zhongyi et al. 1957. Unfortunately most of these old houses have since been torn down and replaced with modern buildings, but in Huizhou (which by Ming times was a rich commercial center that supported a large network of old and distinguished gentry families) many fine houses have survived to the present day, some of which still contain Ming furniture (Huang Yilong, personal communication 1995). In the sixteenth century the cabinetmakers of Huizhou were nationally famous, and many set up in southern cities like Suzhou and even in the northern capital of Beijing (Wang Shixiang 1991: 14).
24. *Building Standards*, a building guide for official use published in 1103 (Glahn 1982).
25. The technical detail of the ground-plans in the *Shinzoku kibun* is altogether exceptional in showing the precise location of every pillar, as well as steps, windows and doors, and naming each of the spaces.
26. Knapp 1986: 21.

Figure 4.   The An Tai Lin residence in eastern Taibei (reproduced from Li Chien-lang 1980, by permission). This is a perfect example of vertical and horizontal symmetry and shows how the geomantic and social status of halls and wings, and the chambers within them, is differentiated by the height and style of the roof; the apex of the building is the roof of the ceremonial hall at the back of the inner court. Note also the elaborate roofed entrance gate.

with large lattice windows and often folding doors opening onto a court-yard. Verandahs or overhanging eaves provided a pleasant intermediary space between inside and outside, shady in the height of summer and a sun-trap in the winter. Ideally the courtyard would contain a well, plants and shrubs. It was a social space, where the family members could relax or chat to each other as they carried out domestic tasks. In poor houses with small rooms, the confinement of the winter months was oppressive, and during the summer the women spent as much time in the courtyard as possible. Even in winter they would come out onto the sunny verandah, sheltered from the wind, to spin or prepare food. It was common to cate-gorize houses by the number of courtyards they possessed, and indeed one could argue that the courtyard was the heart of the dwelling, the point of view from which the buildings themselves were perceived.[27]

27. This was certainly the case in the Muslim societies of the Mediterranean and western Asia, and one might even presume that this tradition drew on the still older courtyard construction of the North African and Mediterranean villas of the Roman empire. Antoine Abdel Nour concludes that the term used in medi-eval Syria for a family dwelling, *dar,* basically referred to a "celestial" courtyard surround by buildings turned inward, without external façades, a materialization of the closed Arab agnatic family (1979: 82–83). In the same volume Roberto Berardi takes this analysis further, to argue how the whole structure of a medieval Arab town worked to enclose rather than to make public all that was prized and

In the north few houses were more than a single story high, but two-story houses were common in the south, in villages as well as towns. Buildings were constructed on a platform of beaten earth that varied in height according to the wealth of the family and the importance of that particular building. In large houses the main buildings would be taller than the others, and the floor was often raised up a flight of several steps. Within a compound, structures differed in height to produce a pleasing variety, with roofs of different pitches and curves, and walls and gates of varying heights.

The usual building materials in China were wood and earth; stone was rare even in mansions and palaces. Rich houses were roofed with good-quality tiles, with elaborate guttering and overhanging eaves that protected the wooden beams and rafters; their walls were of fired brick and good-quality plaster. Poor houses usually had roofs of thatch or mud and straw (cob), and fragile walls of cob or unbaked brick.

The foundation of a Chinese house was a platform of pounded earth, and the load-bearing framework usually consisted of wooden pillars and beams. The Chinese configuration of pillars and beams allowed considerable flexibility in roof design. Roofs in the north were often almost flat, but southerners preferred fantastical curves and upturned eaves.[28] The size of buildings and of rooms was reckoned in bays, or *jian:* the space between pillars.[29] If a house consisted of a single hall of several bays in size it was better to have an odd number, for this made symmetry between reception areas and sleeping quarters or storerooms easier to preserve

---

valuable, and to confine strangers to the blank walls of the streets, excluding them from access. There are certain obvious parallels with Chinese house and city design that might perhaps be connected to similar conceptions of agnatic identity. One wonders whether the common use of the term *heaven-well* to designate a courtyard in northern China might owe anything to Pax Mongolica.

28. This is a quite different construction from the European frame and roof truss. It allows flexibility both of roof curvature and of adaptation to uneven sites (Knapp 1986: 71 fig. 3.36 shows the contrasting structure of northern and southern frames; 76 fig. 3.44 shows building on a slope). Knapp remarks that in domestic architecture walls of brick or tamped earth often serve as load-bearers; it is mistaken to assume that the wooden load-bearing frame, though typical of palaces and temples, was a universal feature.

29. House size was also reckoned by the number of bays, but the scale of the building was determined by a basic module, the cross-section of the bracket arms supporting the roof. All the main timbers of the building were in standard proportions to this module, which varied according to the rank of building. The *Yingzao fashi* (Building standards) of 1103 uses a somewhat smaller basic measurement than the corresponding government handbook of 1734, *Gongcheng zuofa zeli* (Structural regulations) (Glahn 1982; S. Liang 1984: 15).

than if the number was even. Inner walls were not structural, load-bearing walls, but partitions, which could be moved or changed relatively easily.

Not all houses attained the ideal. Poor houses were less likely than rich to display symmetry or axiality, and sometimes did not even face south. Nor were they necessarily enclosed by a wall. A really poor house might consist of a single bay in which strict internal symmetry was impossible: it was unevenly partitioned to mark off a small sleeping space at one side, so the main room containing the ancestral tablets was not central. In the rural regions of the lower Yangzi small houses were often L-shaped, in which case symmetry was clearly impossible.[30]

Yet despite the great variety in details of construction and layout, when these guidelines are taken in conjunction with spatial practices we realize that houses in late imperial China did display a fundamental unity of design, conforming to a clear-cut set of principles. The division of interior space into designated functional categories was much the same in rich and poor houses, all of which contained an ancestral shrine, bedrooms, kitchen, and storage space. Rich houses could afford more diversity and were likely to designate spaces as guest rooms, reception rooms, studies and bathrooms as well. Yang Siqing, building a suburban mansion from scratch in the early fifteenth century, "put up an ancestral temple, a hall for entertaining guests, living quarters, housing for his sons and grandsons, a studio for study, a pavilion set among flower plantings, plus storehouses, kitchen, and stables."[31]

Given the key importance of eating as a social rite in China, it is interesting to note that spaces designated specifically for eating were rare even in large houses, which seldom contained anything equivalent to a dining

30. Liu Dunzhen 1980: 105–10.
31. Dardess 1989: 306. *Qing Customs* tells us that in well-to-do houses a small bathhouse stood next to the latrine in the back courtyard, where the kitchen and the well were also situated (fig. 7). Poor people, farmers and workmen, did not have bathrooms of their own but went to public bathhouses, or for a small payment one could buy hot water by the basinful—which was presumably what poor women did if they wanted a good wash (A: 134, 161). In ancient China officials were expected to take a hot bath every five days and to wash their hair every three, according to the *Liji* (Book of rites). Perfumes for the bath were brought to a fine art in early medieval times, and medicinal baths were also common; Wang Tao's collection of medical prescriptions, the *Waitai miyao* of 752, contains a chapter on washing and cosmetic preparations, including five for hair washes and eight for bathsoaps. Public bathhouses are first noted in Hangzhou in the Song, and large public bathhouses gradually became a notable feature of city life. As for latrines, Han grave models show them built up a staircase above the pigpen. The earliest mention of toilet paper is in a book of family instructions, the *Yanshi jiaxun* of 590, where using any paper on which characters have been written is prohibited.

room or banqueting hall; family members usually ate separately depending on sex and age, and guests were entertained in different parts of the house depending on their intimacy with family members. In well-off households parties of male guests would generally be entertained in the main hall, sitting at numerous small tables. One popular form of dining table was a square table large enough for two to sit at each side, the so-called Eight Immortals Table (*baxian zhuo*); another popular form seated only four guests, and was about three feet square. "The Ming or Qing dinner party did not assume any single invariable form. However one thing about the most formal dinner parties which struck a sixteenth-century Dutch writer as odd was that one small table was provided for each diner, rather than the great feasting boards familiar to him from Europe." Some families used long rectangular tables for less formal meals, though generally in China larger tables were used not for eating, but as sidetables set against the walls on which were placed either the paraphernalia of the ancestral cult or vases of flowers and objets d'art. The bedroom scenes of Ming illustrated novels often include rectangular tables set at the side of the bed; they were used as dressing tables, for writing, painting, or for casual meals when no guests were present.[32]

Even in poor houses that could not afford to set aside whole rooms for special functions and in which formal symmetries and orientation could not be achieved, the arrangement of objects within the rooms themselves permitted the occupants to produce the ritual orientation that was required. In a poor house, the ancestral tablets might be jammed into a tiny niche in the main room, which might face west rather than south. But the underlying principle of orientation concerned the ancestral tablets rather than the façade, so some flexibility was possible. Some humble houses made do with adjusting the site of the altar.[33] In the famous case of Chairman Mao's family home, where an overhanging hill made a southern orientation of the main hall impossible, a tiny well was constructed within the house so that the ancestral tablets looked out southward from the

32. Clunas 1988: 45, 51; see also Wang Shixiang 1991: 24–28 and plates. In section 9, on entertaining, the *Qing Customs* has an illustration of a dinner party where the guests are seated at small tables. The final illustration of the rice farming series in the *Bianmin tuzuan* (p. 16) shows a harvest feast where the landlord entertains his workers and tenants at a long board; the feast is nearing its end, everyone is drunk, some are singing, some dancing, some performing tricks, and one man can hold his liquor no longer. At genteel dinner parties the guests were seated on chairs; at the rustic harvest feast the table is surrounded by benches. The social significance of different forms of seating will be discussed below.

33. See for instance Liu Dunzhen 1980: 83 fig. 45.

main hall onto a "courtyard." If imaginary and concrete architectures are considered together, if social practice is integrated into the analysis of spatial form, then we perceive the complex underlying unity of the Chinese house. We can understand how people ordered their living space, making homes of their houses, and manipulating inadequate material resources to conform to the requirements of decent and respectable living.

SOME AESTHETICS OF HOUSE DESIGN

There are many construction features of Chinese houses that can be interpreted in straightforwardly functional terms, as adaptations to resources or to the environment. In the north, courtyards were often long and narrow so that they caught the winter sun, while in the south they tended to be wide and shallow, to keep out the summer sunlight. Overhanging and upturned eaves were common in the south where rainfall was heavy, and straight-pitched or flat roofs were characteristic of the more arid northern regions. In forested regions like Sichuan and Yunnan houses were likely to have wooden walls, but in the long deforested loess lands of the northwest the use of wood was reduced to a minimum and often houses were simply carved into the soil, like elaborate caves.[34] Although the irregular plans and lack of symmetry that I have mentioned as common in poor houses obviously relate to a lack of the means to buy a suitable plot and to invest in building a larger house, many technical choices cannot be explained as purely functional.

The use of wood and earth as primary construction materials can be seen in strictly pragmatic terms: they were always available and very adaptable. Loose earth was pounded between wooden frames to form a solid foundation or walls, plastered between lathes or branches as wattle and daub, or mixed with straw for cob, which was used for both walls and flat roofs in northern China. Earth was also the raw material for bricks, fired and unfired, and for tiles. But the preference for earth and wood was also a cultural choice. Although stone was used as a building material for graves and certain religious buildings, where dwellings were

34. The cave houses of the northwestern loess lands have attracted much attention from architectural writers (Knapp 1986: 31–39 provides a section on them as well as several fine illustrations). They remain a living tradition: large numbers have been either reconditioned or constructed since 1949. The only other Chinese housing genre that has attracted as much special attention is the communal dwellings of the Hakka (Liu Dunzhen 1980: 152; Boyd 1962; Knapp 1986: 45).

concerned—even mansions and palaces—it was seldom used except for the bases of the structural wooden columns. It has been suggested that this was because stone was associated with the dwellings of the dead (*yinzhai*) and was therefore avoided in the houses of the living (*yangzhai*).[35] At the same time both earth and wood had desirable symbolic associations.

In Five Phase cosmology, Earth represented the center of the compass, the Inner Kingdom, the human domain. The goddess Nü Gua had fashioned the first human beings out of yellow earth. Even ordinary people unacquainted with the sophisticated details of Five Phase cosmology knew that humans had a particular affinity with Earth. "Attachment to earth is a Han tradition; the southern frontiers of Chinese civilization are marked by the limits of the zones where houses are built directly on the ground."[36]

The use of wood as a construction material clearly went beyond strictly structural requirements. Alternative building techniques for roofing were known in China, which could have reduced the need for timber—for instance, the brick vaults and arches made in China from early times but whose use was largely restricted to tombs and temples. In strictly economic terms the loss of forests and woodlands and the consequently high prices of timber made such alternatives desirable in many parts of China by late imperial times. Nevertheless, most houses continued to use large quantities of timber. Two factors probably combined to maintain the tradition, the first an aesthetic preference for curved roofs and broad eaves, the second the cosmological association of wood with patterns of growth and branching, a model of successful reproduction.[37]

35. Ruitenbeek 1993: 8.

36. Métailié et al. 1980: 15. Chinese cosmology is concerned not with essences and distinctions but with the ebb and flow of energies and with patterns of transformation. The Five Phases (water, wood, fire, earth, metal) do not represent distinct and nonfungible elements, as in Greek thought, but rather a sequence of characteristic patterns of transformation. For example, water is associated with patterns of condensation of matter and downward movement, fire with patterns of dispersion and upward movement. All natural phenomena (including human beings) go through successive cycles of phases during the course of their existence, but one phase or pattern may be considered especially characteristic of a particular phenomenon.

37. See Needham et al. 1971: 65 and Liu Dunzhen 1980: 67 on the restricted use of stone. Eaves were so important in the aesthetic experience of the house that Li Yu invented cheap "adjustable eaves" for the poor scholar who could not afford a house with an overhanging roof and large windows (*Casual Expressions* 8.6a–b).

The demand for wood maintained a huge lumber trade linking the forested mountains of the interior with the cities of the plains and deltas.[38] As early as the Song there are descriptions of rafts like small towns floating down the Yangzi, hundreds of yards long and built of innumerable tree trunks, on which the lumbermen's families lived in houses, with their livestock, and sometimes even a temple and a tavern. By the Ming Chinese stocks were severely reduced and hardwoods were imported from Southeast Asia. Palaces and rich mansions might use fine woods even for beams and rafters, but among commoners hardwood was reserved for coffins, and for furniture if they could afford it. Most ordinary houses were built with softwood. A seventeenth-century text tells us that in the south fir was mostly used; in the dry northern plains, where no forests were left, people took whatever wood was available, using "mulberry, willow, locust and pine . . . indiscriminately. That is the reason why their beams and purlins are frequently crooked." In the north and northwest, where rainfall was low and timber scarce, most poor people built houses with a type of almost flat roof that required only two horizontal end-beams and four or five rafters.[39] Wherever possible the Chinese built with a wooden framework despite the considerable expense, producing a richly textured house-scape of harmonious curves that satisfied both geomantic and aesthetic expectations. It is sometimes hard to separate geomantic from aesthetic reasoning: "The shape of a house is of the highest importance. If the shape is unfavourable, the house will be hard to live in definitively. Whether a house is favourable or unfavourable, unlucky or lucky, can be told by the eye. As a rule, a house is favourable if it is square and straight, plain and neat, and pleasing to the eye. If it is too high and large, or too small and tumbledown, so as to be displeasing to the eye, then it is unfavourable."[40]

"Square and straight, plain and neat" did not mean dull or uniform.

38. This brief account is based on Ruitenbeek 1993: 7–15. Other discussions of the use of wood in building include Tong 1981 on crafts and the timber trade, and Needham et al. 1971.

39. Liu Dunzhen 1980: 89; the crooked timbers of the north are mentioned in the *Wu za zu*, tr. Ruitenbeek 1993: 14.

40. *Bazhai zaofu zhoushu* 1: 4b, tr. Ruitenbeek 1993: 38. Feuchtwang (1974: 142–43) discusses the coincidences and parallels between the auspicious and the beautiful in the selection of sites, pointing to the importance of adjectives like "beautiful" *(mei)* and "graceful" *(xiu)* in describing good sites. Geomantic concerns, he says, are integrated even into the most popular levels of spatial experience, "affect[ing] the very perception of the reality of a landscape and of fortune."

Within a house compound a pleasingly dynamic effect was produced by differences in the pitch of roofs and the height of buildings, walls and gates. Yet this effect was achieved within the span of one or at most two stories.[41] Even grandiose buildings such as palaces followed this pattern. The only buildings in a late imperial Chinese city or rural landscape that stood out above the low roofs were drumtowers, pagodas, and city walls.[42] Within these limits, height signified eminence, and the height of the pillars was often a reflection of the owner's self-esteem. Li Yu remarks sourly that while high ceilings and wide eaves are an unmistakable sign of grandeur, such splendid rooms are only comfortable in summer. In winter the owner can no doubt afford thick furs, but a poor guest will shiver in his padded jacket. Yet the tiny house of a poor scholar makes the most carefree visitor sigh and feel oppressed. "Houses should be built to human scale."[43]

Li Yu insisted that houses should be kept clean and neat. Perhaps poverty was one reason why Li took such an interest in housecleaning, for at one point he remarks that cleanliness and tidiness can compensate for cramped quarters. His concern may also reflect a symbolic view, expressed in both Confucian and Buddhist thought, of dust as polluting. The ancestral cult required that a room be carefully swept before any ritual performance, and Buddhism referred to the mortal world as a place of red dust. Sweeping was a purifying act that eliminated pollution as well as dirt. It seems to have been general practice to sweep the courtyard as well as the rooms of the house every morning. Sima Guang incorporates daily sweeping into a structure of gender segregation: "The servants of the inner and outer quarters and the concubines all rise at the first crow of the cock. After combing their hair, washing, and getting dressed, the male servants should sweep the halls and front courtyard; the doorman and older servants should sweep the middle courtyard, while the maids sweep the living quarters, arrange the tables and chairs, and prepare for the toilet of the master and mistress." To stop the dust from flying, water was first sprinkled on the ground. Li Yu deplored the fact that this ancient practice

41. One exception to this rule is the Hakka communal house of the southeast; see n. 34.

42. Needham contrasts the horizontal lines of a Chinese built landscape with the "vertical soaring" that first appeared in the West with the Gothic cathedral, linking the upward impulses of European design to a theology that emphasized transcendence and the fusing of Chinese building into the surrounding landscape to spiritual concepts of immanence. Lefebvre (1974), in contrast, interprets the Gothic thrust, like the skyscraper, as an embodiment of phallic aggression.

43. *Casual Expressions* 8.1b.

was neglected in his day; lazy servants could not be bothered to draw water, and masters were ignorant of the need to sprinkle before sweeping. He gives us a four-page disquisition on how to clean properly, using just the right amount of water, keeping the brush close to the ground and sweeping gently rather than vigorously, with the doors shut.[44]

Li's next section is entitled "Storing Dirt and Disposing of Filth." "For a scholar who loves tidiness, a single object out of place is like a thorn in the eye." Keeping things nice required constant effort, like scholarship. Even the most magnificent mansion would fail to please unless it was kept tidy. There should be a small shed for storing old letters, wastepaper, dirty inkstones and worn out writing brushes until one got around to disposing of them, as well as the ends of rouge and leftover face powder from the women's quarters. Poor families who could not afford a special shed should put their rubbish in a chest until they could bury it.[45]

The problem of rubbish was as nothing compared with the problem of human elimination, Li complained, especially for a cultivated man. Going to the privy to empty the bowels was not too taxing since it was only necessary occasionally. Going back and forth to urinate, however, was a frequent and irksome need. "Sometimes a scholar is buried in his work and fears even a short interruption will break the mood. He can skip meals, but not going to the privy. . . . Do they not say that if you have a perfect phrase at the tip of your writing-brush and you go for a pee, when you get back it will be lost for ever? Since I have frequently had this experience, I have found a way for coping with these emergencies. I insert a small bamboo tube through the study wall, protruding at either end. That way I never need to leave my study to urinate, whatever the time of day or weather."[46] Since the privy was a building that one could safely relegate to the geomantically most inauspicious place in the compound, it often was a long way from the study.

The distinction between formal, public spaces and informal and more intimate ones was also marked by the decorations, the furnishings and their arrangement. "In large halls [furniture] was usually placed in a sym-

44. On tidiness compensating for space see ibid.: 8.2a. The quotation from Sima Guang is translated by Ebrey 1991d: 33. Li Yu's treatise on how to sweep is contained in *Casual Expressions* 8.8a–10a.

45. *Casual Expressions* 8.10a–11b.

46. Just over a century later, the Marquis de Sade inserted a pipe in the wall of his room in the Bastille and used it for the same purpose. Since his room was high up over the street, the effects on passers-by were even more unfortunate than in Li Yu's case.

metrical, somewhat rigid, arrangement. In studios and living quarters it was found in freer, more varied and more practical arrangements."[47] According to the *Qing Customs*, the centerpiece of the main hall where guests were received was an alcove with scrolls hanging symmetrically above a large table, on which were placed incense burners and flower vases. To either side were set chairs and stools of mahogany, rosewood or rattan where guests were invited to sit and chat. The front of the hall consisted of folding wooden doors; the side walls were decorated outside with panels of landscape paintings and calligraphic inscriptions.[48] Chairs were formal furniture denoting high status. "The vast majority of the population never sat on high chairs . . . which have retained to this century in Chinese culture something of the connotations of status and authority with which their origins were associated."[49] When chairs first came into common use in China, around the eighth or ninth century, they were the prerogative of religious patriarchs or of high officials. By Song times chairs were common in all well-off households, but they were seldom used by women when men were around, except by the wife of the household head. In mixed company most women sat on stools; in a female group only the senior women used chairs. Hierarchies were also marked by the type of chair occupied, whether a square-backed or a round-backed chair, with or without arms.[50]

Chairs went together with high tables and with a whole range of furnishings that developed only once the chair came into general use. Previously Chinese furniture had been designed for use from the floor: armrests, tables with legs only a few inches long, low coffers and chests. This kind of furniture did not disappear with the adoption of chairs, but continued to be used in the relaxed setting of the study or the bedchamber, or of the heated platforms on which people spent the winter months in North China, known as *kangs*. The scholar's couch (*ta*), which was used not just for sleeping but also for sitting and for lounging, and low tables and other

47. Wang Shixiang 1991: 41.
48. *Shinzoku kibun* A: 75; B: 1, 78. It was a southern custom, said the merchants who provided the information for this work, to build an inner hall *en suite* with the main hall that could be used for parties; it faced out onto a space planted with trees, or perhaps with bonsai or flowers or a bamboo fence (A: 96).
49. Clunas 1988: 22.
50. In early China everyone, of whatever status, sat or knelt on mats on the floor. The Chinese chair seems to have developed from the raised seating platforms or "thrones" that were introduced sometime after the Han dynasty by Buddhists (see ibid.: 15–17; Wang Shixiang 1991: 14–15).

so-called *kang* furniture continued to be made for use in these intimate spaces (fig. 10).[51]

Furniture could indicate both the means and the taste of its owner. Although Clunas argues that fine furniture in the Ming and Qing was cheap by comparison with other status markers such as antiques, paintings or calligraphy, some people seem to have been prepared to pay extravagant sums, as suggested by the following passage that documents the beginnings of the fashion for hardwood furniture in a small town on the lower Yangzi:

> When I was young I saw but a few pieces of furniture, such as writing-tables and large chairs, made from fine wood. The common people only had pieces made from ginko wood and gold tinted lacquer square tables. Mo Tinghan and the young gentlemen of the Gu and Song families began the practice of bringing a few pieces of fine wood furniture to Yunjian [near present-day Shanghai] from Suzhou. During the Longqing [1567–72] and Wanli [1573–1620] periods, even lower officials began to use fine wooden furniture, and cabinet-makers from Huizhou opened shops in Yunjian where they made wedding furniture and other objects. At that time the wealthy families did not consider *ju* wood good enough and so it had become customary for them to have all their beds, cabinets and tables made from *huali* wood, burl wood, blackwood, *xiangsi* wood and boxwood. This furniture is very fine and exorbitant, each piece costing ten thousand cash, a most extravagant custom.[52]

At the other end of the economic scale, poor peasant families might own no more than a couple of wooden stools and a bed of planks laid across trestles, with a woodblock print of a god pasted up near the stove. A majority of paintings and illustrations show peasant furnishings as very few and simple, though of course some peasants were poorer than others and artists would be likely to highlight the contrasts between rusticity and cultivation. Works like the *Gengzhi tu* (Agriculture and sericulture illustrated) or the *Mianhua tu* (Illustrations of cotton planting and manufacture) depict farmhouses that are agreeably spacious and pleasantly furnished (figs. 14, 17), but we may presume these were construed as the

51. Ecke 1962: 43; Clunas 1988: 29–31, 60; Wang Shixiang 1991: 25.
52. From the *Yunjian jumu chao* (Record of things seen in Yunjian) by Fan Lian (b. 1540), tr. Wang Shixiang 1991: 14. "Ten thousand cash" means a great deal of money. *Ju* is a type of elm native to the lower Yangzi, not a hardwood but harder than most other softwoods and with a beautiful color and grain; the other woods mentioned are hardwoods (ibid.: 16–18, "The best furniture woods"). At first the taste for hardwood furniture seems to have developed among people considered to have more money than taste, but gradually it became the cultivated norm and softwood became typical of more modest homes (Clunas 1988: 41).

dwellings of landowners rather than day laborers. It should not be assumed, however, that most peasants had no furniture of any value, for furniture was part of the family property that was to be divided up between brothers after the father died. Moreover social mobility, up as well as down, was common in the countryside as well as the towns. There were many periods between the Song and the later Qing when overall levels of prosperity were high and peasants formed part of the market for handicrafts such as printed kerchiefs or the carved and lacquered sweetmeat boxes that an eighteenth-century writer tells us became one of the chief products of a small town in the lower Yangzi, selling like hot cakes in all the surrounding areas as wedding gifts.[53]

RUS IN DOMO

A house was not just a shelter but also a symbol of culture, or *wen*. The first humans were indistinguishable from animals or from birds: they built untidy nests in trees or dwelt in lairs in the ground until the legendary sages taught them how to make proper houses. Houses were thus by definition a human sphere distinguished from "nature."[54] The primary reason for putting a roof over one's head is to obtain protection from the

53. Tong 1981. Western observers from the late nineteenth and twentieth century have chiefly emphasized poverty in their descriptions of peasant life. Hommel (1937: ch. 4, "Shelter") documents the construction and the contents of peasant houses in the 1930s. "Chairs are a luxury in the primitive home of the Chinese. Their place is taken by long and short 'forms' [or] benches" (ibid.: 307). Hayes, exploring village houses in Hong Kong for written materials (of which he found few), writes of "their earth floors, dark and narrow interiors, and spartan furnishings—hardly more than board beds, gate legged or trestle tables, and rough benches and stools" (1985: 107).

54. *Nature* is a term to be used with caution in English. There is no single Chinese term that corresponds exactly to the constellation of meanings it has acquired in modern Western thought, and scholars like Marilyn Strathern would argue that projecting our own conceptual polarities onto other societies is a falsification. Nevertheless, a parallel distinction was made in Chinese between the organization of the human world and the "myriad phenomena" (*wanwu*) that did not fall under human rule, as between the regulated comportment of a person in society and the "spontaneity" (*ziran*) characteristic of the myriad phenomena, that one might hope to achieve by withdrawing from the world. Mountains were a prominent symbol of this unregulated domain. "Mountains and marshes" (*shanze*) stood apart from farmed land as "forests" did in Europe. Landscapes were paintings of "mountains and water" (*shanshui*). Mountains were a place of escape from the mundane and of contact with the numinous or divine. (In chapter 9 I address the rather different notion of "nature" as in a child's "natural" endowments, what it is born with, a concept that is rendered by the term *tian*, "from Heaven.")

elements; to borrow a term from physics, a house is a device for damping the effects of the weather, providing an environment that is less cold in winter, less hot in summer, drier when it rains than the outside world. How far this effect is taken depends partly on technical competence, partly on cultural preference. In the rich Western countries today, where central heating and air conditioning are both accessible and affordable, it is not uncommon to keep one's house at roughly the same temperature all year round. If one wants to feel the summer heat or the winter cold, one must go outside. Western visitors to China frequently remarked that, in contrast to their usual experience, a Chinese house with its verandahs and lattices presented no clear barrier shutting off the domestic interior from nature.

The Chinese house embodied the social world, yet at the same time it almost always contained within it a natural retreat, a cultural choice that was closely related to that of keeping the house open to the seasons. Insofar as their means permitted, peasant and gentleman alike brought elements of wild or rural landscapes into the domestic compound. Within the household walls, the human space that housed lineage tablets, husband, wife and children, master, servants and dependents—the whole human structure of an ordered society—a space was set aside that offered escape from the red dust of human commerce into a tranquil contemplative world of mountains and waterfalls where social relations were irrelevant.

The most obvious example of this impulse to create a natural domain within the domestic space was the famous Chinese garden, constructed not outside the house but within its walls. The delights of the great Chinese gardens were restricted to the rich, like the wealthy merchant families of Suzhou whose wonderful and ingenious gardens are now open to the public.[55] For those with lesser means, a landscape scroll, some pot plants or bonsai, carved latticework in the windows or a view of a more fortunate neighbor's trees could serve a similar purpose.[56] The courtyard

55. Public parks did not exist in the cities of late imperial China, though some rich families started to open their gardens to the public in the Ming and Qing (Plaks 1976: 154). Unlike temples up in the mountains, city temples were cramped and so mountain pilgrimages offered a dual attraction, aesthetic as well as spiritual, to rich and poor alike.

56. Georges Métailié (1995) suggests that since most Chinese literati who served in official positions lived an itinerant life, never spending more than three years in one posting, they developed a form of garden suitable to their lifestyle, taking with them a few bonsai and potted flowers that they would set down in or outside the study wherever they happened to be, taking advantage of what trees

was not just the focal point of family life, the space around the well, but a window open to the natural world, to the sky.[57]

It was city dwellers who felt the strongest need to construct wild landscapes and even rural scenes within their boundary walls, as Andrew Plaks points out. "A Ming treatise on gardening, *Yuan Yeh*, lists six possible garden sites: in the mountains, in cities, in rural villages, on suburban plots, adjacent to homes, and in waterfront locations. But since the very impulse towards the garden ideal arises most naturally out of the dust and anxiety of city life, the second, fourth, and fifth of these choices seem to have been favored by China's garden designers."[58] Often these gardens were tiny: a few pots of plants and a strangely shaped rock symbolizing a macrocosm of mountains and forests. Some rich families had large and elaborate gardens within the walls of the compound; the gardens of the city of Suzhou are especially famous for their beauty and ingenuity. Gardens, whether large or small, were spaces of intimacy and retreat. Unless a family was rich enough to have more than one garden, it was not located in the front courtyard, where outsiders were received, but toward the back of the compound by the study, where close friends were invited.

Garden buildings, pavilions, gazebos, studies and the like were not for permanent occupation. Like the garden itself, they were places of retreat from the duties of ordinary life, the setting for music making, drinking, composing poetry. Yet at the same time many of the great gardens also contained vegetable plots, orchards or even small rice fields, aesthetic symbols of productive rusticity that could be turned to material account if the household needed additional sources of income.[59] Rusticity was not an effect that peasant households had to strive for, but often they would bring the aesthetics of untamed nature into their compounds in the form

---

or other permanent plantations might already be in place, and tending them or developing them in an altruistic spirit for the benefit of their successors. Only when they retired were they able to establish permanent gardens of their own. It was therefore those who were not eligible or chose not to serve the state who were the builders of great gardens. (Li Yu, who never took an official post, is a case in point.)

57. One common term for the courtyard is *tianjing*, heaven-well or sky-well.

58. Plaks 1976: 154.

59. The garden in the eighteenth-century novel *The Dream of the Red Chamber* contains a model village with fields, and an orchard. "Since the garden had recently been divided up among the many married women-servants for tending, it was just at its busiest time. Some were tending bamboos, some were pruning trees, some were planting flowers, some were planting beans. Even in the middle of the ponds some women were riding on boats planting lotuses in the mud" (ch. 58, tr. Plaks 1976: 199).

of a flowering tree in the yard, or pot plants on the verandah or window-sill. Lattices carved with plum flowers or bamboo leaves, which trans-formed bleak winter views into a promise of spring, were a widespread form of folk art.[60]

Like a view from a window, the object of contemplation was not neces-sarily confined within the compound. "Theorists of the Ming and [Q]ing periods often turn to the oblique device of 'borrowing views' [*jiejing*] in order to surmount their logistic limitations. The author of *Yuan Yeh*, for example, places great emphasis on site selection and careful planning with an eye toward capturing particularly prized scenic views—even from a neighbor's garden—and making them part of one's own composition."[61] Li Yu devised several ingenious methods for borrowing views suitable for aesthetes of limited means. The most striking consist of visual puns on landscape painting.

To understand the "picture windows" that Li Yu constructs, one needs to know the typical form of a Chinese landscape painting. The most com-mon was a vertically hung scroll; the tall narrow picture was mounted on borders of plain paper and silk. Another popular form was the curved piece of silk that was mounted on a fan; paintings or calligraphy on fans were frequently exchanged as gifts.

> I used to live by the West Lake[62] and I planned to build a boat that would feature a fan-shaped window on each side. Nothing would block the view from the windows, the only openings. The planks of the cabin were to be covered with dark cloths to prevent any light sneaking in through the cracks. . . . Sitting in the boat, one would be able to look out of the fan-shaped windows and get excellent views to either side: the lake scenery, the temples, the bamboo grove, the wood-gatherer, the herd-boy, the drunken old man and the traveler on his horse[63] would enter the window, constituting a series of continually changing scenes as the boat floated along. Such windows are not costly at all: each requires only two curved and two straight wooden lathes, and what extravagant novelty can match their wonderful effect? The fan-shaped window not only provides amuse-ment to oneself, but also gives entertainment to others. On the one hand they bring the outside scenery unfolding into the boat; on the other, they

---

60. Hommel says of carved lattices in peasant houses: "Lighted windows of such pleasing pattern have an indefinable charm and make you stop and gaze at them in silent admiration" (1937: 302).

61. Plaks 1976: 165.

62. An ancient manmade lake just outside the city of Hangzhou, renowned for its beauty and frequently depicted in paintings.

63. All conventional elements of a Chinese landscape.

open up the joyous and festive activities on the boat to viewers. . . . Hiring a sing-song girl, inviting a monk, entertaining friends with chess, games of rhyming and drawing, drinking and singing were just events before the invention of the fan-shaped window. But through such a window anyone can effortlessly turn them into a picture.[64]

Before Li Yu could put this delightful notion into practice he was obliged to move away from the West Lake to Baimen.

> There was a very small mound behind the house, less than ten feet high and no wider than my outspread arms, yet in it I perceived every requirement for life in the mountains—red cliff, emerald water, dense forest, exuberant bamboo, singing birds, resonant water-fall, thatched huts and wooden bridges. . . . To start with I did not intend to put in picture-windows. But after a while I realized how wonderfully picturesque this scenery was, for I could never bring myself to close the windows even after admiring the view all day long. Startled, I said to myself: "This mountain can make a picture, and the picture can make a window." It only cost me a day's drinking-money for the tools to cut out the opening. Then I asked the servant-boy to cut strips of paper to serve as the mount. We pasted them to the top and bottom of the window, with another two strips at the sides, and so we had a majestic scroll, in fact a blank scroll but one in which the empty space was filled by the mountain behind the house. When I sat back and took a look, the window was no longer a mere window. It had become a painting instead, and the mountain was no longer the mound behind my house but a mountain in a painting. When I realized this I laughed myself hoarse, and my wife and children all came in, saw what I had seen and laughed too.[65]

The paradox is that Li substitutes real, living views for painted landscapes: the artistry lies not in the brushwork but in the framing, reminding one of the passage in *Northanger Abbey* where Catherine is taught to turn views into landscapes. Still more paradoxical, in the case of the fan-shaped view the frame works in two directions like Alice's looking glass: it frames the outer world for the delectation of the viewer inside the

64. There is an illustration in *Casual Expressions* of the boat, with its fan-shaped windows, floating on the lake amid willows, temples, passing boats and other fine scenery. Unfortunately the quality of the print in the edition I had available did not warrant reproduction.

65. *Casual Expressions* 8. 18a–20b. Li Yu explains that such windows are best enjoyed in a long room, seated at a distance from the window. In a small room one will tend to lean out of the window, thus missing the framing effect. One might also suppose that few people had a sufficiently imaginative eye to perceive a mountain landscape in a small mound, and the frame was therefore necessary to identify the pictorial potential.

boat, and at the same time it frames him with his companions in a vignette that may catch the eye of the passers-by who are the subjects of his picture. Framing the picturesque and bracketing out unaesthetic elements is a well-developed skill in China, not just among artists but in everyday life. For instance, in a study of traditional courtyard houses in modern Beijing (now all occupied by several families crowded in together), André Casault remarked how each family demarcates its part of the court with untidy piles of bricks, coal or even cabbages. Within this messy boundary a row of pot plants or a fishbowl provides a restful space for the eyes, a token of nature and of open spaces.[66]

THE CONVERGENCE OF ARCHITECTURE

The "Chinese house" acquired its essential and unmistakable Chineseness over the course of centuries. Although no actual houses survive from earlier than the Song, archaeological excavations, clay grave models, bas reliefs and paintings provide a glimpse of housing styles as far back as the neolithic period. This evidence reveals a stylistic convergence over the centuries: many house styles in early China included features that in the minds of the late imperial Chinese were alien, associated exclusively with barbarians.

In the north, the so-called cradle of Chinese civilization, many defining features of later standard Chinese architecture date back millennia. At the site of Banpo, one of the earliest neolithic sites in the north with the earliest strata dating back to about 5000 B.C., both round and square houses have been found.[67] The Banpo houses were built on earth foundations, either slightly sunken or standing directly on the surface of the ground. Contemporary with the Banpo settlements but far removed geographically, the houses in the rice-growing village of Hemudu, located by a marsh near the mouth of the Yangzi, were rectangular wooden constructions built on piles. The neolithic cultures of the lower Yangzi and eastern coasts seem to have contributed at least as much as the northwestern cultures to the Chinese civilization that emerged in the second millennium B.C. But its capitals were built in the northern plains, which perhaps ex-

66. Casault 1987: 39.
67. The cosmological complementarity between round (heaven) and square (earth) is a theme that appears very early in Chinese thought; from the early empire round and square elements were combined in designs for sacred buildings such as the residence of the emperor and imperial temples (see Needham et al. 1971: 122; Du 1994).

plains why earthen platforms and other northern architectural features became markers of Chineseness.[68] The palaces and ceremonial buildings of the Shang (c. fifteenth to eleventh century B.C.) were built on platforms of tamped earth and were oriented north-south, but commoners' dwellings were still subterranean pit-houses showing no concern with orientation; this class distinction was maintained through much of the Zhou period. "It is scarcely an exaggeration to equate nobility with *hangtu* [tamped earth], and commonality with pit-dwellings."[69]

Standardization was a gradual process, reflecting both the geographical spread of Han Chinese orthodoxy (through political conquest and cultural assimilation) and its dissemination from the elite through other strata of society. In the Han dynasty, for example, houses in the south were often built on tall wooden piles, like the houses of Southeast Asia today. But as northern China consolidated its political hold on the south and northerners migrated to the southern provinces in large numbers, houses on piles, well-suited though they were to the subtropical climate, disappeared, to be replaced by the northern practice of building on foundations of tamped earth. The boundary between Han civilization and barbarity came to be marked by building style.[70]

"Chineseness" was not always rooted in an indigenous tradition. One example of an import that came to distinguish the Chinese from less "civilized" neighbors is the chair. As was stated earlier, from antiquity well into the medieval period the Chinese of all regions sat, ate and slept on mats on the floor. Chairs first became known sometime after the Han dynasty, probably through contacts with Buddhist Central Asia, although chairs (for the rich) and stools (for the poor) came into common use only during the Tang and Song. The neighboring cultures—the Koreans, Japanese, Vietnamese and Thai—continued to live on the floor and to use

68. History being written by the winners, it is not suprising that the classical Chinese texts on cultural foundations represented Chinese civilization as a product of the northern plains; moreover, most of the early archaeological excavations were carried out in the north, further supporting the view that this was the cradle of Chinese culture (Ho 1975). Archaeological discoveries in the south, of texts as well as of artifacts, have since required us to think of the production of "Chinese" culture as a much more complex process (e.g., Chang 1977, 1980; Keightley 1983, 1987, 1989).

69. Wheatley 1971: 63; see also Knapp 1986: 9.

70. Houses on piles are mentioned in several of the histories of the southern provinces in medieval times (Liu Dunzhen 1980: 197 n. 2), but such dwellings were by then considered by northerners to be a trait of the Man and other non-Chinese ethnic groups.

chairs only for ceremonial purposes; chairs became a mark of Chineseness.[71]

In early and medieval China, certain features subsequently shared by all classes were restricted to the elite. As mentioned, in ancient China the south-facing orientation of dwellings that later became standard was not found in commoners' dwellings. The ancestral altar, singled out by nineteenth- and twentieth-century visitors to China as the defining characteristic of the Chinese dwelling, was also restricted to the elite in early and medieval times. As late as the Tang, commoners were forbidden the rituals of ancestor worship that marked the status claims of the aristocracy. Sumptuary laws throughout the imperial period imposed visual distinctions between official and private buildings, and between the houses of the elite and those of the lower classes (artisans and merchants as well as peasants). But the sumptuary laws of the Song and later dealt with questions not of kind but of degree: who was entitled to fancy roofs, to multiple courtyards, to elaborate gateways. From the Song what one might call the basic social and cultural structure of the Chinese house became standardized and shared at all levels of society: all houses contained an altar for the ancestral tablets, all faced south if possible, all marked off the inner spaces that were the women's quarters; a poor peasant's house was a module, a stripped-down version of an imperial palace, built according to the principles of the same invisible architectures and calling on the same array of technical expertise.

71. In Korea, Japan and Southeast Asia, the floor of the house must be kept clean (in the physical and ritual sense), and anyone entering is required to remove his or her shoes at the door, as presumably was the case in early China. Perhaps the shift to chairs was connected to the spread of foot binding, another characteristic feature of late imperial Chinese culture. The tiny lotus shoes fitted closely over a woman's foot bandages and were not easily slipped on and off; a woman was likely to remove her shoes only in the privacy of her bedchamber. The importance of mats (*xi*) in early Chinese cultural identity is reflected in numerous expressions that include the word for mat. The connotations mostly derive from the fact that people of similar rank sat on the same mat to share food, especially at feasts. The word for "chairman" (*zhuxi*), as in Chairman Mao, literally means the person who presides on the mat.

2 Encoding Patriarchy

The wall divides inside from outside and separates "us"
from "others."

Casual Expressions

A WALLED DOMAIN

The wall around the house separated the inner from the outer world, defining the Chinese family (*jia*) and its dependents.[1] The Chinese reckoned
kinship according to the rules of patrilineal descent. Although relatives on
one's mother's or wife's or sister's side were recognized as more distant
categories of kin, the close bonds of kinship were traced officially along
the lines of male descent. The group living within a house consisted of
agnatically related men, their wives and children. When a daughter married she left her own parent's house and took up residence with her new
husband in a room or wing in his parents' house. Once she had given
birth to a son she joined the line of family ancestors and became an official
member of her husband's lineage. In some areas it was customary to enforce the separation between a wife and her natal family strictly, and visits
from or to her relatives were limited or even forbidden. In other areas
affines were treated as close connections and visits between households

---

1. Much of what follows in the next few pages on Chinese kinship will be
commonplace as far as most sinologists are concerned. I have included it in the
hope of providing an accessible framework for nonspecialists. The word for "family," *jia*, also means a house or home (as in *jia xiong*, my elder brother—as opposed to other elder male relatives of the same generation—and *jia nei* or *jiazi*,
the person inside the house, i.e., my wife). Other words that conflate the meaning
of family or kin with that of the building in which a family resides are *fang*, or
wing (as in *nei fang*, the women's quarters, and *fang qin*, agnates), and *shi*, house
or room (*shi nei* is the person who has remained inside her room, that is, an
unmarried daughter, a virgin; *shou shi*, literally "to take a room," means to
marry).

were common.[2] But the group that lived within the house compound consisted, apart from servants, of a strictly defined patrilineal segment—"us."

The Chinese house presented a blank face to the outer world. It was surrounded by a high wall, usually unbroken except for a high and elaborate gateway. "You can tell the opulence of the rich and the misery of the poor by the walls of their houses," wrote Li Yu. "As they say: one house builds a wall but two houses enjoy looking at it; it is the only object in a house that is in fact public."[3] The walls and gates that surrounded the family compound provided protection as well as privacy for its inmates, keeping out the ghosts and evil influences that could strike a family down with misfortune or disease. Both ghosts and evil influences were thought to travel in straight lines or "arrows." "Every house has its devices for preventing straight access. The path must wind and many methods are employed to save the house from unwelcome intrusion . . . for instance a *ying-pei* or shield wall is erected before a house door . . . the idea of a winding entrance to the house arises from the desire to keep men at a distance as well as demons and to make a limit between what is public and what is private."[4]

The gate communicated between family and outside world, first as a physical threshold, and second as a kind of notice board. In comfortably-off houses the main gate was about 7 or 8 feet high, with a tiled roof and hinged double doors. It usually had a motto carved or inscribed over the lintel, and pictures of guardian deities and paired vertical inscriptions (*dui-lian*) written on red paper pasted to either side. Wealthy or official households had small side gates, which could be used at night when the main gate was closed; poorer houses might simply lock one side of the main gate. Inside, a little way behind the main gate, was a screen gate that was opened only if a person of high rank visited the house. Wealthy or official households had a small guardroom just inside the main gate. At festivals or special celebrations like weddings, beggars would come to the gate for charity and would be given either money or food. In the cities of the lower Yangzi, according to the *Qing Customs*, on such occasions the chief of the beggars would be informed in advance and given anything from fifty to

2. See Judd 1989; Stockard 1989; Siu 1990. Goody 1990 offers an interesting comparative anthropological overview of the degree to which a Chinese woman was incorporated into her husband's family.

3. *Casual Expressions* 9.1a.

4. J. Edkins, "Feng-Shui," *Chinese Recorder and Missionary Journal* (March 1872): 294, quoted Feuchtwang 1974: 194.

two hundred cash, for which he would issue a receipt. The receipt would be pasted to the front door and no more beggars would come to the house.[5]

The gate was used to communicate family events to the surrounding community. If a member of the household died, the name of the deceased would be inscribed on white paper and pasted to the door. For joyous celebrations such as New Year, weddings or the birth of a son, red paper inscriptions were used. Beyond the community, the gate linked every Chinese family to the structures of the state. The state registered and taxed not individuals but households, and the term for these fiscal units of production was *hu,* literally "door." On the gate or door of the house in late imperial China one was likely to find a small plaque marked with official information about the composition and status of the family inside. At another level, the gate signaled status conferred on the family by the institutions of the state. In the Yunnan town studied by Francis Hsu, good families would put one or two varnished plaques on the portal, inscribed with characters in pink or gold recording official honors bestowed on family members. In most parts of China, Hsu says, only the achievements of immediate family members were displayed in this way, but not so in West Town, where "every honor attained will find itself indicated over the portals of several family homes." "The desire for family honor is so acute that when real honors are not associated with any known member of the family, imaginary or alleged ones are inscribed on such plaques." And a West Town family might even stoop so low as to have a lavish plaque, denoting imperial favor, made to record the purchase of a minor degree— something which families elsewhere in China preferred to keep quiet about.[6]

A MORAL BUILDING BLOCK

The Chinese house faced inward, enfolding its occupants in a protective embrace; from outside one could perhaps glimpse the upturned eaves of the main wall or the tops of the tallest courtyard trees. The wall marked the boundaries of a patriarchal domain. Ideally the house sheltered "five generations under one roof," including uncles and cousins as well as the stem family. Although this was a society where young people were often married in their teens, the ideal of five generations was seldom achieved, but even in poor families three generations at a time were not uncommon

5. *Shinzoku kibun* A: 70.
6. Hsu 1948: 31–32.

at some stage of the domestic cycle.[7] Family finances were communally organized. If family members ran farms or businesses, the income was not theirs to dispose of but belonged to the family. Property within the household was held communally as patrimony; it was divided equally between the sons when they set up separate households, which could occur either before or after their father's death. Daughters did not share the inheritance, though they were customarily entitled to a dowry. Land, buildings and farming equipment all belonged to the category of patrimony in late imperial China. The head of the family, the patriarch, had authority over all household members, and controlled the patrimonial property.

> Heads of families should make every effort to adhere to correct manners so that they can discipline their children and other members of the family. To each of them the head assigns specific duties and responsibilities (such as managing the storerooms, stables, kitchen, house properties, fields, or gardens) and sees to it that the tasks are carried out successfully. . . . He should establish a budget for the household based on its income and resources in order to provide food and clothing for everyone in the family and the expenses of marriages and funerals. Outlays should be graded according to the recipient's rank, in an equitable way. Unnecessary expenses should be cut, extravagances prohibited, and some savings put aside for emergencies. Younger members of the family should always obtain permission from the family head for anything they do, large or small, and at no time act on their own.[8]

In fact although Sima Guang here attributes all the budgeting and management to the male head of household, if he was a scholar involved in studying or in official duties, the complementarity of roles between the couple was so construed that it was considered both normal and desirable for his wife to take charge of such practical domestic duties.

The moral principles that organized family behavior were those of

7. Ts'ui-jung Liu, in a study of five patrilines documented in genealogies over a period of at least ten generations, located in different provinces and spanning periods variously between 1300 and 1900, concludes that overall the chance of becoming a grandfather was about one-fifth, the chance of being born as a grandson about two-fifths. "The predominant family type within a lineage was simple two-generation conjugal families, for even though the family was not divided, sheer demographic conditions [i.e., average ages of first paternity and of death] would not allow three- or four-generation families to become prevalent. It is notable, however, that most of the three- and four-generation families that could have been formed were of the grand type, indicating the complexity of family structure" (1994: 138).

8. Sima Guang, *Miscellaneous Etiquette*, tr. Ebrey 1991d: 25. On daughters and dowries see for example Ebrey 1991d, 1993; Birge 1992.

communality and of reciprocal respect between ranks of the hierarchy. The founding fathers of Confucianism categorized all social dealings into the Five Relationships (*wu lun*)— between ruler and subject, father and child, husband and wife, elder and younger brother, and friends. All except the last were unequal relationships in which the senior or superior had undisputed authority, but also a responsibility to treat the other partner with kindness, consideration and understanding. A correct understanding of the Five Relationships ensured harmonious dealings between all members of society.

Unlike the Greek philosophers, for whom the world of politics was quite separate from the family, Chinese philosophers considered the family as part of a political continuum, the social order in microcosm. "Managing the family is the basis for managing the state" was a tenet undisputed throughout the duration of the empire. Although the Five Relationships defined what was clearly a male-dominated moral order, women were integrated into it in a way that they were not, say, by the classical Greek philosophers. The roots of civic virtue were firmly planted in the family compound. Women were sequestered within its walls, and the public representatives of the family were all male, but a woman's work as wife and mother tied her into the world beyond the inner quarters. Moreover, a man was only a complete and competent social being insofar as he was the male partner in a married couple.

The integration of women into the prevailing moral philosophy did not translate into what we would consider power or freedom—on the contrary, it often made women particularly vulnerable to rigid control in the name of public morality. Nevertheless, it did give a distinctively Chinese cast to unequal gender relations. Although women were spatially sequestered in the home, Confucian ritual and liturgical writings all depended on the couple, on a dignified and elaborate dance in which each sex had its essential role. One without the other had no meaning.[9] Confucian

---

9. Since the hierarchies of the family were structured by generation, and by age within a generation, as well as by gender, it is not possible to generalize that "men were always superior to women." The relationship between parent and child, "filial piety" (*xiao*), usually overrode other principles in determining the relations between two individuals; any man owed respect to the women of senior generations. In such cases, however, although respect did govern etiquette it did not necessarily confer authority. Another tenet that became popular in the late imperial period was that women should conform to the Three Obediences: before marriage they obeyed their fathers, as wives they obeyed their husbands, and as widows they obeyed their sons. This produced a contradiction between law and common practice. The law continued to uphold the earlier view that gave widows

thinkers repeated that of all five relationships the bond between husband and wife was the key social bond, for it was the foundation of human reproduction and of the socialization of children. A husband was expected to treat his wife with respect, consideration and affection.[10] The spatial boundaries between "inner" and "outer" spheres were not so much absolute as contextually defined, for they did not denote separate moral and conceptual worlds. Women were understood to contribute to the social order just as men did, though their contributions were not identical but complementary, and I argue in the course of this book that the nature of what they contributed, and thus the understanding of gender roles, changed in the centuries between the Song and the Qing.

THE HEART OF THE HOUSE: ALTAR AND STOVE

The Chinese domestic group included the dead as well as the living. The family lived, as Francis Hsu put it, "under the ancestors' shadow." The spirits of the four generations of immediate forebears dwelled at the very center of the house in tablets placed in the ancestral shrine. The tablets were tall, narrow wooden strips a few inches high, on which the name and title of the deceased was inscribed. There were different conventions for arranging the eight tablets in the shrine, but generation and gender were always the key principles governing the arrangement (fig. 5).

Until Song times ancestral tablets were restricted to families of high rank. In early Song times the practice of installing ancestral portraits in the family shrine seems to have been common, but neo-Confucians like

---

the status of their dead husbands. According to the legal code, a widow was the household head and her sons could not divide up the family property without her consent (Birge 1992). But the rights of widows started to come under threat as early as the Song, and in the later Ming and Qing they were often helpless in the hands of their husband's family. In the Confucian view there was no necessary contradiction between filiality and the third obedience: a son could show his mother respect while controlling her behavior. The issue most frequently arose when sons tried to dispose of family property without the legally required permission of their widowed mother, or when a widow's remarriage was forced or forbidden.

10. In reality the authority of the patriarch was often exercised as tyranny, and many men treated their women not as partners but as slaves. Since the link between social order and the proper behavior of women was made so explicitly in Chinese thought, it is not surprising that the uncertainty and insecure values of certain periods (like the early eighteenth century) were expressed in a heightened emphasis on the need to control and subordinate women (Mann 1991; T'ien 1989). The Three Obediences are particularly in evidence in popular preaching at such times.

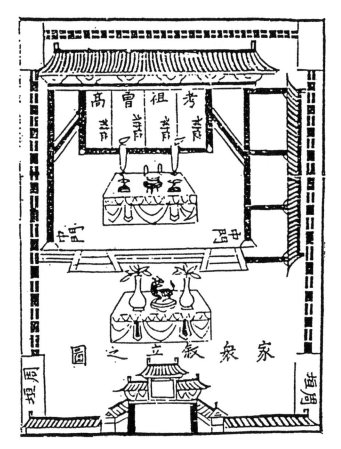

Figure 5. Family offering hall (*citang*), from the 1602 edition of Zhu Xi's *Family Instructions* 7/78a (see Ebrey 1991a: 7). The characters on the screen at the back of the chamber indicate the genealogical order in which the tablets should be arranged. Note the two sets of three steps leading up to the chamber from the courtyard.

Cheng Yi objected to portraits on the grounds that they could never be sufficiently accurate. Instead this school advocated the use of tablets, which seems to have proved acceptable to increasing numbers of people precisely because it had formerly been an aristocratic privilege. The memory of earlier generations was kept fresh in genealogical records and in the lineage temple, where the spirit tablets of earlier ancestors were installed. Orthodox Confucians during the Song and Yuan tended to oppose the use of lineage halls for worship of distant ancestors, arguing that genealogical records were a sufficient bond. But these offering halls became increasingly popular and common during the Ming and Qing, especially in the south where corporate lineages were strong, and an increasing number of orthodox scholars provided rationales for the group worship of first ancestors that took place in the halls.[11]

Ancestors required constant attention from their living descendants, and a Chinese man's first duty was to marry and produce descendants to ensure an unbroken line of worshipers for his forebears. An unmarried person could never be considered a complete human being, or a mature and responsible adult. Childlessness was a personal tragedy, since the childless persons would have no descendants of their own, and it was a breach of filial duty to the lineage.[12]

To most outside observers in the nineteenth and twentieth centuries, the Chinese house appeared as first and foremost an ancestral temple. "The altar is deliberately placed in the central room of the main building, at the heart of the dwelling . . . with a generous façade onto the courtyard. It is the room around which the house is built, on which concerns of orientation and composition focus. The house must have an odd number of rooms so that the ancestral altar retains its predominant role and central position as the pole of the dwelling and center of symmetry." In siting a house, the geomancer set down his compass on the spot where the altar would eventually stand. This was the point of orientation for building the house, "from which all the activities of the inhabitants find their starting point. Thus, the house is linked with the grave and living descendants with their dead ancestors."[13]

As early as the twelfth century, in the *Family Rituals*, Zhu Xi confirms this representation of the house as a ritual space with the ancestral shrine as its heart. The first chapter, "General Principles of Ritual," begins with the offering hall: "When a man of virtue builds a house his first task is

11. Ebrey 1991b: 62, 160–61. Lineages in the south have been characterized as "corporate" because they typically owned large amounts of land and other joint property, the revenues from which funded lineage schools, charities and ancestral halls.

12. Childless couples would often adopt to provide themselves with a descendant to make offerings after their death, and to provide the lineage branch with an heir so that the line was not cut off. Even monks and nuns might adopt heirs, and young people who died unmarried might be married posthumously or have a child adopted posthumously in their name, to ensure that they did not become "hungry ghosts" and cause harm to the living; see A. Wolf 1974 for modern examples, and Waltner 1990 for a general history of adoption in China.

13. Seaman 1992: 88; the previous quotation is translated from Clément et al. 1987: 133.

always to set up an offering hall to the east of the main room of his house." Zhu Xi explains why he places so much importance on the proper construction of this ritual center: "This section originally was part of the chapter on sacrificial rites. Now I have purposely placed it here, making it the first subject, because its contents form the heart of 'repaying one's roots and returning to the beginning,' the essence of 'honoring ancestors and respecting agnatic kin,' the true means of preserving status responsibilities in the family, and the foundation for establishing a heritage and transmitting it to later generations. My arrangement will let the reader sense that what is placed first is the most important."[14]

Zhu Xi is not prescribing an innovation, but rather validating a practice that was becoming increasingly common among the families of the new Song elite, that is to say, consecrating a space within the house to the ancestral cult. Ebrey takes Zhu's hall, the *citang*, to be a specially constructed, separate hall.[15] But it is unlikely that most families could afford such expense, and Zhu in fact seems to be describing a room rather than a building.[16] He advocates a room three bays wide, containing not only the offering tables and shrines for four generations of ancestors' tablets but also a closet for books, clothes, and sacrificial vessels and a "spirit pantry" to hold the dishes used to offer food to the ancestors. Ideally there should be a covered space in front of the room "large enough for all the family members to stand in rows." One important feature of the *citang* is the two sets of stairs leading up from the courtyard to the room; Zhu says that they should have three steps (fig. 5). In rituals the presiding man used the eastern steps, and the presiding woman used the western steps.[17]

Zhu was concerned to involve not only his peers but also lower levels

14. Tr. Ebrey 1991d: 5, 6.
15. The first section of the *Lu Ban jing* contains instructions for the construction of a *citang* that is a separate compound containing a front and a rear hall both some 25 feet wide; the majestic front gate was over 13 feet high (Ruitenbeek 1993: 197–99). Most of this first section comes from the earlier house-builder's manual, the *Lu Ban yingzao zhengshi*, written in the Yuan dynasty, although the uncharacteristic use of vernacular language in this passage may indicate that it is a Ming dynasty addition (ibid.: 129, 132).
16. Kuhn maintains that family shrines (*jiamiao*) in Song times were "rather modest rooms," not separate halls (1992: 373). The word *tang* does mean hall, and pictorial renderings of the offering hall (*citang*), such as the Ming illustrations shown by Ebrey (1991d: 7), one of which is reproduced in fig. 5, could be taken to indicate that it was a separate building. However, given the conventions of Chinese illustration, they could also be taken as showing a centrally placed section of the house compound.
17. Ebrey 1991d: 6.

of society in sanctioned ritual practices. It has been remarked that a change took place between the Northern and Southern Song in the way that social action was envisaged. The educated elite of the Northern Song had also seen ritual and schooling as the main means of cultural transformation (*jiao*, "teaching"), but most thought that this should be brought to local society "by the state and from the center . . . through channels that are still thoroughly institutional."[18] However many of the elite reacted strongly against the highly centralized and radical economic and social policies of the late eleventh century, associated with the reforms of Wang Anshi (1021–86), which they saw as representing an unjustified level of state activism. Meanwhile the relation between education and access to power was changing. In the early Song the high bureaucracy was drawn from a small number of semihereditary official families who saw their vocation as service to the state. During the later Song, however, outsiders were allowed to compete in the state examinations, and the number of degree holders rapidly outstripped the number of government posts available.[19] The rapid expansion of an educated class, only a few of whom could hope to occupy government posts, together with the disastrous and disruptive failure of Wang Anshi's policies and the fall of the north to Khitan barbarians, led many gentry families to lose faith in the state.

Instead the gentry pursued localist strategies of advancement and of social action, emphasizing their role as local leaders in ways advocated by neo-Confucian philosophers like Cheng Yi (1033–1108) and Zhu Xi (1130–1200), who called for the revival of pure Confucian rites and lineage institutions as a way of combating Buddhism, providing cohesion in rural society, and giving educated families appropriate dignity. Many lineage organizations were created during the Southern Song, and the movement continued through later dynasties, incorporating an ever-greater proportion of the population.[20]

Lineage rituals of the kind advocated by the Song neo-Confucians were intended to tie rich and poor, educated and uneducated members of the patriline into a cohesive and harmonious group. The group was not egalitarian—far from it: the point of Confucianism was to maintain the social order by inculcating distinctions of rank and hierarchy (including the gender hierarchy). But the members of the group shared common interests

18. Hymes and Schirokauer 1993: 16.
19. The size of the bureaucracy barely changed in the centuries between the Tang and the late Qing, even though the population grew tenfold (Skinner 1977: 23–26; Hartwell 1982).
20. Ebrey 1993: 113; Brook 1993: 323.

represented by the fact that they shared ancestors. Apart from the group cult these joint interests often took material form in corporate property, the income from which might be used to fund corporate schools open to the sons of all families, or charities that helped out poor families in times of hardship, while the land that provided the basic capital could be rented out to poor members of the group.[21] The educated elite, the prime movers in producing the genealogies that identified these corporate kin groups, justified their place at the top of the hierarchy by their cultural expertise and leadership, educating their kinsmen in practices that would encourage social harmony and cultural conformity. Chief among these practices were family rituals of ancestral worship, marriages and funerals, all of which required some kind of domestic ancestral shrine.

Zhu Xi offered a cheap version of the *citang* for poor families living in cramped quarters: they should use a room a single bay in size as their ancestral hall, substituting chests for the closet and pantry. By late imperial times the shrine was a universal feature of the house, however rich or poor the family.[22] Interestingly, Zhu does not advocate the central location that later was characteristic. Instead he places the shrine off center to the east of the main hall.[23] During the Ming and Qing shrines were placed either in the center of the main hall or in an equivalent position if the house was not symmetrical. In wealthy houses the back part of the central room of the main hall would contain an elaborate cabinetry shrine

21. In some lineages the charter of the corporation stipulated that lineage land should be rented only to lineage members, in other cases this was expressly forbidden. The secondary literature on lineages and corporate property is huge; the classic analysis of how lineage corporations emerged during the Song is Twitchett 1959.

22. The passage in which Zhu Xi advocates a modified version of the shrine for use in poor families is translated in Ebrey 1991d: 7. The number of generations of ancestors whose tablets might be housed in the family shrine stabilized during the Song dynasty at four, a number considered suitable for all classes of society. Although the family shrine itself was egalitarian in allowing four generations to all classes, distinctions between rich and poor appeared at the stage where the oldest generation was superseded. Just as the rich were said to have more children than the poor in China, so too they had more ancestors. Ancestors, though long-lived, were not necessarily immortal. As members of the new generation died and became ancestors, the oldest generation was removed from the family shrine. Sometimes the tablets were simply discarded, but if the ancestors had been distinguished in any way they would be reinstalled in the lineage hall; the rich and powerful dead lived longer than the poor and humble (R. Watson 1985).

23. Zhu's neo-Confucian predecessor Cheng Yi had the shrine facing not south but east; Zhu Xi cited classical evidence to refute this interpretation (Ebrey 1991b: 126).

surrounded by scrolls, under which stood an offering table set with fine incense burners, fruit stands and flower vases. In a poor house the tablets might simply be housed in a niche in the back wall of the main room.[24]

Zhu portrays a household whose life revolved around the shrine. It was the heart of the house, its most precious possession: "Should there be flood, fire, robbers, or bandits, the offering hall is the first thing to be saved. The spirit tablets, inherited manuscripts, and then the sacrificial utensils should be moved; only afterward may the family's valuables be taken." The shrine was something of which all members of the family were conscious at all times. The main ritual actor in this domestic space of decorum was the "presiding man," the senior patrilineal heir. He was expected to look in on the shrine every morning, burning incense and bowing. His wife, the "presiding woman," was his partner in all of the more elaborate ceremonies, and like him was expected to announce all her comings and goings to the ancestors. "When the presiding man and presiding woman are about to go some place, before departing they enter the outer door of the offering hall and perform the 'respectful look.' They do the same on returning."[25]

Every day the ancestors received a visit from the ritual head of the household. Twice a month, at the new and full moon, as well as on New Year's Day and the solstices, a family visit was held (fig. 6). These ceremonies assembled the whole family in front of the hall, the men to the east, the women to the west, standing in rows ordered by generation. The presiding male was responsible for handling the tablets of the male ancestors, the presiding woman for taking the female ancestors' tablets out of their cabinet and setting them on the altar table to receive offerings. As the husband presided over offerings of wine, so his wife presided over offerings of tea. Other members of the family came up the steps into the hall and participated in the offerings, but went down again after they had performed their role. The ceremony ended with presiding man and woman alone in front of the tablets. They made a final bow, went down the steps into the courtyard, and led the family away. A wife was therefore her husband's ritual partner, but this ritual equality was not available to all the women in the household. Only a legal wife could address the ancestors, for only she was presented to them as a family member when she entered the house as a bride. Concubines were barred from participation in the family

24. I know of a Chinese family living in the United States today that keeps its ancestor tablets and other deities in a small shrine on the top of the refrigerator, the heart of the American house.

25. Tr. Ebrey 1991d: 5, 11.

cult just as they were debarred from social motherhood, and a man was not permitted to make a concubine his legal wife, even if he was widowed.

Although all families in late imperial China had a family altar located in some central position in the house, it was not always as central in their minds as the orthodox Confucians would have wished. Li Yu, hardly to our surprise, makes no mention whatsoever of family altars in his essays on the house. But accounts by more conventional authors may be unexpected. Here, for example, is the description of the main hall given in the *Qing Customs* in the early chapter on the house: "As soon as one is past the inner gate, one reaches the reception room for visitors. It varies in size and has two- or four-paneled folding doors, a tiled floor and pillars with stone bases, round, square or hexagonal. *At the center of the back wall there is an alcove; in front stands a long-legged table. A framed painting or piece of calligraphy hangs above the table, and there are paired scrolls hung on either side. On the table are incense burners and flower vases.* Chairs of rosewood or rattan are placed on either side of the table, and guests are invited to sit here and chat. Doors open out of the back wall to allow food to be brought in from the kitchen."[26] It is clear that the italicized passage refers to the shrine, and the accompanying illustration confirms it, yet no mention is made here of the ritual significance of this "alcove." Only in the later chapter on sacrifices is the shrine shown as a place of worship (containing five, not four, sets of tablets).[27] Although strict Confucians deplored such laxity, it was common practice in late imperial China for Buddhist and other deities to share the shrine with the ancestors' tablets.[28] However, the *Qing Customs* shows a second altar, apparently a Buddhist altar, installed not in the main hall but in the "dew

26. *Shinzoku kibun* A: 75, emphasis added.

27. Ibid.: 498.

28. One important stimulus to the formulation of neo-Confucian philosophy was the desire to wean people away from the foreign cult of Buddhism. Confucians were committed to improving the moral order of the world. They claimed that Buddhism was subversive because it denied the importance of the world of the living and concentrated its devotees' efforts on achieving salvation in the hereafter—though the caricature of Buddhism as exclusively otherworldly was exaggerated. Monika Übelhör (1989) has argued that the community organizations proposed by Song neo-Confucians were a direct response to the challenge posed by contemporary Buddhist community and charitable organizations, and Brook (1993) has advanced similar arguments for the late Ming. Most Chinese were able to live quite happily mixing Confucian, Buddhist and Daoist beliefs and practices, but the neo-Confucians were particularly anxious to claim all family rituals for their own. In practice, since Buddhism did not include any celebrations of marriage, this meant a struggle over funeral practices and the kinds of attention paid to the dead.

Figure 6.   Celebration of an ancestral sacrifice (*Qing Customs* A: 496–97). The sacrifice is performed by all the couples in the family, each wife standing behind her husband, and also by the boys. The elaborate ordering of the dishes varied according to local custom, and etiquette books or household encyclopedias would often provide diagrams of the patterns that should be formed by the jars of wine and dishes of rice, meat, vegetables and fruit.

platform." The dew platform was the upper story of the inner quarters, a private room where visitors did not go, and which was mostly occupied by the women, though the men would also spend leisure time there. This seems a fitting place for a Buddhist altar, since in late imperial times Buddhism was considered a religion that was particularly attractive to women, or to men at times when they had withdrawn from public life.

In its representation of the shrine as the heart of the house, moreover, the *Family Rituals* presents only one side of the ancestral cult. The Chinese had worshiped their ancestors since prehistoric times. In the Shang dynasty (c. fifteenth to eleventh century B.C.) the sovereign consulted his ancestors by divination before undertaking any significant action. The spirits of the ancestors took an active part in the affairs of the living, meting out rewards and punishments as well as advice. Their benevolence was courted with sacrifices of blood. The educated understanding of the contract between descendants and ancestors had changed significantly, however, by the late Zhou period (c. 500 B.C.), when Confucius declared himself an agnostic on the question of spirits and ghosts. As portrayed in Confucian writings, the ancestral cult was a way of life rather than a religion. Strict Confucian representations of the cult emphasized the respect and gratitude owed by the living to their collective forebears and the moral values that were inculcated by liturgical practices that emphasized rank and order. The ancestors were worshiped not as individual spirits with appetites and emotions, but as a strictly ranked lineage group that did not actively intervene in its descendants' lives. The ancestors no longer required blood, and offerings were construed not as food for spirits who were hungry but as a symbol of respect. For high Confucians the tablets were not the residence of a dead man's spirit but a concrete symbol of reproductive order: "As one generation succeeds another, the spirit tablets are reinscribed and moved to their new places."[29] This orderly generational succession was mirrored by the living: when sons moved out to set up an independent home they set up their own new shrine.

Only a small, educated elite held this secularized and sanitized view of the ancestors. Most people in late imperial China accepted the equation of the ancestral cult with social order, but at the same time the ancestors were active forces in their daily lives. The spirits of the ancestors really resided in the tablets on the family altar: the soul of the dead person entered the tablet at the moment that the final dot on the character *zhu*, "host" or "owner," was inscribed, usually just after the person's burial.[30] The ancestors no longer demanded blood, but they did demand food and worship. A person who died without male heirs became a "hungry ghost" and rained misfortunes on the living until the cause of these troubles was discovered and someone was found to adopt the ghost as an ancestor. Legitimate ancestors could be capricious and often ill-tempered, likely to bring sickness down on a child because they felt neglected or were not offered their favorite food at a seasonal ceremony.

In the chapter on sacrifices, the *Qing Customs* enumerates domestic offerings to the ancestors. The dates correspond to those of the *Family Rituals,* but the spirit seems different. The work conveys a sense of a more intimate relationship between family and ancestors. Although they are not portrayed as capricious individuals, the ancestors did receive personal

29. *Family Rituals,* tr. Ebrey 1991d: 5.

30. In many parts of China it was customary to prepare the tablet in advance except for this dot (see, e.g., Naquin 1988); in some parts of the south the ancestors' names were all inscribed on a single paper kept in the shrine, and the equivalent of dotting was the writing of a new paper including the name of the recently deceased person (R. Watson 1988).

attentions on their birthdays, when their portrait was hung over the altar and received special offerings. Loving attention is paid to the details of the offerings. A routine offering, for example, might include lichees, longans, candied melon and sweet cakes. The drawing of the main annual sacrifice is so detailed that it would not be difficult to reproduce the feast, from the three roast animals (pig, chicken and sheep) to the dishes of rice and of bamboo sprouts (fig. 6).[31]

Food was inseparable from worship in the Chinese popular mind, just as social life was impossible without eating. The ancestors required food if they were to treat their descendants kindly. In most ordinary households in the twentieth century the daily offerings to the ancestors are made not by the husband but by the wife, who prepares and serves food for the whole family, living and dead. There seems no reason to suppose that the popular practices of late imperial China were any different. The *Carpenter's Canon,* as well as providing accounts of how to build an ancestral hall and the cabinet that housed the tablets, contains passages on inviting the gods and spirits into a new house. Interestingly the ancestral tablets receive no more attention than the Stove God.[32]

Many ordinary Chinese would probably have said that the kitchen was as much the center of the house as the shrine. The encyclopedia *Jiabao quanji* (Complete collection of household treasures), compiled by Shi Chengjin from Yangzhou and first published in 1707, includes a manual on building in which it is stated that the ancestors and the Stove God must both be worshiped before a family moves into its new house.[33] Every home had a Stove God, who reported to Heaven at the New Year on his family's behavior. He was usually represented by a colored woodblock print pasted up in the kitchen, which showed him with his wife next to him, and a variety of other human and animal figures, each with their own story, which were likely to vary regionally.

Unlike the Confucian ancestors, who were not part of any hierarchy of gods, the Stove God linked the occupants of the house to a supreme heavenly deity who sat in judgment on humans, rewarding good deeds and punishing bad behavior by adding to or subtracting from the span of their lives, just as the emperor meted out rewards and punishments to his subjects. It was customary to smear the Stove God's mouth with honey or sweetmeats or to offer him strong wine on the twenty-fourth day of the

31. *Shinzoku kibun* A: 493–524 describes domestic rituals.
32. Ruitenbeek 1993: 307.
33. Ibid.: 114.

twelfth month, just before his New Year visit to Heaven, to ensure his silence on any misdeeds.

Robert Chard has studied the history of the stove cult in China and discusses the likely relations between popular beliefs and elite efforts to channel them into the service of social order and respect. The earliest mention of stove cults and stove spirits comes in Confucius's *Analects (Lunyu)* and in the early Daoist work *Zhuangzi*. In some early texts the stove spirit is associated with "the esoteric lore of . . . magicians, specifically in the areas of alchemy, exorcism, and the placing of curses." In others the stove deity is already described as a kind of official spy who reports to Heaven each month on the behavior of the family. In Han times the cult of the Stove God is mentioned as part of a system of domestic rituals (the Five—or Seven—Sacrificial Cults). By the sixth century A.D. there is mention of a popular god worshiped in South China at the year's end, and Chard believes that this southern cult "is probably the direct ancestor of modern belief; by S[o]ng times, at least in the South, the observances to the stove were very similar to those of modern times, including such things as the paper image and sendoff of the god on the evening of the twenty-fourth day of the twelfth month." [34]

The importance of the stove was not that it represented the hearth of the European cultures, the open fire around which the family gathered together for warmth and comfort. Open flames were avoided in the Chinese house, even for heating. In the north, where winters were long and bitterly cold, people kept warm by sitting and sleeping on a brick platform called a *kang*. This heated communal bed first appears in Han grave models and is still in use today. [35] In southern houses people used a variety of handheld stoves or portable braziers. [36] But although the family group was not associated with an open flame, the symbolic identification of fire with home did exist. A home was inconceivable without its own stove, and those who ate food prepared on the same stove belonged to the same family. When brothers divided the house, or if two separate families in-

34. Chard 1990: 152. Chard's two essays provide references for the original sources on stove cults, for ethnographies and collections of folklore, and for the analytical literature in Chinese and Japanese.

35. On the history of the *kang* as an architectural feature, see Needham et al. 1971: 135. The neighboring Koreans developed a more extensive form of underfloor heating, the *ŏndol*, which heats a whole room, as early as neolithic times. The chimneys connected to this hypocaust system are a striking and attractive feature of Korean domestic architecture.

36. Illustrated in *Shinzoku kibun* A: 116–17.

habited the same house, they not only set up separate ancestral shrines but also made separate kitchens to house their own stove.[37] The Stove God was as much a symbol of family unity as the ancestral tablets. And the women's work preparing food in the kitchen was as essential to the ancestral cult as the men's performance of the rituals at the shrine (fig. 7).[38]

Cooking both for the living and for the dead was the woman's province, at least in domestic settings,[39] and the transformation of raw (*sheng*) ingredients into cooked (*shu*) food was the basic metaphor for the production of social values. Given the symbolic energy focused in the stove, it is not surprising that the gender and character of the stove deity were continually up for renegotiation. Since women were responsible for the daily activities around the stove one might have expected a Stove Goddess instead of a Stove God, and several early myths about the stove deity identify it as a woman, either an old woman or a young and beautiful one. Early myths as well as medieval versions attributed the invention of fire and of cooking to a woman whose title was some variant on the Divine Mother of Cooking, a middle-ranker in the pantheon that governed and controlled the human world. In one Daoist "stove scripture" that Chard believes was written sometime between the late Tang and the end of the Song, the Divine Mother, Mother of Cooking, states: "I have effected the transformation of [those who] once drank blood and ate fur, so that now they go to meals where the raw has been refined [by fire] and turned into

37. "Possession of a stove identifies a family as an independent entity" (A. Wolf 1974: 133); see also Liu Dunzhen 1980: 82.

38. "Womanly work" as specified in the *Liji* (Book of rites) includes cooking and preparing food for the sacrifices as well as spinning and weaving. On raw and cooked offerings, see A. Wolf 1974 and Thompson 1988. Most ethnographic studies deal with southern Chinese, among whom rice is the staple food, and offerings of rice play a central role not only in daily offerings to the ancestors but in reproductive rituals generally, including weddings and the rituals of death and burial that produce ancestors (Seaman 1992; Thompson 1988). Thompson argues that rice is *yang*, male, analogous to semen. One could extend this argument to suggest that women's cooking of rice for funeral offerings on the kitchen stove should be considered an analogous process to the transformation of semen into a fetus in the womb.

39. In most texts that deal with cooking there is no mention of the gender of the cook. Ideally cooking was attributed to women. The classical texts on ritual and etiquette such as the *Liji* include cooking among the duties of women even of the highest rank. However, roughly contemporaneous pictorial materials, like Han stone reliefs illustrating life in large manorial households, show a mixed force of kitchen servants preparing food, with men often doing the actual cooking.

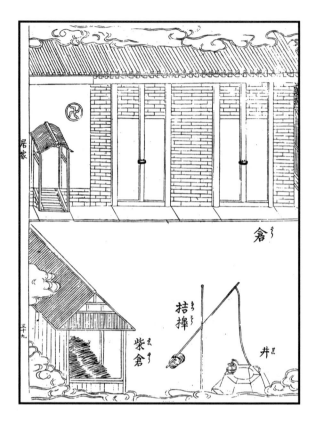

居家

倉

桔槹

紫倉

井

二十九

Figure 7.   The rear courtyard of a house (*Qing Customs A*: 142–43). The kitchen is on the right (*opposite page*), the well in the foreground. The wood-fired stove is just inside the entrance of the kitchen; we can see the chimney and the two circular lids that covered the holes in the stove for the iron cooking pans when they were not being used. All we can see of the other kitchen equipment is a table and benches, a cleaver or two hung on the wall, a couple of large bowls, and some sacks of rice. The illustrations of standard kitchen equipment that follow on the next few pages show storage jars and pouring jugs for wine, oil and soy sauce; cooking pots; the large wooden padlocked chests in which rice was kept; a hand-mill for husking grain; and a kitchen cupboard on high legs, with numerous compartments and drawers for storing sugar, spices, and other cooking supplies. To the left and rear of the kitchen courtyard are the firewood shed, the storerooms for rice and other basics, and a small building raised on a brick platform with the latrine on the left and the bathroom on the right. The drainage pipe leading out of the latrine allowed the waste to be collected and added to the manure heap.

being cooked"[40]; this relatively powerful deity recorded human merits and demerits and reported on them monthly.

As Chard points out, scriptures of this kind were not so much unmediated reflections of popular belief and practice as texts intended to define the proper forms these beliefs and practices should take, preferably in a way that also made them attractive. He gives the example of a later Daoist "stove scripture" where the Stove Goddess has become even more powerful: the Mother Who Seeds Fire controls Heaven and Earth, harmonizes yin and yang, and rules over both the divine and the human realms, like the Queen Mother of the West (*xiwangmu*) and other Daoist primal goddesses. Pointing out that there is no evidence of any such supreme goddesses in popular manifestations of the stove cult, whose deity was by that time usually represented as male, Chard suggests that "by claiming that the stove god was in fact a Mother goddess very like one that was

40. Chard 1990: 158.

becoming increasingly important in popular religion in general, the compilers of the text were seeking to enhance his prestige, thus making the teachings presented in the text more convincing."[41]

In versions of this kind, the Stove God is male but is identified as one manifestation of a superior female deity whose powers extend far beyond the scope of the domestic. But within the tradition of popular tales of the stove deity it seems that over time the need was felt to subordinate primal female powers to male control. This was effected on the one hand through barring women from the cult,[42] and on the other through the classic mechanisms of kinship: having the original goddess marry a man who is then appointed Stove God, or representing the Stove God as a man, though aided by his wife and six or seven daughters.[43] Chard distinguishes between two types in the folklore of the stove: one that represents the male god in a favorable light, and one that either pokes fun at the Stove God or "highlights the female perspective on the cult."[44]

Tales of the first type affirm typical Confucian values and tend to contain typically misogynistic elements. In one tale related by Chard a patriarch dies and the family starts fighting, the farm goes to ruin, and the daughters-in-law become gluttons and behave disrespectfully. In desperation the patriarch's brother paints a portrait of his dead brother and his wife, also deceased, and sticks it up in the kitchen on the anniversary of the patriarch's death, telling his unruly relatives that the patriarch has been appointed Stove God by the Jade Thearch and will report to Heaven on their bad behavior unless they mend their ways immediately. The effect is miraculous, and soon all the families around are begging the artist for their own pictures of the Stove God. In this as in other tales both from folklore and from "stove scriptures," women's lack of economy or restraint in using food (which the anthropologist is immediately tempted to read as a symbol of sexual license) and the disrespectful behavior of daughters-in-law feature centrally as signs of social disorder. Another theme is the need to control women's speech; stove deities might record

41. Ibid.: 162. This was also the period in which the Bodhisattva Guanyin underwent a sex change, becoming not the God but the Goddess of Mercy (worshiped, despite her virginity, as a goddess of fertility and of safe childbirth).

42. "In many parts of China women were completely excluded from the New Year rites to the god" (ibid.: 151).

43. Some Stove God legends identified the youngest of the seven daughters as the Weaving Girl, the patron deity of female textile skills.

44. Chard 1990: 167.

women's oaths, or even lurk in their sleeping quarters listening to their private conversations.[45]

In such versions the male authority embodied by the Stove God is endorsed as part of a celestial order, and transgression is punished by misfortune or early death. The identity of the Stove God was linked with that of the Overseer of Fates *(siming)* as early as the Tang dynasty.[46] Arthur Wolf has discussed the integration of the Stove God into a divine hierarchy that mirrored the Chinese bureaucracy, with its ranks, rules, rewards and punishments, as well as its tendency toward corruption. The ancestor cult tied Chinese families into a much larger group of kin, the values it promoted were nonnegotiable, and—in its more philosophical forms at least—the rewards and punishments it offered were internally generated: the satisfaction of a harmonious household or the pangs of an uneasy conscience. The stove cult embodied a relationship between the household and the outside world that was more like that between a subject and the cumbersome and venal mechanisms of the state. Even though the values it promoted were in essence Confucian and patriarchal, rather than tying a family into a broader kin-group, the stove cult underlined its separate existence: "independent families never share a stove, not even when the heads are brothers."[47]

In tales of the second type, the Stove God starts out as a servant, a wastrel, a glutton or a corrupt official. In many of these tales a principled and determined woman brings about the downfall of the villain and his transformation into a humble god (the kind who can be bribed or tricked into neglecting his reporting duties: here the offerings of sweetmeats are not a sign of respect but a nod toward the deity's mortal weaknesses). In other tales the victim of a grim and inflexible male Stove God who is intent on punishing some minor transgression is rescued by a female deity who is his superior in the celestial hierarchy. In one story the daughter of the Jade Thearch falls in love with a kitchen hand. At last the thearch grudgingly accepts the situation and makes his son-in-law the Stove God. Living on earth with her menial husband, the divine princess sees how miserably many humans live, and when she visits her natal home she tries to bring back food to help them. The story explains the details of the traditional sequence of New Year preparations—sweeping the house, making beancurd, slicing meat, killing a chicken and making dumplings—

45. Ibid.: 166.
46. Chard 1993.
47. A. Wolf 1974: 133, citing Freedman, who argues that this separateness makes the Stove God the supreme domestic cult (1970).

as steps the princess took on a visit home to outwit her father and postpone her departure until she had accumulated plenty of tasty food to take back to her mortal friends.[48]

This is a tale of combating poverty by generosity. Its emphasis is not on feasting within the family but on distributing food to others. This certainly contrasts with the more commonly expressed patriarchal ethos of forestalling poverty by stringent economy and self-restraint within the household. Although I agree with Chard that certain stove tales do seem to express viewpoints that reflect the needs of women rather than men, in this particular instance I think the impulses the tale conveys transcend gender. Chinese New Year is a time when routine preoccupations and precautions are set aside. For the first two days of the New Year nobody works, nobody saves, scrimps or makes do with old clothes: everyone relaxes, puts on new clothes, eats as much and as well as they can afford with no thought to the future. They visit friends, neighbors and relatives to exchange gifts (small amounts of money in a red packet). In short, they live for two days as they would hope to live for the rest of the year, and as they would like to be able to live always, men and women alike.

CONTINUING THE FAMILY LINE: THE COFFIN AND THE BED

In the secular understanding of the Confucians, the ancestors did not intervene in the affairs of the living. The relationship was one-sided: the living strove to be worthy of their ancestors and to show gratitude for the life that had been bestowed on them. Zhu Xi describes how ancestors should be informed of all comings and goings and of any special events such as a betrothal, the birth of a son or an important career event like a passed examination, a promotion or a demotion. A more popular view was that the ancestors were active spirits who thirsted for worship by as many descendants as possible. Both the elite and the popular understanding closely involved the ancestors in all the rituals of reproduction, including in the rituals surrounding death. It may seem paradoxical to propose death as a form of reproduction, but in a society where ancestors are worshiped, the death of the body is the first stage in the birth of an ancestor.[49]

The main ceremonial room containing the ancestral tablets was the

48. Chard 1990: 179–81.
49. Some examples are provided in Watson and Rawski 1988. Since Chinese death rituals and beliefs have been so widely studied by the Chinese themselves as well as by scholars of China, here I deal only briefly with the subject, concentrating on the purely spatial aspects.

place best suited to contain the pollution of death. When the family judged that a person was dying, they put him on a special bed and moved him into the main room next to the altar, then stood by the bed until the sick man breathed his last.[50] This main room was where the first stages of mourning took place: the obligatory wailing by the family women, the washing and dressing of the corpse, the first visits of condolence by relatives and friends. The corpse was moved outside the house to a special ceremonial area, in the front courtyard or beside the house, for the rituals of encoffining and the official receiving of condolences.

This was the first stage in a long, complex and highly variable sequence of rituals that ended with the birth of an ancestor, at the moment when the spirit of the dead person took up residence in the spirit tablet. Though neo-Confucian orthodoxy declared that the body disintegrated into nothingness after death, in popular belief the bones of the dead had enormous power. They did not intervene consciously in the affairs of men, like spirits[51]; instead they served as conductors of natural energy, of wind and water. "The link between the ancestor in his grave and his descendants is a strong and consequential one. The proper placement of one's ancestor's bones in the landscape has a direct effect on the wordly success or failure of the living."[52] In Confucian ideology, the ancestral shrine tied a family through its dead into the orderly moral world of the lineage and the Five Relationships, a world of uniform space that stretched throughout the confines of the Chinese empire. In geomantic terms, the shrine tied a family through its dead into a local landscape of natural forces that could be manipulated to its own advantage but only at the cost of disadvantage to others. In the Confucian ideology the welfare of an individual family contributed to the welfare of the lineage. In geomantic terms, ancestral powers benefited only direct descendants. Because the natural forces were conceived of as a limited good, one family's fortune was another's loss; the siting of a grave could set groups of relatives at each other's throats.

Producing ancestors was one central concern to the Chinese; the other

50. Kuhn 1992: 373; Naquin 1988: 39.

51. This at least is the view of anthropologists who have worked in the Canton area (R. Watson 1988: 206). Ahern, in her study of Taiwan, argues to the contrary that it is the ancestor himself not the geomancy of his grave that brings good fortune (1973: 185). Certainly this interpretation would account for such practices as family offerings at the grave at the Spring Festival, but in most parts of China the channeling of natural forces seems to have been the first concern in the siting of graves.

52. R. Watson 1988: 207.

side of the coin was producing descendants to continue the line, and the ancestral shrine figured centrally in wedding rituals. In the case of a son's marriage, at the stage of betrothal the presiding man took the betrothal document[53] to the offering hall. On the day that the groom brought his bride from her parents' house to his, the presiding man first reported to the ancestors. The bride arrived and was feasted, the young couple spent their first night together, and the next day she was formally presented to her parents-in-law and the family elders. The sealing ceremony of a wedding took place on the third day, when the presiding man presented her to his ancestors at the altar.[54] There is an interesting asymmetry between the two families: the presiding man of the bride's family also presented the initial betrothal gift and the betrothal document to his ancestors, and reported to them on the day of the wedding before the bride left the house. However, when the groom visited his new in-laws, the day after his bride had been presented to his ancestors, he merely paid his respects to the family and was not presented to their ancestors.[55] His family had acquired a new member, his bride's family had lost one.

The classics had said that marriage promoted social morality by illustrating the distinctions between men and women. As Sima Guang put it, "the boy leads the girl, the girl follows the boy; the duty of husbands to be resolute and wives to be docile begins with this."[56] Female subordination was expressed not only in demeanor but also in spatial terms: the groom *fetched* his bride from her house to his, then *led* her into the bridal chamber, out into the main room, and so on. The bride's dependence was made greater by her disorientation: she found herself in a new house full of strangers, never knowing which way to turn.

Although Confucian philosophers across the ages never lost sight of

53. A formal record that varied considerably in length and content. It might list full names and titles of the betrotheds' patrilineal ancestors and mother, or be limited to dates and the full name of the presiding man. Often it would list all the gifts exchanged between the two families (Ebrey 1991d: 51; see also Watson and Ebrey 1991). Most popular encyclopedias describe or illustrate betrothal documents, with instructions on how to fill them in.

54. Although Zhu's liturgy advocates the third day for this presentation, there was considerable disagreement among Song neo-Confucians as to when this ceremony should take place. Sima Guang was willing to accept contemporary practice, which had the bride presented on the day of the wedding; Cheng Yi wanted to reinstate the classical rule that there should be a three-month waiting period (Ebrey 1991b: 84).

55. Ebrey 1991d: 48–64.

56. Ebrey 1991b: 82.

the opportunity a wedding offered to reinforce gender hierarchies,[57] they understood the relationship between spouses in Confucian terms as one of mutual obligation and dignity. They never advocated treating the new bride with anything but kindness and respect, and they emphasized such practices as the parents feasting the young woman after her arrival in their house. Although philosophers stressed harmony and the force of moral example as the means of inculcating Confucian values, family patriarchs often preferred force and felt no moral need to justify this attitude.[58] In practice authority was often construed as tyranny, and the bride might have her subordinate place in her new lineage rammed down her throat as soon as she crossed the threshold of her new home. Wedding customs in imperial times could include raucous teasing or even cruelty of the kind shown in a film of a peasant wedding near Beijing in the 1980s, where a list of male ancestors and seniors was read out to the young couple and the bride was pushed down to the floor to prostrate herself as each name was read.[59]

In many instances of popular practice, however, the focus was as much on joining the couple in happiness and fertility as on imposing male authority. A Song text written at roughly the same time as Sima Guang's liturgy, the *Dongjing menghua lu* (Dreams of splendor in the eastern capital) describes wedding customs in the capital of Kaifeng. It gives us a more playful and egalitarian version of the leading and following that Sima Guang found so appropriate. After the bride was installed in the bridal chamber, the groom had to perch on a high seat in the main hall while the matchmaker and the bride's female relatives took turns drinking wine and challenging him to climb down. Eventually his mother-in-law summoned him and he descended from his stool and went to fetch the bride. "One end of a long sash would be tied to the bride's hand and the other end to the groom's belt-plaque. The groom would back out, leading her to the family altar where she would bow to his ancestors. Next she would walk backward, *leading him back into the bridal chamber*, where they would bow to each other. At this point they would both sit on the bed. Coins and

57. Sima Guang, for example, did his best to reinforce the authority of senior men by denying women any role in the encounters between the two families (Ebrey 1991b: 83).

58. Furth 1990.

59. The scene is shown in Carma Hinton's film *Small Happiness*. Despite the secularizing efforts of the Communist regime, local wedding customs in China seem to have shown remarkable continuity and resilience, and it seems reasonable to assume that this unkind local ritual was inherited from earlier times.

candies would be scattered over the bed amidst considerable merriment and songs. Then a lock of hair from each of them would be tied together. Next they would drink wine from two cups tied together with a cord. . . . Soon thereafter the couple would be left alone."[60]

The couple were then expected to consummate their marriage. In general understanding, the central feature of the bridal chamber was the bed. The *Family Rituals* prescribes the preparation of the room for the couple's first meal together, including mats, tables, armrests and place settings, as well as the "nuptial cup," a fertility symbol consisting of a gourd split in two.[61] But the *Family Rituals* does not mention beds (perhaps because most people still slept on mats), although it is not especially coy about consummation, advising that when the groom enters the chamber after the end of the wedding feast, "he takes off his clothes. The candles are removed. (When the groom takes off his clothes, the bride's followers receive them. When the bride takes off her clothes, the groom's followers receive them.)"[62]

In later representations of marriage the importance of the bed, where children were conceived and born, emerges more clearly. At least in recent times, the marital bed was a part of the bride's dowry, her own property that "remains the possession and the exclusive domain of the wife after marriage. She sleeps there—with her children. The husband enters rather as a guest."[63] The *Carpenter's Canon* shows us what a sumptuous piece of furniture the marital bed was in a well-off household, and how much ritual care went into its production and installation. It gives instructions for making three kinds of beds: alcove beds, summer beds and beds with cane webbing. The bed was not simply for sleeping in, it was also a place where a woman could recline and relax—alone, with her husband or children or with other women of the household, just as men would recline on the couches in their studies, not simply to rest but also to read, to play music or chess, to sip tea or to sew.

The marital bed was the alcove bed; the illustration in the *Carpenter's Canon* shows a married couple standing beside it.[64] The bed was rectangu-

60. Ebrey 1991b: 81, emphasis added.

61. A visual pun on the first intercourse of a virgin (Cahill 1993: 238).

62. Ebrey 1991d: 60. A modern version of this riotous practice, rendered with such delicacy by Zhu Xi, can be seen in Lee Ang's film *The Wedding Banquet*, which depicts a marriage in the setting of Taiwanese immigrant culture in New York.

63. Schipper 1982: 194.

64. Ruitenbeek 1993: II, 35.

lar, constructed on a dais with panels, a canopy and doors, a room within a room (fig. 8). The measurements of the timbers varied, but "on no account may [the inner doors] be 1 foot wide."[65] Ruitenbeek notes that in the whole section on furniture this is the only unambiguous example of a measurement determined by cosmological considerations, a fitting acknowledgment of the bed's symbolic importance as the place where progeny are conceived. The instructions for building the bed are followed by a long list of auspicious dates for installing the bed and hanging its curtains. Beds were usually set against the back wall of the room, so the placement of the bed itself was more or less fixed, but medical texts from early times suggest for procreation not only favorable dates but also the favorable orientations of beds.[66]

The *Qing Customs* shows a scene of a newlywed couple sitting on their bed as maids serve them wine in the split-gourd nuptial cup. The folding doors of the bed alcove are painted with large peaches, a fertility symbol (fig. 20). The same work shows us a woman just after childbirth, sitting propped up on her bed supported by piles of quilts, with a maid (or perhaps the wet nurse) sitting beside her holding the baby (fig. 21).

Birth was popularly considered both a dangerous and a polluting event. In modern times birth pollution was considered if anything as strong as the pollution of death, and passages in premodern medical texts show the ambiguities inherent in understandings of the powerful and disruptive event of childbirth. A dying person was taken from his usual bed and set by the shrine to die, but procreation and parturition were kept strictly separate from the shrine. It is clear from the floorplans of Chinese houses that bedrooms never communicated directly with the room containing the shrine.[67] Medical texts indicate that probably as late as the Tang dynasty parturient mothers were moved outside the main house to give birth and remained outside for a month until the pollution had dispersed. In early China women did not give birth in bed, but squatted on a straw mat that absorbed the blood and afterward was burned, dispelling pollution as well as dirt.[68] By late imperial times women no longer gave birth outside the house, and pollution was contained within the mother's room. Local customs of childbirth varied considerably; in some regions women continued

65. Tr. ibid.: 226.
66. Furth 1990: 163.
67. In smaller houses the rooms next to the main hall were often bedrooms, but to get from one to the other it was almost invariably necessary to pass through the courtyard.
68. A common term for giving birth is *zuo xi*, "to sit on the mat."

Figure 8. Lady's chamber (*Qing Customs* A: 114–15).
The alcoved bed forms a chamber within a chamber; the
bed itself is both broad and long. On the dressing table by
the window are a round mirror, a jewelry or cosmetic case
with several drawers, a toothbrush, a band for tying up
the hair, and a teapot and cup. A washstand is on the
right, and there is a clothes rack by the entrance to the
bed. The alcove beside it on the left is locked and contains
the woman's chests of clothes and valuables.

to give birth on mats on the floor, in others they gave birth in their own bed. A period of seclusion followed, usually of a month. The seclusion could be explained in Chinese terms in one of two ways. Either the birth chamber was still polluting and represented a threat of contamination, or this was a time at which mother and child were especially weak and vulnerable to outside contagion and required protection.[69]

Qing middle-class practice in the lower Yangzi cities, as described in the *Qing Customs,* was for the pregnant woman to give birth on her bed, which was spread with large quantities of absorbent paper. The mother was attended throughout her labor by a midwife; a doctor was called only if serious problems arose requiring the prescription of special drugs. The

69. Charlotte Furth, personal communication 1995. The classic ethnographic analysis of menstrual and birth pollution in China is Ahern 1978; Seaman 1981 explores the historical depth of such beliefs. Furth 1986 suggests that the emergence in late imperial China of medical theories about "fetal poison" may represent a medicalization of popular beliefs about how a mother's polluting powers after childbirth affected her infant.

Qing Customs does not mention pollution beliefs, but takes the same line as most medical texts of the period: the mother was in a delicate state of health and needed careful looking after. After giving birth she squatted between piles of quilts to avoid changing position and causing hemorrhages. If she had not lost much blood during the birth, she could lie down after five or six days, but the normal period was a week. During this time she could not be left: her nurse or some other experienced older maid were in constant attendance, providing her with nourishing foods and decoctions. Her seclusion in her room was represented not as the containment of pollution but as a protective concentration of care and attention.[70]

INNER DIVISIONS: MARKING THE MORAL ORDER

Family relationships were structured by hierarchies of generation, age and gender—power relations continually expressed in terms of address and deportment, as well as space: in the way that domestic spaces were divided and allocated, and in the access that different family members or their servants had to spaces within the house.

Differentiation by rank was fundamental to the Chinese sense of social order. The respect and obedience owed to seniors of either sex were absolute. However, seniors were to treat the people in their power with consideration and affection, so that authority did not degenerate into tyranny. Proper sentiments between family members were cultivated through daily routines of courtesy and consideration. When Zhu Xi introduces Sima Guang's little tract on family etiquette, he explains that "it concerns ordinary matters of living at home and deals with the basis for rectifying personal relationships and principles and deepening kindness and love."[71]

The section of Sima Guang's *Miscellaneous Etiquette* that Zhu Xi appends to the first section of his *Family Rituals* is concerned not with liturgy but with domestic routines; it concerns only relations between the living. He describes a household that revolves around the senior parents' room. Sons and their wives rise early, wash and dress, and as soon as it is light they go to inquire whether the parents have spent a good night.[72] The daughter-in-law prepares breakfast for the senior couple as they rise,

---

70. *Shinzoku kibun* A: 313.
71. Ebrey 1991d: 24.
72. As Sima says, this "morning enquiry" like the following "evening wishes" was already mentioned in the *Liji*. The difference between men and women was marked by the form of greeting: men said "At your service" and women "Bless you" (Ebrey 1993: 34).

and the son gives them their medicines. Then the young husband and wife go about their daily tasks. At night they go to the parents' room to wish them good night. And at any time during the day "whenever one has nothing to do, he or she should go to wherever the parents are to attend them." If a son is given an errand by his parents, he must report back when he has done it. He has to inform his parents when he leaves and returns to the house. "When [sons] receive their own guests, they do not seat them in the main room. (If they have guests, the guests sit in the study. If they do not have a study they can use the side of the hall.) They do not tread the eastern steps to the main room to go up and down. They do not mount or dismount their horses in front of the main room. In nothing should they presume to place themselves on a par with their fathers."[73]

As mentioned earlier, the steps to either side of the ancestral hall were a significant feature. During the family ceremonies, all the family members ascended in turn to the level of the shrine, and then descended again to the courtyard. The men used the east steps, the women the west steps. The dynamic aspect of the steps was as important as the visual aspect. Juniors were always expected to ascend to the level of seniors, to rise when an older person entered the room and never to sit down before the senior did, to mount or dismount a horse away from the presence of their elders, never to "place themselves on a par with their seniors." Writing of the succession of courtyards in the magistrate's court of Song Suzhou, Stewart Johnston remarked that the vertical movement of people climbing and descending the steps between courtyards and raised platforms magnified the awe-inspiring effect of height produced by pillars, roofs and gates.[74] The superior social rank of the occupants was conveyed to outsiders entering the building by the experience or the visual display of physical effort.[75] In domestic architecture, buildings were set on tamped earth or brick platforms of a height proportional to their dignity. Several steps would lead up to the main hall, while the kitchen, latrine or storage sheds

73. Ebrey 1991d: 28.
74. Johnston 1983: 215.
75. "Now . . . of ramps [and steps] there are three kinds, steep, easy-going and intermediate. In palaces these gradients are based upon a unit deriving from the imperial litters. Steep ramps are ramps for ascending which the leading and trailing bearers have to extend their arms fully. . . . Easy-going ramps are those for which the leaders use elbow length and the trailers shoulder height." This is a passage from an early Song carpenter's manual, the *Mujing* (Timberwork manual) (see Ruitenbeek 1993: 24), quoted here by the Song polymath Shen Gua (tr. Needham et al. 1971: 83–84).

would be either at ground level or raised just enough to keep out the rain.[76]

The number of stories and the height of the roof were further indications of the importance of a particular building within the domestic compound. In some regions, for instance Anhui, the upper story in Ming houses was the noble part (in the sense of the *piano nobile*) and was often quite different in layout from the ground floor. Francis Hsu describes a house in Yunnan where the ancestral shrine was in the central south-facing room of the upper story while the rest of the living space was downstairs.[77] In geomantic understanding, it was necessary to ensure that the roofs were of the right relative height to ensure correct family relationships. The first section of the *Carpenter's Canon*, dating from the Yuan, clearly illustrates the principles of ranking inherent in this sympathetic magic: "A family temple is not like an ordinary house: whether or not sons or brothers will attain wisdom depends wholly on this place. Moreover the rear hall, main hall, corridors and triple gate may increase only gradually in height, since only then do sons and grandsons know their rank; and does not the younger aspire to the older's place. The builder must take careful notice of this."[78]

Roofs were not the only architectural features perceived as affecting the proper relations between kin. In the *Carpenter's Canon*, the third section of short rhymes on layout and siting contained precepts familiar to everyone through their reproduction in encyclopedias and almanacs (fig. 11). As well as reflecting concerns about money, health, the number of sons and the virtue of daughters, these rhymes repeatedly refer to family harmony. In a house with two gates "there will be no love between father and son" and "young and old will put each other to shame"; pointed brackets over the roof bring continuous arguments; if the road in front of the house curves like an ox-tail, "there will be division between father and son."[79]

Rank within the family was clearly encoded in the allocation of house space. In a house where several agnatic relatives lived together, each married couple would be given their own sleeping quarters (space permitting). In most cases this would be a single room shared with the children. This was a woman's space rather than her husband's, for he was not expected

76. Pounding earth took a great deal of labor, and expense was no doubt one factor determining how high a platform would be.
77. Liu Dunzhen 1980: 123; Hsu 1948: 33.
78. Tr. Ruitenbeek 1993: 197.
79. Ibid., 278.

to spend daylight hours there, nor did he spend every night there.[80] In wealthy families a couple might have several rooms or even a whole wing. The senior couple were always given the quarters that had the best geomantic location. They would be in a south-facing horizontal hall, not a vertical wing. In smaller houses the senior couple's room would be adjacent to the main room containing the shrine, usually to the east of it. Their sons' family quarters would be allocated according to seniority.[81] The same principles applied to married collateral relatives, uncles and cousins, living in the same house.

Although Chinese law allowed a man only one legal wife, who was also his ritual partner, concubinage was permitted and in late imperial times was apparently common not only among the wealthy but even among peasants in some regions. In such cases each woman would have separate quarters, again allocated according to seniority.[82] Small children would sleep in their mother's quarters, but where there was space they would move out once they began to grow up, and share a room with their siblings and cousins of the same sex. Servants were usually given quarters either in the farthest back courtyard or in the front of the house, neither location being geomantically auspicious. Keeping the sexes separate was an important consideration in allocating quarters to servants. In the merchants' houses described in the *Qing Customs,* the maids' quarters were in the back courtyard above the kitchen. This was their private domain: they kept their clothes and tools and other belongings in their bedrooms, which they could lock from the inside. Married couples lived together, but otherwise the menservants' quarters were built outside the main house.[83]

As children were born and old people died, people moved through the space of the house in paths that were dictated by their rank within the kin-group. At the death of the parents, or the division of the family, there was a general reallocation of quarters. The Janellis in their ethnography of Korean ancestor worship document the movement of the married couple through the house in the course of the domestic cycle as follows: the eldest son and his wife set up after marriage in the "opposite room"; when they

80. He might have concubines as well as a wife, or, in the case of young couples, his mother might control his access to his wife's chamber.

81. In a society where marriages were arranged it was relatively simple to marry one's children in order of age.

82. The wife was the occupant of the main chamber and the polite reference to another person's wife was therefore *shiren.* Concubines, occupying chambers at the back or in the wings of the house, were referred to by the names for these apartments, as *houshi* or *ceshi* (Ebrey 1991c: 7–8).

83. *Shinzoku kibun* A: 141.

inherit the headship of the family, they move into the "inner room," and when they retire and give up the headship to their eldest son, the old couple move into the "outer room."[84] In the Korean case, younger sons did not inherit and old men were expected to retire. In China sons inherited equally, though the eldest son was the ritual heir through whom the descent line continued. Although the senior man remained the ritual head of the household as long as it remained united, a son would often relieve him of managerial burdens sometime in his sixties or seventies.[85] In other cases the sons might urge their father or widowed mother to divide the property between them so they could set up separate households. Orthodox Confucians frowned on household division before the death of the senior male and thought it best if the extended family continued to live together thereafter. But they recognized that friction between the sons might sometimes leave a family with no alternative. As a Song writer put it: "One of the most beautiful things in the world is brothers living together after their father's death."[86]

The principle governing family division was that common property, the patrimony, should be equally divided between stirps. Thus each son received an equal share, but if one son died leaving four sons of his own, each would receive only one quarter of what their father would have received. By late imperial times the rules were quite inflexible, encoded in popular expectations as well as the law.[87] First the property had to be listed, then it was divided up into equal or equivalent portions, and the document was endorsed by a trustworthy third party; then the sons drew lots for a portion.[88]

84. Janelli and Janelli 1982: 44.
85. Although it was usually the eldest son who took his father's place, if the eldest son was judged incompetent or if a younger son was especially good at management, the mantle would fall on his shoulders (R. Watson 1985: 36–54).
86. Yuan Cai, tr. Ebrey 1984: 202.
87. In earlier times there was apparently more latitude in inheritance practices. In Tang and Song times daughters were legally entitled to inherit communal property too (Birge 1992). Moreover, Yuan Cai implies that in the Song a man who divided his property before his death could dispose of it as he wished. "Sons who felt cheated could not take him to court; they would have to wait until he died and then sue their brothers for a more equitable share" (Ebrey 1984: 113). Though a man might try to provide for unequal shares by writing a will, a will was more easily contested than a living patriarch.
88. Models for recording property division have been retrieved from the medieval site of Dunhuang and were a feature in Yuan and Ming encyclopedias (Ebrey 1984: 115). Drawing lots was already standard practice, at least for land. In late Qing and Republican China it was standard for all inherited property (Cohen 1976; Wakefield n.d.).

One of the most important pieces of family property was the family house. The literal division of the house has not been singled out for study by social and economic historians of imperial China, and even ethnographers such as Myron Cohen cannot provide information over a sufficient time span to trace the detailed history of an individual house as it was divided and redivided over generations. David Wakefield, in a comparative study of regional practices of family division based on Japanese ethnographic surveys as well as wills and other legal documents, provides some significant concrete information for late Qing and Republican China. Comparing materials from North China and Taiwan, Wakefield concludes that practices were broadly similar in the two otherwise very different regions, and the principles of division were shared by rich and poor alike. In drawing up portions, the basic principle was to allocate equal amounts of housing to each stirp.[89] Ideally each share would include sleeping quarters and reception rooms; its own, separate courtyard; space for a kitchen; a pigsty and outhouses. In a house with only one courtyard, each brother would receive equal facilities around that courtyard. Where possible, enclaves were avoided, and the eldest son was given the best room for his living quarters, namely the room to the east of the main room containing the shrine. If a courtyard had to be divided, each brother would be given the section immediately in front of his own living quarters, and the boundary lines were marked by walls, gutters, or other architectural features. Some features, like wells or threshing floors, were kept in common.

As the eldest son was the ritual heir, he would inherit the care of the central room containing the shrine, and if his brothers remained in the same compound this became joint ritual property. If they moved elsewhere so that they could not join the ritual heir for daily worship, then they would establish their own shrine. Sometimes a family would stay together for several generations, continually adding to the original house to accommodate new members.[90] But division marked the transfer of legal ownership, and therefore the right to sell. Chinese families, understandably, preferred not to share their living space with strangers, and many division documents stipulate against selling the house share to outsiders.[91]

---

89. In some regions of China, however, it seems that dividing up the house was avoided and junior sons were given realizable capital to compensate.

90. Cohen 1976: 21.

91. Presumably, though Wakefield is not explicit on this point, if one of the new families wanted to move out to live separately, the other heirs would try to buy their brother out.

CONTAINING WOMEN

In late imperial China, all levels of society considered the seclusion of women and the segregation of the sexes inside and outside the house to be not simply a sign of respectability but an essential factor in maintaining public morality. Spatial and social segregation was an expression of a doctrine of separate spheres dating back to classical times. This doctrine was not a simple charter for female subordination; rather it represented the sexes as fulfilling complementary roles of equal dignity (if not equal power). Men and women controlled different domains, into which the other should not intrude. The female domain was the inner, domestic one (although we should beware of presuming absolute coincidence between Chinese and Western meanings of "domesticity"), and the male domain was the outer one; the two were complementary and thus "he should not discuss affairs of the inner sphere, she should not discuss affairs of the outer sphere."[92] Confucian canonical texts like the *Book of Rites* emphasized a wife's dignity and authority as well as obedience and submission, and as Susan Mann points out, on careful reading the *Book of Rites* "could be interpreted to emphasize *distinctions* and *difference* more than hierarchy, dominance, or submission."[93] More usually, however, women were represented as potentially disruptive of the social order, and the doctrine of separate spheres was used to justify their containment and control.

The Chinese house was a box full of tensions and conflicts, held down by the heavy lid of the patriline. The rifts that most threatened the structure of the Chinese patrilineal family were those between father and sons and between brothers, both bonds being sanctified in the Five Relationships. Wise men like Yuan Cai (fl. 1140–95) recognized that the development cycle of the patrilineal family naturally produced tensions between agnates, and that these might be triggered by minor irritations like one son's children making a mess in another son's quarters, or one brother's laziness about the family business. If a father favored one son above the others, or if doubts were raised about the fairness of the division of the property, conflict between brothers was inevitable. Yet even Yuan Cai liked to present women as the root of the trouble: "Many cases of family discord begin because a woman, by what she says, incites animosity between her husband and other family members of his generation."[94] He did not attribute this so much to inherent defects of the female character as to the

92. *Liji* (Book of rites), quoted Ko 1992b: 15.
93. Mann 1991: 209.
94. From the section "Getting Along with Relatives," tr. Ebrey 1984: 206.

fact that in virilocal marriage women had no natural affections for the members of the corporate group whose interests they were now expected to regard as their own. Yuan advised a husband to ignore anything his wife might say against his brothers.

While Yuan is surprisingly realistic about the structural causes of conflict in the Chinese family, the most common version projected all the blame for family problems onto women. Wives were commonly represented, in Confucian moral works as well as in popular proverbs, as gossiping troublemakers eager to stir up strife between otherwise devoted brothers, the root of family discord, requiring strict patriarchal control. Henpecked husbands and jealous wives were common themes in moral tracts and in popular literature throughout the imperial period.[95] Moreover, popular Buddhism represented women as polluted and inferior beings whose best hope for salvation was to be reincarnated as men. The prevailing ethos in late imperial China was that women should be strictly confined and controlled by men, lest the family honor be lost and social and moral chaos ensue.

Doctrines of segregation were elaborated by neo-Confucian philosophers during the Song and formulated in spatial terms that gradually became the orthodoxy at all levels of society. In late imperial China all houses, rich or poor, marked off a separate space for women. Men were expected to spend most of their waking hours outside, and their access to the interior spaces was controlled. Detailed instructions for the spatial segregation of the sexes, and for communication between the two domains, were formulated by Sima Guang and included in the *Family Rituals:*

> In housing, there should be a strict demarcation between the inner and outer parts, with a door separating them. The two parts should share neither a well, a wash room, nor a privy. The men are in charge of all affairs on the outside, the women manage the inside affairs. During the day, without good reason the men do not stay in their private rooms nor the women go beyond the inner door. Men who walk around at night must hold a candle. A woman who has to leave the inner quarters must cover her face (for example, with a veil). Men-servants do not enter the inner quarters unless to make house repairs or in cases of calamity (such as

95. Ebrey, documenting the theme of jealous wives in Song literature, proposes that it was connected to the rapid expansion of concubinage among the elite (1993: 167). Ko believes that a similar rise in concubinage among the well-to-do in the late Ming underlay writers' "obsession" with female jealousy, but suggests that in this case the increasing visibility and assertiveness of elite women was also felt as a threat (1994: 106).

floods, fires or robberies). If they must enter, the women should avoid them. If they cannot avoid being seen (as in floods, fires, and robberies), they must cover their faces with their sleeves. Maids should never cross the inner gate without good reason (young slave-girls also); if they must do so, they too should cover their faces. The doorman and old servants serve to pass messages and objects between the inner and outer quarters of the house, but they must not be allowed to enter rooms or kitchens at will.[96]

Referring to this passage, Yuan Cai comments: "This is over half of what is needed to manage a household."[97]

In late imperial China all families, however humble, observed strict rules of segregation within the house. Young children of both sexes lived with their mothers, but Sima Guang described the usual practice when he said that boys must move out of the inner quarters at the age of ten.[98] Sima Guang writes of a large compound in which the inner quarters were at the back of the compound, separated from the rest of the house by an inner gate. In many large houses the inner quarters were a separate building in a back courtyard, or maybe part of the main hall but with a separate entrance facing the back. The *Qing Customs* says that in the merchants' houses of the southern cities the women's quarters were entered through a curtain, but at night the double doors were closed and locked.

In some houses each married couple was allocated a room or a suite in the main part of the house where they slept and kept their things, but during the day the men would go out or work in their studies, and the women would repair to the kitchen or workrooms. In a poor family's cottage the inner quarters might be demarcated by a curtain hung across the kitchen door, behind which the women retreated when male visitors occupied the single living room.[99] Men were supposed not to stay in the house during the day, but no outside work could be done during the bitter winters of the north, and everyone stayed inside to keep warm. In the Beijing countryside in the early 1930s, in a village where most houses consisted of three rooms (a main room containing the altar, and a bedroom, with a *kang*, on each side), Körner found that during the cold days of winter the men would occupy the left bedroom and women the right bedroom.[100] At night married men entered the inner quarters to sleep in

96. Tr. Ebrey 1991d: 29.
97. Ebrey 1984: 286.
98. Ebrey 1991d: 33.
99. *Shinzoku kibun* A: 112.
100. Körner 1959: 6.

their wife's room, but they were supposed to leave again in the morning and to avoid any unnecessary contact with other female relatives. Men who tarried in the inner quarters were not true gentlemen and were likely to come to a bad end. Baoyu, the hero of the Qing novel *The Dream of the Red Chamber,* is the despair of his ambitious father, for he avoids the outer sphere entirely and spends all his time with his female relatives.

Mealtimes could be occasions when the whole family came together. But even in relatively easygoing households, like those described in the *Qing Customs,* no promiscuous mixing was allowed. Until they were twelve or thirteen, boys and girls ate together at the same table, sitting with their immediate family group of the father, his children, wife and unmarried sisters. Once they reached puberty, the boys had to sit separately. A bride might not eat at the same table as her father-in-law, nor could a wife sit with her husband's brothers. Mostly men ate together in the outer room and women ate together in their own quarters. Sima Guang allows only the senior couple to eat together. They are served first, at a separate table, and then the men sit down at one table, the women at another, ranked in order of age. The children too sit at a separate table with the boys on the left and the girls on the right, in order of age.[101]

Although families might get together for feasts and parties at home, all other respectable social activities were homosocial. Dorothy Ko documents how a busy official, living under the same roof as his wife, might lead a very separate life. Even if her social life was active, it was almost exclusively female. As a Chinese ethnographer writing on Guangdong in the 1920s put it: "There is no social life between men and women in the villages. The custom and ethical teaching of the Chinese are that men and women, unless they are members of the same family, should keep apart as much as possible; so even the male and female members of the same class never join together in a party, a feast, or a celebration. In making calls, extending congratulations or consolations, the men visit the men and the women visit the women."[102] This pattern of behavior was already clear, at least among elite and middle-class women, in the Ming and Qing, as we can tell from sources such as novels or the etiquette sections of encyclopedias.

Men's work and women's work were strictly divided. The idea was that upper-class men studied and went into government, lower-class men were farmers, craftsmen or merchants. Women were responsible for preparing

---

101. *Shinzoku kibun* A: 155; Sima Guang, tr. Ebrey 1991d: 27.
102. Ko 1994: 179–218; Cheng Tien-fang, quoted Hayes 1985: 89.

food, looking after the children and elderly, and producing textiles and making clothes. Generally speaking, the spatial location of their work reinforced women's segregation from men and from the disruptive pleasures of gossip with neighbors. Yet as I show in parts 2 and 3, although these tasks were all supposed to be performed indoors, thus marking the separation between women and men, womanly work was represented as producing social and material goods essential for the world outside, tying women tightly into the polity. Nor were all decent women continuously cloistered, for it was also recognized that certain duties took a wife outside. It was not uncommon for peasant women to work outside the house at times. In many regions they would help out in the fields at busy seasons even though they were hampered by their bound feet, and there were certain field tasks like picking tea or cotton that seem routinely to have fallen to women (fig. 16). And if the fields were too far from the house for the farmer to come home for a quick meal at noon, "he would have his wife or daughter bring a meal in a bamboo basket, together with bowl and chopsticks."[103] Women did a lot of farmwork near the house or in the courtyard, like husking and grinding millet. The courtyard was often not big enough for dressing looms, so that had to be done outside, and washing clothes, going to market or fetching water from the well were other necessary tasks that were likely to take women outside their walls.

In principle upper-class women were expected to work productively too, sitting at their looms or supervising tasks in the kitchen. But by late imperial times, the most productive work that many well-off women did was a little embroidery. The *Qing Customs* tells us that in wealthy homes the ladies themselves did not make clothes for the family, but some did handicrafts or embroidery as a hobby.[104] An illustration shows the inner quarters of a wealthy merchant home as an elegant retreat with every creature comfort (fig. 8). A lady's bedroom would contain an elaborate alcove bed, a dressing table, tables and chairs, and a washstand with bowl and towels. She was well provided with toilet articles, mirrors and sewing boxes. Musical instruments might be hung on the wall, and in a separate alcove, which could be locked, were piled her clothes chests, jewelry boxes and

<hr />

103. *Qing Customs* A: 182. Several of the pictures of farming in the *Gengzhi tu* (Agriculture and sericulture illustrated) show men hard at work in the rice fields while their wives or daughters walk along the bunds bringing them a teapot and lunch basket. Other agricultural treatises show women in the fields picking tea, thinning cotton, or gathering mulberry leaves (though in some areas this work was confined to men).

104. *Shinzoku kibun* A: 155.

household goods. The articles of furniture and equipment that accompany the description of the common rooms of the women's quarters include braziers, lamps and equipment for serving tea and preparing medical infusions.[105]

While the married ladies' rooms were on the ground floor of the inner quarters, the upper floor contained the daughters' bedrooms. It had small windows covered with blinds to protect the young ladies from intruding glances. One reached the upper floor by a staircase. The floor was of polished boards, the entrance was a double door. There were mats and rugs on the floor, with tables, chairs and stools. The panels of the door stood open but a woven blind hung inside. At the front of the top story was built the dew platform (*lutai*), a large balcony supported on pillars and with balustrades of wood or bamboo on three sides, an awning overhead to keep off the sun, a cool refuge from the heat (fig. 9). These balconies served as a family sitting room, a place where women would work at their embroidery and other tasks and where the men of the family joined them to relax in the evenings. Family parties for viewing the moon in the eighth month were held on the dew terrace. So too was the girls' ceremony of the Double Seventh, the night when the Herd Boy and the Weaving Girl met in the sky, and offerings of fruit and cakes were made as young girls prayed to be given skills with the needle. In the homes of poor families the offerings had to be made in the courtyard.[106]

The *Qing Customs* illustration of the dew platform shows a glimpse of a Buddhist altar. Buddhist piety was particularly associated with women and with the lower classes. Since Song times at least, women had been particularly attracted by the Bodhisattva Guanyin, a merciful goddess to whom women who were pregnant or childless turned for protection and help. Although popular Buddhist doctrines held that women were intrinsically polluted and therefore barred from immediate salvation, the prospect of reincarnation and eventual admission to paradise, and the possibility of improving one's spiritual status through good works and piety, made Buddhism an attractive escape from the shackles of the Confucian order.

105. Items of women's furniture, such as chests, coffers and presses, toilet stands and clothes racks, as well as beds and chairs, have survived from Ming and Qing times and examples are illustrated in studies like Wang Shixiang 1991 and Clunas 1988.

106. *Shinzoku kibun* A: 122 on the "dew platform," 40–43 on the ceremonies of the Double Seventh. The Herd Boy and the Weaving Girl were two constellations separated by the Milky Way. They were deeply in love, but were allowed to meet only on this single night of the year.

Figure 9. The dew platform (*Qing Customs* A: 132–33). This was where the ladies of the family relaxed, often joined by the men. The awning protected the verandah from the sun and caught every passing breeze, wafting in fragrance from the plants along the balustrade. The altar on the left is Buddhist, as is the couplet on the paired scrolls to either side. A sleeping alcove can be glimpsed in the room behind: perhaps it was a room belonging to one of the daughters. The little table to the rear of the room is a writing desk, with books, an ink slab, water dropper, brushes and a brush stand, the scholar's "four friends." It seems that daughters were well educated even in merchant families in the Qing.

There were periods when elite men became actively involved in Buddhism, or when an easy acquaintance with its philosophy and symbols was considered a sign of cultivation; at other times they kept a cool distance.[107] But even then they did not forbid their mothers, wives or daughters to practice their faith. Ebrey cites funeral epigraphs of Song wives (written by men) that describe a kind of pragmatic complementarity between Confucian and Buddhist principles. For instance, a stern and dogmatic man might

107. Brook (1993) argues that in late Ming Jiangnan a nonpious involvement in Buddhism and its associated good works, like the use of monasteries as places for lectures and discussions, meant that for elite men the Buddhist connection offered a kind of "gentry society" space autonomous from state control. At the intellectual rather than the social level, the emphasis on self-cultivation inherent in much neo-Confucian thought, from Zhu Xi in the Song through to Wang Yangming (1472–1529) in the Ming, drew explicitly or implicitly on Buddhist theory, and as such was roundly condemned by the "Han learning" school of the late Ming and Qing, who advocated the restitution of pure, original Confucian values.

be persuaded by his wife to temper justice with mercy, to inflect the application of abstract principle with adjustment to human circumstance, to try to develop empathy with others. Such a wife would be admired by elite men for the tactful and supportive way in which she advised her husband. Ebrey also suggests that men appreciated their wives' piety because the tranquility it gave the women permitted them to tolerate concubinage gracefully, to put up with material hardship and to comfort their agitated spouses when misfortune struck. It therefore served the male Confucian purposes of family harmony well.[108]

The gentleman's equivalent of the woman's bedchamber was his study, a room where he could retreat to pass time undisturbed, invite intimate friends and express his individual taste. Unlike the other male quarters, a man's study or "book room" (*shufang*) did not have to be shared. As its name implies, it was supposed to be the preserve of an educated male who spent most of his time with books—it was the scholar's workplace, just as the field was the peasant's workplace, except that it was inside the walls of the house. As well as being the place where a gentleman worked, it was also a place where he could take refuge, like the smoking room of a Victorian mansion. The women of the house were not supposed to follow him there (except perhaps to bring hot water to make tea), and noisy children would be kept away. It was also a place where he might be banished, if his presence in the inner quarters was considered undesirable.

The study was either a room or a separate construction, located behind the main hall in the more private region of the house, and ideally it looked out onto a garden (fig. 10). The contemplation of nature, the sight of greenery and the sound of wind rustling through bamboos brought calmness of mind and inspiration to literary endeavors. Ideally the scholar surrounded himself with fine editions and tasteful appurtenances, and it was in the study that the refined male aesthetic was best expressed. Almost all the objects there were by definition male and not female: the "scholar's four friends" (writing brush, brush stand, water dropper and inkstone), the bookshelves, the writing table, the scrolls of calligraphy and valuable antique bronzes, and the couch or dais (*ta*) that dominated the male study (as the bed dominated a woman's apartment). Books of connoisseurship devoted detailed discussions to good and bad taste in such gentlemanly paraphernalia, while omitting any mention of those considered to be the domain of women and servants, such as cupboards or coffers or other

108. Ebrey 1993: 124–27.

Figure 10. The scholar's study (*Qing Customs* A: 97). This is a study in a merchant's house, which is perhaps why it looks out on a permanent arrangement of rocks and shrubs rather than the more portable potted plants that officials carried with them from one posting to another. This study is a separate building at the back of the compound, constructed in rustic style and simply furnished. The writing desk looks out on the rocks, and there is a curtained couch at the back. Apart from the "four friends" on the desk, the only other furnishings appear to be a calligraphic inscription on the wall and chests of books. Another illustration (ibid.: A: 98) shows a more lavishly furnished study, which this time is part of the main building. The centerpiece is a large couch or dais with a low table, around which friends could sit and read together. On the wall behind the couch is a landscape painting and paired scrolls, and a flute, two-string violin and *pipa* lute hang on the side wall.

containers for clothes.[109] Even the musical instruments that hung on the study walls were different from those that a lady would play.[110]

Because the study was a symbol of elite status, of education and refined virility, in other words of *wen*, which denoted skills both in letters and in social behavior, anyone who wanted to rise in society would build himself a study and buy the objects necessary to equip it. As early as the Yuan there was a market for books instructing people how to consume, and the number of titles and editions grew inexorably through the late imperial period. As Clunas points out in his study of "superfluous things," the fine art of writing books on connoisseurship consists in admitting ambitious newcomers to the outer circle of expertise while reminding them that books can teach you only so much and money cannot substitute for the innate taste acquired through breeding or for true education. Holding out this kind of bait was one powerful stimulus to a form of cultural integration where ever larger numbers of families laid claim to gentility and elite manners. The *Householder's Vademecum* of 1301 contains a section entitled "What One Needs for the Study," which discusses writing brushes, ink and different kinds of paper. In the late fifteenth century Fan Lian (b. 1540), noting the new fashion for hardwood furniture and how it was spreading through society, wrote: "It is strange that even those policemen who had a home would arrange a comfortable place to rest, separated by wooden partitions. In the courtyard they raised goldfish and planted various kinds of flowers. Inside there were good-quality wooden tables and a horsetail whisk for dusting. They called it the study. However I really do not know what books they studied!"[111]

The Jiangnan merchants told the author of the *Qing Customs* that "wealthy farmers' houses included a reception hall, a study, and inner quarters just like merchants' houses," that is to say, they took it for granted that merchants would have a study, just as they would have inner quarters.[112] This is an important connection: inherent in the male aspira-

109. Clunas 1988: 83.
110. The most refined Chinese instrument, much favored by scholars, was the *qin* lute, a horizontal instrument resembling a zither which was usually played unaccompanied. Its pedigree went back to classical times, as did many of the airs played on it. The *pipa* lute (mentioned in the caption to fig. 10) somewhat resembles a mandolin, and is said to have been introduced to China from Central Asia during the Tang. It was considered much less refined than the *qin* and was often played in an ensemble with flutes, violins and percussion instruments.
111. *Jujia biyong shilei quanji*, vol. 5. Fan Lian, *Record of Things Seen in Yunjian*, quoted Wang Shixiang 1988: 14.
112. *Shinzoku kibun* A: 181.

tion to the status of a study-owner was the understanding that the women of the house would live in an equally genteel fashion, secluded in separate quarters. The spread of these material manifestations of male and female cultivation or refinement, *wen*, was paralleled in the domain of medical theory. As I show in chapter 9, during the late Ming and Qing, among the well-to-do there was a boom in the market for reproductive medicine and for books on fertility theory, which discussed the sexual characteristics and fertility of gentlemen and gentlewomen in terms directly related to moral and cultural refinement.

Note that the inner quarters provided married women with a room of their own, where they kept their private belongings. Men in China were heirs to a share of the family patrimony, as mentioned, but patrimony was communal property, held in trust. At no stage in their lives could they be said to own it outright. In contrast, women's dowries were wealth that had been given outside the patriline, and its ownership was in constant dispute. The strict Confucians claimed that it became part of the joint family property; when she came to her new home the bride should give it over to her parents-in-law, or at least ask their approval for any use she made of it. If Confucian moralists made so strong a point of this, we can only conclude that most women thought of their dowries as their private property, to use as they would—not least because they had often produced or acquired it by their own hard work, weaving fine cloths for their own use or selling them for cash to buy other necessaries. A poor woman's dowry might consist at best of some pots and pans, quilts and a few clothes. A rich woman in late imperial times would take to her new home a bed carved in precious wood, a chest of clothes for each season, jewelry, fine textiles and cash as well as household goods.[113] It has been argued that women considered their dowries as family property not of the joint family, but of their own family—themselves, their husband and their children.[114] Historical cases suggest that while women were willing to contribute to the welfare of this group, it was on the understanding that this was a choice and not an obligation. In any case, in the houses described in the *Qing Customs* the wives kept their belongings in a locked alcove, and even the maids had a key for their rooms, but the men had nothing to lock up. Paradoxically the patriarchal order sought to control

---

113. In the Song, girls of good family might be given slaves and even land (Ebrey 1991d, 1993; Birge 1992). For a comparative overview of the meanings of dowry and brideprice in China see also J. Goody 1990.

114. L. Sung 1981.

women by confining them, but in the process created private spaces that served as sites of resistance to its control.

The confinement of women to the inner regions of the house was in part a method for controlling their sexuality, as were the strict rules about contact between male and female relatives within the family. In his section "Managing Family Affairs," Yuan Cai insists on the need to control the comings and goings of maids and concubines, chiefly because they may get pregnant by an outsider and then claim that the child belongs to the master of the house, in which case they might be included among his legitimate heirs. The need to control the sexuality of wives and daughters is not explicitly stated, though when dispensing advice for widowers who wish to remarry to provide a mother for their children, Yuan cautions that "men who marry a widow may find that she has had affairs with other men."[115]

The relation between female virtue and seclusion could be construed in two ways, with different implications for the status of women who ventured outside the inner quarters. Either women were capable of moral choices and the pursuit of virtue, or they were innately immoral and lacking in self-control, so that female "virtue" was rather an absence of vice, imposed by male control.

The first position was consonant with the view that male and female spheres had equal dignity and worth, that women could achieve self-cultivation just like men, and could act as responsible and capable educators of their children. The first manual on how to be a good wife, *Nü jie* (Instructions for women), was written by the illustrious Han scholar Ban Zhao. For many centuries, however, Ban Zhao was "probably best remembered as a celibate widow."[116] The late Ming intellectual Lü Kun was one of the first neo-Confucian scholars to stress the complementarity of the husband-wife relationship and to advocate the education of women; in his own instruction book he states that he is addressing not only elite families but also commoners (by this he probably means not peasants but women in the families of small landowners or urban merchants) who "suddenly have three or five volumes in their chests."[117] During the eighteenth century, as rising living standards and easier access to education expanded the

115. Ebrey 1984: 219.
116. Mann 1991: 213. Ban Zhao was the sister of Ban Gu, the compiler of the *Han shu* (History of the [Former] Han dynasty [206 B.C.–A.D. 25]); after his death in A.D. 92 she took up his unfinished task, completing the work in about A.D. 100.
117. Handlin 1975: 17. Ko points out that in the Jiaqing reign (1522–66) the publishing industry went through "a revolution in the economics of publishing

market for books of all kinds, "commoners attuned to concerns about proper marriage and behavior were avid consumers of works on managing the household. Women were part of this consumer market," which included new editions of earlier works (Ban Zhao's *Nü jie*, a Tang work, and a book of instructions written by a Ming empress) as well as new compositions, a few by women (published by their male relatives) and many more by men. "The eighteenth century was the apogee of instruction books for women."[118]

From this perspective, which was perhaps more typical of the high elite (including statesmen and philosophers) than of any other social group, a woman's virtue was not the product of her seclusion, but stemmed from her moral character. In a study of eighteenth-century gentry women, Dorothy Ko states that "the virtues of domesticity and purity were more contingent upon a woman's moral intentions—her subjective will—than on her physical location."[119]

In the second view, more typical of the majority, moral education and decorous behavior within the confines of the inner quarters offered no safeguard against the perils of the outer world. A woman found in the wrong place was given no credit for purity of intention. This was certainly the perspective embodied in the law. Qing legal records include cases where a woman of a country family was seen in the company of a man in some place such as the garden of the house; the conclusion automatically drawn was that she was involved in an illicit sexual relationship.[120] It was certainly the view of the female character most frequently expressed in the patriarchal genre known as "household instructions" (*jiaxun*), a genre popular among the petty gentry of the late imperial period.[121]

---

and the culture of learning." Demand and supply soared, prices plunged, and books became available to new sorts of people, including women, who could now afford to buy and even to collect books such as romantic stories and plays, primers, religious tracts, travel books and collections of edifying female biographies. Books were still beyond the means of the majority, however; in Nanjing in 1585 the price of a book might range between an ounce and one-tenth of an ounce of silver, the latter still being the price of a third of a bushel of rice or of eight pounds of tea. Ko emphasizes that unlike in Reformation Europe, where a new popular middle-class press expressed values that often challenged those of the establishment, in Ming China the new readership was "more an extension of the traditional elite than its enemy" (1994: 34–37).

118. Mann 1991: 214, 224.
119. Ko 1992a: 2.
120. Matt Sommers, personal communication 1991.
121. Their "stress on moral obligations among kinsmen, the social control of women, and ceremonial observance is typical of the complex of values that gentry

Li Yu, who undoubtedly spent far more time in the inner quarters than a respectable patriarch would have considered proper, never once refers in the *Casual Expressions* to the need to seclude women. But in his erotic novel *The Carnal Prayer Mat*, Li mocks the notion that seclusion produces true virtue: all it does is protect women from exposure to temptation. Even the most delicately nurtured, well-educated and carefully cloistered young lady is—like any man—virtuous only until sufficiently tempted. In any case conventional virtue in either sex may simply mask defects of the soul. The puritanical Confucian scholar Master Iron Door receives no visitors and keeps his daughter Jade Scent literally locked up. "The door to her chambers is always securely guarded. She never goes to temples to burn incense or out into the street to watch processions. In fact in all her fifteen years she has never once shown her face in public. As for women visitors such as nuns and the like, it goes without saying—they couldn't get inside the house even if they had wings." Yet the lewd Vesperus tricks Master Iron Gate into giving him his daughter in marriage, and later, when Vesperus has abandoned Jade Scent in search of adventure, a cuckolded husband seeking revenge easily worms his way into Master Iron Gate's house as a trusted steward, then seduces Jade Scent, who is so delighted with his sexual prowess that she elopes with him. Li Yu explains straightfaced that Master Iron Gate deserves his misfortune despite his Confucian learning and intransigent morality, because of his stinginess toward his tenants. Furthermore, the strictest man cannot keep out a determined intruder. "One marvelous feature of this chapter is the way the straightforward, rough-and-ready Honest Quan manages by devious, convoluted means to work his way inside the 'iron door.' . . . And a second marvelous thing is the way Master Iron Door, who has worried over every possible contingency and taken every conceivable precaution, falls right into Honest Quan's trap." [122]

Master Iron Gate's suspicion of nuns and other visitors was shared by many husbands and fathers in the Confucian elite. [123] Anyone who crossed

---

elders expected to be upheld by a proper Chinese family. By the middle of the Ming dynasty, the composition of such household instructions had become an established convention. . . . The vast majority survive not because their authors were well-known scholars, but because many relatively anonymous gentry members belonged to descent groups that published genealogies into which such writings were incorporated" (Furth 1990: 187).

122. Li Yu [1657] 1990: 36, 204.

123. The anti-Buddhist theme of clerical promiscuity was an antique vein constantly mined in late Ming popular fiction. Brook suggests that this was related to

the boundaries between spheres was suspect, even servants. As proposed by Sima Guang only old servants, that is, people who had outlived their reproductive years, were allowed to cross the boundaries between inner and outer quarters, and even then they were not to move around at will. The only women in late imperial China who mixed freely with men to whom they were not related were courtesans and prostitutes. There were several other groups of women who regularly entered the inner quarters of strange houses for professional purposes. They included matchmakers, women herbalists and healers, midwives and nuns. Except for the match-makers, without whose help no marriage could be arranged (and whose role was sanctioned in orthodox liturgies), all of these women—the "six kinds of old crone" (*liu po*), as they were contemptuously called—were viewed by orthodox male writers as a threat to the morality of their wives and daughters, and as potential swindlers. These women peddled wares and knowledge of which such men had no need, or of which they actively disapproved: fertility drugs and abortifacients, religious comfort and promises of salvation, charms and fortune-telling. It seems probable, how-ever, that many of the herbal remedies and other services for which re-spectable women paid were much less seditious than the men liked to think. Probably one of the greatest attractions of these women's visits for the ladies was that they brought in news from the world beyond the walls of the inner quarters.

Elite women had the fewest opportunities to venture beyond their own walls. Dorothy Ko discusses various forays outside the walls of the house that some women might make: scenic outings, boating and picnics, drink-ing and poetry parties with women relatives and friends, or long journeys accompanying a husband to official duties in a new part of the country. But only a privileged few had this degree of freedom, and their exposure to broad horizons and dramatic nature was often envied by their more secluded friends. The only travels most ladies experienced were proxy journeys, made by reading, looking at paintings, or sending letters to other women equally confined.[124]

Unlike in many other societies, the majority of ordinary women shared the commitment of ladies to demure behavior. Even in the Song poor women seem to have done their best to dress modestly and keep out of

---

the expanded contacts between laity and clergy that were typical of the period (1993: 95).

124. Ko 1992a, 1994.

men's view whenever possible.[125] Poor families were just as jealous of their women's respectability as gentry, but besides the seasonal farm tasks mentioned earlier, their women routinely left the home to buy fresh food at the market, to get water from the well, or to do washing at the river. These were the places where poor women could chat with each other and exchange the gossip that Chinese men condemned so strongly—perhaps because, as Margery Wolf argues, it often operated as a powerful form of social control over people abusing their authority, whether it was a man who beat his wife or a woman who mistreated her daughter-in-law.[126]

Women of all classes liked to visit temples and to go on pilgrimages, if their husbands would give them permission to leave the house. Childless women offered incense to the Goddess of Mercy, Guanyin, or to the many other deities of the late imperial period associated with fertility. Old women, as death approached, wanted to pray for salvation or reincarnation in a better life. Elite men, even when they studied Buddhism and visited temples, affected to be free of vulgar religiosity and the emotionality that went with it. They regarded women's participation in such outings with deep suspicion: in operas as in novels, Buddhist and Daoist temples were depicted as promiscuous places where love affairs were likely to occur.[127] And when women grouped together for a pilgrimage, even if no worse mischief occurred they were still sure to lose all sense of decorum and start behaving like spendthrift hoydens. As a seventeenth-century novelist put it, "like a pack of wolves and dogs, the whole herd of women stampeded their donkeys, overtaking one another turn by turn. . . . Some, before they had gone more than a mile or two, said their bowels were unsettled and wanted to get down and find a lonely spot to relieve themselves; some said they had their period and wanted to pull cloths out of their bed sack to go between their legs; some wanted to suckle their children and asked the man with the whip to lead them along by the reins."[128] Most pilgrims in the late imperial period seem to have been members of the lower class, "unwashed, halitotic, defecating, urinating" crowds consisting mostly of men and women in family groups, in search of a blessing to bring long life, a son, or wealth. But women even of the lower class constituted only a minority of the total number of pilgrims.[129]

125. Ebrey 1993: 25–27.
126. M. Wolf 1968: 15, 19–20.
127. Leung 1983: 64.
128. Dudbridge 1992: 52.
129. Wu 1992: 83; Naquin 1992: 362.

One outing that many country women looked forward to was going to the plays or operas put on in villages and market towns all over China. Plays put on in market towns celebrated the local deity's birthday or the opening of a fair. They were sponsored by the surrounding villages and organized by professional promoters. In smaller villages performances were put on for the souls of the hungry ghosts or to honor the village god; here peasants and local gentry cooperated in the organization. In addition, lineages would organize performances at their ancestral hall on important festivals. Anyone attending a play at the lineage temple would imbibe, through the well-loved tunes, the thrilling pageantry and the breathtaking acrobatics that were part of any dramatic performance, an improving tale of dutiful wives, filial sons and loyal ministers. A play in a market town told subversive tales of romantic love, supernatural powers and martial prowess. The plots often involved cross-dressing heroines, young women who disguised themselves as scholars and passed the examinations with flying colors, or who carried out spectacular martial feats. A village play might carry a message of either kind, depending on whether the farmers' tastes or the landlords' carried the day.[130] From a woman's perspective, while many village performances confirmed conventional Confucian social values and gender roles, others opened up alternative allegories of female roles and relations between the sexes. The freedom of imagination they offered was, however, limited: a woman could escape the conventional spatial boundaries and role models only by disguising herself as a man, and there were no plots in which a man assumed the dutiful role of a daughter-in-law.[131] Even the most daring heroines left the audience in no doubt that a man's lot in life was the more enviable.

What effect did female seclusion have on women's ideas about themselves? In the case of gentry women, Ko argues that seclusion provided freedom and dignity. "In Ming-Qing households, the innermost realm of the private sphere was the prerogative of women. The women's quarters, tucked away in inconspicuous corners of the gentry housing compound, were off limits even to adult men in the family. In facilitating the development of her self-image and identity as woman, this cloistering had a positive effect on women's culture. The identification of women with domesticity was welcomed by mothers and housewives, who took pride in their calling to be the guardian of familial morality. Hence women did not feel

130. Tanaka 1985.
131. Ko 1992a: 39.

the need to challenge the age-old ideology prescribing the functional separations between the sexes."[132] Ko argues that gentry women in this period were "oblivious" to the hierarchical dimension of this doctrine of separate spheres. In my opinion, it is more likely that they were conscious of it but accepted it as a natural fact.

The evidence from the merchants of the *Qing Customs* tends to confirm Ko's revisionist interpretation, except that they portray an agreeable intimacy between men and women. The merchants describe a train of life in which they pass perhaps the most relaxed and pleasant hours of the day in the inner quarters. After the household head had washed and combed his hair in the mornings, we are told, he would repair to the women's quarters to drink tea and smoke a pipe, and then the whole family would sit down to breakfast together.[133] The merchants describe the life of their wives as cloistered but do not lay on the moral interpretations or the fear of cuckoldry. Poor women's lives they portray as necessarily less confined. Though many neo-Confucians rail against the moral perils of embroidery, the merchants speak of it as a charming and companionable occupation. Though they do say that naturally girls cannot leave the house to go to school, they do not condemn educating daughters at home. The sequestered quarters of the women emerge in the *Qing Customs* descriptions as the most pleasant and relaxed part of the house, the place for family parties and cheerful evenings, cool in summer and warmed with braziers in winter.

It was customary in China to represent women as emotional, willful and likely to quarrel among themselves. Was this a natural outcome of seclusion? Were women the worst enemies of other women, or did they see each other as friends and allies? Here it seems essential to distinguish between women who were related by birth and those who were thrown together by marriage, an experience of alienation to which Chinese men were never exposed. The moralistic literature that depicts women as quarrelsome and selfish focuses on the tensions between women related by marriage, and they were undoubtedly considerable.

Incoming brides had no preexisting ties to their new family,[134] and relations between insiders and outsiders were often difficult. In gentry

---

132. Ko 1992b: 14.

133. *Shinzoku kibun* A: 155.

134. Unless one of their female relatives had already married into it. Intermarriage was quite common; see Ebrey 1993: 67–69 on the Song, Ko 1994: 156 on the late Ming, and Dennerline 1986 on the interesting late Qing case of the lineage of the famous scholar Mu Qian.

households a new bride was unlikely to receive physical ill-treatment, but she would still find herself outside her own home for the first time, as a very junior member of the hierarchy. Social historians argue that families did their best to provide their daughters with good dowries so that they would be treated with respect and kindness by their new family. In poor households the most junior bride was likely to be treated as an unpaid servant and set to do all the unpleasant chores. Peasant mothers taught their daughters lengthy songs of despair that were part of the wedding ceremony: torn from her mother, aunts and sisters, the young woman felt as if she had died and was making the descent into hell. "The analogy of the wedding process with death is made explicit: the bride describes herself as being prepared for death, and the wedding process as the crossing of the yellow river that is the boundary between this life and the next. She appeals for justice, citing the valuable and unrecognized contribution she has made to her family. Her language is bitter and unrestrained, and she even curses the matchmaker and her future husband's family. Such lamenting can take place only within her parents' household and must cease halfway on the road to her new home, when the invisible boundary has been crossed." [135]

Relationships between women brought together by marriage were fraught with structural difficulties, and this was undoubtedly exacerbated by the fact that seclusion threw these women into each other's company with few opportunities for avoidance or escape. In many poor families the relationship between mother- and daughter-in-law, at least before the birth of a son, was that between tyrant and slave, and it was common for unmarried sisters to despise and exploit their brothers' new wives. Another source of friction was the rivalry between a wife and her husband's concubines and any of the maids he might choose to favor with his sexual attentions. There are frequent cases of a wife beating a concubine or maid to death; since she was mistress in her own domain of the inner quarters, her husband was often unable to intervene effectively. [136] Women brought together by marriage often did not hesitate to exploit the domestic hierarchies that were so clearly marked in the allocation of space within the household. A new bride's hopes lay in the future, in becoming a respected

135. E. Johnson 1988: 139. Most of the evidence for these laments has been collected by ethnographers among the Hakka and Cantonese of Hong Kong's New Territories. Wedding laments do not seem to be limited to that region, says Johnson (ibid.). But because they are orally transmitted and an intimate female form of expression, their history and geographical distribution are not easy to trace.

136. Ebrey 1993: 167–68.

wife and mother and eventually a matriarch, mistress of her own household and living in the best quarters, with daughters-in-law of her own under her control.

Yet there was another side to relations between women; the attachments between female relatives—far less prominent in moralist writings, jokes or proverbs—were pleasant and loving. Ko proposes that in the inner quarters women forged strong bonds of affection and companionship, and it turns out that the women concerned were usually kinswomen, mother and daughter, sisters, cousins, or other blood relatives. In the case of the women writers from seventeenth-century Jiangnan that Ko has studied, poems between mother and daughter express not just tenderness but a bond of intellect and aesthetic sensibilities. While she acknowledges that few women of the period were as well educated as her subjects, she believes it is likely that the mother-daughter bond shaped social experience in the gentry families of late imperial China just as much as the father-son bond to which Confucian male scholars gave pride of place, or even the mother-son bond (the "uterine family") that Margery Wolf saw as providing the strongest emotions in the lives of Taiwanese peasant women.[137]

Among women of lower social status, too, evidence for a female society of solidarity is emerging. Ellen Judd's ethnographic study of social practices in Shandong documents a long tradition of continuous visits between a mother and her married daughters; in some cases newly married women even returned home to have their first child.[138] The astonishing collection of letters in "women's script" recently brought to light in southwestern Hunan reveals the intensity of affection that could develop between young women of relatively humble families who became close friends, vowing eternal friendship, staying in each other's houses, learning embroidery patterns together and singing the same songs, until they were torn apart by marriage and could communicate only by the occasional but heartfelt letter, written in the form of a long poem.[139] The studies of girls'

137. Ko 1992b, 1994; M. Wolf 1972. See also Hsiung 1994 on the bonds between men and their mothers in the Ming and Qing.

138. Judd 1989. In other regions, however, a daughter-in-law had to beg her mother-in-law for permission to visit her natal home at New Year, and permission was often denied.

139. Silber 1994; see also Gao and Yi 1991. The women's script of Hunan can be traced back into the middle or early nineteenth century; today no writers of the script survive, but a few old women can still read and sing the texts. The script may well represent a very old tradition, but this is not easy to confirm because it was customary to bury or burn a woman's collection of letters and books with her.

houses and marriage avoidance or delayed marriage in nineteenth- and early twentieth-century Guangdong also show that sharing a space created enduring bonds between women.[140]

The bonds between mother and daughter, between aunt and niece, sisters or girl cousins growing up under the same roof were bonds of tenderness and devotion made bittersweet by the threat represented by virilocal marriage. Women clung to such friendships if they could.[141] Letters were one way to cross the forbidden spaces between their husband's house and their natal home, to invite their dear ones into their own secluded quarters and cultivate the precious friendship. A few women were accomplished literary writers, and the poems and letters they exchanged have been preserved; they were able to maintain friendships with other female writers and acquaintances as well as with their own relatives.[142] Ordinary women's scope was more limited, though exchanges of gifts, especially of embroidered objects, were important in cementing such bonds. Few women received formal schooling, and the "women's script" of Hunan was an anomaly. Even so, it is possible that letters played a greater role in women's lives than is usually supposed, permitting them to exchange news with their natal family and friends. Guides to letter writing had been in popular demand since early times, separately published or included in household encyclopedias. Such books "included many letter forms for use between relatives on both the male and female side and across three generations, between friends and between business associates. . . . The female side is more prominent in these books than might be expected."[143] "Basically a woman has no business writing," concludes the *Householder's Vademecum*, at the end of a long section describing exactly what forms of address a woman should use when writing to her natal relatives, friends and other correspondents.[144]

Men and women in China had different ties to domestic space, and correspondingly different experiences of identity and personal ties. A man

140. Topley 1978: 253.

141. The attachment between brothers and sisters was also strong and often maintained after a woman's marriage.

142. See the "Symposium on Poetry and Women's Culture in Late Imperial China," *Late Imperial China* 13, 1 (June 1992), containing papers by Charlotte Furth, Dorothy Ko, Maureen Robertson and Ellen Widmer that all address the issue of female social networks and sense of self.

143. Hayes 1985: 86.

144. *Jujia biyong shilei quanji* 1/83–84. It was not necessary to be able to read or write oneself to engage in written correspondence, so this should not be taken as an indication of female literacy.

was born, grew up and died within the same walls, and with the same male kin around him. He never had to leave his parents or his home, he knew which lineage and which landscape he belonged to from the time he began to understand the world. His house was his home for life, and yet he could walk outside the family compound whenever he pleased. He lived in a kind of commune of shared patrimonial goods, in which his first loyalty was supposedly to the group. A girl grew up on borrowed time. When she married she had to leave the house of her birth, her mother and her sisters whom she loved and depended on, to move into an unknown house and a new group of women, many of whom might regard her with hostility. She would have to be self-reliant until she built up alliances and, as a mother, became an acknowledged member of her new family. The structures of incorporation were such that few women questioned the actual system, because as time passed they gained power and authority. Such resistance to neo-Confucian patriarchy as there was seems to have hinged on privacy and property. A married woman was virtually a prisoner within her husband's compound, and yet within this space she had freedoms that her husband did not. She had a room of their own where she could retreat with her children, and where she kept her dowry in locked trunks under her own control.

3 The Text of the Chinese House

During the Song dynasty a new elite replaced the aristocracy who had previously constituted the ruling class. Membership in this new elite was based on education, and especially on knowledge of the Confucian classics. Confucian thought emphasized the role of education and ritual in improving the moral character of individuals and laid great stress on the continuity between domestic and civil order. The Song saw a major reformulation of this philosophy (commonly referred to in English-language scholarship as neo-Confucianism), a reworking that sought to tie all subjects of the empire into a shared orthodoxy founded on correct relationships within the family and extended patrilineal kin-group. Neo-Confucianism was extremely successful. In the course of the succeeding dynasties it perpetuated its hold over the educated through the curriculum for the state examination system, which provided access to public office; the number of candidates who prepared for the examinations increased continually as the population expanded, even though the number of official posts remained almost static. Neo-Confucian values gradually came to permeate the lower levels of society, too, through joint kinship rituals, public lectures on morality given by local magistrates, primers used in village schools, moral tales in popular almanacs and little books on womanly virtue. Its tenets were disseminated through both texts and practice. Neo-Confucians did not approve of coercion, and for them the standardization of ritual was "an alternative to force."[1] Reforming the rituals of domestic life was a key element in their strategies for propagating orthodoxy.

---

1. Ebrey 1991b: 7. On the dissemination of orthodox values throughout society, see, e.g., D. Johnson et al. 1985; Liu Dunzhen 1990; Elman and Woodside 1994.

The medieval aristocracy had protected their status by exclusion, by marking themselves off as different. The neo-Confucians, on the contrary, imposed their authority through inclusion. Originally "commoners" themselves, they were distinguished from the new "commoners" not by blood but by the degree-holding titles which they had won through educational achievement.[2] As representatives of a meritocracy, they treated society as a ranked continuum rather than as separate castes. For them the performance of rituals served to unite people in a common goal or set of beliefs while reaffirming the proper social hierarchies; ritual gave concrete expression to differences in rank and status within the group. Instructing the people in ritual, wrote the statesman Ouyang Xiu (1001–72), "not only would prevent disorder but also would teach them to distinguish superior and inferior, old and young, and the ethics of social relations."[3] The correct performance of ritual had its roots in the knowledge of written texts and of their philosophical lineages; education provided access to this knowledge and authority over the rest of society.[4]

Given the core role that Confucian thought attributed to domestic propriety in underpinning the political order, it is not surprising to find that the house, its everyday practices and domestic rituals, played a crucial part in neo-Confucian strategies of disseminating orthodoxy. As I stated earlier, the standardization of the ancestral cult was at the core of this effort.[5] Foreign observers over the last two or three hundred years have equated

2. A distinction was classically made between "four classes" in Chinese society, namely (in descending order of status) scholar-officials, peasants, artisans and merchants (Cartier 1984). The first two occupations produced people of merit suitable for education, and one of the central myths of Chinese culture was the peasant's son who studied, succeeded, and became a great and wise official. Conversely, it was respectable for a scholar-official to farm land, but not to engage in trade or crafts. Early bans on merchants or artisans entering their sons for the examinations were gradually lifted in the course of the late imperial period, and by the eighteenth century it was even possible to purchase certain low degrees and the titles that went with them. Even in the Song and early Ming, factors such as a free market in land, commercialization, and the opening up of education meant that the distinction between categories became increasingly murky, as commoner landowners put their sons in for the examinations hoping to acquire gentry status, as gentry families invested in trade, and as lineage organizations offered opportunities for farming families to send their children to school. As Ebrey remarks, even as early as the Song the greater contacts and mingling between social groups played an important role in diffusing orthodox values (1993: 4).

3. De Bary 1960: 443.

4. This had not been the case in earlier times, when scribes and scholars were subordinates who advised the elite, not members of the elite themselves.

5. For a full account and detailed analysis, Ebrey's study of Confucianism and family rituals is indispensable (1991b).

the Chinese house with an ancestral shrine, and Westerners often think of ancestor worship as an immemorial characteristic of Chinese culture. For the lower social orders the official endorsement of their ancestral cult was, however, a relatively recent privilege. It has been suggested that peasants in medieval times may have had a communal village cult of the dead, while in the Tang and early Song educated commoners might use one room in the house as an "image hall" where they kept their ancestral portraits.[6] Until the Song, however, only the highest ranks of society were officially entitled to erect altars to their ancestors.

In part through a desire to affirm their elite status by sharing the privileged connotations of ancestor worship, and also no doubt because the concept of filial piety (*xiao*), the central Confucian virtue, logically extended to reverence for one's forebears, the new educated elite began to establish family shrines for themselves in the early Song.[7] The eleventh-century statesman Sima Guang appears to have been the first person to suggest that the practice should become general among the literati: "When a man of virtue plans to build a house, his first task is always to set up an offering hall to the east of the main room of his house."[8] In the twelfth century Zhu Xi took a much more radical step. His goal was to extend these privileges to the whole agnatic group. So in his commentary on Sima Guang's text, sections of which are included in his *Family Rituals,* Zhu Xi made allowances for disparities of wealth. He wrote that ideally the ancestral shrine should be three bays wide, but poor families could make a shrine just a single bay wide, or even use the east end of the main building. Zhu also makes allowances for other material inadequacies, such as the lack of a south-facing main building: "Here and throughout this book, in organizing the room, *no matter which direction it actually faces,* treat the front as south, the rear as north, the left as east, and the right as west."[9] The absolute requirements of orientation are thus reformulated as a set of transformations, such that anyone can conform to them.

6. Ibid.: 56.
7. "To establish how the educated elite in Sung times should sacrifice to their ancestors would serve symbolically to establish their position in Sung society," writes Ebrey (ibid.: 47). "Compared to aristocrats (who possessed their ritual standards for hundreds of years) the families of scholar-officials had no history which meant that they had no genealogy. On the one hand they needed an ethical justification, on the other hand there was a need for self-strengthening and self-cultivation. The way . . . to create a sort of nation-wide 'corporate identity' was (apart from the examination system) to design family rituals" (Kuhn 1992: 377).
8. Ebrey 1991d: 7, 1991b: 55.
9. Ebrey 1991d: 8, emphasis added.

The *Family Rituals* starts with instructions for making a family shrine. Zhu Xi states explicitly that this section comes first in his book because it is fundamental to all that follows, not only in moral and metaphysical terms but also for the inculcation of proper deportment: the first chapter "provides the basis for understanding the fine points in the later chapters concerning movements and postures, for walking here and there, getting up and down, going in and out, and facing various directions."[10]

Once a family had set up an appropriate ancestral shrine, they were able to conduct the proper everyday rituals and rites of passage that embedded them in a network of orthodoxy and disciplined their bodies in patterns of civility. Daily visits and monthly offerings to the ancestors were internal family matters, but weddings, cappings and funerals involved the liturgical participation of relatives and neighbors and were thus occasions for communal affirmation of orthodoxy. All these rituals centered on the family shrine. By extending the privilege of the family ancestral cult to the lower ranks of landowners, and eventually through the lineage to ordinary and uneducated people, the neo-Confucians created an unprecedented opportunity for molding their lives and thoughts. The household shrine tied its members into a historical and geographical web, and into a new and durable set of traditions.

The core unit for all these liturgical practices was the couple, whose roles were complementary and symmetrical. This is explicit in Zhu Xi's *Family Rituals:* where the presiding man ascended the eastern steps, the presiding woman ascended the western steps; where he offered wine, she offered tea. But although a man might also have several concubines, only his wife, as a ritual member of his ancestral line, was able to fulfill these duties. Every family ritual confirmed hierarchies at several levels: between senior and junior generations, between older and younger brothers and their wives within a generation, and—in any polygynous household—between legal wives and concubines. (We might also note that unlike Christian "family prayers" in early modern Europe, which the servants were obliged to attend even if they belonged to a different sect from their masters, servants had no part to play in Chinese "family rituals.") As liturgical texts on the family cult were disseminated through Chinese society, not only were rituals standardized but so too were the social microhierarchies, including gender relations, that they embodied.

Once everyone was not only allowed but required to have ancestors, even commoners became preoccupied with their family's origins, with ge-

10. Ibid.

nealogies, and with complex kinship networks traced through male descent. People belonged to a lineage as well as a family.[11] Through such lineages large numbers of ordinary Chinese could trace their own descent back to founding ancestors who were heroic generals of the Tang or illustrious scholars of the Song—a tie to history that permits a Malaysian Chinese today to tell you that his home is a county in Henan province, or a semiliterate farmer to claim kinship with a long-dead scholar.[12] Lineage organizations were patriarchal as well as patrilineal institutions, strong enforcers of orthodoxy (in its local variant); the lineage ceremonies in which members participated over the course of the year played an important role in cultural integration.

At the same time domestic rituals and etiquette tied people into a common history that went back to the great moralist Zhu Xi and the household instructions that he penned in the Song dynasty. Zhu Xi wrote his *Family Rituals* in a conscious effort to popularize. The text was clear and accessible, and it described rituals that were easy to follow. Zhu did not mention local customs or ritual variations but simply provided a normative liturgy. As well as liturgical instructions, the text incorporated much of Sima Guang's guide to daily etiquette. The *Family Rituals* was originally designed as a manual for local magistrates to educate the people in their charge. By the end of the Song some editions of the work had illustrations, "most likely . . . adapted from another book to make descriptions of objects and room layouts in the *Family Rituals* somewhat more comprehensible."[13] The text was included in numerous late Song and Yuan reference books of the kind designed for wide audiences, and Zhu's text was broken up under different headings: weddings in one section, funerals in another; sometimes only the main text without the commentary was included.

---

11. New lineage organizations tended to appear in great numbers wherever there were groups of upwardly mobile families anxious to improve their status. In 1536 the censor Xia Yan memorialized the emperor, advocating that all ranks, not just the upper elite, should now be allowed to establish lineage shrines (Brook 1993: 194).

12. R. Watson provides the classic account of how a lineage is constructed back in time to provide a glorious past and reconfigured to adapt to present contingencies (1985: 12–35). She also analyzes the duality of kinship relations: lineage dealings demonstrated the solidarity of kinsmen against the outside world, but clearly marked the power of high-ranked members over their inferiors. Lineage ceremonies were occasions of considerable tension, with the privileged striving to maintain their rank against ambitious competition, and vying for the support of the lineage members as a group.

13. Ebrey 1991b: 148.

As an example, the popular encyclopedia *Jujia biyong shilei quanji* (Householder's vademecum), a Yuan work first published in 1301 and widely circulated in the revised Ming edition of 1560, begins with a section entitled "Master Zhu on What the Young and Ignorant Should Know." It contains a variety of prescriptions for clothing, speech and deportment, washing and cleanliness, reading and writing, including quotations from Sima Guang as well as the *Family Rituals*. The fourth volume of the encyclopedia deals with building and moving into a house; in it the resolutely secular advice of the neo-Confucian Yuan Cai jostles with chunks of the *Carpenter's Canon* and assorted geomantic prescriptions. The text also includes models for writing letters and contracts; sections on civic virtues and offenses; on auspicious and inauspicious days; on the interpretation of dreams; on farming, horticulture and sericulture; on tea, infusions, and dietetics, medicines and longevity techniques; and a historical and geographical cyclopedia. The popularity of such works reflected the growth of what one might almost call a middle class, relatively well-off families with aspirations to gentility and culture, the basics of which could, at least in part, be learned from books.[14] They were as hungry for ritual as they were for etiquette.

As a concern with proper ritual spread both socially and geographically, neo-Confucian thinkers became increasingly preoccupied with the problems posed by "vulgar practices" and "local customs"; they wrote commentaries on Zhu Xi's work, or general reconsiderations of ritual, that tried to negotiate these problems so as to include even greater numbers within the circle of orthodoxy.[15] State techniques for extending orthodoxy, which frequently overlapped or coincided with gentry initiatives, included legislation on ritual conformity, the setting up of schools, the organization of lectures, and the granting of honors to subjects of outstanding merit. It would be wrong to think of the relationship between neo-Confucian elite and ordinary people as straightforward domination. If the former were successful in producing a high level of cultural conformity, this was precisely because of the flexibility with which they treated local customs, alien beliefs or unorthodox practices. Compromise and accommodation, a

14. Clunas 1991: 12–13.
15. Many problems arose from the need to accommodate families that already had lineages stretching back many generations, with long-established rituals of their own. Often these were not simple stem families but were organized in forms resembling the complex lineage systems that later became common in South China. But since these were essentially variations within an acceptable neo-Confucian paradigm, I do not dwell on them here.

suitable relabeling or reframing, were often preferred to confrontation and extirpation. This preference for negotiation allowed the authorities to coopt and assimilate local groups who would otherwise have been alienated.[16]

Some writers on domestic ritual incorporated prayers or offerings to the Stove God in their works—perhaps, as Ebrey suggests, to discourage people from resorting to priests or shamans in case of illness or misfortune.[17] Lü Kun (1536–1618) was anxious to include even women in the circle of ritually literate. Lü did not wish to force people into a ritual straitjacket that offended their feelings, but "offered a consistent rationale for his choices between custom and ritual in terms of emotions and naturalness." His follower Lü Weiqi (1587–1641) tried to counter the popular preference for Buddhist services for the souls of the dead not by banning them but by holding ancestral sacrifices on the same days.[18]

While neo-Confucian scholars usually preferred to negotiate acceptable compromises rather than trying to enforce orthodox practices, rulers often showed greater confidence in the power of law. The first Ming emperor declared that marriages should conform to Zhu Xi's *Family Rituals,* and

16. Local deities, for instance, were often given titles that assimilated them into the Han hierarchy of deities, so that in continuing to worship their own gods, the local people paid homage to the structure of the Chinese state (J. Watson 1985). In fact Watson and other scholars have argued that neo-Confucian authority was concerned not with orthodoxy, correct belief, but with orthopraxy, correct practice (J. Watson 1988).

17. Ebrey 1991b: 176. Chard argues for a gradual taming of the stove, from a dangerous locus associated with magic or sorcery to a moral outpost of the heavenly empire. This was at least in part accomplished by the production and circulation of texts about the Stove God, starting probably in the Tang or earlier. There were both Daoist and Buddhist moral tracts that gave accounts of the stove deity, the latter apparently largely derived from the older Daoist tales. Chard holds that these texts were expressly "created to influence popular belief and practice," and that therefore at least by the late Qing "an effort was made to circulate them [and the messages about moral behavior that they contained] among as wide an audience as possible" (1990: 155). It was common for the state establishment to tame foreign or unorthodox gods by repackaging them as Han culture heroes (J. Watson 1985). Daoism and Buddhism coexisted in a state of tension with Confucian orthodoxy. On the one hand, they contained many social precepts and beliefs inimical to conventional Confucian views of society (the celibacy of monks and nuns, for instance, was condemned by Confucians as profound unfiliality). On the other hand, there were also many manifestations of Confucian orthodoxy that were not incompatible with Daoist or Buddhist beliefs, and preaching adherence to this orthodoxy could therefore be turned to good account. Including prayers to the Stove God appears to be a case in point, as do the pervasive messages in Chinese Buddhist scriptures about the religious inferiority of women to men.

18. Ebrey 1991b: 181–82.

this rule was incorporated into the Ming legal code—one more reason for ordinary households to own an encyclopedia or ritual handbook that they could consult on such occasions. The Qing state also gave prominence to the *Family Rituals* in its official compilations. Since the aim was not to exclude but to include the common people, however, it was not required that the rituals as prescribed by Zhu Xi be followed accurately in every detail; it was the correct moral spirit that was important, and the absence of Buddhist, Daoist or other "unorthodox" practices.[19]

I have already alluded to the fact that the market for books in the Ming expanded well beyond highly educated circles. The ideas contained in texts reached even further; it was not necessary to be literate to absorb these messages. Evelyn Rawski believes that by late Qing times and probably earlier, "even illiterates lived in what was basically a literate culture." Educated experts (a member of the local gentry, a village schoolteacher) would be called on to serve as sponsors or advisors for ceremonies like weddings and funerals, to write in the characters on a recently deceased person's soul tablets, or to choose an appropriate name for a child.[20]

Popular encyclopedias, widely disseminated in the Ming and Qing, included orthodox ritual and etiquette between the same covers as information on astrology, geomancy and building magic. The most popular printed book in late imperial China was the almanac, which indicated auspicious and inauspicious days for the coming year. It is impossible to tell how widely almanacs were distributed, but even people who could not afford to buy one themselves would certainly have consulted a copy before undertaking even a mildly important undertaking, such as making a trip or concluding a deal. "When people cannot read the instructions and advice, they simply select those days under which the most text occurs, for they consider the large sections or the sections printed in red ink as particularly felicitous for important occasions."[21] As well as the calendar, almanacs contain a range of materials rather similar to the encyclopedias; one I bought in Kuala Lumpur in 1977 contained neo-Confucian morality texts, a section on health in which Chinese and Western medical ideas were intermingled, an illustrated section on house design copied from Qing editions of the *Carpenter's Canon*, and an English-Cantonese lexicon. In these works, as in the popular encyclopedias, representations of the house overlapped: the Confucian space of decorum, the energetic space

19. Ibid.: 151.
20. Rawski 1985: 24; Alleton 1993: 36.
21. Kulp 1925: 186, quoted Hayes 1985: 106.

of the geomancer, and the magical site that required protection by charms and amulets.

Rawski has analyzed the dissemination of published texts to argue that functional literacy was relatively widespread in late imperial China.[22] However, I am inclined to agree with James Hayes when he contends that the majority of the rural population did not need books as such, but relied heavily on specialists in geomancy, fortune-telling, and the complicated rituals of popular religion as well as orthodox ceremonies. In Hayes's study of written materials in village life in Hong Kong since the turn of the century, he found that practitioners of geomancy, fortune-telling and divination often came from "the respectable classes": "many appear to have been scholars who dabbled in such matters in their leisure time, practicing them within their families or circle of personal relationships, producing manuscripts, and publishing new books or commentaries on old works."[23] Only well-educated people were in a position to distinguish accurately between true Confucian norms and the many other rites and ideas that jostled together in people's daily lives, encoded in domestic space and in the written texts they turned to for guidance. Even in the minds of scholars trained in the Confucian classics, the multiple grammars of domestic space overlapped; in most people's minds they were inextricably entangled, as can be seen from the range of experts or technicians whose skills were called on in the construction of a house.

TEXTUAL EXPERTS

To build a house, one needed a plan, a carpenter, perhaps a bricklayer, a geomancer and money. The Song writer Yuan Cai includes a section on construction projects in his well-known work *Precepts for Social Life.*[24] Yuan makes it clear that building a house was a project that even rich families did not undertake lightly. His description of the manipulation of the owner by the builder has a contemporary ring.

> To build a house is a very difficult project for a family. Even those in their middle years and familiar with the ways of the world are not expert in construction. Naturally it is even worse with those of little experience! Very few of them escape ruining their families.

22. That is to say, a partial literacy adapted to the particular requirements of a person's occupation (Rawski 1979, 1985).

23. Hayes 1985: 99.

24. The *Shi fan* of 1178 (tr. Ebrey 1984). This passage comes at the end of the book's third section, entitled "Managing Family Affairs" (ibid.: 320–21).

When a man begins to build, he starts by discussing his plan with a master builder. The master builder's primary fear is that the man will decide not to build when he hears the price, so he keeps the scale small and the cost low. The owner considers the project within his means and decides to go ahead. The master builder then gradually enlarges the scale until the cost has increased several-fold before the house is half done. The owner cannot halt the project in the middle, so he borrows money or sells land elsewhere. The master builder, delighted, goes on with more construction, increasing the charges for labor even higher.

I have advised people to build houses gradually over a decade or longer. That way, when the house is done the family will still be as rich as before. First consider the foundation: level the high spots and build up the low ones. Perhaps build the walls and dig out the ponds. Do this in stages, planning to take over ten years. Next consider the scale and the quantity of materials needed, down to details such as the number of logs for beams and the bamboo for fences. Each year buy some according to the numbers needed and have them hewn right away. Plan to have them all ready in ten odd years. Again, calculate how many tiles and stones you will need; plan to use whatever resources you have left to gradually store them up. Even the wages should not be handled on the spur of the moment. With this method the house can be finished with the family as rich as before.

Yuan's "master builder" was in all likelihood a carpenter, for carpentry was viewed as the most important element in building. There were building experts in late imperial China who could be considered architects. After consultation with the owner about his project, they would produce drawings, plans, a cross-section, or even papier-mâché models of their intended work. Some families produced a succession of architects, like the Lei family who designed palaces around Beijing in the seventeenth to nineteenth centuries. For most domestic building there was no architect. The owner himself might produce a paper model to show to the builder what he wanted, or he might ask the carpenter to copy parts of other people's houses he had admired.[25]

In the classics and in the late imperial popular encyclopedias, the carpenter is treated as the representative par excellence of the artisan class. His skills (*qiao*) were encapsulated in a term that contained the same ambiguity as "craft" or "artfullness" in the English language: it included implications of mischief-making as well as the notion of a skillful, diligent and honest artisan. In late imperial times, carpenters in cities were professionals organized in guilds, learning their trade through an apprenticeship,

---

25. *Casual Expressions* 8.4a–b. On professional architects, see Ruitenbeek 1993: 49–50.

then working as journeymen until they could afford the fee to join the guild and set up shop. But in the villages it seems as if they may have been part-timers who did not even own a full set of tools. Ruitenbeek cites a text of 1850 which says that in the villages the proprietor has to provide all the tools and materials. This makes building projects tedious, says the author, but does ensure the quality of the final building. Although the poorest peasants must often have built their houses themselves with the help of family or neighbors, it seems that carpenters were regularly hired even for small-scale projects, like "a thatched house of three bays" built in 1790.[26]

Yuan Cai's account of what was involved in building a house is purely secular, as befitted a representative of the educated elite, and omits any mention of geomancy or of the tensions that could arise between the houseowner and the workmen. But as Ruitenbeek makes clear in his survey of sources on building, the purely technical knowledge required of carpenters and bricklayers was inseparable from magic and ritual (fig. 11). The rituals associated with state buildings were few, but in the case of vernacular architecture almost every stage required cosmic calculations and the performance of rituals. Carpenters, geomancers and houseowners were often in conflict, each trying to manipulate cosmic forces in different ways. Educated gentlemen might imply a disregard for house magic, but popular encyclopedias and almanacs set Yuan's advice in a series of entries on building in which material and magical techniques are inseparably entwined. Here is an example from the encyclopedia *Wanbao quanshu* (Complete book of a myriad of jewels):

> If in a dwelling house the second column is omitted,
> The adjoining room will be hard to live in.

And here is another from the *Carpenter's Canon*:

> *Design of a three-purlin house with one additional purlin.*
>
> Whenever this little house is built, it may not be too high and big. The columns supporting the eaves may only be 10 feet 1 inch high, the columns under the ridge 12 feet 1 inch. The horizontal distance between two purlins is 5 feet 6 inches. The (central) bay is 11 feet 1 inch wide, the side bays are 10 feet 1 inch wide. In this way (the parts) are well balanced. The poem says:

---

26. Ruitenbeek 1993: 20, 23.

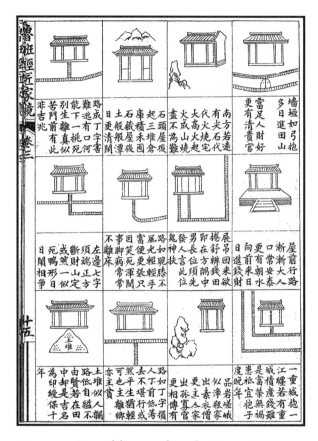

Figure 11. Page of diagrams from the *Carpenter's Canon* depicting lucky and unlucky building forms (*Huitu Lu Ban jing* 3/14b–15a).

Whoever builds a house with three purlins,
On Ban's Rule must look for favourable measurements.
If width and height are determined according to this method,
In the future many good sons will be brought forth.[27]

When a carpenter calculated the width of a lintel or the length of a beam, he was carrying out a series of cosmological computations. The

27. *Wanbao quanshu*, tr. Ruitenbeek 1993: 51; *Lu Ban jing*, ibid.: 177. The modest three-purlin house with its simple uncurved roof must have been fairly representative among poorer people. Knapp gives a good contemporary illustration of such a house just north of Beijing (1986: 29).

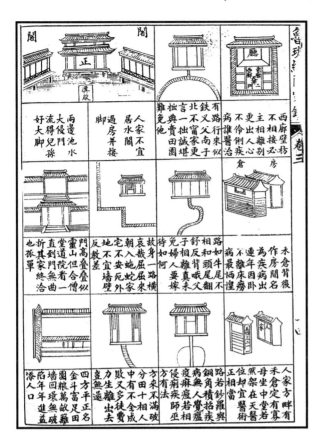

carpenter's rule was considered to have been invented by Lu Ban, the patron saint of the trade. It was marked with lucky and unlucky inches. The "balance" mentioned in the previous quotation referred to the fact that the measurements ended on lucky inches: "wealth," "righteousness," "plunder" and "wealth." The carpenter had to know the favorable and unfavorable days for the various tasks, from initiating building to hanging the curtains on a bed, and to remember the proper order of the various tasks. The encyclopedia *Jiabao quanji* (Complete collection of household treasures), compiled by Shi Chengjin from Yangzhou and first published in 1707, says, for example: "Only after having erected the columns and hoisted the ridge-pole may the surrounding wall be built. It is not permitted to tamp a wall first and then build the house. In this way, the character *kun*, 'trouble,' is formed, which brings ill luck."[28]

Some parts of the structure held particular ritual or magical importance. They included the main gate and the interior doors, the main columns at each corner of the principal building, beds, and the main ridgepole or roof beam. In magical terms, the roof beam represented the fate of the family that would live in the house. Raising the roof beam could only be done on a particularly auspicious day; the owner would prepare and burn amulets, and provide festive fare for the workmen such as pastries, tobacco and wine. These provisions were partly a celebration of good work done, but the owner might well think of them as a bribe to prevent the workmen performing any black magic at this extremely sensitive juncture. Magical objects or amulets that affected the family fortunes might be concealed in several parts of a house. Often they were buried in a wall or a lintel, or tucked into the eaves, but perhaps the most frequent location was the roof beam[29]:

> A shard of a roof-tile and a broken saw,
> Hidden in a joint of the ridge-pole,
> Cause the husband to die, the wife to remarry, and
> The sons to abandon the house. . . .
>
> If two coins are put on the ridge-pole, one left and one right,
> Long life, wealth and happiness will prevail.
> The husband will win fame, the son will obtain a noble rank,
> and titles of honour will be bestowed on the wife.
> Sons and grandsons will wear robes of office for generations to come.[30]

Once the building was completed, a special amulet written in cinnabar was written and pasted to the roof beam, and then the altar was dedicated and the God of the Soil and the Stove God "invited to their respective seats."[31]

Because the carpenters commanded esoteric knowledge that they could use at any point during the construction of a house to influence the family fortunes of their employer, the relationship was filled with mistrust. The first two sections of the *Carpenter's Canon* represent the carpenter as an honest craftsman taking pride in his skills; the last section (apparently a

---

28. Ruitenbeek 1993: 109. The character *kun* consists of the sign for wood (here used to denote the wooden construction of the house) inside the sign for an enclosure.

29. In rural Korea one of the tutelary deities of the house resides in the roof-beam and is worshiped by men, the other is the Stove God, who in Korea (unlike in China) is worshiped by women (Kendall 1985: 172).

30. *Carpenter's Canon*, tr. Ruitenbeek 1993: 302–3.

31. Ibid.: 307.

separate work connected to the *Carpenter's Canon* only in the late Ming) is written from the perspective of an employer preoccupied with the need to forestall or neutralize sorcery. The eighteenth-century *Jiabao quanji* explains: "In general, sorcery is suggested to the carpenters by the clients' exaggerated stinginess and preoccupation with trivialities. In my opinion it is absolutely necessary to serve meat once every four or five days. If in addition to that you put on a friendly face and speak kind words, if you treat them leniently when you know that they are suffering from hunger and cold, then the carpenters will no doubt produce their best efforts for you."[32]

The final section of the *Carpenter's Canon* advocated taking no chances, however generous one might have been to the workmen. It advises presenting the workers with wine mixed with dog's blood during the ceremony of raising the roof beam, to ensure that "whoever has practised magic will fall a victim himself [and] all things will end luckily [for the owner]."[33]

The site for the house was selected by someone with geomantic skills.[34] Some geomancers specialized in siting houses, others in siting graves, still others in siting wells. Feuchtwang and others who studied geomancy in the villages of southern China felt that geomantic experts were regarded by their clients as belonging to a literate elite, and in Taiwan today the title of *xiansheng*, meaning master or scholar, is given to geomancers.[35] Professional geomancers were certainly not considered by the true elite to be their social equals, but local gentry might well be called on for geomantic advice by uneducated neighbors. Hayes found that in Hong Kong in the 1970s "geomancers operating in our area . . . fell into two groups: sought-after itinerants with good reputations from other places, and local persons, usually of the class of schoolmasters and minor local gentry. The latter undertook the work out of interest and the need to have something to do, and, of course, in cases involving requests from their friends and relatives, out of reciprocity and obligation." Things seem to have been much the same in late imperial China, where someone who had failed the

32. Ibid.: 111; on the dual representation of the carpenter in the *Carpenter's Canon*, see ibid.: 141.

33. Ibid.: 305.

34. Certain passages in the *Carpenter's Canon* indicated that many householders were able to make certain geomantic calculations for themselves (ibid.: 159); for the poor and illiterate, if there was no money to hire a professional geomancer, "a carpenter could do the geomancer's job as well" (ibid.: 6).

35. Feuchtwang 1974: 115; Seaman 1992; on specialization in geomancy, see Hayes 1985: 94.

civil service examinations might well decide to make a living out of his philosophical expertise by setting up as a geomancer.[36]

Not all the experts involved in the construction of the house, therefore, had real book learning, yet their knowledge and skills always invoked the authority of the written word. This was not true of all forms of technical expertise in China, and perhaps it has to do with the gendering of techniques. For example, the skills of weaving, often exercised by men in the late imperial period but traditionally considered female, were transmitted without any reference to textual authority. But all the expertise that went into designing and building a house was male. Individual carpenters were often illiterate, yet every workshop had a tattered handwritten copy of their sacred text, the *Carpenter's Canon*, and their practical woodworking calculations were all dictated by the magical numbering of the carpenter's ruler.[37] In fact every stage of the construction of the house was marked by an act of writing, from the geomantic calculations involved in siting, through the marking and hewing of the rafters, to the final penning of an amulet for the roof beam to mark the completion of building. This magico-cosmological text, like the moral and historical text of neo-Confucian space, was woven into the very fabric of the house.

It will have become apparent from the previous chapters that the Confucian or neo-Confucian thought and practice that in shorthand I conveniently refer to as "orthodoxy" cannot be treated as monolithic. Quite apart from historical changes or regional variation, I have found it useful to distinguish between three strands or perspectives in Confucian thought. The first was best represented by the emperor and the scholar-statesmen who served him. When the Yuan emperors incorporated Zhu Xi's marriage rituals into the legal code, when the early Qing emperors mandated that public lectures on morality be given in the villages, or when a magistrate tried to introduce regulations to reform local funeral rituals, they were acting in the belief that the state and its institutions had an active top-down role to play in reforming society. Taken to the extreme, this could imply that the only necessary mediators between the ruler and his people (*min*) were serving officials. Such extreme interpretation was rare, however, and at the very least help from local scholar-gentry was always welcome.

36. Hayes 1985: 95; Benjamin Elman, personal communication 1994.
37. Ruitenbeek 1986.

The second perspective was predominant among most of the neo-Confucian philosophers of the late Song and their intellectual successors. They reacted against state interventionism in a way reminiscent of many schools of social thought in the United States today, such as communitarianism. These thinkers believed that individual self-cultivation and the practice of family values lay at the heart of reform. This stance should not be understood as a withdrawal from society: moral self-cultivation permitted its practitioners to set an example and to take a leading role in organizing local communities and in disseminating orthodoxy through institutions in which they were key figures, such as lineage groups. These thinkers never denied the legitimacy of the state, but they felt that its role should be limited.

Both these perspectives took a rather generous view of human behavior, in which it was understood that education was likely to achieve far more than coercion, producing moral agents who could be relied on to act responsibly and virtuously. Women's moral nature was in no way inferior to men's and daughters should be carefully educated in the "womanly way" so that they could become capable wives, fitting partners for their husbands and wise mothers to their children. As we shall see in the section on "womanly work," subscribers to this view were wont to state that the political order of the state was rooted in the inner chambers; women's daily activities of running the household, rearing children or weaving cloth were essential social contributions that tied them firmly to the world beyond their walls and integrated them into the fabric of the state. From this viewpoint the seclusion of women conferred dignity and responsibility, marking a division between complementary spheres of activity rather than a barricade against the temptations of the world.

The third perspective was less generous and more authoritarian. It paid little attention to the articulations between family, community and state but viewed strict patriarchal control at the level of the family as the linchpin of an ordered society. Individuals would be virtuous only as long as they were controlled and protected from temptation. Women were by nature morally weak, spiritually inferior to men and unable to resist temptation; seclusion was necessary to ensure the family honor. Within the enclosure of the inner chambers, however, women not only quarreled with each other but also fomented trouble between otherwise loving brothers: the threat they offered to the social order was merely transposed by seclusion. Women must work to keep the household going, but they were not to be trusted as managers; it is the patriarch, not his wife, who is shown as keeping a watchful eye on every financial transaction. This point of view was commonly expressed in works such as the lineage rules that proliferated among the petty gentry of late imperial China.

These three strands of Confucian or neo-Confucian expression and action were in no way exclusive. People generally felt that the state, the local gentry and the family all had a role to play in maintaining the social order, though individuals might differ in how they saw the balance between these groups. Views on the meanings and effects of female seclusion were likely to vary between social groups, but were not necessarily absolute: a man might trust his mother absolutely, while remaining convinced that only the strictest control could contain the follies of his son's wives. And naturally even the most humane of patriarchs or matriarchs would experience a tension between trust and authoritarianism in their daily running of the family. The house itself, as a physical structure, aided them in both capacities, for it served as an educational space as well as a set of concrete controlling boundaries.

During the Song dynasty many features of what one might call the archetypal or ideal Chinese house were systematically formulated in treatises on household rituals, composed by neo-Confucian statesmen-philosophers anxious to disseminate correct practices throughout society. Through printing and the consultation of experts, during the Ming and Qing the principles of layout and behavior contained in these works gradually became orthodoxy. At the same time less orthodox cosmological beliefs—many dating back to the Tang or even the Han and recorded in the *Carpenter's Canon* and in geomantic works—also became common coin and were often printed between the same covers as the ritual works in popular encyclopedias and almanacs with huge circulation. Even the illiterate were familiar with the gist of these ritual and geomantic works, with their overlapping spatial grammars and visions of the human condition. With the dissemination of textual conventions about what a house should be, its material structure was increasingly effective in tying ordinary folk into a web of orthodoxy experienced as domestic routine. Despite great differences in size, quality, individual layout and regional style, by late imperial times Chinese houses codified a common set of principles, of visions of the world, shared by people of all ranks across the vast expanse of territory that constituted the Chinese empire.

Many contemporary social scientists have remarked on the importance of tacit, embodied knowledge in forging cultural conformity. The Chinese were keenly aware of the power of bodily habit to form mental patterns: "the moral virtues of filiality and fraternal love were not qualities that anyone imagined could be cultivated independent of the ritual practice that symbolized and reaffirmed them."[38] In the view of the neo-Confucians, *li* (ritual, etiquette or proper behavior) was the key to attaining both individual self-cultivation and social reform. The neo-Confucian order offered people of low degree and little education the opportunity to join the ranks of the respectable by exercising domestic authority on the same terms as their social superiors, through a patriarchal system of intersecting ranks and hierarchies that operated within every family.

It seems that the seclusion of women, stressed by neo-Confucians as a pillar of the moral order, must have held particular attractions for men of low rank or few means, first as an attainable badge of respectability, and second because of the domestic authority it conferred. It is not possible to say to what extent seclusion of women was practiced among peasants or other commoners in medieval China, though it is generally accepted that patrician women in the Tang were relatively free. (They could not only own land, but also go riding and play polo.) But it does seem that the institution of female seclusion became more widespread and more systematic as commoners were increasingly drawn into the practices of neo-Confucian orthodoxy.

Although Tang noblewomen had a freedom of movement that most nineteenth- and twentieth-century women in China did not, I would hesitate to qualify the development of seclusion as a simple linear trend. The urgency with which Song moralists insisted on its importance (and also on the need to forbid women the right to private property) may well have been a response to the perceived threat of disorder posed by the rapid urbanization of the period, a growth in middle-class prosperity, a blurring of the boundaries between classes and, no doubt, visible female involvement in running businesses and other improper activities. Similar situations recurred several times in Chinese history, when, as T'ien Ju-k'ang, Susan Mann and Katherine Carlitz have argued, anxieties about social instability or the failure of male virtue were projected onto women. Moral austerity was likely to prevail even in the cities after disasters like the Mongol invasion, the fall of the Ming or the humiliating wars against the Western powers. But after a few decades of peace the economy would recover, the cities would flower again, and respectable women would creep out of seclusion. Some would be humble women desperately seeking waged employment, others would be partners in the family business taking over the silk shop or the pharmacy while a husband was off on a buying trip. Other women had the money to go on pilgrimages, take

38. Furth 1990: 191.

boating trips, or otherwise make a public display of themselves. Such decadence would provoke a flood of moralistic writings on female virtue that families who wished to confirm their respectability, to marry their daughters up or to prevent their sons marrying down were bound to take seriously.

As far as the urban population was concerned, in the post-Song period female seclusion and the adherence to the other domestic hierarchies favored by neo-Confucian moralists were progressively extended from the elite to all levels of society. However, there were probably repeated fluctuations in the strictness with which respectable people felt they must be enforced.[39] In rural areas there was a parallel penetration of orthodox practice to every layer of society, but I suspect that the special care given by local officials to stamping out "lewd" customs achieved a more unwavering commitment to puritanism and strictness among the men under their jurisdiction than it did in the cities, so that the development of a culture of female seclusion in rural areas was cumulative rather than fluctuating.[40]

It also seems probable that the burdens seclusion imposed were harsher in poor families, where there was little space for women to retreat to, and where the men had little control over other areas of their lives—although even in these conditions we should not presume that seclusion was invariably experienced by women as oppressive: for many of them, as for their menfolk, it was an affordable method of demonstrating respectability and contributing to the family reputation. In wealthier or more educated families the moral and social rewards of life in the inner chambers could be considerable: by virtue of their secluded lives, women were sometimes considered to possess a moral purity and clarity of vision beyond that of men; their role as educators and their contribution to orthodoxy was thus paramount. At the same time, certain women (but not all) had considerable freedom to act in domains that we now consider important to self-image, such as running the family finances or taking reproductive decisions that affected not only their own lives but also the development of the patriline into which they married. I deal with this subject at more length in chapters 6 and 9, where I discuss the prescribed and real complementarities between the roles of wife and husband, and the hierarchies

39. This idea was suggested to me by Bettine Birge.
40. Susan Mann (personal communication 1995) believes that regional differences were more important than those between urban and rural areas.

among women that were just as important as gender hierarchies in the construction of different versions of Chinese patriarchy.

When considering the significance of female seclusion in late imperial China we also should remember that it does not translate into a simple gender polarity in which women were controlled and men were free. Patriarchal control and family rules meant that men in late imperial China had very little freedom in the sense that we in the contemporary West understand the word. Male identity was embedded in the patriline; in a sense a man's primary identity was communal, just like his access to patrimonial property. Insofar as a man had rights to private space or to private property, it was through his wife. Wives in China were outsiders to the family, popularly characterized as persons of unsure loyalty whose selfish aims posed a constant threat to familial harmony. On the one hand the institution of seclusion allowed the family to contain and control this threat, on the other it constructed spaces where alternatives to the strict patriarchal order could flourish.

A newly married couple were given a room for themselves. Because women stayed inside and men were expected to spend the days outside the house, this marital chamber was the bride's own room, under her control. In it stood her bed, where her children were conceived, and the closet or chests in which her private property was locked. This capital she might spend on her own needs or those of her husband and children, she might use it to help natal relatives, or she might invest it in a business; it was property under her individual control that she could leave to her children, girls as well as boys, unlike patrimonial property that was shared out among all the male heirs. Moreover, if she lent it to her husband or his family it could be used to exercise control over the patrilineal group. No wonder neo-Confucian moralists repeatedly urged good wives to contribute all their dowry unconditionally to the joint family fund, where it came under the immediate control of the patriarch. But women resisted. They continued to hold on to their dowries, and even when they did not use them in ways that subverted the power hierarchies of the patriline, the very existence of this personal property seems to have been a considerable source of satisfaction.

The institution of female seclusion allowed men in late imperial China to control their wives' reproduction, to ensure the legitimacy of the sons who were, from the male perspective, not so much their own children as joint heirs to the family line. It also allowed senior women to control those women who were junior to them in the family hierarchy. At the same time seclusion gave wives, the outsiders to the family, a quasi-private space in which to assert a different and potentially subversive form of autonomy and control, animated by the loyalties not of male-centered but of female-centered kinship. Beside the marital bed that symbolized her contribution to the reproduction of her husband's patriline, a woman kept the locked chests that represented a rejection of patriarchal solidarity. Virilocal, arranged marriage in conjunction with the institution of female seclusion tore a woman from her family roots and subjected her to the control of a male-centered group of strangers. But control is never total, and for Chinese men the seclusion of their wives was as often a source of unease as of confidence.

The meanings of "domesticity" in late imperial China were interestingly different from those of the industrial West, precisely because the house was not a separate, private domain, but formed a political and moral continuum with community and state. Throughout parts 2 and 3 I argue that whether seclusion translated into dignity or into oppression was related to how a woman's contributions to the world beyond the inner quarters were construed. These contributions might be material, for example the textiles used to pay taxes, to earn income, or to exchange between families as betrothal gifts and dowry. They might be social, as in the production of offspring or of well-trained maids. Or they might be moral, as when a wife supported and advised her husband through challenging times, or when a mother educated her sons and daughters in the ways of virtue. The inner chambers were secluded but not cut off from the wider world: the importance of the boundary was that it was neither fixed nor impermeable.

PART TWO

Women's Work

*Weaving New Patterns
in the Social Fabric*

The difference between women and men was signaled not only by the spatial domains they occupied, but also by the work they performed.[1] The significance of work in the definition of gender roles in premodern China has largely been ignored; however, we cannot understand the specifically Chinese nature and meanings of "domesticity" or of gender difference unless we take into account "womanly work" and the historical changes it underwent.

Women's work in China was classically defined as the making of textiles; the inner quarters were identified not as a zone of dependence but as a site of essential productive activity, tying the household into the polity. The technical and management skills that went into producing cloth, whether simple weaves or highly valued patterned fabrics, were considered a female domain of knowledge well into the Song. However, the Song dynasty saw the beginnings of a sustained trend toward commercialization and specialization in textile production. New divisions of labor brought about the progressive marginalization of women's real and perceived contribution to this economic sector. The process was slow, complex and uneven, but by the end of the Ming, weaving of all but subsistence homespuns had essentially become a male task. What did it mean for

1. Parts of this section have appeared in French in the *Annales* (Bray 1994) and in English in *Chinese Science* (Bray 1995b) and are reproduced with permission. I am particularly grateful to Dieter Kuhn, Sophie Desrosiers, Pierre-Etienne Will, and Susan Mann and to the participants in the "Table-ronde sur techniques et culture en Chine" (held under the auspices of the Maison des Sciences de l'Homme, Paris, in January 1994) for their advice on the interpretation of textile history.

women to lose their status as primary producers and as the repositories of an important field of technical knowledge and skills?

To link changes in the organization of production to changes in gender roles, it is necessary to go beyond straightforward quantitative evaluations of women's productivity or of the strict cash worth of their work. One must take into account the symbolic as well as the market value of different kinds of cloth in Chinese society. Women's work in China was classically equated with the production of cloth, an artifact that is particularly rich in symbolic values.[2] Throughout the world the making of cloth has been variously associated with human life and fertility, with the exchanges between families and communities that reproduce societies, and with the obligations between subject and state. Clothes mark status and gender differences. Some textiles transmit ascribed value or a sense of corporate identity, like the robes of state handed down from one ruler to another over centuries, regalia that turn a man into a ruler and embody a whole nation's sense of history; or like a wedding dress handed down from mother to daughter, tracing a female genealogy in a patrilineal culture. The commercialization of the cloth industry breaks the personal or ritual links between producer and consumer, and tends to demystify the skills and devalue the role of the producer. The historical change in Chinese women's fiscal responsibilities as cloth producers that I document here was particularly significant for female status in that it broke an acknowledged material interdependence between women and the state, and thus paved the way for a revised representation of female roles that emphasized various forms of reproduction and downplayed what we consider productive work.

As the quintessential form of womanly work, textile production was at the core of Chinese gynotechnics, a set of practices that manufactured femininities as it manufactured cloth. Roger Friedland and A. F. Robertson note: "Work provides identities as much as it provides bread for the table; participation in commodity and labor markets is as much an expression of who you are as what you want. Although economists typically assume that work is a disutility to be traded off against leisure or income, it actually contains other kinds of utility, ranging from the expression of an identity (I am a metal worker), to relative performance (I am a good metal worker), social value (It is good to be a metal worker—or—It is good to work), gender (It is good for a man to be a metal worker), or prestige (It

2. Schneider 1987; Schneider and Weiner 1989.

is better to be a metal worker than a salesperson)."[3] The identities that work provides are not always positive, of course, and we cannot always use the hierarchies of occupation, knowledge or productivity which we consider natural in order to understand the meanings of work in other societies. Yet in every human society work (or nonwork) is a fundamental element in the construction of roles and of hierarchies; this is true of gender just as it is of class.

Why, then, has women's work been neglected both by economic historians of the late imperial period and by feminists studying gender? Apart from my own work only one other short essay, as far as I know, has focused specifically on how long-term economic development in imperial China affected women.[4] In the period between approximately A.D. 1000 and 1800 China experienced a long-term elaboration and expansion of the economy, marked by urbanization, commercial growth, the development of large-scale markets, and complex new divisions of labor in all productive sectors, perhaps most notably in the production of textiles. Textiles were, after food grains, the most important commodity produced in China throughout that period. Given the importance of the textile sector in propelling Europe's industrial revolution, it is not surprising that economic and technological historians of every ideological stripe have pondered the nature and implications of the development of Chinese textile production.[5] They have documented changes in market structure and relations

3. Friedland and Robertson 1990: 25.
4. Hill Gates has published an interesting marxist-feminist analysis of what she calls the "commoditization of Chinese women" in the late imperial period, which hinges on changes in the nature of women's participation in productive labor, including textiles (1989). Gates's article is innovative in its interpretation, but it still relies on previous scholarship for its assertions about the nature of women's work throughout the late imperial period and pays little attention to the detailed articulations of production processes.
5. Most scholarship in this field ultimately addresses the broader historical question of whether China was developing toward capitalism, and if not, was the undeniable increase in economic activity simply a form of involution, in essence the millennial stagnation suggested by Marx in his allusions to East Asia's brand of "precapitalist mode of production." One of the scholars most influential in arguing against stagnation while rejecting the notion of "capitalist sprouts" is the Japanese scholar Nishijima Sadao ([1949] 1984). A powerful if much criticized argument for the involutionary nature of the Chinese economy, and one that focuses on the technology of textile production to argue its case, is given by Elvin (1973). While not denying the developments in production and marketing documented by Nishijima, Elvin argues that such development produced only quantitative and not qualitative changes in productivity, and therefore could not be sustained beyond certain limits.

of production, in accumulation and investment, in technology and labor productivity. Total production increased as markets grew, and competition sharpened. Merchant capital steadily consolidated its control over rural textile production, and the proportion of cloth made in urban workshops increased, as did the size of the hired labor force.

As in other cases of proto-industrialization,[6] right through this period, and even after the introduction of Western-style factories in the late nineteenth century, household production remained central to the Chinese textile industry. Economic historians acknowledge that women as well as men were involved in this household production of textiles. What no historian has yet done, however, is to look precisely at how the gender division of labor in textiles changed within the household during this period. Since textile production was originally seen by the Chinese as a female productive domain in which men had at best a subsidiary role, this seems a serious omission.

The omission is not confined to economic historians. Feminist historians have devoted considerable attention to this formative period. They note that the Song dynasty (960–1279) marked a turning point for Chinese women. They have suggested that changes in property and inheritance laws, the organization of kinship, the rules of ritual performance, and the ideals and role models of elite and popular culture, initiated during the Song and elaborated in subsequent centuries, contributed to diminish women's autonomy and consolidate their subordination to men. Some have noted that women were increasingly portrayed in terms of motherhood or marital fidelity to the exclusion of other roles. Yet with one or two exceptions,[7] feminist scholars have so far paid little attention to women as producers in premodern China, nor have they explored how changes in this domain might have modified or reinforced the changed gender relations inscribed in property law, medicine or moral tracts.[8]

---

6. See the introduction and case studies in E. Goody 1982.

7. I have already mentioned Hill Gates, who is an anthropologist rather than a historian. Another exception is the historian Susan Mann, who has recently published several essays on women's work in the Qing and early Republican periods; she will soon publish a book that looks at women and work in the Qing dynasty.

8. Patricia Ebrey devotes one chapter of *The Inner Quarters,* her study of marriage and the lives of Chinese women in the Song, to textile production (1993: 131–51). Her chief purpose is not so much to analyze the technical or social implications of the changes that took place or took root during this formative period as to describe the daily tasks characteristic of women's lives. Two studies by Dieter Kuhn, one on the significance of Song changes in material culture (1987) and the

This inattention to women's participation in productive work probably stems in part from theoretical and methodological preference. While many of the foundational analyses of the "woman question" in modern China are written from a marxist-feminist perspective, the current surge in the United States of feminist studies of imperial China coincides with the prevalence of a more idealist cultural history.[9] A second contributing factor lies in the gender division of disciplinary labor: most economic historians of China are men, and none that I know of takes a feminist perspective.[10] While acknowledging the importance of women's work in anecdotal fashion, they have been centrally concerned with other levels of analysis and have not made clear the historical patterns of change in women's productive roles that might have allowed feminist historians to incorporate those findings into their own work. Third, and closely connected, the significance of women's work is masked by the enduring importance of household production in China—an indisputable fact, invariably remarked on but insufficiently probed. The household can remain the basic unit of production over centuries, yet within this "unit" the basic composition, the division of labor, the control of skills and the

---

other a general history of textile production in China (1988), are suggestive as to the gendered effects of the reorganization of textile technology in the Song and Yuan dynasties. Kuhn explicitly distinguishes in his work between female and male contributions and roles. My debt to him is great; however, he has not yet attempted a gender history of Chinese textile production. When it comes to the modern period, we find that historians make women's textile skills and earning power central to their arguments about female status and autonomy. Topley 1978, So 1986 and Stockard 1989 give studies of "marriage avoidance" or "delayed marriage" in late nineteenth- and early twentieth-century Guangdong that are key examples. And the many studies of gender in the People's Republic of China (PRC) take employment and pay into account.

9. The study by Hill Gates referred to earlier is in the marxist tradition. In China itself, whether we speak of the PRC or of Taiwan, feminist history is still in its infancy. The few "women's histories" that have been published to date mostly compile passages from historical texts and add little in the way of analysis or theory. Women's work is frequently given less space than what one might call "lifestyle" (clothes, festivals), and often mundane tasks like textiles and food production are relegated to a brief section after more picturesque occupations such as imperial concubine, prostitute, flower seller and midwife (e.g., Yin 1984; Bao 1988).

10. Philip Huang's account of gender divisions of labor in lower Yangzi peasant households is a promising exception (1990). It is particularly interesting for its description of changes in work in the recent years since decollectivization: the least rewarding tasks are usually designated "traditional" women's work, but should tasks such as mat weaving suddenly find a lucrative market, miraculously the men suddenly discover that these are really "men's work" after all.

claims to managerial or earning power may change drastically.[11] If we break open the carapace of the Chinese household, what historical processes may be revealed?

Perhaps one reason why social and economic historians have been slow to deconstruct the Chinese household is the enduring influence of what Dorothy Ko has called "the May Fourth view" of Chinese history. In the later nineteenth and early twentieth century, foreign observers and Chinese reformers produced a series of images of all that was wrong with China, contrasting it unfavorably with the West in every respect including its treatment of women, who were represented (not totally without grounds it must be said) as the helpless victims of patriarchy, imprisoned and illiterate, and rendered incapable of productive work by their bound feet. This powerful image, which represented the "inner quarters" as a dependent domain that had always been cut off from the public world of economics and politics, was presented not as a product of historical circumstances but as a "tradition."[12]

In fact, Chinese women had a long tradition of integration into the world of economics and politics through their work. The real and perceived role of their material contributions to the state, to the social order, and to the family finances, however, changed significantly in the course of the late imperial period—as did the nature and meanings of men's work. The Western separation of home from workplace and the resulting distinction between a domestic (unwaged, reproductive, female) and a public (waged, productive, male) sphere, to which Engels attributed the subordinate status of women in capitalist society, resulted from a complex series of shifts in production patterns in response to proto-industrialization and then industrialization proper. In China, the expansion and elaboration of the economy that began during the Song also brought about significant and in some ways parallel reformulations of gender roles. By the end of the late imperial period Chinese women were no longer represented as making significant independent contributions to material production, even though the majority of them continued to work hard at productive tasks. This was a dramatic contrast to the classical formulations of the gender division of labor, which had represented women's work as

11. See Yanagisako 1979; Moore 1988. Among recent studies of the conflicts of interest between the state and family, and within the family, resulting from the One-Child Family Policy and the New Economic Policies in the PRC, Anagnost (1989) is less interested in how a woman's productive activities might affect and be affected by household group interests and decisions than is Croll (1987).

12. Ko 1994: 7.

being as essential as men's, both to human survival and to the maintenance of a well-ordered state. Although one might suppose that this shift toward an image of dependence served the interests of patriarchal control well, many late imperial statesmen and philosophers lamented or even attempted to reverse the decline in "womanly work" that they observed.

The first chapter of this section discusses the canonical formulations of "womanly work" and the political, social and symbolic meanings of textiles in China, concluding with an account of textile production in the pre-Song period, when it was still unquestioned as a female domain of expertise. Chapter 5 is an exercise in economic history, in which I document the complex processes of commercialization, expansion and specialization of the textile industry that took place from the Song to the Qing and the new divisions of labor they produced, in which women's contributions were gradually marginalized. In chapter 6 I discuss how the new divisions of labor and the new meanings attributed to female and to male work affected the reformulation of gender roles in an ostensibly neo-Confucian society.

4 Fabrics of Power
The Canonical Meanings of Women's Work

THE CONCEPT OF "WOMANLY WORK": WOMEN AS SUBJECTS

The classic gender division of labor in China was encapsulated in the saying "men till, women weave" (*nangeng nüzhi*). The growing of food grain and the production of textiles were considered equally fundamental in providing for the welfare of the common people and the strength of the state: this belief remained central to Chinese statecraft for more than two millennia, ever since it was first formulated by the political philosophers of the fifth century B.C. and institutionalized in the tax system. In early texts "weaving" was a synecdoche for the whole process of textile production; women were responsible for making cloth from start to finish. In the sense that we are what we do, womanhood in early imperial China was defined by the making of cloth: with a few rare exceptions, a weaver was by definition a woman, and a woman was by definition a weaver. Although men worked outside the home and women inside, both were thought of as equally productive members of society.

Like many proverbs describing ideals, however, the saying "men till, women weave" persisted long after its universality had lapsed. In the early Song dynasty, textile production was still considered an exclusively female domain; by the late Ming or early Qing it had come under male control and was no longer automatically identified with women—indeed, one historian writing of the hiring of women workers in the new industrial silk filatures of South China in the nineteenth century thought of this as the "feminization" of Chinese textile production.[1]

Except for the field work involved in raising textile crops, women in China were originally responsible for every stage of cloth processing, from

1. So 1986.

hatching silkworm eggs and twisting the ends of ramie fibers together to weaving the cloth and making the clothes. But this is by no means a natural division of labor, a universal trait. There are cultures where men spin, or weave, or tailor, while women work in the fields.[2] It is therefore necessary to explain why textile production was women's work in ancient China and to examine the fiscal system that reproduced this division of labor for many centuries.

In early China one important way in which gender difference was marked was through the category of "women's work" or "womanly work" (*nügong*), the labor that women of every class were expected to perform. Womanly work was one of the four attributes—along with womanly virtue, womanly speech and womanly conduct—prescribed by Ban Zhao, the famous female scholar of the Han period, in her primer for wifehood, *Nü jie* (Instructions for women).[3] The second character in the expression *nügong* was written with one of three homophones. The first was the usual word for work of any kind, male or female. The second literally meant "merit" or "value"; Michel Cartier has argued that the use of this term by early political philosophers in China denoted their view that the textiles women made contributed not only to basic needs but also to the creation of potential surplus value. I would add that it was not just any kind of surplus value. The kind of surplus value that could be translated into private profit was despised and distrusted as socially disruptive, not just by Confucian moralists but across most of the political spectrum, in early China and throughout Chinese history. *Gong* as in "crafts" was viewed dubiously as one source of this disruptive kind of surplus—such work would have been demeaning for a superior man. But the kind of surplus that women's work produced was meritorious because it was seen as being transformed not into private profit but into tax payments. As Susan Mann puts it, writing of the late imperial period, "[for] a woman . . . manual labor suited to her station was never demeaning."[4] The third form in which the *gong* of *nügong* was written included the signifier for "silk" or "textiles," and in fact "women's work" was usually defined as the production of textiles, basically the processes of spinning and weaving, but also including sewing and embroidery.

There was no single corresponding category of "manly work" or "men's

2. Schneider 1987; E. Goody 1982.
3. Ban Zhao elaborated the four attributes as part of a reciprocal, complementary relation between husband and wife, as expressed in the *Liji*.
4. Cartier 1984; Mann 1992a: 82.

work." The basic needs of society were filled by the complementary efforts of elite men, who labored at government, and of farmers, who labored in the field; these were considered the fundamental occupations (*ben*). The two other categories of male labor, crafts and trade, were viewed rather ambivalently: although it was acknowledged that they too were necessary for the functioning of society, since they lured peasants away from the primary task of growing grain, and since they also tended to produce disparities of wealth, they were stigmatized as secondary or even parasitic, "branch" occupations (*mo*). "Women's work" was an intermediate category, for it was a fundamental occupation and at the same time a craft.[5]

In early China the basic tasks of raising silkworms and reeling and weaving the silk took place in spring and early summer, conflicting with the high season for farming activities.[6] This was an important factor, according to Cartier, in defining a gender division of labor, with textile production allocated to women and farming to men. Cartier's argument does not explain why farming was considered more male than female in the first place; perhaps it was connected to the use of the animal-drawn plow, as suggested by Goody in the contrast he draws between plow and hoe

5. In contemporary usage, domestic textile work is treated as a handicraft and textile production in state or private workshops as a manufacture. Historical studies of handicrafts and manufactures, such as the works by Chen Shiqi (1958) and Tong (1981), bring together information from a wide range of sources, including dynastic histories, local gazetteers, poems, travel accounts and personal writings; Chen and Tong both work in terms of class analysis and pay no specific attention to gender. Nevertheless, both works have been valuable for this study. In classical terms agriculture and textile production were treated as complementary aspects of basic rural production, and almost all the great agricultural treatises include sections on sericulture and textiles as well as on the cultivation of fiber crops and mulberries; they include the *Nong shu* (Agricultural treatises) of Chen Fu (1149) and of Wang Zhen (1313), the *Nongzheng quanshu* (Complete treatise of agricultural administration) by Xu Guangqi (1639), and the *Bu nongshu* (Supplemented treatise on agriculture) by Zhang Lüxiang (1658), all of which provided important materials for this section. Wang Zhen supplemented his text with woodblocks illustrating, inter alia, textile equipment and machinery. They served as a model for many later works, in particular the *Nongzheng quanshu*. Illustrations and paintings are extremely important for tracing the technical development of the Chinese textile industry, and there is a huge iconography of textile work from imperial China. Here I have relied greatly on Kuhn's work in uncovering and analyzing rare or obscure works.

6. In early China only spring silkworms were known. The Chinese subsequently bred varieties of silkworm that could be raised later in the year. Though the spring silkworms continued to provide an essential part of the year's silk, one or more extra broods could be raised depending on the length of the warm season (Kuhn 1988: 301).

cultures in Africa.[7] Whatever the background to this gender division of labor, it fed into a patriarchal organization of society early on, according to Cartier: since women were not active in farming they were not allowed rights in land, which were transmitted solely in the male line.[8]

Although women stayed inside the house to do their work, the cloth that they produced there tied them to the state through the fiscal system. In the introduction to his study of the effects of fiscal policy on Song Sichuan, Paul J. Smith argues that fiscal history can serve as a prism for a whole society since it focuses on the relationship between social structure and economic policy, and thus on the state's exercise of power.[9] A strong argument can be made for connecting taxation policies with the ideology of gender in China.

Cloth was a key symbol of the power of the state over its people. In the eyes of the early Chinese state, man and wife were equal contributors to reproducing the social order. "Men till and women weave": the basic tax unit was the peasant household, whose tax dues, from the Zhou dynasty until the Single Whip reforms of the late sixteenth century, included both grain produced by the male workers and textiles produced by the female workers, generally of roughly equal value.[10] Nonpeasant households were taxed on similar principles. The women in landlord households also produced textiles for tax, and in periods when commutation to cash was not permitted, urban households that did not produce textiles themselves had to purchase cloth in order to pay their taxes. The tax system thus imposed

7. J. Goody 1971.

8. This did not necessarily apply in elite landowning families, at least up to the Song: their daughters were entitled to a share of the family land (Birge 1992). It does seem that among the peasantry from pre-imperial times on, however, land was allotted only to men, as actual or potential family heads. This was the case whether the land was owned by the family and divided between sons, or distributed by the state under one of the medieval "equal holdings" systems; in late imperial China a tenant's sons might inherit his right to rent a particular plot of land from the landlord. The restriction of landownership to men has also been linked convincingly to the practice of virilocal marriage.

9. Smith 1991.

10. Sometimes the tax rate was based on numbers of people, sometimes on size of holding, but at a rough average, rates of taxation for peasant households from the Han up to the Ming varied around two bushels of grain and two bolts of plain-weave tabby silk (somewhat more for plant fiber cloth) per taxable couple (able-bodied persons aged between fifteen and sixty). There was an ideal equivalence between a bushel of food grain and a bolt of plain silk, although market prices often departed greatly from this standard depending on fluctuations in relative supply and demand; see, e.g., Tong 1981: 66, 108; Liang Fang Zhong 1980. On the circumstances leading to the Ming reforms see R. Huang 1974.

a generalized gender division of labor in which women of all classes produced cloth "inside" (*nei*), while peasant men labored outside growing grain and fiber crops. So the demands of a state redistributive economy maintained a discrete female productive sector and highlighted the prominence of the female contribution both to the household economy and to the fulfillment of its responsibilities toward the state.

Textiles were fundamental to the functioning of the Chinese state. From the Zhou dynasty until the late Ming, a period of over two millennia (roughly 700 B.C. to A.D. 1580), every household was liable for taxes in cloth and yarn as well as grain. The government needed huge quantities of basic textiles to clothe the army. Initially hemp and ramie were levied, but in the Yuan dynasty cotton started to replace them in taxes as well as domestic use. Silk cloth too was required in huge quantities by the state: for the court to clothe itself in fitting majesty, for the government to pay bureaucrats and soldiers, alleviate hardship, reward loyal service, purchase horses from the Tibetans, buy off the current nomadic enemies in the north, or impress tributary monarchs in Southeast Asia. Silk yarn was levied from peasant producers to be woven into satins, damasks and brocades in imperial manufactures. Until the late Ming, hundreds of millions of bolts of cloth were levied and redistributed directly by the Chinese state every year; thereafter merchant middlemen played the predominant role in distribution. Even after the Single Whip tax reforms of 1581 substituted cash for payment in kind, state levies of cloth continued and the state remained by far the largest consumer of textiles, but by then the direct symbolic link between women as the producers of cloth and the state as consumer had been broken.

CLOTH AND SOCIETY

The cloth that women wove also tied the family into the community. The walls around the house separated "us" from "others," but the cloth made in the inner quarters bound the family to neighbors, kin and marriage partners. Textiles were an essential element in the forging and reinforcing of social bonds. Gifts of cloth were indispensable for most ceremonies and social exchanges, as is made plain by etiquette books and popular encyclopedias.[11] Their role was especially prominent in weddings. Marriage was a joining of families, and fine cloth was one of the gifts of the groom's family to the bride. Marriage was also a transition: "The wedding is not

11. Sheng 1990: 125.

[a cause] for congratulations; it is [a case] of generations succeeding each other," said a Han philosopher.[12] The parental generation had lost their powers of biological reproduction, but were often reluctant to cede the reins of other forms of power to the new couple. The intergenerational struggle was classically demonstrated in the tyrannical treatment of a new bride by her mother-in-law. But a bride could hope to sweeten her reception by coming with capital in the form of a dowry or bridal goods. At certain periods this might consist of land or bond servants given to the young woman out of her natal family's possessions. As a more general rule, it comprised clothes, jewels, quilts and household goods, and cloth in large quantities. Girls from poor families usually had as dowry only the textiles they had produced themselves (or goods purchased with the money they had earned making textiles).

Throughout Chinese history young women worked hard on their trousseau or dowry. The twelfth-century writer Hong Mai mentions a young woman who died unmarried at twenty-one and was buried with the thirty-three bolts of open weave, seventy bolts of plain silk and about fifty meters of coarse silk that she had woven for her dowry.[13] The cloth that a bride made and received was both trousseau and marriage capital, a symbol with a real cash value. It was female property over which the bride herself generally retained control. Hong Mai relates the tale of a dog butcher who converted to Buddhism and wished to give up his business; his wife told him she still had several bolts of cloth in her wedding chests that they could use as capital to start up in a new trade.[14] Among the elite the cloth was more likely to be used to make fine quilts and clothes, a trousseau to astonish and overawe the groom's mother and sisters. Like the poorer woman's marriage chest of salable cloth, the elite trousseau was a means to establish the new bride's high status and right to respect.[15]

Textiles also played a fundamental role in another ritual of transition: funerals and mourning. With their death, the old regained the power they

12. *Bohu tong* (Comprehensive discourse in the White Tiger Hall), a first-century A.D. philosophical work, quoted Mann 1991: 208.

13. *Yijianzhi* (Record of the listener): 10/1642, cited Sheng 1990: 137.

14. Ibid.: 3/1574, cited Ebrey 1991d: 111.

15. It was also a medium for maintaining intergenerational bonds, not those of hegemonic patrilineal descent, but of descent through the female line. Some articles of clothing, like the jewelry passed down from mother to daughter, might become heirlooms. Song elite families were likely to pass wedding robes down from one generation to the next (Sheng 1990: 110). And elite dowries could also be converted into capital, to buy land or set up a business (see, e.g., McDermott 1990: 26).

had lost to their children, acquiring the status of ancestors. Thus the warp threads of the descent line were unrolled another generation into the future. As with weddings, funerals played an important role in affirming or renegotiating rank, and in cultivating the links between the bereaved family and the community in which they lived. Clothing played an integral role in funerals and mourning. The Chinese did not wear black as a sign of bereavement, but rather undyed or white cloth. In the first stages of mourning the coarsest, untailored and untrimmed hemp cloth was worn. In the later stages of mourning, softer plant fibers could be substituted for hemp and the edges of the cloth could be trimmed. The Han compendium of ritual, the *Book of Rites*, says kudzu-vine cloth may be worn in the later stages of mourning, but most people were likely to substitute ramie, or later on cotton. Mourning grades and the corresponding variations and sequences of mourning garments were determined by the mourner's degree of relatedness and relative status to the deceased. Thus mourning clothes made visible the hierarchies of the social web.[16]

So far I have stressed the social and political value of cloth, but it also represented straightforward monetary worth. Cloth served as a medium of exchange and as a standard currency in early China. In later times it continued to be the usual medium of exchange in many local markets, and its use as currency revived whenever coinage was short or its value in flux. I have already mentioned that women might convert their dowry cloth into ready cash; the fruits of their loom could also bring a cash income for their family.

By spinning and weaving, women produced not only objects of value but also persons of virtue. Learning textile skills inculcated the fundamental female values of diligence, frugality, order and self-discipline. In early China little girls of gentle birth were taught to spin and weave from the age of eight or nine, when their brothers started learning to read and to carry arms. "The wife is the fitting partner of her husband, performing all the work with silk and hemp," says the *Book of Rites*.[17] Long after elite households had turned to buying the cloth for their needs on the open market, patriarchs admonished their daughters to spin in order to learn respect for the hard work of their inferiors and to weave hemp to learn frugality. The moral value of personal involvement in spinning and weaving is clearly illustrated, for example, in the popular encyclopedia of 1607,

16. *Liji*, cited Kuhn 1988: 22; on the use of mourning to mark social connections and distinctions see, e.g., Freedman 1970; Ahern 1973; Watson and Rawski 1988; Ebrey 1991b.
17. Quoted Kuhn 1988: 20.

Bianyong xuehai junyu (Seas of knowledge, mines of jade). It contains a sequence of woodblock drawings modeled on the Song work *Gengzhi tu* (Agriculture and sericulture illustrated) showing the women of a gentle household working in harmony to spin and weave patterned silks which, in the final tableau, they present to the grandparental couple so the elders can choose their clothes for the coming year (fig. 24). This is not a realistic depiction of contemporary life among the rural gentry (who by then would be more likely to buy patterned silks than to produce them at home). It is rather a parable of virtuous femininity and of the role of women's work in upholding the social order.[18]

Finally I would like to touch on the philosophical meanings of textiles in China and the metaphors that they provided. Like the house, cloth is a symbol of the human. In Chinese thought clothing distinguishes humans from beasts, and among humans it distinguishes between the rulers and the ruled. "The noble wear sweeping robes, resplendent as mountain dragons they rule the empire; the humble wear coarse wool or hemp garments, in winter to protect them from the cold, in summer to shield their bodies."[19] Clothing was fundamental to the Chinese idea of dignity and propriety; the naked body was neither beautiful nor erotic.[20] The legendary Yellow Emperor invented proper clothing, replacing the skins of animals and the feathers of birds with silk and hemp, "making jackets in the image of Heaven." Of the silkworm the early Confucian philosopher Xunzi says: "Its merit is to clothe and ornament everything under Heaven, to the ten thousandth generation. Thus rites and music are completed, noble and base are distinguished, the aged are nourished and the young reared."[21] Clothing is the mark of civilization. Not only does it distinguish ranks and provide ornament, it is linked to the reproduction of human society through descent, the care of the old, the raising of children, and the proper distinction and complementarity between the sexes.

It is no coincidence that the making of cloth provides several of the

18. See Mann 1991 and McDermott 1990 for examples of the training value ascribed to textile work in late imperial gentry families. Stone-Ferrier 1989 offers an interesting parallel, showing the moral importance attributed to traditional gender divisions of labor in a period of social instability in Holland.

19. *Tiangong kaiwu* (Exploitation of the works of nature) 31. This work is a technical treatise written by Song Yingxing and first printed in 1637. Although it includes descriptions of peasant production of food and other basics, Song's main interest is in the most advanced and productive specialized commercial enterprises.

20. Elvin 1989: 266.

21. *Huainanzi* (Book of the prince of Huainan), a compendium of natural philosophy compiled c. 120 B.C., quoted Kuhn 1988: 250; *Xunzi* (Book of Master Xun), a philosophical treatise written c. 240 B.C., ibid.: 301.

most fundamental metaphors of social and intellectual order in Chinese thought. The disentangling, ordering, smoothing and combining processes that produced yarn, the timeless continuity of the long, strong warp threads and the regular patterning of weft threads that joined them provide many of the metaphors by which the Chinese understood the world. As the seventeenth-century writer Song Yingxing points out, "to govern" (*zhi*) is the same word as "to reel silk," "civil disorder" (*luan*) as "raveling a skein," "canonical texts" (*jing*) as "warp threads," and "philosophical discourse" (*lun*) as "silk yarn."[22] From these moral threads were woven the fabric of Chinese civility.

To give a taste of the range of metaphorical uses derived from textile terminology, I give as one example some common uses of the word *jing*, whose primary meaning is "warp threads," as listed in the standard dictionary *Ciyuan* (Source of words). That meaning is extended to denote the principal direction or the guiding principle. *Jing* means the cosmologically and ritually important north-south axis of a city, and it is also used for the acupuncture tracts or meridians along which *qi* energy circulates through the body. It denotes the canonical texts that are passed down from generation to generation, weaving them into a tradition of knowledge. And by extension the term implies regularity and regulation, as in the phrase in the *Zuo zhuan*, a historical work supposedly compiled by Confucius himself: "Ritual is the means by which the state is regulated [*jing*]." It also refers to cyclical regularity, most commonly the menstrual cycle that regulates female health.

MEDIEVAL DIVISIONS OF LABOR
AND THE VALUE OF FEMALE WORK

There were four main types of establishment producing textiles up to the Song: (1) peasant households, which relied essentially on family labor; (2) large elite households, rural or urban, in which the mistress organized the production of textiles by family members, servants, and hired female workers; (3) state manufactures, run by officials, using permanent or temporary conscripted workers, male and female; and (4) urban workshops of various kinds. State manufactures and urban workshops owned complex looms or draw-looms on which fancy weaves and designs (damasks, brocades, satins or gauzes) could be produced.[23] They specialized in

22. *Tiangong kaiwu* 31.
23. When the draw-loom was first used in China is a matter of controversy. Kuhn (1995) believes the Chinese draw-loom was an indigenous development and

the production of high-value textiles, mostly complex silk weaves; they did not produce their own raw materials but acquired them from tax goods or on the open market. Peasant and manorial households produced their own raw materials, both silk and plant fibers (hemp in the north, the finer ramie in the south), which in peasant households were all made up into simple weaves (tabbies or twills) using cheap and simple looms; manorial households frequently owned draw-looms as well as simple looms and produced complex silk weaves too (fig. 12).[24]

Up to the Song redistribution of grain and cloth was almost exclusively the prerogative of the state. The taxation system required that all peasants everywhere produce grain, yarn and textiles for tax. Changes in regional impositions helped redefine the map of textile production and specializa-

---

that it was first used in some state workshops during the Han dynasty. In this he agrees with Chinese scholars, who argue that the ancient Chinese could not have woven figured silks such as those discovered in later Han tombs (A.D. 25–220) without a draw mechanism. Most Western scholars believe that the techniques of weft-faced weaving developed in Central Asia between the fourth and fifth centuries A.D. were at the origin of the draw-loom; they argue that the Chinese had no indigenous expertise in the production of weft-faced fabrics, and either the draw-loom was introduced from farther West or the Chinese themselves were inspired to develop a draw-loom by Syrian fabrics imported at a much later date than the Han. (On the difficulties of analyzing complex silk weaves and attributing them to different loom forms, see Desrosiers 1994).

24. For a good basic introduction to the development of Chinese textile machinery and technology, as well as to modern Chinese conventions of weave terminology, see Chen 1984. Gao Hanyu also begins his study with brief and accessible historical accounts of the development of Chinese weaves and weave terminology, well illustrated with diagrams and photographs (1986: 8–36, 258–67). Kuhn 1988 is a more detailed and critical study of the development of Chinese spinning technology (a parallel study of weaving technology is in preparation; Kuhn forthcoming). Because textiles have been so important in the history of almost every society, the historical interpretation of weave vocabulary presents enormous difficulties. The same term might be used for different kinds of cloth in different regions, or different names applied to the same cloth. The modern convention, which arises out of the industrialization of textile production, is to attribute names on the basis of the processes of production: the form and quality of weave, as well as the materials used. Even so, the discrepancies between English and French weaving terminology alone demonstrate the difficulty of developing a standard terminology even on the basis of the technical details of production (Burnham 1981 provides the standard English definitions with their equivalents in French, German, Italian, Swedish, and other European languages wherever possible). Before this production-oriented approach it was common to take a more consumption-oriented approach. Textiles were often named according to their regional origin, or the uses to which they were put, or their general quality, so that the same name might be applied to cloth produced on looms that were set up differently (Reddy 1986). The case for confusion in historical Chinese textile terminology is enormous, and despite the touchstone of modern process-oriented terminology,

tion. Up until the Song, the northern regions were taxed in silk and hemp, the southern provinces chiefly in ramie and other bast-fibers.[25] But with the loss of sericultural regions to invading nomadic rulers in the tenth century, the state fostered the development of a sericultural industry in the lower Yangzi provinces—encouraging it by providing information and credit, imposing it by levying heavy taxes in silk.[26] It was not possible for individual households to opt out of producing silk if they lived in an area with a sericultural tax, or for individual households, whole villages or even districts to give up subsistence production and specialize in commodity production as many did in the Ming and Qing, buying their food on the open market.

Peasant men were obliged by tax requirements to grow hemp or ramie or mulberries, but in medieval times they were not involved in producing yarn or cloth. That was women's work. The following equipment was required: each household needed the basic flat loom (fig. 13) used to make tax cloth; it also served for subsistence needs. If a household raised silkworms,

---

discrepancies are still to be found among the interpretations of modern scholars. Not being a textile specialist, I have certainly erred in certain choices of terminology, but not, I hope, to the extent of undermining my arguments about historical trends.

25. The fibers taken from hemp, ramie, kudzu vine and other native Chinese plants are of the kind technically called bast-fibers: they are long and must be spliced together by hand before being twisted into weavable yarn. Cotton has very short fibers which, like wool, require true spinning.

26. The high point of state demands for silk was perhaps the Tianbao period of the Tang (742–56), when the state levied 7.4 million bolts (*pi*) of tabby and 11.1 million ounces (*liang*) of silk floss a year from 3.7 million taxpayers, plus 16 million lengths (*duan*) (equivalent to 7.2 million bolts) of bast-fiber cloth from 4.5 million taxpayers (Tong 1981: 108–9). The Northern Song quota for the ten most important sericultural provinces, representing 65 percent of the total, was almost 3 million bolts of silk and 9.1 million ounces of floss. The total tax in bast-fiber cloth was much lower, around 1.5 million bolts. Between 1131 and 1162, the annual silk quota for the Liangzhe region alone (the two provinces of the Yangzi Delta) was 1.17 million bolts of tabby (Kuhn 1987: 170). Chinese measures changed slightly from one dynasty to another. The foot, ounce, pound and bushel are roughly similar to European equivalents, except that there are 10 ounces to a pound and 10 inches to a foot; I have not bothered to give precise metric equivalents here. As far as tax requirements went, the standard length for a bolt of light plain-weave tabby silk (*juan*) was 40 Chinese feet, which depending on the dynasty worked out at about 10 meters; it was generally 2 Chinese feet 2 inches in width (around 50 cm), and weighed 1 Chinese pound (about 450 g, a modern imperial pound). The standards for plant fiber cloth were similar. There were regional variations in standards. The rather narrow width of the bolts is determined by the length of the average weaver's arm, reflected in loom structure; it is typical of handwoven cloth before the invention of the flying or automatic shuttle.

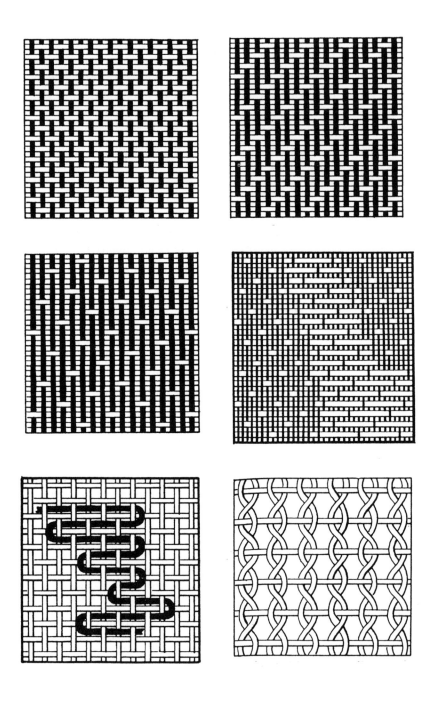

Figure 12.   Weaves (reproduced from Burnham 1981: 6, 7, 32–33, 62–63, 14; by permission of the Royal Ontario Museum).

TOP LEFT: tabby: binding system or weave based on a unit of two ends and two picks, in which each end passes over one and under one pick. The binding points are set over one end on successive picks.

TOP RIGHT: twill: binding system or weave based on a unit of three or more ends and three or more picks, in which each end passes over two or more adjacent picks and under the next one or more, or under two or more adjacent picks and over the next one or more. The binding points are set over by one end on successive picks and form diagonal lines.

MIDDLE LEFT: satin: binding system or weave based on a unit of five or more ends, and a number of picks equal to, or a multiple of, the number of ends. Each end either passes over four or more adjacent picks and under the next one, or passes under four or more adjacent picks and over the next one. The binding points are set over two or more ends on successive picks, and are distributed in an unobtrusive manner to give a smooth appearance.

MIDDLE RIGHT: damask: a self-patterned weave with one warp and one weft in which the pattern is formed by a contrast of binding systems. In its classic form it is reversible, and the contrast is produced by the use of the warp and weft faces of the same weave, usually satin. Most silk damasks are of unbalanced weave with a fine, closely set warp, producing a shiny warp face and a heavier, more widely spaced weft and giving a dull appearance in the areas where the weft predominates.

LOWER LEFT: brocade: a term in general use without precise denotation. It has been used for any rich figured textile, and by extension is applied to any textile with a woven pattern, especially one with a pattern in gold or silver. The diagram shows a simple form of the brocading technique, with a brocading weft carried back and forth as required through the shed opening of the tabby ground weave.

LOWER RIGHT: simple gauze: gauze is an ancient and widespread method of interlacing warp and weft, differing in concept from the three basic systems (tabby, twill and satin). In gauze the binding is achieved by displacement of the warp threads between the passage of the weft. On the simplest looms, gauze can be woven by twisting the warp threads by hand as weaving progresses. With more complex equipment, warp ends called doup ends are made to cross over warp ends called fixed ends. There are many variations according to the complexity of the movements made by the doup ends in relation to the fixed ends. Various gauze bindings may be combined to produce a pattern, or gauze may be used with another binding, frequently tabby.

圖式機腰

Figure 13. A simple loom (*Tiangong kaiwu*, original Ming illustration of 1637 [Sung 1966: 57]). The loom depicted here is a waistloom, that is to say, the tension in the warp is maintained by cords fastened to a belt around the weaver's waist. Waist-looms were popular for domestic weaving because they took up so little room; other simple looms had a rather more cumbersome timber frame. Note that the seventeenth-century author, Song Yingxing, has chosen to show a man at the loom. The same loom is illustrated as the characteristic cotton loom (with a woman working it) in the section on textiles in Wang Zhen's *Nong shu* of 1313.

it needed trays and mats and a room or shed to keep the silkworms, as well as a basic reel for reeling the raw silk off the cocoons, and a spindle wheel for spooling and quilling—twisting and combining the threads into yarn. The spindle wheel could also be used for spinning hemp and ramie. This equipment was almost entirely made of cheap materials (ordinary wood, bamboo, hemp cords) and could be made and maintained at home or purchased from a village carpenter. But peasant households could not afford the capital or the space for the elaborate looms needed to make complex cloth (even though peasant women might have acquired the skills to use them working in a nearby manorial household).[27]

Apart from equipment, the limiting factor on output in most peasant households would have been the amount of raw materials they produced; during this period peasant households did not purchase extra cocoons, raw silk or raw cotton to process. Nor did they hire additional labor. Although there were periods of frantic activity when the silk cocoons had to be reeled, or when the ramie was retted, most spinning and weaving could be spread out over the year.

A skilled worker could produce fine-quality yarn from plant fibers just with a spindle, though she could produce it faster with the help of a spindle wheel. Silk could be reeled and twisted using the same spindle wheel. So almost every household had the wherewithal to produce fine-quality yarn; whether they chose to do so depended on how much time they had and on the kind of cloth they intended to make: tax cloth had to conform to certain standards, cloth for home use did not.

Silk took longer to weave than bast-fibers, perhaps eight to sixteen days as compared to two days for a bolt, though it varied according to whether the loom had treadles and how skilled the weaver was. The Western Han mathematical treatise *Jiuzhang suanshu* gives an example in which "a woman skilled at weaving" is said to weave at rates of between 2.5 and 5 Chinese feet a day, depending on how fresh or how tired she might be. At 40 feet to the bolt, that implies that it took a good weaver eight to sixteen days to produce a bolt, presumably of tabby silk. A somewhat later mathematical work, the *Suan jing*, also implies that the average weaving speed would vary between 3 and 5 feet a day. An Eastern Han song talks about a gentleman's concubine who is scolded even if she completes a bolt in four days, and the Tang poet Wang Jian, in "Weaving at the Window," talks of women from poor families who weave for the rich being urged on

27. On the materials used for basic textile equipment, see Kuhn 1988: 4. A draw-loom could be as much as 16 feet long, with a tower as high as 15 feet (*Tiangong kaiwu* 31).

to produce a bolt and a half in two days; this was presumably plant-fiber cloth. Plain weaving speeded up from the Song as the market in yarn grew and loom technology was refined. Sheng gives anecdotal evidence of weaving speeds on home looms in the Song: perhaps one bolt of plain silk in three days full-time.[28]

It is not easy to find figures to calculate the value added by weaving at different periods. For the early Han (first century B.C.), the mathematical treatise *Jiuzhang suanshu* gives the price of raw silk at between 240 and 345 cash for a *jin* (Chinese pound); the price of a bolt of tabby (which if it was made to tax standards would weigh a *jin*) was put at 512 cash or something over double the price of the lower quality raw silk. Hemp cloth was priced at a mere 125 cash per bolt.[29]

These market values indicate that as well as contributing half the household tax, peasant women could sometimes earn income from the textiles they produced.[30] Both local and long distance trade were underdeveloped compared to the period from the Song on, but there were markets for certain peasant-produced textiles. Plant-fiber textiles (except for the finest ramie) were less valuable and less easily transported than silk and had only local markets.[31] But silk cloth was transported throughout China and beyond: light and valuable tabbies that peasant women could produce on their simple looms were in demand everywhere. They not only served as a universally recognized currency, but also formed the basic material for elite clothing.[32]

28. Tong 1981: 67–68 gives the Han figures, Sheng 1990: 53, 60 those for the Song. Karine Chemla, whose translation of the *Jiuzhang suanshu* will soon be published, pointed out to me that the examples in mathematical texts cannot be taken as necessarily accurate. This applies particularly to figures such as prices, but also of course to weaving speeds. It seems likely, however, that the mathematicians who used such examples would probably select realistic rather than completely arbitrary values.

29. Tong 1981: 50–51.

30. Not all peasant women would have had surpluses to sell: poems of the period tell us of country women desperately working through the night to produce enough cloth for the tax collector.

31. There was no market for bast yarn: hemp was too cheap, and though fine ramie cloth was valuable, the yarn had to be woven immediately after spinning.

32. Although sophisticated brocades and damasks cost much more bolt for bolt, the value of total tabby output was probably higher than that of any other commodity. Nor do the price differentials necessarily mean that a weaver made a vastly greater income from making fancy cloth. To cite a well-documented comparative example, in early seventeenth-century Florence piece rates for figured silks were over ten times as much as those for taffeta (or tabby), but a length of taffeta could be produced in about one-sixth of the time. So in the early modern Florentine silk industry, sophisticated knowledge and skills were rewarded at a

Given the rarity and extremely high cost of luxury weaves, most well-to-do people's everyday clothing was made from silk tabbies, and fine garments were often also made from plain silks embroidered, painted, or decorated with borders of fancy silk.[33] Before the advent of cotton, tabbies had no competitors in the lower range of the luxury market. The needs of officials and their families were partly provided for by state distribution of tax cloth, but there were also markets, local and interregional, for silks. In pre-Song times sericulture was typical of the north, and tabbies were widely produced in peasant households all along the Yellow River.[34] The demand for silks was great throughout China, not least in the luxurious courts of the southern dynasties, and prices in the south were very high. Texts say that southern households involved in sericulture made large profits, and officials made efforts to promote the establishment of silk production in the south, encouraging southern soldiers to find skilled brides from sericultural regions in the north.[35] But the development of sericulture in the south was slow until the invasion of northern provinces by Central Asian nomads sent waves of migrants southward, starting in the early tenth century; just a century later the Northern Song was able to impose the heaviest provincial silk quotas on the lower Yangzi provinces. Through all this period the demand on the open market for plain silks such as peasant households could produce seems almost always to have exceeded supply.

Elite women were also involved in textile production, often profitably, in urban mansions and on rural manors. The involvement of city ladies in

commensurate level with more routine capacities (Goodman 1993: 240). I return to the relationship between skills and rewards later; here I just wish to point out that given the patterns of demand and distribution in medieval China, the production of simple silks could be relatively rewarding.

33. Kuhn 1987: 351.

34. During the Tianbao period, for example, roughly 3.7 million households out of a national total of 8.2 million were taxed in silk cloth; this represented a substantial proportion of the population of northern China.

35. "At first the people of Yue [the South China coast] did not work at the loom and shuttle. When Xue Jianxun was in charge of regulating expenditure in Jiangdong, he gave generous amounts of money to those enlisted soldiers who were not yet married and secretly ordered them to marry weaving women from the north and return. After a few years he thus obtained several hundred people. This caused a significant change in the customs of Yue: the people vied to produce the best patterns, and their gauzes were considered the most delicate south of the Yangzi" (*Guoshi bu* 2, quoted Tong 1981: 109). By the time the first dynastic history of the Tang dynasty (*Jiu Tang shu*) was completed in 945, silk cloth was probably the most important of all the regional products sent as tribute from the southern provinces (Tong 1981: 114).

textiles seems to have been most marked in the period from Han to Tang[36]; thereafter their place was apparently taken by an ever-increasing number of private workshops. But rural manors or gentry households continued to be involved in textile production, in some regions at least until the Ming. Unlike the peasantry, manorial households could afford the considerable investment for complex looms (fig. 14) and were thus able to produce fancy silks commanding higher prices than tabby, although not the finest kinds, all of which were produced in city manufactures and workshops by professional weavers.[37] They also disposed of sufficient labor and equipment to organize time-saving practices: one set of women could reel raw silk from the cocoons and make yarn while the others worked at the loom; or spinners could prepare ramie yarn to supply the weavers while they worked. Manorial households produced raw materials for textiles in their own fields, but probably were glad to purchase any surplus raw silk or yarn that might have been available in local markets to keep their expensive looms working all year round.

Although there is not much textual evidence on the organization of manorial production before the Ming, it is frequently depicted in fine art and in specialized works like the famous treatise *Gengzhi tu* (Agriculture and sericulture illustrated).[38] The mistress of the house was the person in charge. Just as her husband worked with his mind to organize the labors of those below him in the social hierarchy, so his wife contributed the skills of government to the operation of weaving, while her juniors (concubines or servants) contributed the skills of craft. Weaving was thus a task that reinforced the social ranking of the inner quarters.

Skilled or inventive women could add greatly to the wealth of a household, even one that was rich to begin with. The sixth-century *Xijing zaji* (Reminiscences of the western capital) tells us that "[a concubine] of Huo Guang [commander-in-chief in the late first century B.C. and an extremely wealthy man] presented to Chunyu Yan twenty-four bolts of silk brocade with a design of grapes, and twenty-five bolts of damask patterned with scattered flowers. The damask came from the home of Chen Baoguang,

36. See the range of examples cited in Tong 1981: 37–42, 65–77, 101–15.
37. Kuhn 1988: 387.
38. A set of poems and illustrations, depicting twelve stages of rice growing and twelve of sericulture and weaving, by Lou Shou; he presented the manuscript to the emperor in 1145. Succeeding editions through the Ming and Qing show variations of style and detail in the illustrations. Various agricultural works and popular encyclopedias also included series of illustrations of farming and sericulture more or less closely modeled on the prototypes of the *Gengzhi tu* (Kuhn 1976). Some of the most attractive surviving versions are Japanese or Korean.

織更曲殷照心女時攀
作將折勤眼手工慕華
雁無續拋華慕精新尚
背限回暗錦相勤巧
雲思文字紜應

Figure 14.   A draw-loom (*Gengzhi tu,* Kangxi imperial edition
[*Yuzhi gengzhi tu*] of 1696). A tall, spacious room was required
to set up a draw-loom, which was used for weaving figured silks.
Here the loom is shown in a shed in the women's quarters of
a well-to-do household; both the weaver and the young person
sitting up above the loom manipulating the draw-threads are
female. The third line of the poem describes "hand and mind
[working] in obscure resonance" to produce the complex designs.

whose [concubine] could teach the technique. So [Huo Guang's wife] Huo
Xian invited her to come in, set up the loom and make the cloth. The loom
used 120 patterning devices [nie[39]] and it took sixty days to make a bolt
worth ten thousand cash."[40] To give a rough idea of the value added by
this exceptional weaving technique: a bolt of ordinary tabby, according to
the roughly contemporary Jiuzhang suanshu, probably took between
eight and sixteen days to weave and was worth something over five hundred cash. Huo's colleague, General Zhang Anshi, was even wealthier. The
Han shu (History of the [Former] Han dynasty), by Ban Gu and Ban
Zhao, tells us that his wife worked at textiles with her own hands, managing a workforce of seven hundred servants and producing textiles for sale
which contributed substantially to the family's riches.[41]

Not many manorial establishments were on such a large scale even in
Han times, and by the early Song only royal households could match
them. In many country manors the mistress of the household had a small
labor force consisting of the other household women (concubines, daughters and daughters-in-law, and servants), and perhaps some hired "weaving women," who would presumably come from the villages nearby. The
Nong shu (Agricultural treatise) by Chen Fu, written in 1149 and describing rural conditions in the lower Yangzi, devotes a section to sericulture.
Chen makes calculations of quantity and profit based on a family of ten
with enough labor to raise ten frames of silkworms. The total output of
tabby was calculated at 31.2 bolts of silk, worth almost 3,000 kilograms of
rice at current prices; this would have been more than enough to feed the
family of ten through the year.[42] In these larger households women did
all the spinning and weaving. Small girls or boys were often given the
task of sitting up in the tower of the draw-loom, changing the patterns
(fig. 14).[43] Whether urban or rural, manorial textile production was a fe-

39. For the interpretation of this term, which in modern Chinese means
"tweezers," see Kuhn 1995: 78.
40. This is a slightly modified version of the translation by Kuhn (1988: 203).
"Ten thousand cash" is a figurative term meaning that the cloth fetched a very high
price.
41. Tong 1981: 51, 39.
42. Ten frames of worms yield 120 jin (72 kg) of cocoons; each jin gives 1.3 liang
(50 g) of basic silk thread (grège, raw), and 5 liang make one small bolt of light
tabby (half the tax weight). Using three hand-driven reels, it would take ten days
to reel all the cocoons (i.e., each reel produces enough for one bolt a day). One bolt
was worth 1.4 shi (93 kg) of rice, says Chen Fu (Nong shu 21); calculations of metric
equivalents for these Song dynasty measures are given by Kuhn (1988: 388).
43. I have not been able to find any material on the status of the "weaving
women" at this early period. The seventeenth-century Bu nongshu by Zhang

male domain, organized by the mistress of the household. Young boys might be involved, but no man gave orders.[44]

As late as the Song, complex weaves made on draw-looms formed only 4 percent of total production even in the most urbanized and advanced silk-weaving regions of Sichuan and the lower Yangzi.[45] The most valuable silk textiles were produced in state manufactures and increasingly in private urban workshops. Until the fall of the Northern Song, the most sophisticated looms and the most skilled workers were to be found in the silk-weaving centers of Sichuan and the north. Since earliest times the Chinese state had tried to control the production and use of luxury fabrics. Sumptuary laws (frequently flouted) laid down the weaves, dyes and decorations to which different classes and ranks were entitled. And the state itself ran the manufactures that produced the most elaborate and valuable silks. These manufactures were run by officials and obtained their raw materials from the silk yarn or raw silk levied in taxes. The looms and much other equipment used in state manufactures were specialized and expensive, constructed by skilled carpenters. Xue Jingshi's handbook on loom construction, the *Ziren yishi* (Traditions of the joiner's craft), prefaced 1264, describes the construction of various looms: draw-looms, standing looms, gauze looms and combination looms. It makes clear the high cost of construction, the need for skilled maintenance, and the complexity of setting up the loom for weaving. A rather later text says a draw-loom included *eighteen hundred* components of water-milled bamboo.[46]

Lüxiang describes them as being hired full-time by the year, but that was after the textile tax had been abolished. Maybe in earlier periods weaving women worked part-time after they had met their own household's subsistence and tax needs, or maybe peasant families would send their daughters out to be trained.

44. "An anonymous scroll from the Southern Song gives us a glimpse into the weaving-house of a private household in a rural setting. We see women involved in the preparatory tasks and a woman weaver sitting at the loom, just pressing the treadle, with the shuttle in her left hand. . . . In the tower of the draw-loom sits a child, pulling the harness-cords [to control] the pattern"; the configuration of the loom and its double warp beam suggest that patterned gauze is being produced (Kuhn 1988: 377).

45. Kuhn 1987: 378.

46. According to Kuhn (1977, 1987: 376–86) there were no significant changes in loom construction after the *Ziren yishi* was written, so we may assume that Song draw-looms were comparable in complexity and value to the 1,800-piece loom described by Song Yingxing in the *Tiangong kaiwu* of 1637 (p. 31). It has been suggested to me that perhaps Song—who was keen to display the sophistication and complexity of all the crafts and manufactures he described—exaggerated the number of pieces required for the draw-loom. His account tallies, however, with other late imperial references to the cost and complexity of specialized looms.

The state manufactures were divided into separate workshops for different stages of production (dyeing, reeling, quilling, weaving), and the workforce was correspondingly specialized. Depending on the period, the workforce consisted either of unfree hereditary craftsmen and women, or of conscripted free artisans. Scanty documentation means that it is difficult to say much about the gender division of labor. We do know that weaving could be performed either by men or by women (in later periods women were usually restricted to reeling and quilling). Texts refer both to *gongjiang,* (male) artisans, and to *nügong,* female workers; for instance, the dynastic history of the Song dynasty (*Song shi,* c. 1345) tells us that when the emperor Taizong closed down the state silk manufactures in Chengdu, Sichuan, between 967 and 984, fifty-eight women workers were dismissed.[47] We cannot be certain if the work of each section was always run by a male foreman (*hutou*), but this was standard by the Song, and the living and working conditions of all the workers, male and female, were hard.[48] Plainly this way of organizing production was radically different from that of the peasant and manorial households: first, it depended on outside raw materials and labor; second, the work process was divided between separate groups of specialized workers; and third, a large part of the workforce was male, and men were the managers.

In state manufactures most raw silk was obtained through the tax system, but private workshops had to purchase raw silk or yarn on the open market. Sichuan had been famous as the foremost sericultural region since before the empire was founded, and in medieval China the state manufactures of Chengdu had a virtual monopoly on producing the finest brocades; the luxury-loving monarchs of the medieval southern dynasties were among their best customers.[49] Interestingly, by the time of the Song most of the Chengdu manufactures obtained raw silk not through the tax system but directly from local peasant producers who had more or less abandoned the practice of weaving to specialize in sericulture and reeling (fig. 19). When the early Song emperors closed down the Chengdu silk manufactures, transferred them to the capital, or turned them over to the production of coarse cloth for the army in the 980s, not only were tens of thousands of skilled textile workers out of a job, but the rural producers of Chengdu were reduced to penury, and in the 990s a bitter rebellion broke out.[50]

47. Tong 1981: 147; Kuhn 1993.
48. Kuhn 1993, citing Eichhorn 1955.
49. Tong 1981: 69.
50. Kuhn 1993, citing Eichhorn 1955.

State manufactures, originally concentrated in Chengdu and around whatever city happened to be the capital, were found in many Chinese cities by the Song.[51] But outside the Chengdu Basin, rural producers were not likely to specialize entirely in the production of raw silk or yarn. There was always a market for these products, however, since private urban workshops had to purchase their raw materials. Private workshops varied from family-size establishments to the occasional huge enterprise with more looms than a state manufacture. One rich Tang merchant specialized in lined garments; his workshop had five hundred looms, more than the Song imperial manufacture in the capital, which had only four hundred.[52] In his historical survey of handicrafts, Tong Shuye hypothesizes that the majority of pre-Song private workshops were much smaller, relying principally on family members and one or two hired workers for labor. Since respectable women worked only in their own or in some other family's inner quarters, urban hired workers were almost invariably men, and many craftsmen had received their training in government service.[53]

To summarize: all but a tiny proportion of the textiles produced in China before the end of the Song were simple weaves made by rural women in peasant or manorial households. It is not just that the workforce was female: rural textile production was a female domain, in which technical knowledge as well as the responsibility for production were controlled and managed by women. Furthermore, although most of the textiles produced in this female domain were simple weaves, they were not merely subsistence products but had a high recognized value both as tax payments and, in the case of silk yarn and tabbies, as marketable commodities.[54] Rural women in peasant and manorial households produced the bulk of the low-value cloth used for common wear as well as by far the major part of the high-value cloth in circulation.

51. Kuhn 1987: map 19, table 13.
52. *Taiping guangji* 243, quoted Tong 1981: 103.
53. Tong 1981: 104–9.
54. The *New History of the Tang Dynasty* (*Xin Tang shu*, written by Ouyang Xiu and completed in 1061) says that at the beginning of the Tang, when much farmland lay waste, a bolt of tabby was worth just a pint of husked grain, but after several years of good harvests its value rose to several tens of bushels (or over ten bushels according to the *Tang huiyao* [Administrative statutes of the Tang dynasty]) (Tong 1981: 136). It would be more accurate to give the value of grain in terms of silk, since silk cloth provided a standard during many periods when coin was in short supply. It was also an important medium of exchange: a merchant would set off to a distant province to buy fine paper or dried fish, taking with him a dozen or so bolts of tabby to pay for his purchases (Tong 1981: 137 gives several examples from Tang sources).

5 Economic Expansion and Changing Divisions of Labor

The scope and value of women's work in textiles was affected by a series of factors starting in the Song. Not all were unfavorable, at least initially. Sericulture and silk weaving spread to new areas, so that a larger number of women became involved in the production of high-value textiles. The increase in commerce and prosperity and the growth of urban populations increased demands for silk cloth, not simply because there were greater numbers of people able to afford to wear silk, but also because urban dwellers who did not weave themselves had to buy tabbies to pay their taxes. But tax demands were high and grew during the Song, because of the constant threat of invasion and the need to maintain large armies. This meant that women had to work increasingly hard just to pay their taxes, and in peasant households with restricted workforces and limited means to invest in labor-saving equipment, producing any salable surplus must have become a real challenge.

During the Northern Song the state made great efforts to encourage the growth of sericulture in the southern provinces. But until the northern provinces were invaded by the Khitans and then the Mongols, the north remained far in advance of the south, both in the quantity of silk it produced and in the sophistication of its processing techniques. Various handbooks to help officials improve peasant sericulture were written and circulated in the Song, but the real triggers for change were the loss of the north in 1126, the mass migration of northern peasants and artisans to the Yangzi provinces and farther south, and the establishment of the Southern Song capital in Hangzhou. With imperial manufactures and myriad private workshops producing luxury silks for a growing market of literati and wealthy merchant families, Hangzhou and the other lower Yangzi cities became the nucleus of a regional and eventually a national economy, buying up raw materials and processing them into high-quality goods that were sold all over the empire.

As the supply of fancy silk fabrics made in urban workshops increased, so too did the demand for raw silk. At the same time there is some evidence to indicate a change in fashion affecting elite demands for plain tabbies that peasant households could produce. The most spectacular textile finds from the Han to just before the Song are rich polychrome brocades, often patterned with motifs reminiscent of Persia: phoenixes, fabulous animals, heavy bunches of purple grapes. Elites of this period favored brocades, embroidery, and rich colors as a mark of rank. The total demand for silk luxury fabrics increased and changed in the Song as the literati class consolidated their control over an increasingly elaborate bureaucracy, and the numbers of well-off urbanites with high living standards increased. But a change in fashion affected how this demand was expressed. Dieter Kuhn suggests that one way in which the Song literati claimed legitimacy as a new elite was through establishing new fashions in material culture, rejecting the exuberant, cosmopolitan tastes of the Tang and Five Dynasty aristocracy and substituting a subdued and to us unmistakably Chinese refinement, whether in textiles, ceramics or painting.[1] As is often the case, the simplicity of the products required a significant increase in the complexity of the production process.

Two recently excavated late Song tombs give an idea of the change in tastes.[2] The scholar Zhou Yu (1222–61) was buried with what seems to have been a complete wardrobe, all of silk. It included gowns, long and short, padded and unpadded, jackets, trousers, shoes, stockings, underwear and hats. Forty-five percent of the textiles were silk gauze. Huang Sheng (1226–43), the wife of magistrate Zhao Yujun, was buried in a triple tomb,

1. Kuhn 1987.
2. Ibid.: 326–51. Zhu 1992: 227 has diagrams depicting six types of gauze weave from the Song. Sheng 1990 also argues that demand for gauzes increased significantly during the Song and was satisfied at the lower end of the market not by true gauzes but by open-weave tabbies that peasant households could produce on an ordinary loom. (See also Gao 1986: 258 on *sha*, open-weave tabby.) Of course two excavations cannot be taken as firm evidence of a general change in taste, and several of my colleagues who are far more expert in textile history than I disagree with Kuhn's interpretation. I myself thought the argument was convincing enough to be laid out here, given other aesthetic trends during the Song that together demonstrate an effort by the new elite to create an authentic and appropriate style for themselves.

her husband's in the center and his concubine's on his left; only Huang's survived intact. In her grave 354 fabrics were found, including 201 pieces of clothing (from official robes to handkerchiefs and even a sanitary napkin–holder of silk); 56 percent of the textiles were gauzes. The prevalence of gauzes does seem to tally with a preference among Song literati for polished but unobtrusive mastery of material; no heavy polychrome bands (typical of Tang wealth) were found in either grave, and light gauze took the place of light tabby silk as the basic clothing fabric.

Gauzes, whether plain or figured, require a loom with a double warp beam, beyond the means of peasant weavers even if they had the skills to work it. Manorial households could afford them: the Southern Song scroll described by Kuhn shows women in a rural mansion weaving on a gauze loom that is probably making patterned gauzes.[3] But the majority of the complex weaves (damasks, satins, brocades and gauzes of various kinds) that constituted maybe one-twentieth of total production during the Song were produced in state manufactures and the rapidly expanding sector of private urban workshops, where production was organized by men, and women participated only as auxiliary workers (fig. 15).

Government manufactures used both conscripted and hired workers, and still employed some women weavers. Private workshops used family and hired labor, and the hired labor seems mostly to have been male. Some men acquired their skills through apprenticeship. Others were taught a craft during their military service, working in an army or imperial manufacture, and weaving of complex silks was one of the skills they might learn.[4] Craftsmen looking for work would assemble in public places, standing in groups by a bridge or a temple waiting to be selected; often jobs were given out by a guild chief. Young workers could be hired and trained in a kind of apprenticeship. While foremen were usually hired long-term, other workers might be hired as journeymen.[5] Chinese mores did not allow women to stand out in public places competing with men to be hired, or to work with a different group of strange men every few days; in addition, if a woman had small children it was unlikely that anyone would want to hire her. (Contemporary illustrations of household production of textiles depict it as inseparable from child rearing: they include such vignettes as women

3. See p. 203, n. 44. The Ming illustrations to Wang Zhen's *Agricultural Treatise* also include a draw-loom with two warp beams (*Nong shu* j.18, p. 407). (The abbreviation "j." stands for *juan*, fascicle. In Chinese works the *juan* is roughly equivalent to a section or long chapter.)

4. Sheng 1990: 195, 207.

5. Tong 1981: 164.

Figure 15. Peony-patterned satin brocade (after Xu Zhongjie 1985: 120). This was a polychrome fabric, but similar patterns in monochrome silk damasks were also popular.

taking time off from spinning to breastfeed an infant or toddlers playing beside the loom.) Moreover, men were more likely than women to have been trained in the special skills increasingly needed to compete in the fancy silk market. In sum, increasing numbers of urban men were acquiring specialist skills in textile production, but urban women at this stage played little role in the production of fancy textiles, except if their family owned a workshop.

The late Yuan anecdote "What the Weaver Said" describes a workshop in a village in the Hangzhou region, where four or five looms were set in a row in a tumbledown building, with more than ten men working through the night, singing as they worked, even though they were pale and dazed. The writer asked how they could be so happy when their work was so hard. One replied: "Although my profession is humble, my wage is 200 strings of cash, and I am clothed and fed by the master, so that with my daily earnings I can feed my parents, wife and children."[6]

6. Xu Yikui, *Zhigong dui*, c. 1400, quoted Tong 1981: 201. The men's singing may have been not a sign of happiness but a weaving song: such songs were mnemonics for the successive steps of complex weaves, an auditory equivalent of

Meanwhile, rural women were still producing both raw silk and tabbies (and some fancy silks in manorial households), but the demand for raw silk and silk yarn was growing, prompting an incipient division of labor along the lines already observed in pre-Song Chengdu, whereby rural sericulturalists specialized in producing raw silk for urban workshops and gave up silk weaving. Sheng argues that Song peasant weavers tried to step up the production of silk cloth and compete in the luxury market by producing open-weave tabbies that resembled gauze. But even if this is correct, the switch by the Yuan state from taxing in cloth to taxing only in raw silk and yarn must have encouraged many rural households to abandon weaving tabbies and concentrate on sericulture and reeling.[7]

Several technical improvements disseminated in the Song and Yuan must have allowed sericultural households to increase and perhaps improve their production of raw silk. These included better breeding methods and the development of several types of reel that improved the quality of the thread or increased the speed with which it could be reeled off.[8] In a society without engineers, it is the workers directly involved in a technical task who are most likely to think of improvements and innovations. Of pre-Han and Han inventions Dieter Kuhn notes that "the spindle-wheel and the treadle-operated loom were invented within the circle of women workers, for they alone would have had both the working experi-

the Jacquard card. Some songs were still remembered by the weavers in a Chengdu workshop that Dieter Kuhn visited in 1979.

7. Sheng 1990; Dieter Kuhn, personal communication 1990. The Yuan state, avid to have as many craftsmen as possible working under its control to produce luxury goods to order, shifted the silk tax from tabbies to raw silk for use in its own workshops. It also conscripted almost all the craftsmen in China. In 1236, 720,000 craft households were called up, and in 1279 there were 420,000 households registered under hereditary artisan status, quite apart from other levies on craft labor. "The sons must practice [their father's] craft, the daughters embroider" (*Yuan shi, Xingfa zhi*, quoted Tong 1981: 192). The Eastern Weaving and Dyeing Bureau controlled 3,006 households, with 154 looms, producing a quota of 4,527 bolts of cloth and 1,152.8 pounds of wild silk (ibid.: 198). The 1328 tax in raw silk amounted to 655 tonnes (still less than 10 percent of total production, not including the private use of fabrics and silks) (Kuhn 1988: 288).

8. Breeding improvements included heating the room or shed in which the silkworms were raised so that they matured faster, or using trays that allowed any sick or dead worms to be spotted and removed more easily; there were also improved techniques for killing the moths inside the cocoon, so that reeling could be postponed or spread out over a longer period (Kuhn 1988: 318, 340–43, citing among other texts Wang Zhen's *Nong shu* of 1313). On improvements in reeling see Kuhn 1988: 357.

ence and technical skill required to see which alterations were necessary and practicable. In the S[o]ng dynasty the women were also in charge of silk-reeling, and it was evidently they who stimulated improvements in the silk-reeling frame" (fig. 18). One Song woman who was important in innovation, if not in invention, was Xu Wenmei, the wife of the poet-official Qin Guan (1049–1100), who wrote the *Can shu* (Book of sericulture) in or just before 1090. The *Can shu* is one of the key documents describing improvements and innovation in silk production during the Song. It is a short work of just ten paragraphs: half treat silk reeling, half other sericultural equipment and machinery. The details are precise, and the text depicts Shandong methods which Qin prefers to those of the south. In the preface he indicates that his knowledge came from his wife, whom he married in 1067 and who had been trained in Shandong methods as a girl.[9]

Some of the improvements in sericulture and reeling were expensive or required several workers, and were probably useful only in manorial households. Only better-off households could afford to keep the breeding room at a constant temperature. The cheap and simple treadle reels that rapidly became common during the Song were two and a half times as fast as hand reeling, but did not twist the thread as more complex and slower machines did. The most efficient way to organize reeling was for five women to work together using two silk reeling frames, a combination of labor and capital investment that most poor households would be unlikely to afford.[10] From contemporary descriptions of reeling Kuhn concludes that it was mainly wealthier rural households that took advantage of the increased market for raw silk, but adds that the best methods required too much concentration and time, and with the urgent demand lower standards of silk were produced, especially after 1300 or so. There were several types of simple and cheap but efficient roller reels that did not require teamwork to operate and so would be appropriate for peasant households. Although there was a small market for cocoons even as early as the Song and Yuan, reeled silk—whatever the quality—paid much

9. Kuhn 1988: 204, 355.
10. Two people prepared the cocoons in a pan of hot water, loosening the ends of the silk fibers, while another fed the fires. The two others each operated a reel. By this method about 36 kg of cocoons could be reeled a day, producing about 2.9 kg of raw silk depending on the cocoons, the quality of the thread, and the weather. A single worker doing everything herself could produce only about 480 g of thread, so the combination allowed the five workers to produce a total of about 500 g more thread per day, while using only two reels instead of five (*Nongzheng quanshu* 1639: 2: 861; Kuhn 1988: 388).

better, so it seems probable that many peasant households also came to specialize in silk reeling.[11]

To summarize, over the Song and Yuan sericulture spread to new regions. In response to new taxes and to the growing market for yarn from urban workshops, numerous peasant women raised silkworms and spun silk yarn, but many must have given up weaving silk tabbies as fashions changed and both tax and market demands declined.

THE COTTON BOOM

Another good reason for many rural households to abandon the slow and painstaking weaving of silk tabbies, indeed to give up the exacting tasks of sericulture altogether, was the advent of cotton, a light, fine cloth, warm in winter and cool in summer, of which a bolt could be woven in a single day on a simple loom.[12]

Cotton had been grown in the border regions for centuries. Cloth made in Tonkin or Yunnan from perennial varieties was a highly priced curiosity in medieval China. Chao Kang argues that the annual cottons of Central Asia, which might normally have been imported through Gansu and Shaanxi and naturalized like other crops introduced from the West (grapes, walnuts, alfalfa and the field pea among them), were effectively barred from China for many centuries by the huge silk industry of the capital Xi'an. Cultivation of the southern perennials gradually spread to Guangdong, Hainan, and Fujian, and it is thought that annual varieties were developed from perennials as cultivation spread northward into nontropical zones. They were probably established in the lower Yangzi by the twelfth century and had reached the Huai and Sichuan by the Yuan. Annual cottons were very adaptable. They grew in a wide range of soils and climates, and in the process of acclimatization the length of the staple and quantity of lint were improved, increasing yields, making processing easier, and improving the quality of the cloth, so that cotton became competitive with native Chinese textiles.[13]

Cotton is mentioned here and there in economic documents from the Song, but the industry was really established under the Yuan and expanded rapidly; by the late Ming cotton was worn by everyone and was cultivated all over China. Late Ming texts tell us that by the Wanli period

---

11. See Kuhn 1988: 388 on why the methods for reeling high-quality silk became less popular, and ibid.: 377 on the prices of yarn versus cocoons.

12. *Shouyi guangxun* 2/9–10.

13. Chao Kang 1977: 6–18.

(1573–1620) it was planted on half the best land in Hebei and Henan; of 2 million *mu* (roughly 130,000 hectares) of land reclaimed by the state and army in the Songjiang regions of the lower Yangzi, over half was planted with cotton, and it was replacing rice in upland regions of the lower Yangzi.[14]

Once again it was the taxation system, in conjunction with technical innovations, that stimulated the growth of the industry. The Mongols must have acquired their respect for cotton in the course of their travels through South Asia and the Middle East. Undeterred by ecological or social obstacles, they believed firmly in innovation by fiat. Efforts to enforce the adoption of pastoral nomadism in the North China plains and to establish orange groves in the frost-prone Shandong Peninsula failed, but the Yuan government's policies to promote cotton cultivation must be counted a resounding success. In 1289 official cotton bureaus were established in various provinces (Fujian, the lower and middle Yangzi) to provide technical information and encouragement to local farmers. State-commissioned agricultural works like the *Nongsang jiyao* (Fundamentals of agriculture and sericulture, published in 1273) included detailed sections on cotton cultivation. Then in 1296 cotton was incorporated into the tax system at very favorable rates compared to other textiles. Sericulture had been severely damaged by the wars of invasion, especially in the north. Yuan taxes on silk producers were high, but the amount of silk brought in was still inadequate to the state's wants. The incentives to the state to encourage cotton production, and to peasants to switch (if they could) from silk to cotton, were equally compelling.

No sooner did cotton become available than it became indispensable. The cloth was strong and durable, cheap, warmer than ramie or hemp in the winter, and it made padded garments that were almost as warm and much less expensive than silk; for summer wear it was absorbent and cool and made fine, light cloths that could be dyed in rich colors and calendered to a shine approaching the gloss of silk.

The Ming government, which used as much as fifteen to twenty million bolts of cotton a year, continued to promote cotton cultivation through taxation.[15] An edict of 1365 made cotton cultivation compulsory for all farmers with holdings over 5 *mu* (roughly a third of a hectare), but this proved unworkable because the soil was not always suitable and the farmers did

---

14. *Tiangong kaiwu* 41.

15. At 40 Chinese feet to the bolt, 20 million bolts would be the equivalent of some 260 million meters of cotton; compare this to the more than a thousand

not necessarily know the cultivation techniques; this edict was soon replaced by another stipulating that all farmers must pay part of their tax in cotton, which could also be substituted for grain in other quotas.[16] The demands of court and state were not diminished by the tax reforms of the late Ming, but the role of private entrepreneurs in procuring and distributing cloth was boosted, and the cloth industry continued to grow and develop, the largest in the empire until well into the twentieth century. By the late Ming cotton was grown and made into cloth in every corner of China. "In ten houses there will be at least one cotton loom, so there is no need to illustrate it," wrote Song Yingxing in 1637.[17]

The cultivation of cotton, however, spread much faster than did its processing, and one of the earlier effects of its adoption was to create a regional division of labor. The regionalization of the cotton industry was paralleled by the increasing fragmentation and commercialization of textile production in general; meanwhile agriculture was also becoming increasingly specialized, and the proportion of the population who were no longer primary producers but earned their livings by craft or trade increased. Cash commutations of basic taxes in kind became increasingly numerous and complex, and eventually in 1581 the Single Whip tax reforms did away with the traditional taxes in kind altogether. This consolidated the trend whereby women gave up weaving if more profitable occupations were available; conversely, where home weaving was more profitable than grain farming, peasant men might join their wives and daughters at the loom.

The regional division of labor in cotton production consolidated the role of the lower Yangzi as the manufacturing center of China, reducing the northern provinces to the status of an underdeveloped periphery that exported raw materials and imported finished goods. Big merchants controlled every stage of production. They bought up raw cotton, put it out at local markets for peasant women to spin and to weave, had the cloth dyed and calendered in town or city workshops, and then exported it all over China for sale. The system of putting-out in cotton production was different, however, from the system of putting-out that was growing up around urban centers of silk production, because it involved the manufac-

---

million yards of cotton goods exported annually by the Manchester warehouses to British India alone from the 1870s up to World War I (China was also an important market, but not as big as India) (Kidd 1993: 104).

16. Chao Kang 1977: 19.

17. *Tiangong kaiwu* 41.

ture of a relatively low-value commodity that required no specialized skills and only minimal capital investment in technology.[18]

The Yuan state would have been unable to enforce its promotion of cotton had it not been for a remarkable woman known as Huang Daopo, or Mistress Huang, said to be responsible for introducing all the equipment and techniques for ginning, bowing and spinning cotton to central China from the south. Weaving cotton presented no problem: traditional looms were perfectly suitable, provided the air was humid enough to produce good yarn. But before the end of the thirteenth century the Chinese did not have efficient techniques for cleaning the raw cotton, preparing the rovings and spinning them into yarn. Huang Daopo provided the solution. After her death Mistress Huang became the patron saint of cotton, with shrines in her honor as "The First Cotton Cultivator"; today she is still the heroine of a popular nursery rhyme. Born in about 1245, at the age of fifty she introduced the entire process of cotton cultivation and processing from Hainan Island to the district of Songjiang, just outside modern Shanghai. It is not clear whether Huang Daopo was born in Hainan or went there from Songjiang as a child. What is certain, as the fourteenth-century writer Tao Zongyi says in his short biography, is that all by herself this middle-aged woman developed a poor region into a prosperous center of cotton cultivation and manufacture.[19] Huang is credited with introducing to Songjiang in the later 1290s the cotton gin, which eliminated the seeds; the technique of bowing, which untangled and fluffed up the fiber ready for spinning; and the multiple-spindle treadle-operated wheel, which allowed one woman to spin several threads simultaneously.[20]

The cotton gin supposedly introduced by Huang Daopo was several times faster than the rollers that it replaced and much more economical. A large, three-person gin was invented between 1290 and 1313, but smaller gins that could be set up on a table and worked by two people were common from the outset, and gins worked by a single person were widely used by the Qing.[21] Cotton, which unlike bast-fibers requires true spinning, needs a smaller spindle wheel because the rovings have to

---

18. Nishijima argues that it is wrong to equate this merchant-controlled system with putting-out, since there is no evidence that the same merchants were involved in all stages ([1949] 1984).

19. *Chuogeng lu* of 1366, cited Kuhn 1988: 212.

20. The latter method was in fact already known at least eighty years earlier (Kuhn 1988: 212).

21. Ibid.: 190.

be fed in from a short distance to control the thickness. Otherwise the spindle wheels were much the same as those used to quill silk or twist ramie yarn, except that more than one thread could be spun at a time. The cheap wooden three-spindle treadle wheels that rapidly became an everyday piece of equipment could spin as much as 4 to 6 ounces of cotton in a working day (Kuhn says the sophistication of Chinese cotton spinning was unparalleled until the 1760s in England[22]). The single threads had to be doubled into yarn before weaving; Fan Guangcheng's eighteenth-century monograph on cotton, *Mianhua tu* (Illustrations of cotton planting and manufacture), reckoned it took a woman four days to prepare the pound of yarn needed for a day's weaving.[23]

The use of this new technology was circumscribed by climatic factors. To spin good-quality cotton thread the air must be humid, as it is throughout southern China in the summer. Although summers are extremely dry in the north, and thread spun there was brittle and uneven, as long as well water or river water was available cotton grew extremely well there and there was a great local demand for cotton cloth. A regional division of labor developed quickly. The southern provinces grew cotton but had the capacity to process much more than they grew; the northern provinces could produce raw cotton but could not process it. Commercial capital seized the opportunity. Brokers and merchants bought raw cotton from peasants in the north and transported it to the lower Yangzi and the Huai, where it was put out through local markets to peasant women to be spun and woven. The merchants returned to the north with finished cloth, which they sold in the same markets where they bought the raw cotton. What is striking about this arrangement is that the northern producers were in no position to strike any bargains, since it was impossible for them to process the raw cotton on the spot.

Songjiang in the Yangzi Delta became the proto-industrial heart of China, the center of cotton cloth production and the hub of a complex network of national trade. During the Ming, peasant women in Songjiang and the Shanghai region produced a wide range of cotton goods, mostly plain, but also patterned cloth and twills, as well as bolts that were narrower and longer than usual and went to the inland regions of the south, and other special types for the northwest and Beijing. Cloth from Chang-

---

22. Kuhn 1988: 201.

23. *Shouyi guangxun* 2/9–10. The *Mianhua tu* was written to encourage the development of cotton production in the northwestern region under Fan's jurisdiction and published in an expanded and imperially endorsed edition in 1808 under the title *Shouyi guangxun* (Expanded instructions on procuring clothing).

shu went to Shandong for peasants' clothes. Throughout the lower Yangzi, villages produced cotton cloth that was said to "pay for their taxes, their food and clothing, their equipment, their entertainments and ceremonies, all the costs of living and dying."[24]

The interregional cotton trade was huge and extremely lucrative for the merchants, but much less so for the cotton growers and for the peasant women who made the cloth. As cotton became everyday wear for all, cultivation spread, competition increased, and prices fell, but the merchants were not the losers. In the Shanghai region cotton merchants from other provinces, who worked through brokers, were treated like princes when they arrived each year in the local market towns to buy up cloth. They might bring anything between ten thousand and several hundred thousand ounces of silver with them to trade. The customer's price for a bolt of plain cloth was only 0.3 or 0.4 ounces,[25] so the peasant women who ginned, carded, spun and wove the raw cotton each earned just a fraction of this amount for their work.

Clearly under this system anyone who sold raw cotton but had to buy readymade cloth was getting a bad bargain. The terms of trade were so unequal in the Ming that the lower Yangzi provinces were buying northern cotton and exporting some of their own to Jiangxi and Fujian. "Raw cotton is cheap in the north and cloth is dear, while in the south the contrary is true," wrote Xu Guangqi in 1639. But at the beginning of the seventeenth century, the peasants of Suning in Hebei discovered that cotton could be spun and woven during the northern summer if it was done in underground cellars where humidity could be conserved. The situation changed rapidly. Xu added: "A few years ago the cloth made in Suning was not a tenth as good as that of the lower Yangzi. At first it was dreadfully coarse, but now it is very fine, almost up to the lower Yangzi quality." He goes on to say that the northern provinces still produce 20 percent less cloth than the east, and it fetches only 60 to 70 percent of the price: nevertheless, this was quite an achievement for a region that just two or three decades previously produced no cloth at all.[26] At roughly the same date the (lower Yangzi) Jiading gazetteer is already complaining that the northern market for Yangzi cloth has dried up, and the early Qing *Mianhua pu* (Treatise on cotton) says Jiangnan now has to import raw cotton from the south since it gets none from the north.[27]

24. Wanli (1573–1620) gazetteer of Jiading, quoted Tong 1981: 223.
25. Chao Kang 1977: 44.
26. *Nongzheng quanshu* j.35.
27. Quoted Tong 1981: 237.

Figure 16. Picking cotton (*Shouyi guangxun* 1/
14b–15a). Cotton thinning and picking were among
the few agricultural tasks that were considered appropriate for women (along with picking tea and
mulberry leaves), despite their bound feet. This picture shows a group of younger women hard at
work, while a granny and a little boy, helpfully carrying a wicker basket round his neck, look on.

With the dissemination of the Suning-style cellars, peasant families in the north became essentially self-sufficient in cloth. The men planted the cotton, their wives and daughters thinned out the bolls, picked them (fig. 16), processed them to yarn and wove a sturdy homespun that lasted two or three years (fig. 17). "Whole peasant families assemble, young and old: the mother-in-law leads her sons' wives, the mother supervises her daughters; when the wicker lantern is lit and the starlight and moonlight come slanting down, still the clack-clack of the spindle wheels comes from the house."[28] Any surplus was sold in the local shop or market, and went from there to nearby towns or to the riverboats. Salable surpluses per household were probably small, although by the late Qing the trade in northern cottons had reached considerable proportions; Chao Kang cites the remark of an eighteenth-century governor of Zhili that more cotton was now woven there than in the lower Yangzi. Large quantities were

28. Ninghe gazetteer, quoted Tong 1981: 306.

Figure 17.   Setting up a cotton loom (*Shouyi guang-xun* 2/18a). This picture shows that women routinely made use of the mechanical skills needed to assemble complex machinery; they did not just turn the handles or throw the shuttles on machines that had been set up for them by men.

exported to Korea, and the demand for raw cotton in the Hebei-Shandong plain stimulated cotton cultivation and eventually weaving too in peripheral zones.[29] However, homespun fetched very low prices, though presumably a little higher than the price of raw cotton. Women did not get high cash rewards for their work, but the equipment they needed was simple, they no longer had to buy clothes, and they were not exploited by a put-

29. Chao Kang 1977: 34. P. Huang remarks that the initial development of cotton cloth markets in the north depended on access to river transport (1985: 118–20).

ting-out system, as were many southern cotton weavers. Chao Kang sees this type of cotton cloth production as a "subsidiary activity" carried out by women and other "marginal labor." In fact, women's work in clothing the family was an important subsistence activity that substituted for otherwise unavoidable expenditure, even if it did not generate cash income. But since the families in question were no longer called on to put a monetary value on the cloth made by the women, it may well have counted in their eyes too as a "subsidiary activity." Where cloth was marketed, as Huang remarks, the sale of surpluses "often helped to sustain small family farms that would otherwise have collapsed under the pressures of population." What women could earn through spinning and weaving might be enough to "stave off tenancy or landlessness."[30] Officials certainly saw such contributions in a favorable light, but I have found no evidence as to whether it translated into general esteem for women's work.

The northern provinces were perhaps unique in that what Esther Goody calls "cottage-craftsman production" of cotton cloth,[31] once established, persisted into the twentieth century. That is to say, peasant families performed all stages of the production of cloth, owning their equipment and exercising direct control over their raw materials and labor; they also had direct access to the market for any salable surplus.[32] In other, economically more advanced regions of China the steady development of commerce and changes in comparative advantage affected the level of peasant involvement in cotton, but although merchants were involved, putting-out did not necessarily develop. Cotton cultivation had been profitable in Fujian, but by the Qing most farmers had given it up in favor of sugar, which was exported throughout China and overseas. Local merchants would pay for part of the sugar with raw cotton from the lower Yangzi, which the sugar farmers' wives spun and wove mostly for family use. As markets grew not just for Fujianese sugar but also for its excellent teas, it became more advantageous for peasant women to give up weaving, buy cloth, and use their time processing the sugar grown on their farms, and tending, harvesting and curing tea. Fujian started to import cotton cloth, as did neighboring Guangdong. In the nineteenth century Sichuan and Shanxi peasants started growing opium on their cotton land. But opium did not require female labor, and so these provinces imported raw cotton from Hebei, not finished cloth from the lower Yangzi. In Hebei between

30. P. Huang 1985: 120.
31. E. Goody 1982: 3–5.
32. See the various remarks quoted by P. Huang 1985: 119.

a fifth and a third of all farmland was planted with cotton, some of which was exported to Korea.[33]

It was in the lower Yangzi provinces that merchant control and the putting-out system were most developed. There we find what Goody calls "cottage-laborer production": merchants controlled access to raw materials and to the market; although they were not paid daily wages and did not work in large manufactures, the cloth workers were essentially wage laborers paid for piecework. While elsewhere in China spinning and weaving cotton were exclusively women's work, in the proto-industrial villages of the lower Yangzi whole families toiled at the wheel and loom, producing various qualities of cotton cloth that were exported all over China. Peasant families were organized by merchant capitalists and locked into a system of mass production, with levels of self-exploitation typical of proto-industrialization elsewhere in the world.

There are many parallels with the organization of the luxury silk industry of the period, also centered in the lower Yangzi, but there are significant differences too. The bulk of the cotton cloth produced was cheap, plain cloth. No special skills were required for any of the processes of its production, nor did any stage require specialized and expensive equipment comparable to the looms used for fancy silks. Ginning, carding, spinning and weaving were all carried out under the same roof. Peasant households sold the plain cloth back to the merchant, and a large part of the value added to the finished cloth came from dyeing and calendering, which the merchants organized (again through a putting-out process) in separate urban workshops.[34]

Some fancy cottons were produced, but although they often borrowed the names of silk weaves they were not nearly as complex, and most could be woven on an ordinary flat loom with three or four treadles, though they took longer to make than plain cloth and could cost several times as much. In country towns near Songjiang up to twenty different kinds of cotton cloth might be on display in the market, including the nationally famous "three-shuttle" cloth which the emperor used for his underwear; it was woven in the style of silk gauze, and cost 2 ounces a bolt as compared to 0.3 or 0.4 ounces for ordinary cloth.[35] Much fancier cottons were produced in the state manufactures and some urban workshops of the Ming and Qing, including velvets and patterned cloths made on a draw-

33. Chao Kang 1977: 23.
34. Tong 1981: 304.
35. Chao Kang 1977: 48.

loom. By the end of the Ming dynasty Songjiang was to cotton what Hangzhou and Suzhou were to silk. "The common occupation is spinning and weaving (other skills are rare), and their fine [cotton] damasks, three-shuttle cloth, lacquer gauzes and cut-nap velvets are all the best in the world. Their craftsmen command all the same skills as those of cities like Hangzhou and Suzhou. The products of the Songjiang region are all good for practical use, for example their damasks and plain cloth, which clothe the empire and are unequalled even by [the silks of] Suzhou and Hangzhou."[36]

Where fancy cottons were made, or in close proximity to urban weaving centers where cloth was made in family workshops (*zuofang*), there was often a further division of labor, similar to that in the silk industry, by which weaving households purchased their yarn from poorer spinning households. "Poor people without capital cannot afford to make cloth from cotton yarn; they sell a few ounces of yarn every day for food," says a sixteenth-century local history.[37] A century later the encyclopedist Chen Menglei cites a text on the Shanghai region which says: "The spinners and weavers are not confined to the villages but are found in the towns too. The old women from the villages go to the market in the mornings to exchange yarn for raw cotton; the next morning they bring the next lot of yarn and so on without a break. The weavers can usually produce a bolt a day; some don't even go to bed at night."[38] These texts do not tell us the sex of workers, but we can assume that the village spinners were women, while in the urban weaving households, as in silk-weaving families, the weavers were male and used yarn spun by their wives and daughters as well as what they purchased from outside. Until the advent of industrial filatures in the late nineteenth century, only the barest living could be made by spinning cotton.

Even near Songjiang weaving was still a female activity in some villages. The Kangxi (1662–1723) gazetteer for Songjiang says: "In the weaving villages they make very fine cottons; during the agricultural off-seasons they produce some ten thousand bolts daily. The women work hard to supplement farming income by weaving."[39] Presumably the high

36. Songjiang gazetteer, cited Tong 1981: 232. Chen Weiji (1984: ch. 8) gives a disappointingly cursory account of patterned cottons; almost all scholarship on Chinese woven patterns has focused heavily on silk.

37. Wanli gazetteer for Jiashan, quoted Tong 1981: 223.

38. *Gujin tushu jicheng* of 1726, j.690, quoting a description of rural and urban cotton production in the Shanghai area (quoted Tong 1981: 233).

39. Quoted Tong 1981: 348.

figures given for the agricultural off-seasons mean that men took over at the looms when they were not busy in the fields. In other villages men were also involved, part- or full-time, often abandoning agriculture altogether in places where the land was poor. Huang Ang's early Qing monograph on the Wuxi region tells us that in Wuxi, "farming only suffices to feed the village people for the three winter months; they begin weaving in the spring, exchanging the cloth for the rice they eat. . . . Even if there is a bad [rice] harvest, as long as the cotton ripens elsewhere the Wuxi villagers do not suffer too badly. . . . In villages where the soil is very poor, both men and women work exclusively at spinning and weaving."[40] In Wuxi the peasants produced some types of cloth (20 or 30 feet to the bolt) that they exchanged with local merchants for raw cotton, and another type (24 feet to the bolt) that was exchanged for rice or cash and was taken by the merchants to sell in the Huai region; total production in the district was said to be at least several tens of millions of bolts yearly.[41]

Qing texts from Shanghai and elsewhere show that even in regions where fancy cottons were produced in urban workshops, though buying and marketing became increasingly complex and competitive, the source of production remained domestic. A Kangxi memorial talks of "requisitioning 300,000 bolts of indigo-dyed cotton made in Shanghai prefecture: after the autumn all the peasant households weave cloth and depend on this for their living." Another early Kangxi text tells us that most lower Yangzi villages had cloth depots with dyers and calenderers who were all hired from the district of Jiangning. In the Hangzhou environs "the men and women of the villages all weave cotton."[42] The population of the lower Yangzi increased steadily during the Qing, and as the cotton business became more competitive, exploitation became more severe and production standards declined. The Qianlong (1736–96) gazetteer for Shanghai says, "Some of their cotton cloth used to be as fine as silk tabby, but now the weavers compete for profits, skimp over width and length, and everywhere you find that quality has declined."[43]

With increasing subdivision of the labor process, the differentiation in the labor force became pronounced. It was especially marked in Songjiang, the most advanced of all the cotton regions, but in the late Ming and Qing Nanjing too became a huge center of fancy silk and fine cotton production (not to mention all the other luxury crafts that a Chinese capital

40. Huang Ang, [Wu]xi Jin[kui] zhi xiao lu, quoted ibid.
41. Tong 1981: 349. See also Elvin 1973: 270–74 on putting-out.
42. Quoted ibid.: 302.
43. Quoted ibid.: 301.

needed).[44] In these centers, households that could afford to weave (that is, to invest in a loom and to make regular purchases of yarn) were privileged compared to those that had to sell yarn for a living.[45] Another resource for poor village people without capital was to make up fancy items that were then sold nationally. For instance during the Wanli period (1573–1620) "Songjiang started making kerchiefs so light and pretty that they were soon in demand even far away, and the town authorities allowed over a hundred shops to set up in the western suburbs to sell them; men and women in nearby districts made these kerchiefs for a living, a new source of income for the population."[46] "Many of the women who cannot weave take the cloth at market price and use it to sew [kerchiefs]."[47]

By the late Ming and Qing we can distinguish three distinct relationships of peasant households to cotton production. First was subsistence production. In economic backwaters where the only exports were raw materials, there were few alternative productive occupations for women, and cotton was spun and woven in every home; either the cotton was grown on their own farms, as in Hebei, or if other crops were more profitable raw cotton was purchased, as in the opium districts of Shanxi. Second, if peasant women could contribute more to the family income by processing commodities like sugar or tea, they would give up weaving and purchase the necessary cloth. These two systems of production were essentially independent of the control of the cotton brokers. But in the manufacturing conurbations of the lower Yangzi, and eventually of Nanjing and Guangdong, the previous interregional trade in raw cotton had given merchants tight control over production, which they exercised through a putting-out system. As exploitation intensified, the division of labor within and between households changed. In some families men continued to work in the fields while women spun and wove, using raw cotton distributed at the village market every morning by brokers; in other families men gave up farming and took over from their wives at the loom. In the poorest households that could no longer afford to weave, women were still involved in textile work, either as spinners or as pieceworkers making fancy goods, both of which were very poorly paid.

44. L. Li 1981: ch. 2.
45. Simple looms by then seemed to count as an investment that only the relatively well-off could afford. In earlier times when cloth was a tax requirement, every household had to own a simple loom. It could be that timber prices increased, and also that ordinary families no longer had the basic carpentry skills needed to build a loom.
46. Fan Lian, *Yunjian jumu chao,* quoted Tong 1981: 235.
47. *Gujin tushu jicheng* j.690, quoted Tong 1981: 235.

SILK PRODUCTION IN THE MING AND QING

As commercialization intensified in the late Ming and Qing cotton cloth production spread all over China, dividing regionally between a rural subsistence sector and a commercial sector, also dependent on peasant household production but concentrated in the suburban villages and market towns of the economically most advanced regions of China. Since cotton competed favorably with silk, its development had important repercussions on the evolution of the silk industry. During the Ming and Qing the rural production of silk tabbies almost disappeared except in the villages of the lower Yangzi. The balance of products shifted markedly from plain to fancy silks, which were mostly woven in workshops concentrated in the cities and suburbs of the main economic centers in the south. Raw silk was still produced in rural households, again largely concentrated in the lower Yangzi: sericulture died out in regions that could not produce high enough quality thread for fancy silks (fig. 18).

One reason for the shift out of rural production of silk cloth was that silk tabbies, which had been made both in peasant and in manorial households, suffered badly from the competition from cotton, especially after 1581 when the state no longer provided any direct demand for silk tabbies even in traditional silk-weaving regions. Another factor was that the fancy silks made in manorial households or even in certain long-established urban centers were no longer able to compare with the price of fine cottons or the sophistication of the highly specialized silks of the southern conurbations. Even rural production of raw silk and yarn was affected, because all the best Jiangnan businesses preferred to use raw silk from the local district Huzhou, which was of exceptionally high quality.

During the later Ming silk tabbies were still produced in Zhili and Jiangxi for sale in the central markets like Hangzhou, but the quantity was insignificant compared to what was produced by urban workshops run with hired labor in Hangzhou and Suzhou, the lower Yangzi centers of fine silk weaving.[48] Sichuan, Guangdong and Fujian also continued to produce some homemade tabbies, but mostly they exported raw silk to the lower Yangzi. The Sichuan monopoly of the finest brocades was now a thing of the past, and the silk industries of Hebei, Henan and Shandong had also fallen into decline, in part because of effects of war, in part because of shifts in the regional economic balance.[49]

48. Hangzhou gazetteer, j.53, quoted Chen Shiqi 1958: 7.
49. Tong 1981: 231.

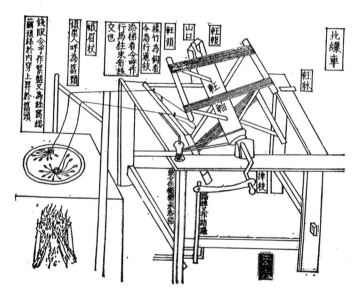

Figure 18. Southern (above) and northern (below) silk-reeling frames (early Ming illustrations to Wang Zhen's *Nong shu* j.20). In the fourteenth century, northern silk technology was more advanced than southern; the northern frame shown here reels two yarns simultaneously, the southern only one. The lower illustration names and explains the parts of the machine, but the drawing does not make all the necessary connections and notably omits the treadle that turns the reel. The upper illustration gives a clearer idea of how a reeling frame actually worked. The cocoons were floated in a pan of water heated in a stove. The hot water loosened the gum around each cocoon so the single long fiber could be wound off. The threads from several cocoons were fed together through an eyelet (the square hole in a copper coin), and as they emerged from the water they were twisted into a single yarn and wound onto a reel.

A typical case was Luzhou in Shanxi, which had produced famous tabbies for centuries: "The gentry all wear Lu tabbies," according to Lü Kun,
who served in the region in the sixteenth century. The tabbies were produced not in peasant households, however, but in workshops in small
towns, and in much of the countryside women had apparently lost the
skills of textile production. "[Governor Lü Kun] ordered all female adults
without occupation in certain districts of the province to learn spinning and
weaving."[50] The women's involvement in silk making lasted no longer
than Lü's tenure, and by the fall of the Ming even the Lu workshops had
come to a sad end. A document of 1660 tells us that

> the weaving of these tabbies used to pay all the official expenses and pro-
> vided support for poor people. But winding, twisting yarn, dyeing and fill-
> ing bobbins, while all extremely painstaking work, brought only tiny prof-
> its, and since the local conditions of these mountain towns were not
> suitable for sericulture, the raw silk had to be bought from Shandong,
> Henan and Zhili. . . . At the end of the Ming there were over 3,000 looms,
> but all the weavers had to take out loans and their debts piled up and ru-
> ined them, so by 1644 there were only two or three hundred looms left. Al-
> though the weavers worked hard for themselves and for official exactions,
> toiling day and night with their wives and children, they had to pay all
> their expenses out of their own pockets and accumulated only debts—how
> could they go on? Now in 1660 they are thinking of burning their looms,
> repudiating their debts and, in great sorrow, running away.[51]

The collapse of the Luzhou silk-weaving industry must also have had
severe repercussions for the peasant sericulturalists nearby, as well as
those in Sichuan, Shandong, Henan and Zhili who had sold raw silk to
Lu, for it is unlikely that the raw silk of these regions was able to compete
except in local markets. Sericultural skills died out completely in whole
provinces. P.-E. Will tells us that by the time Chen Hongmou served as
governor of the neighboring province of Shaanxi, on and off between 1743
and 1758, a local tradition of sericulture stretching back to the Zhou dynasty had been entirely forgotten, except for a handful of places where
officials or gentry had made efforts to revive the lost skills. A silk bureau
was established in Xi'an in the 1740s after an official named Yang Shen
had spent some years promoting mulberry cultivation, and Chen coordinated his efforts with the bureau. "The trees became productive just one
or two years after the shoots had been planted, and once silkworm eggs
had been imported and the breeding techniques had been taught to volun-

50. Chao Kang 1977: 21, emphasis added.
51. Lu'an gazetteer, j.34, quoted Tong 1981: 298.

teer farmers, the problem was to import the skills and install the machinery and infrastructure for textile production."[52]

The intention was not to reestablish Shaanxi as a national center of silk weaving. Chen's policies of resuscitation, like many others of the time, were intended to "enhance local self-sufficiency" so that local people did not have to sell scarce food grain to buy imported cloth. Peasant households were to be educated to see that mulberries, cocoons and raw silk were all sources of income, and the silk cloth was initially to be woven in urban workshops, though Chen hoped that eventually peasants (presumably "females without occupation," as in the case of Lu) would learn to weave tabbies again at home. Like Lü Kun's project, Chen's did not long outlive his tenure in the district, but similar projects were temporarily successful in Yunnan and Guizhou, and local household weaving also survived in peripheral regions far from the lower Yangzi metropolitan vortex, like Zhili and Jiangxi.

Even at the Ming-Qing transition, there were places where the domestic weaving of tabbies for sale remained a profitable activity, but the increasing involvement of brokers in rural household production is evident. The rural districts around the Taihu Lake, near the great silk-weaving centers of Suzhou and Hangzhou, produced the best raw silk in all China, the famous Huzhou silk. Given the ever-expanding demand for raw silk from the workshops of Hangzhou and Suzhou, it is surprising to observe the vitality of rural tabby production in Huzhou in the seventeenth century. Perhaps it was the high quality of the locally produced yarn that kept these tabbies competitive.

The *Shenshi nongshu* (Agricultural treatise of Master Shen), composed in about 1640 just before the fall of the Ming, describes sericulture in a landlord household in Huzhou:

52. Will 1991: 12. Susan Mann reminds us that such proposals took as their model an essay by the seventeenth-century scholar Gu Yanwu, who had written an essay entitled "The Profitability of Weaving," advising the state to promote silk weaving in households on border areas (Mann 1992a: 83). Both Gu and Chen suggest that "master weavers" and skilled craftsmen able to construct looms should be brought in to transmit their skills to the local people. It would be interesting to know whether such plans to teach women new skills were thwarted by the reluctance of families to let their women go outside the home to be taught by strange men. There is a paradox here. "In the minds of Qing statecraft writers, those regions in China where 'women wove' were culturally and even morally superior to those areas where women had no specialized home crafts" (Mann 1992a: 86). At the same time morally and culturally superior women were not supposed to leave their own quarters, nor were they supposed to consort with strange men. Perhaps the husbands went to the weaving classes for them?

Men till and women weave: these are the basic tasks of a farming household. And especially in my area, every household weaves. Some are extraordinarily skilled and work from early morning till late at night, and
they produce an incalculable amount. Two women will weave 120 bolts of
tabby a year. Each ounce of tabby is usually worth 1 string of cash [one-
tenth of an ounce of silver], so for 120 bolts, after paying for 700 ounces
of warp thread worth 50 ounces of silver and 500 of weft worth 27, plus
the cost of reels and other equipment and wax for the yarn at 5 ounces,
and 10 ounces for the women's food—altogether something over 90
ounces of silver—there remain 30 ounces' profit. If you breed your own
silkworms, the gain will be that amount more. There is no doubt that a
household should weave, but if it lacks capital, then buying raw silk on
credit will incur extra costs, as will selling the cloth [back to the broker]
and the exchange rate against silver, and then there will be the amount
lost to "rat pilfering" which is hard to calculate. But if a household has
weaving women, whether they weave or not they will still eat, and [if they
do weave,] without counting their food and wages there will be a natural
profit, even if it is just a few coins a day, that the household can count
upon in its calculations.[53]

Shen is describing a landlord household that purchases its silk thread,
already made up into warp or weft yarns. From the figures he gives, we
can calculate that weaving tabby added 50 percent to the purchase price of
warp thread, and almost double to weft. Since the thread was probably
purchased through middlemen, we can assume that the price paid to the
reeling or spinning household would have been substantially less. The
returns to the investment in looms and skilled labor were thus relatively
high and reliable, especially if one had the ready cash to avoid going
through a broker to obtain the yarn. Hiring two women weavers who
wove 120 bolts brought a profit equivalent to thirty bushels of hulled rice
a year, whereas the hire of male labor for agricultural work often brought
a net loss, but was necessary, said Shen, if you wanted to farm at all.[54]

Although Shen declares that every household in his district weaves

53. *Bu nongshu* 84. In 1647 Zhang Lüxiang transcribed a work describing agriculture and sericulture in a landowner's household, known as the *Shenshi nongshu* (Agricultural treatise of Master Shen) because it was composed by a Huzhou
landlord called Shen. In 1658 Zhang completed his additions, based on his own
experience in nearby Tongxiang, and the two works were subsequently published
together under the title of *Bu nongshu* (Supplemented treatise on agriculture).
Shen and Zhang were both unusual for the time in that they were resident landlords actively involved in farming. In both the localities described, silk is of central
importance, but ramie, fish ponds, pigs, poultry and goats are also described as
profitable ventures, as well as domestic industries like brewing. Growing rice, it
turns out, was more a labor of love than a source of profit.

54. *Bu nongshu* 76–77.

silk, it seems probable that poorer peasant households, which had limited labor and insufficient capital to buy extra looms, would content themselves with the lower profits of sericulture and reeling, as well as hiring out their women to weave in landlord workshops. If they did weave, using only family labor but assuming other costs to be equal, the profits would be one-third instead of one-quarter of an ounce of silver for each bolt. If they also raised their own silkworms, net profits would be about 0.4 ounces of silver or 0.4 bushels of hulled grain for each bolt woven (compared to 0.25 bushels per bolt in Shen's gentry household). If we compare Shen's figures with those given by Chen Fu for sericulture in the Yangzi Delta in the mid-twelfth century, we see that profits have dropped enormously. Chen says that a family of ten, raising ten trays of silkworms, would have enough raw silk to weave 31.2 bolts of tabby at a profit of 1.4 bushels of hulled grain per bolt. Even so, and despite the high demand for raw silk, five centuries later it still seems to have been considered worthwhile for sericultural households in Huzhou to invest in weaving tabbies, but obviously the intervention of brokers, providing raw silk on credit and buying back the cloth at their own prices, greatly reduced the profits of any family that was short of capital.

In the nearby district described by Zhang Lüxiang, the land was unsuitable for draft animals so the fields had to be tilled with hoes, and nobody could manage more than 10 *mu* (about 0.66 hectares). Most land was given out to tenants, and since the population was dense rents were high: half the crop. Women's income was crucial to survival. Zhang devotes a whole section of his short treatise specifically to women's work and its importance; he is the only agricultural writer I know of who is so explicit about the female contribution to the household economy.[55] In the western half of Tongxiang, he says, the village women's work consisted of weaving coarse tabbies from waste silk and ordinary tabbies, as well as ramie cloth; in the eastern villages they helped in the fields, tended the mulberries, raised silkworms and wove silk. In Zhang's own village the women made cotton cloth and bred silkworms for floss.[56]

The market for raw silk or even cocoons continued to grow as the

55. The essential nature of women's textile work is implicit in all the agricultural treatises that include sections on textile production—that is to say, almost all of them—as it is in specialized monographs on sericulture, cotton, or other textiles. Although most treatises allude in general terms to the importance of women's work for the welfare of state and people, Zhang alone gives precise figures for the relative contributions of men's work and women's work to the household to back up his contention that women's work is just as important as men's.

56. *Bu nongshu* 148, 151.

number of urban workshops and the amount of fancy silks they produced grew. Huzhou, where Shen came from, produced the best raw silk in all China, and in the Wanli period (1573–1620) "even a plot the size of a handkerchief will be planted with mulberries ... the rich have mere patches of rice field but thousands of acres of mulberry land." Huzhou continued to export raw silk right though the Qing, in fact it almost monopolized the market. At the end of the Ming the weavers of Fujian and Guangdong as well as Hangzhou and Suzhou depended on Huzhou silk; only the silk weavers of Luzhou (soon to become extinct) bought raw silk from Langzhou in Sichuan. Luzhou produced only tabbies, but Fuzhou made satins both for internal markets and for export; Guangzhou (Canton) produced "satins of a fine, even texture and fresh, bright and rich color, while its gauzes and monochrome patterned silks outshine even those of Suzhou and Hangzhou, so that the gauzes are bought all over China and the satins almost as much." Since southern yarns lacked luster, Fujian and Guangdong were both dependent on the lower Yangzi for the raw materials to make their luxury products.[57]

Meanwhile in Huzhou and nearby, profits from weaving were declining. "The income from weaving gets smaller day by day," says a lower Yangzi gazetteer for the Qianlong period (1736–96). Giving figures from the tax records, it compares the value of raw silk and of the equivalent weight of woven tabby over the two centuries up to Qianlong 12 (1747). As table 1 shows, according to this source the value added by weaving fell from 300 to 350 percent in the Jiaqing to 150 to 200 percent in the Kangxi and to a mere 55 to 110 percent in 1747.

As a result many lower Yangzi sericulturalists preferred to specialize in cocoons or raw silk instead of cloth. For many peasant women the demanding tasks of sericulture must have provided small rewards, but since the land was poor and the taxes high, few peasant households had any choice but to produce silk. Large households with capital had an advantage over peasant families, since they could afford the capital and labor to reel faster.[58] I have already mentioned the arrangement considered most economic by the end of the Ming, where five workers together managed two reeling frames. But as Kuhn remarks, even women in large silk-producing households only worked seasonally at reeling, so their skills could never equal those of professional silk workers in workshops.

57. Huzhou gazetteers, j.29, quoted Chen Shiqi 1958: 7; *Nongzheng quanshu* j.31, and Qianlong (1736–96) gazetteer, both quoted Tong 1981: 231.
58. Kuhn 1988: 388.

Table 1. Value Added by Weaving Silk

	Price 1 oz Raw Silk (fen)	Price 1 oz Tabby (fen)	Value Added by Weaving (%)
Jiaqing (1522–67)	2	8–9	300–350
Kangxi (1622–1723)	3–4	10	150–200
Qianlong 12 (1747)	6–8	13	50–110

SOURCE: Qianlong gazetteer for Wujiang; adapted from Tong 1981: 296.

Although the scale of the Ming and Qing imperial silk-weaving workshops was still huge, by now they accounted for only a minor share of the total urban production of luxury silks. Artisans no longer had permanent duties of state service but were expected to serve on a rota system: in the early Ming embroiderers and patterned gauze weavers had to serve annually; reelers, dyers and ordinary weavers every three years; quillers every four and tailors every five.[59] The rest of the time they looked for hire in private workshops. Since the most elaborate silks were still those made in the imperial workshops, artisans' skills were important in maintaining levels of technical expertise in the private sector. The private silk industry of Nanjing began to rival that of the lower Yangzi cities after the Ming dynasty established its capital and state manufactures there.

In the private sector there were significant changes in the relations of production in urban silk production. At the end of the Ming, an urban "loom household" owned its own loom or looms, and used either domestic labor or hired hands to spin and weave raw silk purchased on the market. Unlike rural landlord households, the urban loomowners did not hire women.[60] Urban male weavers were highly specialized, but despite their valuable skills they had less security than their rural sisters who were hired

59. *Ming huiyao* 189, quoted Chen Shiqi 1958: 72.
60. While Ming and Qing texts on rural subsistence silk production have illustrations showing women involved in all the processes, the *Tiangong kaiwu*, which concentrates on the production of commodities, shows men not only weaving but also quilling or twisting silk. The significance of these illustrations is that the author, Song Yongxing, wished to emphasize the most advanced forms of technology in use at the time. He therefore devoted far more space to urban workshops than to household production of textiles. It is notable that he also includes the finishing processes like dyeing and calendering—which do not figure in the treatment of textiles in agricultural treatises.

by the year and fed whether there was weaving for them to do or not. The urban artisans were paid a wage only for the days they worked, and were employed only to work at their speciality. If there was no work for them, they starved. "There is a master who calculates the number of days and pays them accordingly; if there are additional tasks he may call in freelance workers, who assemble at the bridges waiting to be hired, satin workers at one bridge, gauze workers at another. Those who twist silk are called wheel-workers. Several dozens or a hundred may stand together in the Xianqi quarter craning their necks expectantly; after eating their congee they break up and go home. If the loom households lack work then this class has no way to make a living." "The loom households provide the capital, the loom-worker the labor, and they both depend on each other for a steady living."[61]

As new centers developed in Fujian, Guangdong and then Nanjing, and the silk trade became more competitive, the advantages of owning capital became more marked and exploitation intensified. Employers played off ruined peasants looking for city work against experienced textile workers. While it was still possible to write convincingly of the interdependence of the loomowners and their workers in the late Ming, during the Qing no worker imagined that the resources were equally pooled.[62] A memorial of 1734 speaks of a shift from daily wages to piece rates for hired weavers.[63] Meanwhile the loomowners were displacing more and more of the burdens of production through the process of putting-out. Poor women were employed to wind the silk for workshops, but many silk merchants, instead of weaving silk on their own premises, hired out their looms to weaving families. In this way the owners did not have to deal with intran-

---

61. *Wanli shilu*, quoted Tong 1981: 226 and Chen Shiqi 1958: 7.

62. Weavers were always a rebellious lot. During the Ming the loomowners (who had to pay taxes on their looms and output) usually allied with the weavers against the state. By Qing times, the weavers rebelled not against the state but against the loomowners (see the essay on urban riots in the Ming and Qing by Tsing Yuan [1979], who also documents a series of riots by calenderers in Qing Suzhou). An early Qing memorial says that "the loom households of Suzhou used to hire many workers to weave ... and paid them a daily wage, and originally everyone agreed that both sides gained from this arrangement. But journeymen without training, who didn't know the work, were fined by their employers, which engendered great resentment. They grouped together into a union and called a strike for higher wages. This put the loom households out of work, and they sacked the weavers. Then loom owner He Junheng and others requested that a stone be engraved registering a perpetual ban on such strikes" (Tong 1981: 345).

63. Tong 1981: 294.

sigent groups of male workers, and the work of the professional weavers was supplemented by that of their whole family.

A late Qing work describes a Nanjing satin that used seventeen thousand warp threads made from Huzhou raw silk, "first dyed and then parcelled out to winders, who are poor women who wind three or four reels a day, earning money for rice, enough to get their daily food."[64] It goes on to say that "constructing a satin loom requires the work of many skilled craftsmen and it is the piece of equipment that requires the most capital in all China." The author tells us that Nanjing silk production was concentrated in the southwest suburbs. "The households that run looms are called *zhangfang* [credit houses]; the loom households borrow the looms and take the raw materials from them, then weave the silk which their masters control for quality; small households without capital generally depend on the *zhangfang* for a living." Four satin companies bought up the products organized by the *zhangfang*, and throughout the period from Qianlong to the late Qing there were apparently some thirty thousand looms making satins in Nanjing, not to mention looms for gauzes, damasks, brocades and carpets, products exported all over China and abroad.

The main rural contribution, still predominantly female, to fancy silks between the Song and the late Ming was the breeding of silkworms and reeling of raw silk. With the development of the new putting-out system, rural women were once again involved in the production of fancy cloth—not as managers or skilled weavers, but rather as auxiliary workers, reelers and spinners, even within the context of family production. As the putting-out system developed in the late Ming, silk weaving overflowed from Suzhou into surrounding villages like Shengze, many villages abandoned agriculture altogether, and everyone in the family worked together: "Poor people all wove themselves, and had their offspring change the patterns, while the women's labor was insufficient to prepare the yarn and they reeled silk from morning to night. As soon as their sons and daughters were ten, they all toiled day and night to earn their bread."[65]

Producing silk cloth was no longer a female domain: the women were reduced to the indispensable but inglorious task of making the yarn while their husbands wove and took the finished cloth to market. This division of labor was a symbiosis, an interdependence, just like that between the workshops and the hired laborers—but the inherent hierarchy is clear in both cases. Furthermore, women's contribution to the production of cloth

64. Chen Zuolin, *Fenglin xiaozhi* j.3, quoted Tong 1981: 292.
65. Wujiang gazetteer, j.38, quoted Tong 1981: 227.

and to the income earned by its sale was no longer distinct, it was subsumed. Where once they had been in charge of the whole process of producing silk fabrics, now they were neither managers nor weavers but
humble spinners and reelers. This was true in urban and rural "loom
households," where all the tasks were performed under the same roof, as
well as in the urban workshops where most weaving had been performed
by men since Song times. In short, in both commercial and household
divisions of labor, women were now restricted to the worst rewarded and
technically least demanding tasks. It is not surprising, then, to see a modern scholar, writing on the industrialization of silk production in the late
nineteenth century, describe the changes in the workforce as "the feminization of silk-weaving."[66] By the end of the Qing, what reason was there
to remember that once women had woven almost all the silk in China?

66. So 1986, summarized Schneider 1987: 435.

6 Women's Work and Women's Place

The canonical expression "men till and women weave" expressed a relationship of complementarity rather than of subordination between husband and wife, at least at the level of work. The complex changes in the textile industry that took place between the Song and the Qing, however, by and large displaced women as weavers; women were deskilled, and their contribution to textile production was devalued, marginalized, or subsumed within male-headed household production. What might the meanings and consequences of such changes have been? It seems as if the changes in the Chinese textile industry I have described, and the consequent shifts in women's economic contribution to the household, must have contributed to an alteration in conceptions of gender roles. But how should material changes of this kind be translated into social meaning, and what other factors need to be taken into account?

The masking or marginalization of women's economic contributions through new divisions of labor is not a uniquely Chinese phenomenon. It is a process familiar from many other societies in transition to a commercialized economy. In *The Origin of the Family, Private Property and the State*, Engels argued that in the process of social differentiation which accompanied the development of the means of production and private rights to property, women became restricted to an unwaged sphere of reproductive activities distinct from a male sphere of socially recognized productive work. In this way women lost the status of full social adults to become subordinate "wives and wards." From Engels on, marxist and feminist scholars have argued that the reduced importance accorded to women's work under the pressures of commercialization and proto-industrialization has been a central factor in the consolidation of patriarchy around the world. But patriarchy takes many forms, even within a single society. To understand what these changes in the Chinese gender division of labor signified at the time, it is worth noting that they were paralleled in the proto-industrial textile industries of many regions of early modern Europe, as they were in other parts of the world under the influence of colonialism.[1] But if we wish to use evidence from the Chinese textile industry to clarify the nature and history of Chinese patriarchy (or patriarchies), we must try to unravel the complicated tangle of meanings attributed to "women's work" or "womanly work" in late imperial China— and this in the context of a historical trend toward commercialization and specialization in which the meanings of different kinds of men's work also changed, reflecting new social hierarchies and tensions. There are three aspects of textile production that I consider in this regard. They include the attribution of specialist knowledge and skills; the specifically Chinese construction of the economic, social and political value of women's work; and the role of cloth in transcending the spatial boundaries of gender segregation to link the inner and outer worlds of Chinese society.

I would like to signal at this point one noteworthy and initially surprising feature of the increasing marginalization of women in textile production to which I return later, namely the response it generated among powerful men. If the masking of women's productive contributions to the family economy served to strengthen the patriarchal power structure of the Chinese family, then one might expect that the Confucian theorists and legislators of Chinese patriarchy would accept such masking with approval, or at least let it go unmentioned, rather than actively contesting it. But far from accepting the dwindling of women's recognized earning capacity as a mark of their subordinate position, by the late Ming and early Qing many members of the educated male elite, from the emperor down, were dismayed by what they perceived as an unnatural phenomenon that threatened the social order. In both their private and their public capacities they made numerous efforts to restore women's role as weavers. When we consider the nature of the policies devised and the reasons they gave for bringing women back to the loom, for restoring to women their work and the dignity that work implied, we are faced with an apparent paradox. The men at the apex of imperial China's patriarchal hierarchy did not want women's productive role to be masked within the family— they wanted it restored, made clearly visible, and honored as a specifically female virtue. In her recent publications Susan Mann argues that such opinions relate to the growing and broadly recognized economic contribu-

1. E. Goody 1982; Weiner and Schneider 1989.

tion that women in late imperial society made to the family finances. In my view the elite discourses about "women's work" represented a more complex situation. In this chapter I try to disentangle what the various writings or silences about "women's work" tell us about the tensions within late imperial Chinese society and about variant concepts of patriarchy and gender.

SKILLS, KNOWLEDGE AND STATUS

I have described a complex process whereby Chinese women gradually lost control of what had been a female domain of skills and knowledge. In the Song dynasty spinning and weaving were accepted without question as "women's work," but as women's contributions to textile production shifted, so did the representations of their skills. Historians recorded that the family wealth of the Han ladies Huo Xian and Mme. Zhang was substantially increased by their skills in weaving,[2] while the knowledge of the late thirteenth-century Mistress Huang, an expert in cotton processing, was said to have transformed the economy of the Yangzi Delta.[3] Contrast the earlier attribution of textile skills and their economic worth with the following examples from the late Ming:

> In Shengze market during the Jiaqing period (1522–67) there lived a man named Shi Fu, who had two wives. Neither had any children, so they set up a silk loom in their house and every year they would raise several frames of silkworms. The women wound the thread and the man wove, and so they lived very well. . . . The cloth was so lustrous and colorful that when the people at the market saw it they would all compete to buy it at the highest price. Shi always got several more cash for a bolt than the normal price. This allowed him to add 3 or 4 looms over the years so that his family became extremely well-off.[4]

> [Zhang] Yian was a brewer by profession; in Chenghua 7 (1561) there were disastrous floods everywhere. . . . His brewing materials were all spoilt so he gave up brewing and bought a loom. On it he wove colored ramie cloth of extremely fine workmanship. People competed to buy every piece that came off the loom, and it fetched a profit of 20 percent. After three weeks he added another loom, and subsequently acquired over twenty.[5]

Combing through the literature on textiles I found that almost all the anecdotes about textiles written up to the Song (and in the case of

2. *Xijing zaji*, see Kuhn 1988: 203; see also p. 202 herein.
3. Tong 1981: 203; Kuhn 1988: 212; see also p. 215 herein.
4. Quoted Tong 1981: 228; unfortunately he does not name the original source.
5. Zhang Han, *Songchuang mengyu*, quoted Tong 1981: 229.

Mistress Huang, the Yuan) featured female protagonists as skilled workers, as inventors of devices or processes, or as expert managers. In many
cases these women were named. With one exception, men are not mentioned. (The only man to figure in accounts of textile production during
this period is the third-century engineer Ma Jun, who is credited with
inventing a loom that could produce complex patterns with only a few
treadles.[6]) In his *Can shu* of c. 1090, which describes improved techniques
for reeling silk, Qin Guan tells us that it was in fact his wife, Xu Wenmei,
who had provided the information. This was a period when it was considered natural to associate knowledge or skills in textile production with
women. In the case of Mistress Huang, we have no incontrovertible proof
that she existed, or that she brought all the devices with which she is
credited from Hainan to Songjiang (one of them at least was in current
use almost a century earlier). But it is significant that a scholar like Tao
Zongyi should have considered it appropriate to attribute the birth of an
important local cotton industry, for which it seems improbable that any
single individual could have been responsible, to one peasant woman.

Already in the Yuan, however, we find men replacing women as the
protagonists in such anecdotes, sometimes as anonymous workers,[7] sometimes as named entrepreneurs. Shi Fu and Zhang Yian both demonstrate
great skill in weaving, which makes their families rich; they fill the role
that in the Han anecdote was played by concubines. Shi's wives are acknowledged to have contributed to his business, raising the silkworms and
reeling the thread, but they are not named, and although Zhang certainly
did not spin his own thread, we are not even told if he had a wife or
daughters to help him. The shift from giving to withholding (or ignoring)
women's names is also significant, for names were closely bound up with
personal identity and worth in China.[8]

---

6. Ma also invented a chain pump for irrigation, a rotary ballista and a mechanical puppet theater; he held the position of policy review adviser at the Wei
court (Needham and Wang Ling 1966: 39).

7. As in the late Yuan tale by Xu Yikui, "The Weavers' Reply," quoted in
chapter 5.

8. Naming practices were one important aspect of gender differentiation. Great
care was given even by uneducated people to devising a propitious name for a son,
but daughters' names either came from a rather rote list of flowers and jewels or
expressed their parents' chagrin that their child had not turned out to be a boy
("precursor to a son," "little mistake," "[the mother] can bear males"). Men acquired a succession of personal names as they progressed through life (pen names,
sobriquets, and so on), but women did not. Indeed in Cantonese villages in the
twentieth century, many women never had any personal name at all but went
through life as somebody's child, wife or mother (R. Watson 1986). The possession

As late as the Song and Yuan, textile production was still represented as a female and predominantly domestic domain. But this gradually changed with the expansion and commercialization of the textile industry between the Song and the Qing. It is important to remember that the transformation of the textile industry did not involve any radical technical improvements or inventions; as with most cases of proto-industrialization, changes in markets, investment and the organization of labor were much more important than technical innovation. We are not dealing here with a male refashioning of textile technology and skills or with a spate of male inventions; the shift in representation does, however, reflect new divisions of labor. If we compare earlier paintings or woodcuts of textile production with the illustrations in Song Yingxing's *Tiangong kaiwu* (Exploitation of the works of nature) of 1637, we notice that there are no men in the former, whereas men are shown in all the illustrations of the latter (fig. 13) except those depicting the rearing of silkworms and the spinning of cotton. This is significant because Song wanted to portray the most advanced methods of crafts and manufacture: in the textile sector at the end of the Ming dynasty this meant showing men at work.[9]

The possession of technical knowledge and competence does not necessarily translate into high social status or greater autonomy, even when it produces objects that a society considers valuable. A ruling class may well exercise strict control over the artisans who produce the luxury goods that symbolize their status. During the Shang and Zhou periods fancy textiles were so precious as symbols of political power that the women who knew how to produce them were controlled as slaves.[10] Many centuries later, when the Mongols put large numbers of Chinese subjects to the sword,

---

of a personal name meant that one could be recorded as an individual and have a historical existence. Men were granted this kind of identity through genealogical records that named all male members of the patriline, but women were recorded only as wives and mothers, and by late imperial times were usually identified only by their family name, without any personal name. In some strictly neo-Confucian genealogies in late imperial China women's names were omitted entirely, even if they were the mothers of heirs (Meskill 1970; Birge 1992).

9. In agricultural treatises of the late imperial period the illustrations continued to show women as the producers of textiles, in woodcuts modeled directly on either the Song series *Gengzhi tu* (Agriculture and sericulture illustrated) or Wang Zhen's *Nong shu* (Agricultural treatise) of 1313. The authors of these treatises were usually committed to the old ideal of a self-sufficient rural economy, as I discuss in the introduction. Given the changed conditions in most of rural China, this often meant advocating a kind of revivalism in which women would be brought back in to local textile production.

10. Sheng 1995: 58.

they spared all the craftsmen who produced the artifacts that represented high civilization, but reduced them to the hereditary status of unfree families under direct state control.[11] But when we try to understand what the loss of their previous identity as the possessors of weaving skills meant for the majority of women in late imperial China, we must think of them as free women and members of a family. We should also remember how closely body and morality were linked in Chinese thought. By performing wifely work a woman practiced both family and civic virtues. When a little girl was taught to spin and weave, she was not only acquiring the skills to produce useful goods—through them she was learning diligence, orderliness, and respect for labor, the dignity of a wife and the responsibility of a subject of the state. In the cloth that she produced, her skills were transmuted into worth and virtue. That is one reason why so many social reformers and moralists of the late imperial period were anxious to revive women's weaving skills.[12]

WOMANLY VIRTUE AND THE
PRESERVATION OF THE SOCIAL ORDER

When women abandoned proper women's work, the whole fabric of society was threatened. As early as the fifteenth century the writer Hu Juren (1434–84) was lamenting that commercialization and the spread of artisan activities meant that weaving had now become a man's job.[13] In Confucian

11. Tong 1981: 187–92.

12. In her chapter on women's work and textiles in the Song, Patricia Ebrey expresses the view that women's contributions were even then so effectively subsumed into the notion of a joint household economy that their textile skills did nothing to affect their status. She correctly points out that the majority of Song writings on women weavers are poems depicting peasant wives and daughters slaving to produce tax cloth in time for the collector's visit, too poor to wear the silks they weave for the state, or even to set a portion aside for their own dowries. Women are portrayed as oppressed victims rather than as enrichers of their families, and as Ebrey says, this indictment of the rapacious central state is made the more poignant by focusing on the plight of exploited women thus deprived even of the basic right of marriage (1993: 194). On the one hand, we need to remember that poems like these were part of a widespread elite reaction against the state that followed the failed reforms of Wang Anshi and the fall of the Northern Song state. It was therefore desirable to represent the state as preventing women not only from earning money by their work but even from meeting family subsistence needs. On the other hand, the poems show that elite men at any rate admired and respected the role such women played in working to keep the family going, even if they deplored the ways in which the work could be exploited.

13. McDermott 1990: 30.

terms this was a threat to the social order in part because basic production had fallen into the hands of artisans and merchants, but equally because it signaled a failure to distinguish properly between male and female work. Men weaving or women tilling the fields were deeply disquieting occurrences, because they were signs of a world turned upside down.

Where the social order of the state forms a continuum with the conduct of family life, women's behavior is a matter of political concern even though they live in seclusion from what we might think of as the public sphere. The 1712/13 preface to Lan Dingyuan's popular text *Women's Learning* voices a typical opinion when it declares: "The basis of the government of the empire lies in the habits of the people. The correctness of the habits of the people depends on the orderly management of the family. The Way *(dao)* for the orderly management of the family begins with women." [14] "Private" virtues were considered to underpin the "public" order in many ways, and for late imperial moralists women's weaving incorporated several levels of virtuous behavior.

As mentioned in chapter 4, in popular encyclopedias as well as agricultural works of the Ming and Qing, spinning and weaving were still depicted as the daily occupations of respectable ladies, even though in reality most elite households had long since abandoned cloth production and supplied their needs through the market. One significant way in which texts of this kind represented domestic textile work was not as a commercial activity, but as an exercise in filial piety: the end product of the women's labors was shown as warm and delicate cloths that would be used to make new clothes for the patriarch and matriarch each year (fig. 24). Spinning and weaving taught both the gender-neutral virtue of filial piety and the more specifically female virtues of thrift, frugality and diligence. These were considered essential not only for poor households but also for the proper management of elite households,[15] in which parents still admonished their daughters to spin in order to learn respect for the hard work of their inferiors, and to weave hemp to learn frugality. The eighteenth-century conservative Chen Hongmou wrote bitterly of spoiled young women whose children were raised by nurses, while maids and concubines did their needlework. "All they have to think about is making themselves beautiful. Everything is done for them, so they don't know that rice comes from a stalk and silk is unreeled from cocoons. They treat money like dirt,

14. Lan Dingyuan's *Nü xue*, quoted Mann 1994: 23.
15. Mann 1994: 30.

and living creatures like bits of straw."[16] The statesman Zeng Guofan (1811–72), a key figure in the conservative movement that developed in China in response to Western domination, insisted that his daughters start the day in the kitchen, then spend half of every morning weaving cotton and hemp, the afternoons doing needlework and making shoes, and end the frugal and virtuous day by spinning yarn after supper.[17]

Most educated people in late imperial China saw idleness as a danger, and as wealth grew, more and more women were perceived as being idle and therefore under moral threat. The sign of being idle, in orthodox eyes, was that the women did not weave textiles. In chapter 5 I gave several examples of official attempts to recreate a textile industry in poor regions where women no longer wove. These women were described in the proposals for reform as being "without occupation" or some such expression—even though they were probably working hard all day long, and may well have been involved in farming tasks, handicrafts or other economic activities as well as housekeeping and child rearing. The only women's work that reforming officials considered worthy of being called an "occupation" was making textiles. In contrast, there was a growing number of well-off households whose wives and daughters did now have what we would recognize as leisure time, time they might occupy with reading, painting, or embroidery. Such leisure was considered especially threatening to women of the commoner class; as well as attempting to revive the silk-weaving skills of the poor women of Luzhou, the sixteenth-century official Lü Kun composed a work entitled *Gui fan* (Regulations for the women's quarters) specially to provide moral instruction for commoner women who now had "three or five books in their chests" and less work than was good for them.[18]

In her essay "Household Handicrafts and State Policy in Qing Times," Susan Mann provides a series of examples of official efforts to eradicate peasant women's idleness and its attendant dangers by encouraging what she terms "handicrafts"—though it turns out that we are dealing here not with a whole range of acceptable handicraft activities, but invariably with textile production and especially home weaving. In regions that were not yet fully sinicized, teaching Chinese-style weaving skills was seen as a powerful method of enculturation. Mann quotes a touching lament by an official posted to the Xiang region of Hubei, where the local women (who

16. Mann 1991: 220.
17. McDermott 1990: 26.
18. Handlin 1975: 17.

I presume were of some other ethnicity than Han) were shamelessly unfaithful to their husbands by Chinese standards. They thought nothing of marrying several times, nor did families in search of a bride mind this loose behavior.[19] The trigger to the official's concern was the sight of the women "breaking up clods of earth with a hoe." This shocked him deeply since such a confusion of gender categories indicated that "it would not be long before these same wives would be suing their husbands, and husbands their wives." Only sericulture, he felt, could save them: "I especially pity the women of Xiang. They have no way to develop specialized work of their own and thereby affirm their commitment as faithful wives. The woman who has no work of her own should take up sericulture. Whether she comes from a gentry or a commoner household, a wife can personally tend silkworms in order to clothe her husband. When she sees that her own strength is sufficient to provide for her family's subsistence, her heart will be pure."[20]

Within the traditional Chinese heartland, too, Qing statecraft writers believed that "those regions in China where 'women wove' were culturally and even morally superior to areas where women [did not]." Many tried to introduce the skills of advanced areas like the lower Yangzi to more backward areas where they held office, even though the local population would sometimes refuse to learn them.[21]

One reason why local populations did not always welcome these attempts was precisely because they had developed alternative and more rewarding means for earning a livelihood. In another article Mann documents the real range of home handicrafts that women of various classes practiced in the Ningbo region during the late Qing period. They included embroidery in well-off families, and also "handwoven cloth, rush mats and matting, hats made of straw or bamboo splints, and the canopies of oiled-paper umbrellas. All were counted among the specialities that made

19. This was a period when there were strong moral pressures on Han women to remain faithful to their husbands by refusing to remarry; however, widows often came under severe pressure to marry again, not least because of legislation that allowed the in-laws to keep the dowry if the woman remarried. See T'ien 1988; Carlitz 1994.

20. Mann 1992a: 87, quoting from a collection of essays on agricultural policy that comprise three chapters in the *Huangchao jingshi wenbian* (Collected essays on statecraft of the august dynasty), first published in 1826. "More than half of the forty-nine essays in these chapters refer to home weaving, and one entire chapter containing nineteen essays (*juan 37*) focuses exclusively on cotton and silk home handicraft industries" (ibid.: 92 n. 8). See also Will on official attempts to restore "correct agriculture" and to revive the sericultural industry (1994).

21. Mann 1992a: 86.

Ningbo famous" throughout Southeast Asia as well as China.[22] But these activities were not the type of women's work that a late imperial official was likely to encourage or promote, for they fell squarely under the orthodox category of craft, and were therefore—unlike textile production—considered not basic but subsidiary and commercial activities. Even in the Qing, officials still tended to treat commerce as a drain on the state's resources and the people's welfare. When late imperial officials encouraged home weaving or sericulture, they did so for two reasons: first, it allowed women to contribute to their family's subsistence needs, and second, it meant they could pay their taxes.[23]

Late imperial officials and moralists did not neglect the economic value of women's work, but they reduced it to its political elements: family subsistence underpinning a moral contract between subject and state through the payment of taxes; the same was true of their attitudes toward men's work. It was not that they objected to modest prosperity, and many felt that a moderate involvement in commercial production or trade was legitimate and even desirable—so long as it was firmly underpinned by subsistence production. As mentioned in the introduction, Qing emperors and officials did all they could to coax commoner men out of trade and crafts and overreliance on commercial cropping, and back into subsistence production of grain. In their minds such agricultural policies served as a fetish: the restoration of "correct agriculture," that is to say subsistence farming, would not only reestablish a firm tax base for the state but also revive the ancient social contract between ruler and subject, even though the material symbol of the exchange had disappeared since the abolition of taxes paid in grain.

I see late imperial official efforts to restore a traditional textile industry as representing the female side of the gender equation underpinning this moral order. Traditionally both husband and wife had been responsible for paying taxes, both had been active subjects of the state. Weaving like grain farming served as a metonym: it represented not just the private female virtue of "womanly work," or an essential element of the family's subsistence, but also the necessary female contribution to a desirable public and political order—again, even though taxes were no longer paid directly in cloth, and even though the contribution of man and wife was no longer

22. Mann 1992b: 249.
23. Mann points out that these statecraft writers took as their model an essay by Gu Yanwu, *Fangzhi zhi li* (Profitability of weaving), in which he argued that the state should promote sericulture in border regions both to increase self-sufficiency and to increase the tax base (1992a: 83).

materially distinct, visibly complementary, as it had been when taxes were levied in kind.

It is ironic that the lower Yangzi was the region most often held up by officials as an example of proper women's work. Although it was true that in the sericultural regions around Huzhou even the poor (or most of them) could afford to pay their taxes, by the Qing the local economy was definitely not based on self-sufficiency but on a highly developed market economy. The paradox is even clearer in the case of the cotton industry. Qing officials in areas like Fuzhou were trying to persuade the locals to grow cotton and weave their own cloth, even though the local women were profitably involved in processing tea, tobacco and sugar and could well afford to buy cloth on the market. At the same time officials in the lower Yangzi were trying to stop farm specialization in cotton crops because they did not wish grain to be neglected, even though the farmers told them that cotton was far more profitable than rice.[24]

As far as Confucian officials were concerned, modest self-sufficiency was infinitely preferable to the kind of wealth that generates what we would call economic growth, for the latter involved the risks of dependence on the commercial economy. One doubts whether this view was often shared by commoner families in the late imperial period. It is true that where transport networks were not well developed, abandoning subsistence production made a region vulnerable to famine. But more than that was at stake when officials urged the local farmers to stop growing so much cotton, or sugar, or oranges, and turn their fields over to rice. It was not even true that taxes on subsistence farming were more reliable or easier to collect than taxes on other livelihoods after the complex reforms of the late Ming. Something else lay behind the dogged economic conservatism of the Qing officials. As Hill Gates puts it, the late imperial state did all it could to maintain a "tributary mode of production" and to deny the reality of the "petty capitalist mode of production" that shaped people's daily lives and decisions.[25] It was almost as if the late imperial officials who held up the lower Yangzi cloth industry as an example were deliberately blind to what was going on—cloth was being produced and taxes were being paid, and from this they deduced that the women of the region were fulfilling their traditional role, even though the articulations of the lower Yangzi cotton industry had been completely transformed.

The sericultural industry of the same region did develop in such a way

24. Ibid.: 84–85.
25. Gates 1989; see also Will 1994.

as to fulfill both the moral expectations of officials and the material needs of the local population. The hatching and raising of silkworms in order to produce cocoons was one area of textile production that was an exception to the deskilling and marginalization of women. As the illustrations in the *Exploitation of the Works of Nature* suggest, it remained a female and domestic domain of competence through all the specialization and subdivisions of textile production of the late imperial period. In a sense, the splitting up of the various silk-making processes (into sericulture, the reeling and quilling of yarn, and the actual weaving) enhanced the importance of raising silkworms—it was so clearly the rock on which the silk industry was founded, and silk thread had always been a valuable commodity in its own right. By the late Ming, in certain regions of the lower Yangzi where the best cocoons were produced, the whole economy depended on sericulture, and dry land on which mulberries could be grown was much more valuable than rice fields. "In my village," writes Zhang Lüxiang, "the profits from sericulture are greater than those from grain, and the public and private sector alike depend on them. If the silkworms don't spin well then public and private alike suffer terrible hardship."[26]

Although the whole family was involved in sericulture, the women were responsible for the quasi-maternal role of hatching and tending the worms and giving them food. The short story *Spring Silkworms* by Mao Dun (1956) vividly conveys the deeply physical involvement and intense commitment required of women raising silkworms. Mao describes a silkworm season in a sericultural village in the lower Yangzi during the Republican period. The whole family labored day and night throughout the months of the silkworm season to raise its precious brood of "children." The eggs were bought in the market on sheets of paper. The women tied the sheets around their bodies next to the skin so the steady temperature would hatch the worms more quickly. They knew the hatching had begun when the paper started to tickle. Then the tiny worms, the "ants," were laid out on trays and the constant work began of feeding them new leaves, picking out the droppings, and inspecting for sick or dead worms.

While the worms were feeding the men were busy too, rushing back and forth with fresh leaves. But the women's role of tending, feeding and cleaning involved constant attention and physical devotion of the kind required for raising a human child, and the explicitly maternal imagery connected with hatching silkworms fits in with the increasing centrality

---

26. *Bu nongshu* 108. The "public sector" means the official administration, but also presumably community institutions like local schools, temples and charities.

of reproductive roles in late imperial representations of women. (As I make clear in part 3, I do not mean that women in late imperial China were confined to the role of biological mother, but that there was a tendency to translate other kinds of roles into reproductive terms.)[27] Throughout the late imperial period sericulture continued to be represented in nonofficial writings as women's work, and extremely valuable work at that. As mentioned earlier, Zhang Lüxiang is remarkable among the many writers on agriculture in that he insists on the absolutely essential contribution that the wife makes to the domestic economy, through both her productive and her managerial skills: "If a woman works diligently, her family will flourish, and if she is negligent, it will decline— exactly as with a man's tasks. Because a woman's occupations are limited to such things as hemp or silk, it seems as if her diligence or laziness would have only a slight effect on the way the household runs. But in fact if she is diligent then all the tasks will prosper and if she is lazy they will all be neglected. So they say, 'A poor family hopes for a wise wife as a state in disorder hopes for a good minister.' The degree of help and cooperation is the same in both cases."[28]

Zhang presents the wife as an active partner in the domestic economy: "Of husband and wife, the man can manage 10 *mu* of land, wet or dry, and the woman can rear ten frames of silkworms. In one day she can weave 2 bolts of ramie cloth, or spin 8 ounces of cotton yarn—how could such a family go cold or hungry?"[29] Zhang points out that a skilled and diligent wife can even reverse the family fortunes. But more than that, he tells us that the local people compared a wife's role to the dignity and responsibility of a minister of state. This takes us even beyond the formulation in the *Book of Rites* that "the wife is the fitting partner of her husband." Zhang also indicates that in sericultural regions not only did the household depend on female sericultural skills but so did the whole local economy, including the public institutions that were funded by tax money.

---

27. The maternal parallels of sericulture were explicitly developed in Japan when the silk industry was being industrialized in the late nineteenth and early twentieth centuries. The main sericultural workforce consisted of unmarried girls who left their villages to live in factory dormitories. To justify keeping young women far away from the moral control of their families, legislators and public moralists made great play of the essentially feminine, maternal qualities required for the tasks of sericulture. The silkworms were likened to babies, and through tending them the factory girls were said to be receiving a training as future "good wives and wise mothers" (Tamanoi 1990, 1991).

28. *Bu nongshu* 151.

29. Ibid.

Huzhou sericulture was not in fact a traditional subsistence activity. Only a small proportion of the silk thread was woven within the household that produced it (and in such cases the men often did the weaving while their wives and daughters spun and reeled the thread). Instead sericultural families were tied into a complex commercial chain that linked them to weaving workshops in Suzhou or Hangzhou that produced cloth for the national market, or even into networks that extended far beyond the provincial borders through the national and international manufactures of Nanjing and Canton. However, women still were at the center of this domain of traditional "womanly work." State ideologues chose to emphasize that this work allowed sericultural families to subsist in dignity and to pay their taxes; when they offered it as an example to other regions they ignored the commercial networks that played on relative advantage and allowed this form of sericulture to flourish in the Yangzi provinces where the silk thread was especially fine. The work was hard and the rewards slender even in Huzhou, where the best silk thread was produced. Little wonder that few households in remote areas like Luzhou were tempted to persist with silk production once the eager official who devised the program had been transferred to a new post.

Despite the realities that restricted sericulture in Ming-Qing China to a few favored regions, to orthodox thinkers it still represented a powerful symbol of the traditional social order, and that, I suggest, is what lay behind the late imperial revival of court rituals in honor of the goddess of sericulture.[30] This ceremony, in which the empress and her ladies tended silkworms in a special shrine at the capital, was first developed during the Han dynasty along with the parallel "first furrow" ritual in which the emperor himself set hand to the plow. Although it has been argued that these rituals were intended to ensure good harvests of grain and of cocoons throughout the empire, I think they were equally concerned with the reproduction of a moral and political order, serving as symbols of the interdependence between emperor and subject and of the ruler's respect for the fundamental occupations that defined and supported the Chinese agrarian state.

In 1530 an official called Xia Yan (1482–1548) urged the Ming emperor Shizong to revive the imperial sericultural ritual not because he thought silk production was falling, but as a means of encouraging women to prac-

---

30. The historical sketch of the different varieties of sericultural ritual that follows is based largely on Kuhn 1988: 251. A detailed description of the Qing ceremonials, which were particularly lavish, is given in Mann 1992a: 80–81.

tice feminine virtues. The court sericultural ritual had been practiced fairly regularly during the early dynasties, but by the Song it had fallen into disuse, although two short-lived attempts at revival were made in 1132 and 1145. Considering the heavy dependence of the Song state on silk production, this decline in ritual would be curious if the purpose of the ceremony had been simply to ensure good crops of silk throughout the country. But the discontinuation of the ceremony does make sense if it is seen as an exercise in political symbolism, for this was a period in which the commercialization of silk production, together with tax changes, was eroding the traditional interdependence between the ruler and peasant women raising silkworms. The attempts at revival of the ceremony in the Ming and Qing coincided with other official attempts to repudiate commercialization and to reinstate a more old-fashioned economic (and political) order.[31]

At the local and domestic level, the decline of the imperial ritual overlapped with the rise of local shrines to the Silkworm Goddess in cities and districts where sericulture was an important part of the economy, and of domestic altars set up during the breeding season to honor a silkworm deity. One can suppose that at this level such religious rituals were more concerned with ensuring good harvests than with acting out political theory. At the end of the eighteenth century the silk-weaving cities of the lower Yangzi all maintained popular shrines to silkworm goddesses, and during the fourth lunar month when the silkworms started to hatch (known locally as "the silkworm month"), a series of "silkworm taboos" was observed to avoid disturbing the little creatures: social visits, weddings and other celebrations, and even tax collection stopped. Domestic sacrifices to the Silkworm Deity are first mentioned in the *Can shu* (Book of sericulture) of 1090, though they probably began in very early times, and they are depicted in the *Gengzhi tu* (Agriculture and sericulture illustrated) of 1145 and in all the works modeled on it. Just after the first eggs hatched the family would set up an altar and offer fowl and wine or special rice balls shaped like silkworms to the Silkworm Deity. At the end of the breeding season they would give thanks, hanging the altar with skeins of silk and burning paper money (fig. 19).[32]

Although the court sericultural rituals performed by Qing empresses were careful reconstructions and elaborations of much earlier ceremonies, the popular industry they were intended to promote had changed almost

31. Will 1994.
32. Kuhn 1988: 269.

Figure 19. Domestic sacrifice to the Silkworm Deity (*Gengzhi tu*, Qianlong imperial edition of 1742 [Franke 1913, fig. 88]). A makeshift altar is set up in the shed where the silkworms were raised, on which skeins of the newly-reeled silk and vases of incense and flowers are set before a tablet to the Silkworm Deity; the maid is approaching with a tray of wine or tea to offer the god. The ceremony is noticeably more casual than the ancestral sacrifice depicted in fig. 6. The two men of the household are in front of the altar invoking the deity, although it was their wives (now much concerned with a hungry baby boy) who produced the silk. In the villages of western Sichuan, where this scene is supposedly taking place, silk was the primary source of income.

beyond recognition. Conservative officials and elite moralists still clung to such comforting shreds of gender tradition as Huzhou sericulture that could be proposed a model for regeneration elsewhere, but it seems that for most ordinary people the understanding of women's work and its importance must have changed considerably. Next I discuss how women's productive work might relate to ordinary understandings of man and woman, and in particular of husband and wife.

WOMEN'S WORK AND FAMILY STATUS

The marginalization of women's productive roles is typical of societies in the process of proto-industrialization. But only by examining the broader context in which such changes take place can we understand how they might contribute to reconfigurations of gender roles in specific instances. In the case of medieval Europe, David Herlihy argues that changed work roles in the textile industry do not account in themselves for the contemporary decline in women's social status; they must be set in the context of shifting marriage and inheritance practices:

> Women were valued members of the household in early medieval society. [Aristocratic women managed estates and fulfilled other important administrative functions.] On lower social levels, they played an indispensable role in many processes of production; they dominated the manufacture of cloth, including such skilled operations as dyeing. In the central and late Middle Ages women lost some of these functions. The growth of bureaucratic offices limited, though it never fully extinguished, their importance as administrators. . . . Their role in economic production also diminished, especially in the cities. Guilds dominate cloth production within towns, and only under special circumstances could women become guild members. Males now take over nearly all phases of cloth manufacture, including dyeing. The contribution of women is limited to such relatively unskilled work as spinning and washing. Late in the Middle Ages, the rise of an important silk industry enhanced the role of women, who were apparently more dexterous than men and better able to work the fine threads. But this is a late development. The contributions women made through service or skill to their families thus diminished, especially in the middle ranges of society and especially in cities. Families were no longer eager to retain the services of daughters. In the fifteenth century, a Florentine matron, Alessandra Micinghi-Strozzi, complains that nothing can be accomplished in a household, as long as marriageable daughters are present. She clearly regarded daughters as a burden and not an asset.

However, Herlihy continues, the main reason why daughters came to be considered a burden was a change in inheritance and marriage patterns. Not only did war reduce the number of marriageable males, but after about A.D. 1200 families with property preferred to concentrate it rather than dividing it equally. They encouraged only eldest sons to marry and bequeathed them the patrimony. Younger sons had to make their own way in the world, and many could not afford to marry—so it became difficult and expensive to marry a daughter. Herlihy considers that the changes in women's contributions to household production and management were of only secondary importance in the medieval reconfiguration of gender roles.[33]

33. Herlihy 1985: 100–102. I am grateful to Ellen Widmer for drawing my attention to Herlihy's work.

In the case of late imperial China, too, we may contend that changes in women's legal status and in kinship practices defined a matrix that structured the effects of changes in women's work roles. Throughout the imperial period marriage was universal, and partible inheritance, whereby all sons inherited equally, was practiced—so we are not dealing here with a surplus of marriageable women of the kind that Herlihy describes.[34] But taken in the context of the switch from bridewealth to dowry that accompanied the rise of the new Song elite,[35] and of the neo-Confucian success in excluding daughters from rights to a share of the patrimony as well as rights to inclusion in the lineage,[36] it does seem that the erosion of women's productive capacities—or at least of their acknowledged productive capacities—provided fertile soil for a growing emphasis on the reproductive roles of wives: as childbearers and as managers rather than generators of the household economy. Moreover, one can see how these conditions taken together could translate into the view that women consumed without producing, an ethos that at least at popular levels could develop into negative perceptions of daughters and even of wives.

Dowries, for example, were less of a burden when women were still active in weaving; at that time women not only contributed to tax payments and earned extra cash, but they were able to manufacture large portions of their own dowries. By late Ming times official reports on the distressing phenomenon of female infanticide inform us that most peasant families had difficulty providing dowries, and the problem was compounded by the fact that daughters did not—could not—contribute to household earnings.[37] As in fifteenth-century Florence, such daughters were considered a burden. This view was reflected in innumerable popular sayings about the worthlessness of girls, sayings resurgent in China today with the growth of a market economy in which employment opportunities for women have noticeably declined.

Hill Gates sees the changes in textile production as one factor in the

34. Practices like polygyny and female infanticide resulted in a shortage of available women for poor men.

35. Ebrey 1991d illustrates how criticism of buying brides (as a way of gaining entry into aristocratic circles) gave way in the Song to complaints about buying grooms (or at any rate those grooms who were reckoned to have good minds and a brilliant career in government ahead of them).

36. If daughters had been considered members of the descent line they would have been able to worship their own ancestors and to contribute heirs to their own lineage, in which case, no doubt, female infanticide in China would have been as rare as the male counterpart.

37. T'ien 1988: 28.

"commoditization of Chinese women," in which the patrilineal, patriarchal Chinese kinship system permitted men to appropriate the fruits of
women's economic and reproductive labor. She has argued that the unprecedented economic growth of the Song in fact provided all kinds of
new opportunities for women as producers and earners of income,[38] and
hypothesizes that this perceived threat to male control underlay the misogynistic severity of the neo-Confucian doctrines of gender hierarchy
elaborated at the time, as well as legal changes that strengthened the control of the male-centered lineage over any female claims to property. At
the same time she sees the family economy operating within the rationali-
ties of a market-driven "petty capitalist mode of production" in which
households or patrilines strove to increase their incomes, or, in the case of
poor families, struggled just to survive.[39] The interests of these private
economic units, says Gates, frequently clashed with those of the state,
which operated in the interests of a "tributary mode of production," in
which a ruling class of officials extracted taxes from the great body of
commoners. Despite its secular growth throughout the late imperial period, and its flexibility and sophistication, the petty capitalist mode of
production never came to dominate the Chinese economy, argues Gates,
because the state always acted to contain it. I have given examples of such
state action in the introduction and earlier in this chapter.

Although I feel misgivings about Gates's hypothesis linking the economy and the birth of neo-Confucian gender doctrines during the Song
period, her particular formulation of two economic systems in continual
tension[40] helped me unravel some of the contradictions I saw in the attitudes toward women's productive work in late imperial times, contradictions that seem to crystallize in the ambivalence of the term *nügong*.
Throughout this chapter I have alternated between translating *nügong* as
"womanly work" and as "women's work," and in the course of writing I

38. A survey of references to women's occupations in Song sources yields
rather sparse evidence to support Gates's view (1989: 826–29). There are only a
few mentions of women running tea shops, herbalist stores, or other small shops,
and also to women earning at home-based textile production as well as tailoring,
sewing and embroidery; otherwise, the chief occupations mentioned are the perennial ones of maids, kitchen maids, and various kinds of entertainer or prostitute
(Jin 1988).

39. In my own work on the relations between agricultural technology and
economic diversification in China, I have made use of the term "petty commodity
mode of production" (Bray 1986).

40. The contradiction between state goals and private interests is a rather tired
commonplace of Chinese economic history. By bringing gender *and* class into the
equation, however, Gates has opened up new possibilities for dynamic analysis.

came to realize that this is an illuminating distinction. Of course it is not a distinction that a Chinese speaker or writer needed consciously to make, hence some of the confusions past and present in dealing with what is apparently a single category.

"Womanly work" is the translation I decided to use (following such scholars as Mann and Ko) principally to denote moralists' and officials' use of *nügong*. What these writers see in female work is a moral activity linked to a gendered identity and embodied in weaving. This notion of work corresponds to the first two formulations of neo-Confucian doctrine that I distinguished in chapter 3, with their positive view of human nature and respect for the couple as active partners; it also corresponds to Gates's tributary mode of production. It implies that the woman is an active subject of the state, and that her role is an essential complement to that of her husband. The work performed is the production of symbolically charged cloth, an essential good like food grain; the straightforward monetary value of the commodity produced by this work is of no real interest. This is why late imperial officials were able to describe women who did not weave as having "no occupation," and why they were able to see in the highly commercialized sericulture of Huzhou an exemplar of traditional wifely occupations.

The translation as "women's work" I see as operating at the level of the private household economy, within the framework of a market economy of the type that Gates calls petty capitalist mode of production. In this context, *nügong* could mean any kind of work women performed that produced recognizable commodities. This included the kinds of handicrafts that a Ningbo survey of 1907 documented as women's home-based work[41]: weaving mats, making umbrellas or hats, processing foods, all kinds of work that fit nicely into our Western concept of handicrafts and all of which date back several centuries as commercial activities in various regions of China (as is clear from documents like local histories or agricultural treatises), but which as far as Confucian orthodoxy was concerned did not qualify as "womanly work." Modern scholars like Tong Shuye, Philip Huang and Susan Mann tend to categorize weaving as a "handicraft," thus eliding a distinction between basic and subsidiary activities that was fundamental to orthodox Confucian economic thought, but that probably became alien to most ordinary working people as commercialization ad-

---

41. In 1907 a native of Ningbo, Nyok-Ching Tsur, conducted a survey of Ningbo industry ([1907] 1983), which Mann (1992b) uses as one of her key sources.

vanced and specialized divisions of labor became the norm, not only in the textile industry and in crafts and trades, but also in the canonical male activity of farming. As work of all kinds came increasingly to be evaluated in terms of cash wages or prices, and as working people scrambled from one crop or one occupation to another in order to survive, the idea that work was a dignifying sign of a particular social identity must have faded and eventually disappeared.

Reforming officials and moralists in late Ming and Qing China seem to have held to the hope that "women's work" could be transformed into "womanly work," with all its moral powers and its implications for the revival of a more desirable social order. But most ordinary people, struggling to survive in a commercialized economy by any occupation that offered a living, probably shared our modern view that weaving was an occupation like any other: it was of little importance whether the female members of the household wove cloth, cured tea, painted fans or brewed soy sauce, provided it brought in some cash. Although there is no systematic popular equivalent to the elite discourses on the value of *nügong*, I suspect that in working families in an increasingly market-driven economy, one factor that powerfully affected women's status vis-à-vis their male kin was their *perceived* ability to contribute to the family finances.

Philip Huang remarks that the commercialization of the Chinese peasant economy in the late imperial period increased the involvement of all family members in production, including women.[42] This may seem to contradict the arguments I have been making about marginalization, but it does not, for Huang is talking about the facts of economic activity, and I am interested in its representations.

In attributing responsibility for a particular kind of work, carrying out the final transforming process is often what counts. It was the finished products that were counted, weighed, wrapped and carried from the inner quarters to the marketplace; the preliminary stages of processing did not so obviously link the inner to the outer world. In China whoever sat at the loom was considered the real maker of the cloth. Cocoons and silk thread were valuable commodities considered to be the product of women's work. Perhaps the same was true of curing tea or other processed or handicraft products where women were responsible for the key transformation. But more often the splitting up of production processes that accompanied the commercialization of the late imperial Chinese economy not only produced new and specialized divisions of labor and increasing

42. P. Huang 1990: 52, 54.

degrees of exploitation but also deprived women of primary responsibility for various products and rendered invisible the value of female work. For instance, in a world where most goods had an explicit cash value, if a woman wove cloth for family subsistence needs, what she produced was only attributed a proper value in cash terms if she failed to clothe her family and extra cloth had to be bought. The masking of the value of homemade cloth was reinforced by the tax reforms that made cloth payments obsolete. And women who worked in the commercial production of cloth either were the poorest paid workers in the new divisions of labor between households and workshops or worked as the auxiliaries in a household team where the men wove the final product. In this system both men and women workers were exploited and alienated, but men were usually allocated the more remunerative work. Women who produced cotton yarn for sale, or who worked as silk quillers or reelers, were paid mere pittances; the male weavers or weaving families worked under slightly better conditions, though as I argued earlier these tended to deteriorate with the development of the market economy.[43] So in many families the value of women's work was either perceived as less than that of men's work or rendered invisible, appropriated (as Gates would say) by their male kin.

In the cases where women were still seen as primarily or solely responsible for the production of a valuable commodity, the value of the work they performed does seem to have translated into respect. Women who practiced sericulture and those who wove cloth for sale were respected by

43. A variation on this "feminization" of low-paid work can be observed in the Florentine silk industry. The expansion of markets for fancy silks between the fifteenth and seventeenth centuries brought about a shift in the range of cloths produced. In the earlier period the emphasis was on producing unique pieces at very high prices for a rather limited group of high-ranking customers. At that time the male weavers who produced these elaborate cloths worked closely with the designers; they were not mere workmen but maestri, connected by the requirements of their work to the Florentine artistic community. Moreover, unlike the women weavers who produced much simpler silk taffetas, the maestri's firms offered them advances (necessary because each piece took so long to complete) and credit, for example for the replacement of damaged loom parts. By the seventeenth century the Florentine silk firms were producing standardized designs in large quantities. Design was distinct from the processes of weaving. The majority of silk weavers were female and there was no longer "any sign of a financial relationship between the firm and the weavers other than the regular weekly or fortnightly payment" (Goodman 1993: 242). "If one accepts the wage as the symbol and substance of alienation," says Goodman, "then the experience of the silk industry in the seventeenth century must be one of alienation, a feature of work culture which was female and not male."

their families and by the community, as well as being honored for their womanly qualities by officials. Zhang Lüxiang's account of the positive image of peasant wives in late Ming sericultural families is one example of how people who visibly earned money for the family were well regarded whatever their sex, even at a time when neo-Confucian orthodoxy about female subordination had filtered down to the lower levels of society. In the sericultural families that Zhang describes, the role of a wife was compared to a minister, and the relationship between spouses was represented as one of complementarity and interdependence. It would be interesting to know whether women who cured tea or made fine handicraft products for sale were similarly regarded.[44]

Where remunerative work was available, the stage of the domestic cycle a woman had reached was likely to affect her earning power and how her fertility weighed against her work. Unmarried daughters had many advantages in this respect: they were not responsible for household management, or for caring for their own children; the task of serving old parents fell mainly on wives; and girls still had the keen eyes and smooth fingers that allowed them to undertake fiddly tasks like embroidery. Pregnant women and women with small children were prevented from working to their full capacities, even if other family members helped with the childcare. For young married wives, the future value of the children they bore had to be balanced in poor families against their earning capacities. In larger, better-off families women at different stages of the domestic cycle could team up to work more effectively.[45]

Having argued thus far that "women's work" rather than "womanly work" was the issue at stake in ordinary working families, I should also point out that even in working families "women's work" was delimited in

44. T'ien (1988: 27) tells us that where outside employment opportunities for girls were frequent (the examples he gives are singers and prostitutes) rates of female infanticide were much lower among poor families than elsewhere. But we know much less about more respectable forms of employment within the household.

45. In her study of women's employment in Ningbo at the end of the Qing, Mann describes how foreign markets for fine embroidery opened up new opportunities for women in middle-class families to earn money by their work. Young unmarried women and able-bodied widows were best able to devote their energies to such work, and in some families servants would be hired to do the childcare so that the ladies could work at their handicrafts (1992b: 247). In such families, Mann remarks, "the elaborate division of [female] labor was an emblem of the organic unity . . . of the grand Chinese family" (ibid.: 257)—so in this case the textile or embroidery work involved was serving the dual function of "women's work" and "womanly work."

certain ways that held the moral implications of "womanly work." Though within the walls of their home women might perform a wide range of tasks that generated income without compromising their reputation, women who worked outside the home lowered the status of their family. Female seclusion was a basic mark of respectability and orthodoxy that every family hoped to retain, and only the poorest and most desperate familes would allow their women to go out to work.[46]

This brings us back to the question underlying the chapters on the construction of space: what was the relation between inner and outer spheres? Are modern distinctions between "private" and "public" adequate for understanding what was at stake in various forms of gender relations in late imperial China, and to what extent did the spatial boundaries marking female seclusion translate into a real or perceived separation of worlds? I argue that most work performed by Chinese women continued to tie them into the outer world even after the reorganization of textile production documented in chapter 5, but that "womanly work" implied different kinds of ties from "women's work."

CONNECTION AND SECLUSION:
CLOTH AND THE SEPARATION OF SPHERES

Engels's thesis about the relation between socially recognized work and social status underpins a range of marxist and feminist analyses of gender hierarchies that circle warily around explanations evoking a hierarchical distinction between "domestic" and "public" spheres. Fruitful as this notion has proved to be for understanding the modernization of Western societies, the use of these terms has also generated a number of necessary critiques. One important criticism is that oppositions such as domestic and public take as natural categories and values that in fact derive from

46. See, e.g., Bao 1988 on premodern China. The advent of Western-style textile factories in late nineteenth- and early twentieth-century cities offered a particular challenge to Confucian morality. The Western tradition of industrial textile production led them to seek a large female labor force, but the labor pool was limited by local attitudes toward what such employment implied. Initially at least, the majority of the women employed in factories were either from the poorest classes locally or from the villages of the hinterland (Mann 1992b; Honig 1986). Although having daughters or wives who worked in factories was a stigma for this class of family, within the family the economic control that such women gained could translate into status and considerable freedom. For instance, a daughter who earned good wages in a silk-reeling factory was able to use her income as a bargaining chip with her family to allow her to defer marriage (Stockard 1989).

nineteenth-century Western experiences of capitalism: not all societies assume that there is a natural division of labor whereby women's primary role is as mothers responsible for raising children, and men work outside the home to support them; not all societies rate reproductive work less highly than other forms of labor; nor are the boundaries between home-based work and outside work everywhere as clearly marked as the domestic-public opposition implies.[47]

The gendered spatial distinction between "inner" and "outer" in China may seem to parallel the Western categories of domestic and public, but the Chinese categories of "inner" and "outer" are not so much distinct, exclusive domains as boundaries shifting along a continuum. Lan Dingyuan's statement that the roots of correct government lie in the women's quarters expresses this clearly. The fruits of *nügong*, the products of the inner chambers, integrated women into networks that connected inner and outer worlds. However, between Song and Qing times the nature of these products and of the links they created changed, and in consequence there was a growing divergence between the social meaning that *nügong* held for the educated elite and for ordinary people.

The social value of an activity like textile production cannot be restricted to its monetary equivalent alone, as I suggested in chapter 4 when I drew attention to the multiple levels at which cloth contributed to cultural reproduction in China. Annette Weiner argues that in Oceanic societies the cloth women produced should be analyzed as a "soft" currency or possession that contributed as much to the reproduction of a society as did the "hard" currencies or possessions (such as precious metals, shells, weapons) produced and exchanged by men. "In Oceania, the development of ranking and hierarchy depends upon the work of women in their economic roles as the producers of wealth and, most important, in the power of their sacredness in confirming historical and cosmological authentication" through the keeping-while-giving of the inalienable possessions such as special cloths and regalia that women produce, thus defining the

---

47. E.g., Rosaldo and Lamphere 1974; Sacks 1974; Ortner and Whitehead 1981; Moore 1988: 47, 21. Marx first analyzed the role of unpaid domestic "reproductive" work in sustaining capitalist production. Now that *paid* domestic labor, in the form of home-based piecework and hired domestic help, has come to play so clear a role in reproducing the capitalist system of production in advanced economies like that of the United States, there is renewed analytical interest in the validity of distinguishing between "public" and "private" spheres, in the overlaps between women's productive and reproductive work, and in the linkage between gender systems and the global economy as it affects both rich and poor countries (e.g., Collins and Gimenez 1990).

political domain for both men and women "in terms of reproducing relationships and possessions in the face of loss."[48]

Weiner's study is a critique of the reciprocity theory of exchange. She affirms that if analysis focuses only on male, "hard" objects of exchange, a fundamental dimension of meaning is lost. Societies are all threatened by the "loss" of authenticity, authority and continuity through the death of individuals, through change, through the inexorable passage of time. Weiner suggests that one important meaning of the goods that are exchanged reciprocally lies in their contrast with what she calls "inalienable possessions," goods that either must not be given or must eventually return to the original owner. These "inalienable possessions" (heirlooms, regalia, family lands) are emblems of permanent identity, suffused with cosmological meaning; even when they are (temporarily) given away, their existence serves to maintain the identity and status of the givers. "Cloth may be the most apt metaphor to visualize the paradox of keeping-while-giving as societies in all parts of the world associate weaving with acts of tying and unravelling, sacred threads and dangerous dyes, woven warps and unworked woofs, expressions of longed for unity juxtaposed against the realities of death, destruction, and change." In a society with a gendered division of labor that attributes cloth making to women, "intricate symbolic meanings semantically encode sexuality, biological reproduction, and nurturance so that such possessions, as they are exchanged between people, act as the material agents in the reproduction of social relations. Most important, cloth possessions may also act as transcendent treasures, historical documents that authenticate and confirm for the living the legacies and powers associated with a group's or an individual's connections to the ancestors and gods."[49]

In the case of China, women's work of spinning and weaving is represented prosaically, in a totally demystified mode, in most of the historical documents that are available to us. There are no sacred texts of the weaving profession as there are for carpentry. We do not know what cosmological lore or imagery of descent and renewal might have figured in women's weaving songs, for the songs are not recorded.[50] I do not know if the pedigrees of precious cloths in China might at some stage have included the names of the women who produced them. It may be that the records of imperial collections do contain information of this kind of which I am

48. Weiner 1992: 153.
49. Ibid.: 154.
50. One contemporary exception is Elizabeth Johnson's study of Hakka women's weaving of ornamental bands for their clothes (1977).

unaware, but since the most precious textiles were produced in state manufactures it seems unlikely that they would have a pedigree analogous to
the cloaks of office and other previous cloths that Polynesian noblewomen
wove themselves.[51] But the role of exchanges of cloth between subjects
and state and during the ceremonies of marriages and funerals is proof
enough that textiles in China played a central role in maintaining unity
in the face of "death, destruction and change."

I have shown that by the late Ming the reduced participation of women
in "womanly work" caused considerable anxiety among members of the
male elite. Their concern with getting women back to their proper work
has to be considered as parallel with their worries about the moral and
political effects of a decrease in "manly work," as increasing numbers of
men sought employment outside subsistence agriculture. I have also argued that ordinary people were more concerned with the material results
of "women's work" than its political implications. Nevertheless, the
changes in the valuation of "women's work" in China cannot be simply
understood as an example of a universal materialist rule whereby economic earning power determines status. In the Chinese case the shift in
perceptions of gender roles even among ordinary people was intimately
bound up with women's loss of status as active subjects once a household's
tax dues were no longer partly payable in cloth. Once wives in poor families no longer contributed directly either to the state or to the family
income, the spatial seclusion of the inner quarters took on new meanings
of separation and dependence.

As the value of women's productive work was veiled, their reproductive
role became more dominant, both in elite philosophy and in ordinary life.
In elite philosophy and in well-off households, the reproductive responsibilities of a wife were conceived of as far broader and more important
than the simple bearing of children, and these duties continued to tie her
explicitly into the social and political world outside the walls of her chambers. A whole set of reproductive practices such as polygyny also tied elite
women and their families implicitly into the broader society—through
the interlocking of an internal and external reproductive hierarchy of
women. In poor families, however, such options were scarcer and there
were now fewer opportunities to counterbalance childbearing by the skills
in production that had formerly translated into economic and political

51. Precious textiles made in the Han manufactures were stamped with names
that might have been those of female weavers (Sheng 1995), but the significance
of this practice is not clear. On the robes and regalia of the Qing court, many of
which have survived, see Wilson 1986.

worth, integrating women into the world beyond the walls of the inner quarters. Gates argues that this was an important factor in reducing a woman's worth to her ability to bear sons; in part 3 I qualify this argument somewhat by suggesting that reproduction has to be understood more broadly across the social spectrum: even in poor families wifely success did not depend on natural fertility alone.

Although the central reason given for marriage in China was to produce descendants for the lineage, the couple were also jointly responsible for the ritual performances that maintained the social and spiritual fabric of society. Women in China classically contributed three indispensable items to the ritual reproduction of community and of family: offspring, food, and cloth. Marriages could not take place without the exchange of textiles, nor could funerals be conducted without the special archaic homespun that was worn at funerals and during the mourning period. These ceremonies served to reproduce male-centered Confucian patrilines, yet as Weiner remarks of Oceania, men depended on women to provide the "soft treasures" that constituted the key paraphernalia of these rituals.

The wife's contribution to rituals did not disappear with the changes in her productive role, but it was impoverished. After women gave up weaving they were still regarded as the people in charge of textiles within the household, so the effects of change in the textile industry in this domain should not be exaggerated. But the actual making of the cloth surely must have imparted a specifically female meaning into the rituals that was partly or wholly lost when commercial products were substituted.

Beyond the respectable Confucian interpretations of ritual textile uses, inscribed in liturgies and books of etiquette, there must have been other dimensions, magical for example, that were not recorded. To read cloth in patrilineal terms, the long threads of the warp resembled the male lineage, the weft threads wove in and out like brides—but how did men view the power that lay in women's hands as the weavers of these social metaphors? And did women read these symbols of social continuity in other than purely patrilineal terms? What did it mean to a bride when the fabrics and clothes she took with her to the new family on which her parents had bestowed her were fabrics she had woven herself, or embroidered in a group with her mother and sisters—a pretty twist on keeping-while-giving? One suggestive ethnographic example of a use of cloth to bridge the generations and transmute loss into keeping is cited by Emily Martin in an essay exploring possible differences between female and male ideologies of death: "If women as a gender are deeply involved in the nitty-gritty of the actualities of death, they seem in other ways to bring into

funerals concerns that at first glance have no place there. James Watson
... records that women of childbearing age, daughters and daughters-in-
law, wear a piece of green cloth on their person throughout the funeral
rites, in which they deal closely with the corpse and take its pollution on
themselves. Later this cloth is passed over a fire in purification, and then
*made into the centerpiece of the back-strap harnesses they use for car-
rying infants."*[52]

Even though domestic weaving declined, gifts of cloth remained an essential element of betrothal exchanges through the twentieth century.
Most of the dowry goods a bride took to her new home were cloth items
of some kind—clothes or bedding as well as bolts of cloth—many of which
she had woven or embroidered herself; it would be interesting to know
what importance was accorded to whether certain items of the dowry were
purchased or homemade. The centerpieces of the dowry were all destined
for the conjugal bed, and the motifs that a young woman embroidered on
her quilts, pillowcases and bed hangings were symbols of conjugal bliss
(phoenixes, mandarin ducks, and butterflies) as well as fertility.[53]

Although they embodied the orthodox wifely role in so many ways,
nevertheless dowry goods constituted a female form of property that
stood outside orthodox Confucian beliefs about joint family ownership.
As domestic weaving declined, embroidery seems to have played an increasing role in adding both economic and personal value to the goods
that a bride took with her as dowry. Whether woven or embroidered, these
goods were particularly precious because they constituted material links
with the bride's natal home. As well as a female, nonhegemonic form of
property, the quilts and robes and shoes and handkerchiefs also embodied
a nonhegemonic network of female kinship that was complementary to
the patriline, a bond between female kin that transcended the spatial
boundaries imposed by seclusion to link women separated by marriage.
The embroidered goods showed the groom's family how skillfully the
bride's female relatives had trained her.[54] And they were precious memen-
tos linking women who might never meet again.

Commoners produced the basic material goods necessary for human

52. Martin 1988: 172 (original emphasis), citing J. Watson 1982: 173–74.
53. See, e.g., Mann 1994: 31. Zhang Lüping's *Kunde baojian* (Golden guide to
feminine virtues), an almanac first printed in 1777 and written in a colloquial style
suitable for women who were not highly educated, contains numerous embroidery
designs as well as recipes, patterns for hats and shoes, prescriptions for pimples,
and tales of virtuous women (Ko 1994: 57).
54. In Ming times a bride-to-be in certain regions was expected to embroider
shoes for her mother-in-law or for other female in-laws (Ko 1994: 92, 170).

life, and within this sphere weaving was the female counterpart of tilling the soil. The elite worked with culture, *wen*, and within this sphere embroidery was a female counterpart of writing.[55] *Wen* denotes both the written word and decoration, as part of the complex of notions associated with cultivation, refinement and civility. The acme of maleness in late imperial China was represented not by physical strength or bravery, but by the intellectual, moral and bodily refinement of the male scholar, manifestations of *wen* that were also accessible to women of gentle nurture. As a physical apprenticeship in a conventionally female form of *wen*, embroidery was sometimes seen as a substitute for literacy and the moral cultivation it permitted, sometimes as its complement (as when male scholars took up embroidery), or sometimes as a distraction (certain late imperial scholars argued against parents allowing their daughters to embroider when they should be studying the appropriate classics). It was also an apprenticeship in womanly refinement that, unlike the study of the classics, was available to girls of low class, even though they were never able to advance as far in the art as girls who had servants to perform the rough work.

At the age when boys were sent off to the schoolroom to start grappling with the writing brush, girls were given their first training in plying the needle (fig. 25).[56] The skills were not simple, and "young girls began practicing at the age of ten so they could turn out elegant pillow-cases by the age of sixteen."[57] For fine work one needed fingers so smooth they

55. The Chinese word for embroidery is *xiu*; embroidery patterns are denoted by the term *wen*.

56. For descriptions of the main stitching techniques of Chinese embroidery and their historical development, see Gao Hanyu 1986: 28–36, 264–67. According to Gao, archaeological finds demonstrate that chain stitch embroidery was used early in the Zhou dynasty. By the Han techniques were already much more elaborate. Embroidered garments were a sign of high status, and special manufactures were established to produce the embroidered clothes and hangings used at court. Increasingly subtle techniques for approximating painting and calligraphy were developed in the Tang, Song and Ming, reaching their apogee in the Qing, by which time distinct regional styles of embroidery had developed. Embroidery served a variety of purposes. In its most exalted form it produced works of art that would be displayed just as paintings were. More commonly, it was used to decorate interiors, in the form of quilts, cushions, curtains, screens and hangings. As for clothing, fashions changed. Although embroidered bands were sewn onto fine garments in medieval times, they seem to have fallen out of fashion during the Song; a revival apparently began in the late Ming, and embroidered clothes were typical among well-to-do classes throughout the Qing.

57. Mann 1992b: 262. Men also worked in commercial embroidery shops, at least by the latter half of the nineteenth century, when Western observers were

would not snag the silk, so rough work and fine embroidery were incompatible; young commoner women did embroider their dowry goods, but such work could not be compared to the works of art that gentry ladies created. Dorothy Ko argues that in seventeenth-century Jiangnan embroidery took on the characteristics of the male art of painting: it became a means of expressing individual creativity. Although the most famous exponents of this art were women, some male scholars also took up embroidery at the end of the Ming and in the early Qing.[58]

Significantly perhaps, embroidered clothing seems to have come into fashion in the late Ming, at a time when elite women were seldom involved in the production of fine cloth for family use, and when many poor girls were no longer able to weave their own dowries. At the end of the seventeenth century Ye Mengzhu noted that there had been a shift from woven to embroidered designs. There is not sufficient evidence to say whether most of the embroidered sleeve-bands and slippers that elegant ladies wore were embroidered domestically or professionally. However, Li Yu talks disparagingly of hiring poor women as embroiderers, and we are told that it was possible for women of gentle birth to earn money by their embroidery skills if necessary—as shown by the late eighteenth-century case where "Shen Fu's future wife Yun took in embroidery work to pay her brother's tuition fees." In the late Ming and early Qing it is unlikely that there was the same commercial stimulus to embroider we see in certain port cities in the later nineteenth century, when the Western appetite for Chinese embroideries had gentlewomen in towns like Ningbo hard at work, and Lucy Soothill observed that in poor families women and girls were sometimes able to help out by working at embroidery.[59]

In the Ming and early Qing embroidery had a rather ambivalent status

---

often surprised at the proportion of male workers. However, the majority still seem to have been women and young girls (Wilson 1986: 106).

58. The most famous embroiderers were the women of the Gu family, who founded what we might think of as a school of art embroidery (Ko 1994: 173–75). It was a man, Imperial Candidate Gu Mingshi, who first won renown for his embroideries in the 1550s. But the wife of his second grandson, a woman named Han Ximeng, brought the Gu embroidery art to its acme, "blend[ing] the theory of painting with the skills of embroidery to the betterment of both" (Gao Hanyu 1986: 34). Several of her works have survived, and most of them bear her seal— the mark of art, not of craft. Gao (ibid.) offers an analysis of the motifs and techniques of Gu embroideries, mostly modeled on famous paintings of the Song and Yuan dynasties and remarkable for their bright colors and realistic textures.

59. For Ye Mengzhu see Wilson 1986: 58, and for the case of Shen Fu's bride, see ibid.: 105. On the Ningbo embroidery industry see Mann 1992b; Wilson 1986: 105 mentions Lucy Soothill's comments.

in the eyes of elite men. For an agrarian like Zhang Lüxiang writing of how to make a decent living by farming, embroidery was a frivolity that distracted from proper work: women should weave cloth, not decorate it. For well-off families it was the symbol of the leisure they could give their women: it marked them off from rough-fingered peasant women toiling at rush mats, and it contributed symbolic rather than material capital, an enhancement to the family's material surroundings produced within the seclusion of the inner quarters by women whose embroidery skills marked them as gently nurtured. Because there was as yet no real commercial market for fine embroidery, it was work and yet it was not work, "the hallmark of Qing domesticity."[60] No doubt as gentlewomen sat together over their sewing they were prompted to talk and dream in ways of which a strict Confucian would not approve. The gentlewomen of Huizhou used to keep their embroidery patterns folded between the pages of the popular romance *The Peony Pavilion*, a tale of a talented and unconventional beauty who died in the cause of true love but came back to life to enjoy marriage with her lover. As more conventional women sat sewing in their chamber, their imaginations roved through romantic landscapes far beyond.[61]

Both Lü Kun and Chen Hongmou deplored the fact that parents who loved their daughters were satisfied with training them to embroider. This they saw as second-best, an inadequate moral and practical education: instead girls should be taught to read so they could study moral principles for themselves.[62] Li Yu complained instead that gentlewomen of his time were abandoning embroidery for letters: "They pursue only men's skills, and sneer at women's work ... [and] even hire old women and poor daughters to make their three-inch arch shoes for them."[63]

As far as a woman's view of work and kinship was concerned, embroidery was very much productive labor in the social and symbolic sense, a form of "womanly work" that did not serve men, or the family, or the community, but consolidated bonds between women. All girls left their families on marriage and went to live with strangers, at which point the sternest forms of orthodoxy required that they cut the links with family and friends. They were accompanied on this frightening journey by embroideries that they had worked in the company of their mothers and

60. Mann 1992b: 260.
61. Ko 1994: 82.
62. Handlin 1975: 36–37.
63. Ko 1994: 175.

sisters, aunts and cousins, or friends of their own age from outside the family. Even an ordinary girl embroidered the shoes and quilts she took as dowry to her new home; the hard work and skill she had devoted to the task showed her fitness to serve as a daughter-in-law.[64] Though few women were literate, embroideries or woven patterns conveyed messages of affection and solidarity that otherwise could not have been expressed, and affirmed bonds between related and unrelated women that neo-Confucian orthodoxy did not encourage, or at any rate hardly recognized. (To give an extreme example, embroidery was the main occupation of girls in the famous "sworn sisterhoods" of late Qing South China, as they sat together in their special house in the evening singing and telling stories.[65]) The objects that women exchanged as tokens of friendship, such as handkerchiefs, fans, or shoes, were mostly embroidered.[66] They symbolized a life that reached beyond the walls of the inner quarters, a female network that transcended the spatial boundaries laid down for them by their male kin. No wonder the rituals of the Double Seventh festival—needle-threading competitions and the like—were celebrated enthusiastically by women throughout society.

WOMEN'S WORK AND PATRIARCHY

Henrietta Moore remarks that "cultural ideas about gender do not directly reflect the social and economic positions of women and men, although it is true that they originate within the context of these conditions. This is because gender stereotypes are developed and used in the strategies which

---

64. Mann 1994: 31.

65. Topley 1978: 253–56; Stockard 1989: 39–40. Hard evidence for institutions like sisterhoods is so far confined to South China and does not date back further than the second half of the nineteenth century. In the cases described by Topley and Stockard, working-class girls were able to maintain their sisterhood houses, often in the face of family opposition, at least in part because well-paid work was available for them in Western-style textile mills. But the sisterhoods of these peri-industrial zones were certainly rooted in older traditions. Drawing on evidence from local histories and other local writing, Helen Siu argues that in the Canton Delta delayed marriage and other practices that gave women unconventional freedom of action had been noted much earlier. What is interesting is that in the course of the cultural assimilation of the Canton region these practices were sometimes used as signs of gentility, sometimes of uncouthness; sometimes of non-Chineseness and sometimes of Han orthodoxy (Siu 1990).

66. The "women's script" poems of Hunan were often written on pieces of embroidered fabric (see the plates in Gao and Yi 1991). Ko gives examples of poems written in thanks for a gift of embroidered shoes (1994: 170).

individuals of both sexes employ to advance their interests in various social contexts."[67] This stricture applies not only to the relations between
ideology and material conditions within the societies that we study, but
also to our scholarly analyses of other societies. To explore the meanings
of women's work in imperial China, we have to try to disentangle the
relations between representations and experiences of the time, and also to
recognize and account for the stereotypes we have created for ourselves. I
think this is especially important when we try to understand how work
and changes in work fit into perceptions of the relations between men and
women in late imperial China.

In the retrospective analysis of female roles in premodern China, reproduction has loomed much larger than production. Until recently little
theoretical attention has been paid to the place of productive labor in the
construction of premodern women's roles. Daughters have been represented as essentially no more than future brides, and wifely identity has
been construed principally in terms of biological motherhood. But as I
discuss in part 3, though at one level this characterization of the wifely
role is an accurate reflection of Chinese sensibilities, one cannot help observing how closely the womb-focused image of Chinese wives mirrors
our own cultural predilection for construing female identity in terms of
biological reproduction and its control.[68] Moreover, as Dorothy Ko and
others have pointed out, such constructions of "traditional" women in
China are rooted in distorted and totalizing images generated by the nineteenth-century confrontation between China and the Western powers. In
the late nineteenth and early twentieth centuries, Western writers as well
as Chinese critics of the crumbling Qing state elaborated an Orientalist
image of the "traditional" Chinese woman—imprisoned in the inner
quarters, deprived of all freedom and true dignity, a powerless object of
exchange between patrilines, a baby machine physically deformed by the
practice of foot binding and morally deformed by the tyrannies of patriarchy, so crippled she was incapable of productive work—an image that still
directs the rhetoric and scholarship of many politicians and historians to-

---

67. Moore 1988: 37.
68. Weiner 1992: 13. Nor is this predisposition confined to the modern West,
remarks Weiner. "Hawaiian priests, Inka rulers, Greek philosophers, Christian
clergymen, and Western capitalists, to name only a few, systematically strip away
women's control over cosmological resources, thereby denying women's roles in
cultural reproduction and restricting their influence to reproducing the species"
(ibid.: 153). Note that the control over cosmological resources that Weiner attributes to women was frequently acquired through their material work, and in particular through the production of textiles.

day.[69] We have to bear in mind that this feminine image was not so much a true picture of the condition of Chinese women at the time as an expression of the historical crisis that then faced the Chinese nation.

One reason why Western perceptions of the wifely role in China have continued for so long to be preponderantly negative relates to the distaste that modern Western feminists feel for distinct and exclusive gender roles (especially if associated with social segregation of the sexes). The fact of women's seclusion in imperial China has disposed scholars to visualize women's work as being restricted simply because it took place within the inner quarters; we have therefore assumed that it was more or less limited to the reproductive activities that our own historical experience of industrialization leads us to associate with the domestic sphere. In the nineteenth and twentieth centuries, foreigners and Chinese reformers argued that a nation that bound the feet of its women and deprived them of education was crippling itself by crippling half its subjects. Bound feet supposedly confined women to the inner quarters and excluded them from productive labor. This was a double misunderstanding, however, first of what female seclusion in China was about, and second of how productive labor was organized in a preindustrial economy.[70] Nevertheless, the essentialization of a "traditional Chinese woman" certainly found some basis in the realities of the period during which it was formulated: late Qing women were secluded and subject to many forms of male control, they did have bound feet, and their role as economic and political actors was in many cases much less visible to themselves and to those around them than it had been in earlier times.

The changes in the textile industry in late imperial China served to consolidate a reconfiguration of gender roles structured by changes in kinship practice and in inheritance and property law. In part 1 I described the processes by which neo-Confucian values and practices associated with the seclusion of women were gradually diffused throughout society. Spatial seclusion did not in itself imply the inferiority or dependence of women,

69. What Ko calls the May Fourth view of Chinese history (1994: 7) continues to color the interpretations of much of the emergent feminist history within China, as well as the work of such Western scholars as Hill Gates, whose 1989 article concludes: "This essay speaks more to women's victimization than to their resistance."

70. Another misunderstanding concerns the extent to which bound feet impaired women's mobility and their capacity to work. See Blake 1994 and Mann 1992b on women's important contributions to the home-based industrial economy of rural and urban regions in the late Qing; Blake (1994) and P. Huang (1990: 55–57 and passim) discuss women's contribution to farm work outside the home.

however; whether seclusion translated into dignity or oppression depended in part on how those in control viewed human nature, to which form of neo-Confucian doctrine they subscribed. It also depended on the extent to which the secluded women were seen as participating in the world outside.

The veiling of the material value of women's work and woman's loss of status as active contributors to household tax payments provided fertile ground for acceptance of popular doctrines on male dominance and female subordination, such as the Three Obediences, that circulated widely during the late Ming and Qing; the situation also contributed to a revised view of women in which reproductive roles were much more prominent than productive roles. At the same time some elite views of the period expressed a contrasting though equally neo-Confucian formulation of gender relations that insisted on the inherent dignity of women as well as men, and on the need for active partnership between husbands and wives. Here too we see a growing concern with a wife's reproductive rather than productive roles. But as I argue in the following chapters, these reproductive roles extended far beyond the biological fact of giving birth. A gentlewoman's contribution to the state, formerly depicted primarily in terms of her work at the loom, came to be portrayed increasingly in terms of her moral worth, and in particular of the moral education she gave her children before sending them out into the world.

PART THREE

Meanings of Motherhood

Reproductive Technologies and Their Uses

The virgin Jiang Yuan stepped unaware in the footprint of God and became pregnant, giving birth to Hou Ji, Prince Millet. When he was born his mother regarded him "as unnatural and loathsome" because of his strange conception and abandoned him. But he was rescued; he grew up to teach humans to plant grain, and to found the royal dynasty of Zhou. Although Jiang Yuan abandoned her son, Liu Xiang (80–7 B.C.) included her under the rubric of "Maternal Paragons" in his *Lienü zhuan* (Biographies of exemplary women).[1] In the late imperial period, we find a whole corpus of memorial essays, genealogical entries, letters and autobiographies in which men wrote little that is personal about their father, but related in detail how their mother had struggled against poverty and adversity to educate them and push them on in life; these sons portrayed their mother's life as "a symbol of virtue and suffering." Often, however, the "mother" was not the woman who had given them birth, but the principal wife of their father, their "formal mother" (*dimu*).[2]

Women in the late imperial period are often portrayed as victims of their own biology, trapped by the pronatalist, patriarchal drive for sons. If they were fortunate enough to escape being drowned as infants, they were given less love and poorer treatment than their brothers. They were married or sold off young, and their new family accepted them only once they had given birth to a son. Bonds between husband and wife were weak, but those between mother and son were strong. A woman's success and happiness depended on her fertility, over which she had no control. She was, as the village women Margery Wolf worked with in Taiwan in the

1. Kinney 1993: 129.
2. Hsiung 1994: 88.

1960s put it, a "rented womb." There are many elements of truth in this stereotype, but it is far from the whole truth.[3] I have suggested that the maternal aspects of female roles came to figure more prominently, or even exclusively, in late imperial China than in earlier periods, and in the following chapters I show how this was reflected in medicine as well as in other domains of ideological orthodoxy. The important point is that maternity took many forms; it did not always correspond to the bundle of values and images we assign to it today, as the examples of Jiang Yuan and the beloved *dimu* suggest. I also show that there were different forms of maternal status in late imperial China, and different techniques—social and biological—for acquiring them. Not all women were victims of their wombs. Women could and did act to control their own fertility.

In the following chapters I treat the various material and social techniques used to produce desirable families in China, taken in the context

3. M. Wolf 1972. Like other versions of the "traditional woman as victim" stereotype, this particular version has served the modern state very well. In the first three decades after 1949 the state established a systematic network of rural health care services and pursued a successful campaign, based not on coercion but persuasion, of educating families in modern birth control techniques and encouraging them to have fewer children so that they could provide for them better. The experience of childbirth for most Chinese women was transformed. Rates of maternal and of infant mortality fell dramatically, as did birth rates (Banister 1987). At the same time women were integrated into the public workforce and rewarded at rates that were comparable, if not identical, to male rates. Women were not men's equals under the new regime, for the political structure still retained, indeed depended on, patriarchal mechanisms at every level. However, the transformation in individual women's lives, the dramatic contrast between the new and the "traditional" Chinese woman, helped mask the persistence of gender inequality (K. Johnson 1983; Stacey 1983). With the dismantling of socialist production units and the New Economic Policies pursued since the beginning of the 1980s, individual households once again became independent economic units struggling to survive in the marketplace. Many rural families then wanted more sons to help run the farm. (Since the state had never intervened to discourage patrilocal marriage, rural people still felt that sons were preferable to daughters, although the opposite is now sometimes true in the cities; M. Wolf 1985.) At the same time the state introduced draconian birth control policies that attempted to restrict families to a single child. As a result young rural wives have come under severe and contradictory pressures from their marital relatives and the state (Croll 1987). The often tragic results include forced abortions on the one hand, and savage beatings or even murder for giving birth to girls on the other, not to mention divorce and a resurgence of female infanticide. One response to the dilemma has been a resurgence of fertility magic and witchcraft (Anagnost 1989). The state is conveniently able to argue that in rural areas "traditional" views of women and reproduction were never properly eradicated and are now coming to the surface once again, rather than admitting that this is a thoroughly contemporary crisis caused largely by the contradictions and negligence in its own policies.

of theories of fertility and reproduction, as a set of "reproductive technologies" and as such an essential component of Chinese gynotechnics. It
may seem contrived to speak of "reproductive technologies" in premodern
China, since the term was coined to describe the modern products of scientific experiment, of the laboratory and the operating theater, involving artificial inserts and the synthesizing of drugs and tissues. Today we have the
technology to make fertile men and women effectively sterile, and we are
developing technology that we hope will make sterile men and women fertile. Implicit in the term *technology* is the notion of deliberate and effective
control.[4] When we think of the transformations we have wrought in "natural" reproductive processes by means of the oral contraceptive pill, the
intrauterine device, or in-vitro fertilization, we can hardly imagine that the
premodern world had parallels. But no human reproduction is "natural":
in every society people put immense effort into shaping and controlling
their reproductive processes. If we think of a technology as a system of
techniques for producing a specific material world, as I proposed earlier,
then every society has its own reproductive technologies, in which understandings of the fertile body and of kinship bonds translate into techniques
that are applied to bring about specific reproductive goals.

It is true that by the standards of modern science most of the direct
techniques of intervention employed by premodern societies to enhance
or diminish their fertility were at best unreliable. By direct techniques I
mean methods intended to produce or prevent a particular conception or
its consequences, including for instance coitus interruptus or other sexual
techniques, the consumption of herbal drugs, or the use of prayers or
spells. Some of these techniques were probably more efficacious even according to modern criteria than is usually assumed today, and I discuss
later the question of efficacy and whether such techniques might have
affected real fertility rates. When demographic historians try to explain
a society's fertility patterns, however, they reasonably presume that the
individual and cumulative effect of "proximate determinants"—social factors such as rules of marriage and nuptiality (who might get married and
at what age), the custom of employing wet nurses, or a general preference

---

4. The efficacy of most modern fertility-reduction techniques is high, but in
fact the New Reproductive Technologies, or NRTs, designed to overcome problems
of infertility, often produce conception rates almost indistinguishable from those
of comparable untreated couples (Sandelowski 1991). Nevertheless, the market
for NRTs is growing rapidly, and labeling these difficult, intrusive and expensive
treatments "technology" is clearly one important ingredient in commanding consumer confidence.

for accumulating family wealth rather than dispersing it among multiple heirs—was more likely than most direct interventions to translate into real demographic effects.

Real demographic effects, however, are only a point of departure for understanding reproductive behavior. Appealing for the investigation of "demographic mentalities," William Lavely and his colleagues call on fellow sinologists to cast their analytical nets wider so that "eventually we will understand not just how frequently individuals marry and give birth, but why."[5] For even the "how" cannot be fully understood unless we understand the "why." Every society has different notions of what children are for, where they come from, what parenthood is, what the desirable and what the attainable family might look like, and who may legitimately contribute to its composition. Lavely and his colleagues have labeled this web of ideas a "demographic mentality." Developed by *Annales* historians in the Durkheimian tradition, the term *mentality* primarily denotes common ways of thinking or casts of mind shared and accepted throughout a society. For myself I prefer to use the term *reproductive cultures*. The majority of anthropologists and social or cultural historians today treat culture not as homogeneous but as a shifting arena of contested definitions and conflicts over power—a big argument as much as a national anthem. By using "reproductive cultures" in the plural, I mean to convey a sense of different groups within Chinese society, groups with different resources, interests and identities, and of a corresponding heterogeneity and conflict in their strategies of reproduction, as well as overlaps and commonalities.

The techniques that people resorted to in order to achieve the family they wanted may not always have worked, even in their own estimation, but they tell us a great deal about how they understood their bodies, the nature of family relations, duty and pleasure, and about the goals they thought feasible and the forms of intervention they thought likely to achieve them. They throw light not only on collective goals but also on the different resources individuals might have at their disposal to fulfill their own hopes or ambitions. It therefore seems preferable to consider a society's reproductive techniques together as a set, "effective" and "ineffective" alike, and to presume that each of them had meaning and usefulness in the eyes of at least some members of that society.

Not all past societies have left the kind of traces that allow fruitful studies of their population history; the same applies to the qualitative

5. Lavely et al. 1990: 818.

study of their reproductive cultures. For imperial China we are fortunate in having rich legacies of both kinds. Genealogies and censuses are key sources for the former,[6] medical texts for the latter. Distinct disciplines do not always enter into dialogue even when they focus on the same object, and cultural historians are often suspicious of demographers. Barbara Duden seems fairly typical when she complains that techniques of historical demography "silence the body," reducing individuals to clusters of probable attributes construed in terms of the modern, biomedical body.[7]

In the case of late imperial China, however, it seems that demographic historians and cultural historians of reproduction have decided, at least temporarily, to profit from the essential tension between their disciplines rather than ignoring it.[8] Certainly it would seem foolish to construct self-contained hypotheses about reproductive behavior in late imperial China on the basis of qualitative documents alone, without reference to the fundamental work that demographic historians are carrying out on the structure of the family. My own research has concentrated on medical writings, but the writings of orthodox physicians deal with only a restricted proportion of the population, and in addition it is not easy to tell from the evidence internal to medical writings alone how medical theory and advice might have translated into behavior. What we know about actual family structures and demographic patterns is a necessary touchstone.

The family composition that demographers excavate from the historical records is like the material shell of the house. Beneath the visible structure lies an invisible architecture constructed according to plans and struggles that we only dimly apprehend, but that an investigation of reproductive cultures and techniques may help clarify. The visible structure of recorded births, marriages and deaths only hints at all the successful and unsuccessful actions, the varied techniques that went into its construction. They

6. Each type of data presents its own problems. Ho 1959 is the classic study of census data, their inadequacies, and how they may be addressed. Genealogies include all male members who live long enough to marry and have sons. But as one might expect in a Confucian culture, even the way males are treated is based on rank. Sons who die young may sometimes be omitted from the record, as may sons who leave the community and die elsewhere, while sons without issue of their own may be included in some genealogies only if a posthumous heir is adopted for them. It is usual to omit daughters. Wives and concubines, their names and vital data may or may not be recorded. All this makes it extremely difficult to reconstitute real historical populations from lineage records. Telford 1990 argues that "formal" demographic techniques should be applied not only to patch recognized holes in the data but also to identify holes that have hitherto been ignored.

7. Duden 1991: 192 n. 3.

8. See, e.g., the range of essays in Lee and Saito forthcoming.

include magic as well as medicine, abortions and infanticides as well as children raised to maturity, and the renaming and repositioning of off-spring born in one position but thought to fit better elsewhere. This con-struction, like the house that contains it, is an embodiment of domestic hierarchies, family status and good or bad fortune.[9]

The following chapters do not attempt to deal with all the elements that constituted the reproductive cultures of late imperial China. I am interested primarily in two related aspects: first, what the maternal role consisted of and how Chinese women could act to achieve it, and second, how the role of mother was embedded in the broader reproductive respon-sibilities of the wife.

In our own society we like to conflate biological and social parenthood, presuming that giving birth or contributing genetic material forges a bond between parent and child that is more real and more "natural" than any other kind and that lays the necessary groundwork for successful upbring-ing. This is by no means a universal understanding, as anthropologists have pointed out.[10] China also had a nature-nurture debate, but even in medical representations of fertility and maternity it is apparent that the

9. In exceptional cases where genealogical or registration data are particularly detailed, demographers have been able to demonstrate not only the differential fertility rates between rich and poor branches of the same lineage (Harrell 1985), but also the control exercised within the household over junior members' repro-ductive behavior (Lee and Campbell 1996: ch. 8).

10. E.g., Strathern 1992; Weiner 1992. The question of what constitutes "real" motherhood has surfaced repeatedly in the United States in the last few decades, requiring us to rethink the relative claims of different levels of the "natural" as well as of natural versus social kinship. Because in our society motherhood tends to be considered as integral and indivisible, any sharing between different kinds and degrees is discouraged. One arena of contest has been that of adoption, in which women often benefit from the childbearing of others lower in the prevailing class, race and/or national hierarchies. The NRTs have created further moral dilem-mas in which middle-class, middle-aged couples seem to be exploiting inequities of economic class, and often also of ethnicity or of generation. The paradox of what constitutes "real" kinship is clearly demonstrated in the contrast between surrogate motherhood and egg donation. In the first case, the claims of the em-ployers of the surrogate to be the "real" parents are based on the argument that *genetic* maternity, the provision of the ovum, is what really counts. In the second case, the contrary is argued, namely that the real child is produced not by the genetic blueprint in the ovum but by the social commitment implicit in the gesta-tion of the woman who has purchased the egg. To a cynical eye it seems that these contradictions are easily resolved if biology is set aside—money, not genetic material or gestation, determines kinship, and the "real" parent is the one who pays.

balance was more heavily tilted toward nurture than ours is at present, and nurture in the social rather than the biological sense at that. The medical specialisms concerned with fertility and childbearing blossomed in late imperial China; however, this medical literature does not convey the childbearing imperatives that one might have expected in a society organized around patrilineal descent. In chapter 7 I discuss how medical history can be explored to illuminate the issues of power and agency inherent in reproductive cultures, and I look at the extent to which physicians in late imperial China represented or were able to enforce orthodox values. In chapter 8 I discuss the understandings of physical fertility and of legitimate and effective reproductive interventions contained in the medical literature, and the dual meaning of motherhood, biological and social, implicit in orthodox Chinese gynecology. I then follow up the medical image of dual maternity to see how it fits into the broader social organization of gender and kinship. The legal code, social practice, personal biographies and literary tropes all concur in representing biological motherhood as less binding, less "real," than social motherhood. In the first part of chapter 9 I explore the social complementarities of the two aspects of motherhood, examining how polygyny and adoption, institutions commonly understood as serving the reproductive interests of men and of the patriarchal lineage, allowed high-status women to acquire social offspring. The marriage system allowed senior women to benefit from the fruits of junior women's wombs: bearing a child did not necessarily make one a mother, nor did infertility necessarily make one not a mother. What was overwhelmingly important, at least among the elite and well-to-do, was the bond forged between mother and child during the processes of upbringing and education.

Maternal identity must be understood as embedded within wifely identity in late imperial China, because the various tasks of reproduction that were a wife's responsibility went far beyond giving birth to babies. A wife was responsible for managing the inner domain, which is to say, not just what lay inside the household walls, but whatever fell outside the domain of masculine responsibility. In an elite family this included bringing up the children and seeing to their education, as well as organizing and overseeing the work of all the other women in the house—daughters, sons' wives, concubines and maids. Running the house meant making sure that all were clothed and fed, that the old were cared for and attended to as well as the young, and that the ancestral cult was carried out properly. Running the household meant taking responsibility for the family finances, which in well-to-do or elite families frequently involved running the estate, making investments, paying wages and keeping the accounts.[11] A wife's responsibilities were therefore not bounded by the walls of the inner chambers. Furthermore, she formed persons in order that they could cross those boundaries successfully. A woman trained her own daughters to become wives themselves; when her sons married, she made proper daughters-in-law of the new brides. Her sons she educated and then sent out into the wider world as representatives of their lineage, and of her own maternal virtue.

But not all women in late imperial China were wives, even though the majority were attached to men through forms of marriage. Not every woman who gave birth was a mother, nor was every woman who married a wife. As social historians have argued, it makes sense to think of legal wives, minor wives, concubines and maids as occupying different rungs on a single ladder of gender subordination[12]; as in all Confucian hierarchies, the meaning of the continuum lay in its ranked differences. Institutions such as concubinage served to reinforce the social hierarchies among women—and among men, and among families. They not only permitted the reallocation of children, but also took material form in everyday divisions of labor, in the occupation of household space, and in the differential allocation of reproductive responsibilities in the broadest sense. I therefore conclude chapter 9 with a consideration of female reproductive tasks in general and of how they fit into broader notions of male and female complementarity and the historical shaping of Chinese gender roles.

11. Many scholar families, though of high social status, were far from well-off, and there are many stories of wives whose hard work and astuteness enabled them to keep the family going until at last their husband or their son managed to pass his examinations and gain a well-rewarded official post.

12. Gates 1989; R. Watson 1991.

7 Medical History and Gender History

As the earlier chapters on domestic space and the symbolic importance of the bridal bed made plain, it was expected of married women in imperial China that they would produce children, and in particular that they would give birth to sons who would be heirs for the lineage (fig. 20). "Five sons and two daughters" were what the wedding guests wished a bride during the Song period.[1] The gravest offense against filial piety that a man could commit, not only toward his parents but toward his ancestors in general, was to fail to continue the line.

Up until the Song the ancestral cult was organized according to aristocratic values and honored primogeniture. The neo-Confucian reformulation of kinship included all family branches in the joint ancestral cult. The proportion of the Chinese population incorporated into such patrilineal webs expanded steadily from the Song and Yuan on. One significant effect, as Charlotte Furth remarks, was that this revised and more egalitarian system of patrilineality, with its dual focus of lineage and domestic shrine, "made every elder the potential ancestor of his own individual line of descent."[2] The failure to produce sons was seen in late imperial times as both a private and a public problem. The founder of the Ming dynasty, the Hongwu emperor (r. 1368–99), ordered that village altars should be set up to solace those without heirs, and the Ming code "stipulated that a man who had reached the age of forty and had no sons by his wife could take a concubine," although under other circumstances concubinage was

1. Ebrey 1993: 172.
2. Furth 1990: 189, discussing the genre of household instructions (*jiaxun*), written by elders to keep their heirs in line after their own death. This genre became increasingly popular among the petty gentry in the late imperial period. On the neo-Confucian reformulation of kinship principles, see Ebrey 1986.

Figure 20. "The split gourd" (*Qing Customs* A: 382–83). The new bride and groom are sitting in her chamber on the rumpled quilts of the bed the bride brought with her as part of her dowry. Both look awkward and shy as one of the maids pours wine into each half of the split gourd cup that symbolizes the loss of the bride's virginity. The peaches on the folding door of the sleeping alcove are symbols of fertility.

punishable by "forty blows with the light bamboo."[3] Furthermore, failure to bear sons was a legitimate reason for a wife to be divorced. In this context it is not surprising to find in the medical literature from Song times on a growing concern with producing descendants, with fertility, female health, childbirth, and the care of infants, which presumably mirrored the preoccupations of the population at large.

The relevant categories of medical specialization include *fuke* (women's [or rather wives'] medicine) and *erke* (children's medicine), both of which became well established in the Song; specialist texts on the medical approach to childbirth (*chanke*) also appear at this period. Although in the Song some physicians developed these specialisms along lines that went beyond direct reproductive concerns (based on the theory that, given their different natural endowments of *yin, yang* and *qi,* men, women and children would experience similar complaints in different forms and require different treatments), later this aspect was assimilated into general

3. Waltner 1990: 17, 22.

medicine, except in the field of pediatrics. *Fuke* came to concentrate on all aspects of female health related to conception, pregnancy, childbirth and postnatal problems, corresponding quite directly to our own term *gynecology*. There were also cross-gender categories like *guangsi* (multiplying descendants) or *zhongzi* (begetting sons) which dealt with problems like *buyu* (infertility).[4] One might also note a shift in medical theories of sexuality. The medieval emphasis on conserving semen or male essence, *jing*, as the source of longevity faded into the background in medical writings on sexuality, which now became preoccupied with how best to dispense male and female essence in order to achieve conception.[5]

Both medical theory and popular belief recognized the existence of male as well as female infertility. In medical theory, male infertility was generally caused by such factors as excess of emotion or of sexual activity. Remedies included diet to build up the male principle and sexual restraint or abstinence.[6] According to popular religious belief, Heaven might punish individuals for their own sins or for those of their ancestors by depriving them of offspring. Ann Waltner cites a Yuan text that says infertile men were referred to as "natural eunuchs": their childlessness was interpreted as divine castration. Ming ethnographic authors report a widespread pop-

4. Furth 1986, 1987; Hsiung forthcoming. The historical trajectory of these genres, the early roots of these branches of specialist knowledge, their consolidation by Song and Yuan physicians, and the exponential growth in the number of titles during the late Ming and the Qing are clearly demonstrated in the many excellent bibliographies of Chinese medical works, e.g., Guo 1984–87 or Xue 1991.

5. Hsiung forthcoming; Furth 1994. The early and much of the medieval discourse on sexuality—popularized in the West by the writings of Van Gulik—showed a male making use of multiple female partners, building up his male essence by absorbing their female essence. The ideal female partner was young and immature, well below the age before which pregnancy was advisable. But the point of intercourse was for the man to take advantage of his partner's orgasm, in which she exuded female essence, while fending off orgasm himself in order to conserve *jing*. Impregnation was therefore not part of the ideal sexual encounter. The "child" that such intercourse aimed to produce was the man's spiritual "inner child" (Schipper 1982). As Furth points out, the practices advocated in the medieval texts imply an aristocratic lifestyle. These ideas continued to circulate in later imperial China, but largely within the rubric of writing on *yangsheng* or longevity, or of Daoist practices that were viewed by the orthodox as transgressive. The *guangsi* writing of late imperial China, heralded by Sun Simiao (c. 581–682), emphasized sexual moderation and firmly presented the goal of intercourse as conception. Intercourse itself was now represented as a long-term partnership between a man and his wife, both of suitable age to beget and bear healthy children. Writers such as Wan Quan "encouraged women, like men, to strive for continence and self-mastery, and offered both the reward of erotic fulfillment through the begetting of children" (Furth 1994: 144).

6. See Furth 1994 and Hsiung forthcoming.

ular belief in the Celestial Hound, who caused sterility and infant disease and was fought with peachwood arrows by Immortal Zhang.[7] Offending one's ancestors by carelessness in performing the ancestral offerings, the poor placing of graves, or general immorality could also cause childlessness. Prayers, rituals, amulets and fertility potions could all help.

As one might expect in a society organized around the continuation of the male descent line, however, it was female fertility that came under most immediate and frequent scrutiny. The gynecologist and pediatrician Wan Quan (1488–1578?) was a renowned physician and a prolific writer in all the fields just mentioned.[8] In one of several works that he wrote on "multiplying descendants" he includes a passage on "selecting a mate" in which he lists the popular notions of how to recognize fertile women and sets forth five types of women considered unsuitable for marriage on account of their presumed inability to have children.[9] Women anxious to conceive paid large sums for fertility potions. The cults of fertility deities flourished, and most supplicants prayed for sons.[10] Boy preference was clearly expressed at every cultural level, from medical advice on "planting sons" (*zhongzi*) to popular imagery.[11] Woodblock prints of plump, rosy-cheeked

7. Waltner 1990: 18. Peachwood arrows were considered from ancient times the most effective weapon to ward off evil spirits, and the fruits of the peach symbolized the related blessings of fertility and immortality. The earliest explicit medical discussion of "natural eunuchs" is probably by the sixteenth-century physician Wan Quan (see Furth 1994). In the late sixteenth-century pharmacopeia *Bencao gangmu*, Li Shizhen provides further discussion of the five "false males" and the five "false females" in the section on "human categories." The "false females" are rendered infertile by anatomical abnormalities that prevent effective penetration. However, the natural eunuch *(tianhuan)* is a man whose *yang* is too weak to be of use (*Bencao gangmu*: 2971–72); it is not clear whether this signifies irremediable infertility or not.

8. On Wan Quan see, e.g., Li Jingwei et al. 1988: 10 and Furth 1994.

9. Hsiung forthcoming, referring to the sixteen-section *Guangsi jiyao* (Essentials for multiplying descendants). As mentioned in note 7 of this chapter, this list is also included in the *Bencao gangmu*, which was widely read and cited. These categorizations of infertile types were not developed on the basis of medical theory, however, but seem to have been drawn from widespread lay ideas.

10. On the use of fertility potions depicted in the late Ming novel *Jinpingmei*, see Cullen 1993. Fertility cults included goddesses like Gaomei the matchmaker and Nine-Son Mother, who dealt specifically with infertility, safe childbirth and infants' health, as well as deities whose powers ranged much further, like Guanyin. Interestingly, several of the deities were women who had never married or borne children (J. Watson 1985: 320). Bodhisattva Guanyin was originally depicted as male, but began to be represented as female in the course of the Song.

11. Both classical Chinese medicine and folk beliefs offered methods for conceiving a child of the desired sex and for diagnosing the sex of a fetus. Many medical works on pregnancy and childbirth, as well as more popular writings such

infant boys playing with peaches were pasted up in peasant homes at New Year, while in the inner quarters of prosperous ladies lacquer chests were inlaid with motifs of baby boys at play.

Infanticide was a common method of dealing with unwanted births in late imperial China, and as far back as records go, girls were far more likely to be killed than boys.[12] There is abundant evidence of female infanticide in late imperial China,[13] often explained by shocked observers as a wish to avoid the burden of dowries. There is also evidence that before their thorough integration into Chinese culture the inhabitants of many regions (especially the southeast coast and the lower Yangzi) killed male as well as female infants to achieve their ideal family size.[14] Moreover,

---

as household encyclopedias, give magical methods for changing the sex of an un-born child—from male to female as well as from female to male (Leung 1984; Hsiung forthcoming). Presumably a child of the desired sex was born sufficiently often for many people to have faith in these techniques.

12. See Kinney 1993 on the period up to the end of the Han, and Li Zhende 1995 on the period from the Han to the Sui. At that time infants were likely to be killed not only because their family could not support them, or because they were deformed, or because they were girls, but because they might bring misfortune on their family. Numerous children born under an unlucky astrological combination were killed or abandoned. Given our ignorance of actual birth rates, it is difficult to say with any confidence just what proportion of infants, male or female, were killed at birth. Nor, since we know little about infant mortality at present, and since children were not registered in Chinese genealogies or local records until they reached the age of three or four, is it possible to say anything much about selective neglect. Confident comparisons between dynasties are not possible either, though some comparisons between regions and classes in the Qing have now been published (e.g., Telford 1990 and Lee forthcoming). In a study of a particularly well-documented community in eighteenth- and nineteenth-century Liaoning, James Lee and Cameron Campbell "estimated that approximately one quarter of all daughters were victims of sex-selective infanticide. . . . The general rule was the higher the position, the more children and the larger the proportion of boys" (Lee forthcoming, citing joint research). The Liaoning group studied here lived on restricted banner land and may not have been typical of the Chinese population at large, if "typical" behavior can ever be expected in a matter of this kind.

13. Indeed in recent years it has been widely practiced in the People's Republic, along with sex-selective abortion made possible by the increased availability of amniocentesis. Elizabeth Croll, Amartya Sen and many other analysts have pointed out that the combination of the One-Child Family Policy and the liberalization of the economy has had a disastrous effect on sex ratios (Croll 1987; Sen 1990). However, Susan Greenhalgh and Jiali Li conclude that infanticide is a possible, but not proven, contributor to current skewed sex ratios and in any case would play only a minor role (Greenhalgh and Li 1995).

14. In around 1079 the poet and government official Su Dongpo wrote about the regions that now comprise Zhejiang and Hubei: "The commoners of Yue and E regions customarily want to rear only two boys and one girl. Newborn babies after that will be killed" (T'ien 1988: 26). T'ien cites several other cases from the

even in a culture that generally valued sons, a sudden crisis might also cause harassed parents to kill newborns of either sex, including in well-to-do families.[15]

Infanticide is the most effective way of controlling family size in response to sudden crisis. It is also a foolproof way of exercising sex selection if all other means fail. It may therefore have much to recommend it if we presume some kind of impersonal patriarchal establishment, or even the husband or mother-in-law rather than the new mother herself, to be the principal agent in reproductive decision making. But quite apart from any moral scruples or aversion to cruelty that other members of the family might feel, it can hardly be the fertility-control technique of choice as far as the mother is concerned: she has to go through the burdens and anxieties of pregnancy and the agonies of childbirth, only to suffer the further agony of the death of her infant.[16] If women in late imperial China were indeed more than the passive victims of their wombs, one might expect that they would try to deal with unwanted pregnancies at an earlier and

---

Song dynasty of regions where "local customs imposed heavy burdens on child-rearing." A Song memorial of 1112 uses the same rice-farming term that was used in Japan, "weeding out of children," to describe and condemn practices that occurred in the southeast (ibid.: 27).

15. The dramatic fluctuations in grain prices in eighteenth-century Liaoning represent one such crisis (Lee et al. 1992). In earlier dynasties the requirement to pay poll tax on children, or oppressive military or corvée labor requirements, also often led parents to kill their infants. An edict of 1109, banning the practice of infanticide in Fujian, reads: "Many in this province were apt to kill or drown newborn infants without distinction by sex as soon as the official taxes and corvée regulations had been periodically fixed, in order to avoid an increased reassessment of their lot" (T'ien 1988: 26).

16. There was apparently no Chinese equivalent to the Japanese practice where parents of "weeded-out" *(mabiki)* children set up small gravestones where they make offerings to them in expiation. The common term for these children in Japanese is *mizuko* (water children), and LaFleur 1992 traces the notion of the liquidity and fungibility of early human life implied in this term back to pre-Buddhist beliefs. Discussing infanticide in early modern Japan, LaFleur characterizes Confucian condemnation of this practice as an objection to *waste,* that is to the waste of potential subjects of the state. This seems to have been true of pronatalist Japanese ideology in the early modern period, and it may have been one element in the revulsion for the practice expressed by the Chinese bureaucrats of the earlier imperial period and up to the Song (see, e.g., Kinney 1993 on Han conscription, and the request of the minister of war in 1109 that the imperial prohibition of infanticide be extended from Fujian to all the Yangzi provinces [T'ien 1988: 26]). Although as a feminist I am not particularly sympathetic to most forms of neo-Confucian morality, I do think LaFleur's interpretation undervalues the role of human-heartedness in Confucian aversion to infanticide, at least in the late imperial Chinese case.

less painful stage. Chinese medicine, folk and learned, contained enormous numbers of drugs thought to abort fetuses, several of which were probably quite effective.[17] And moral writings, novels and so on tell us that men in the late imperial period frequently worried that their wives would consort with disreputable women who could sell them such drugs.

THROUGH A GLASS DARKLY: THE QUESTION OF EFFICACY

Even if the Chinese believed they possessed a whole range of effective techniques for fertility control, including drugs that would cause abortions, did these methods actually work in individual cases, and were they effective (and often enough used) to the extent of influencing population trends?

Let us for the moment assume that the answer to the first question is yes. The second question presumes that we can tell the difference between a population's actual fertility rate and the "natural" rate that would represent unmodified reproduction (unmodified, that is, within that society's specific framework of social structures like marriage practices). One problem here is that Chinese population records make it difficult to reconstitute live birth rates and natural or induced infant mortality with any certainty, and the records tell us nothing about pregnancy rates, only about the number of children that lived long enough and were considered important enough to be recorded.[18] The records do show a consistent skew in favor of sons, proving that female infanticide and/or neglect were important factors in affecting population trends; evidence for male infanti-

17. Kong et al. 1976.
18. Chinese demographic history still raises at least as many questions as it answers. The documentation of family data through genealogies and household registration becomes more widespread over time, and this in itself makes comparisons between periods difficult. For instance, we cannot realistically compare rates of male celibacy or of concubinage for the Song and the Qing, nor can we document trends in female fertility rates. Because the genealogies and household records that have provided so much of the fundamental data treat offspring as belonging to the father rather than the woman who bore them, in a polygynous household we cannot always be sure which children were whose. Even when the number of a woman's children is recorded, we usually have no means of knowing if that was all the children she ever gave birth to or whether it was only those who survived infancy. The practice of registering pregnancies, which Ohta and Sawayama (forthcoming) describe for late Tokugawa Japan, is the only example I know of any premodern society where records might permit us a rough reconstitution of total pregnancy rates across a community. Apparently official attempts were made to register pregnancies and to supervise births in order to prevent unwarranted infanticide in early China, but no family records were kept at the time (Kinney 1993).

cide (or perhaps for temporary abstention from procreation) in times of stress can also be recovered from these records.[19]

One challenge is to explain the overall flatness of Chinese fertility curves, where married women bore few children of either sex. James Lee shows that Chinese women's fertility during the eighteenth and early nineteenth centuries was very low compared to Europe in the same period. "[Women] who married at age twenty and remained in a monogamous union until age forty-five gave birth on average to only five children; similarly situated European women had ten. . . . European wives in their twenties were twice as likely to give birth as similar age Chinese wives."[20] These low fertility rates were not unprecedented in Chinese history. Ebrey, working with the funerary biographies of 189 couples during the Song period, finds only slightly higher rates of marital fertility among her elite population. Married in their late teens, the women who survived to forty-five without being widowed averaged 6.1 recorded children.[21] Again, six live children over a fertile period of some twenty-five years is not many, even when high infant mortality, natural miscarriages, still-births, and other causes of premature death are taken into account.

China demographers are no longer content to attribute the phenomenon of low marital fertility to infanticide alone—they have now started to take the contemporary cultures of reproductive control more seriously. Lee and his colleagues explain the flatness of the late imperial Chinese fertility curve in two ways. One is through the exercise of sexual moderation, that is to say, a "preventive check."[22] Once conception has occurred,

19. Lee forthcoming; Lee and Campbell 1996.
20. Lee forthcoming; see also Li Bozhong 1994 on low fertility curves in mid-Qing Jiangnan.
21. Ebrey 1993: 172.
22. Lee forthcoming; Lee and Saito forthcoming. The hypothesis of a culture of sexual moderation is also invoked by Li Bozhong 1994. The rationale behind such a culture, according to these authors, is the wish to maintain or improve living standards. See Hsiung forthcoming for a detailed account of popular and medical prescriptions for sexual moderation. However, it has to be recalled that medical texts advocating sexual moderation are normative, not descriptive. The extent to which they translated into behavior in the bedroom remains hypothetical. Some demographic studies claim to be able to deduce coital frequency from fertility curves, and may adduce surveys of sexual habits to support their findings. I confess to being deeply dubious about such claims. In the late imperial Chinese case, on the one hand, there is a flourishing medical and moral literature, with a long historical tradition, that advocates sexual moderation. On the other hand, there is profuse evidence that prostitution was widespread and increasing, and that even the puritanical cultural clampdown of the Qing was unable to stamp out the "decadence" (sexual and otherwise) to which the decline of the Ming was

however, they apparently do not consider that any intervention would be likely to be effective before the child was born, which means that for them abortion is effectively ruled out as a fertility check. Other historians are more open-minded about the effectiveness of abortion.[23]

A few years ago Basim Musallam castigated demographers for assuming that effective birth control was a product of Western modernity. One reason for this widespread assumption (which seems to have carried over into contemporary East Asian demography) was that until recently most premodern methods of contraception or postconceptive intervention were presumed not to be effective. As well as Musallam, Norman E. Himes, George Devereux and Angus McLaren have each shown that premodern societies were familiar with a far greater range of fertility control methods than we imagine, a number of which were "effective" even in modern scientific terms.[24] Himes, writing in 1936, documented an astonishing range of contraceptive methods practiced in premodern societies, including charms, spells, suppositories, douches, inserts and condoms, and a vast range of oral medicines. In those days it was possible for him to classify the oral medicines along with charms and spells as "superstitions," asserting authoritatively that no oral preparation could possibly have been effective in preventing conception! Himes acknowledged, however, that many of the barrier methods, as well as coitus interruptus, were effective

---

frequently attributed. How are we to reconcile these two conflicting images of a sexual culture and translate them into an ordinary couple's bedroom behavior? Moreover, we might note that in late imperial China sexual moderation was advocated both for reasons of health and as a means to conceiving "good-quality" offspring—a theory also in vogue in modern Western medical fertility treatment. How confident then can we be in linking coital frequency with conception rates?

23. E.g., Hsiung forthcoming. Kong et al. (1976) conducted laboratory analyses of a number of drugs from the Chinese materia medica believed to produce abortions, and found a great many of them to be effective; they went on to suggest that several of them should be investigated as potential antifertility treatments. Many of the traditional prescriptions are still used by Chinese physicians today, sometimes to abort, other times to expel a dead fetus or the placenta.

24. Musallam 1983: 4; Himes [1936] 1970; Devereux 1976; McLaren 1984, 1990. Himes drew mainly on writings about contraception, and his scope was therefore largely limited to the literate traditions of Eurasia. Obliged as he was to work principally with translations and secondary sources, Himes's work can be criticized for misrepresenting some of the cultures he discusses (Musallam points out that Himes was apparently unaware of one of the most important scientific Arabic texts on fertility control and mistakenly took popular texts as representative of the scientific knowledge of the period [1983: 73–75]). Devereux, an anthropologist, used reports of abortion from about 350 "primitive" societies for his analysis.

if not foolproof. Musallam, in his study of Muslim attitudes toward contraception, goes a step further, to argue that in Egypt and Syria under Mamluk and Ottoman rule, the use of premodern contraceptive techniques affected population patterns significantly.[25]

Two important methodological points arise from Musallam's fine study. The first concerns the concept of efficacy and the criteria by which it is judged. From the point of view of the historical demographer, it makes perfect sense to ask of a birth control technique whether it *really* worked, and to discount analytically those practices whose efficacy cannot be demonstrated in scientific terms. Did Tibetan crocus really cause abortions, and if not, do we need to know that Chinese pharmacology said it did, and that Chinese women dosed themselves with "red pills" that included Tibetan crocus if they wanted to terminate a pregnancy? If one is looking at fertility rates, then the question of efficacy is important, but partial efficacy has to be taken into account as well. And if one is looking at cultures of reproduction, then the implications of efficacy or inefficacy have to be thought about differently. What is significant is the intention to abort, and the attempt to do so—and here it is the belief that the procedure worked that counts. How such belief and practice translate into demographic evidence is not something one can predict a priori, but it is something we need to consider carefully.[26]

Medical anthropologists have criticized the application of biomedical criteria of efficacy to nonbiomedical therapies on the grounds that healing is a complex and subjective process, not necessarily equivalent to the elimination of a biological pathogen.[27] One might argue that in the case of fertility control the case is more clear-cut: either a new baby joins the family or it does not. The only premodern method of fertility control that can be considered truly effective is infanticide; together with neglect,

25. Although absolute population figures for Egypt and Syria, from the time of the Black Death in the fourteenth century to the mid-nineteenth century, are difficult to reconstruct, demographers do agree that the population actually declined during this period. Musallam argues that this unusual pattern cannot be explained in Malthusian terms but must have been the result of deliberate birth-control efforts (1983: 105–21).

26. As Hsiung (forthcoming) points out, Chinese medical theory advocated the first few days after menstruation as the best time to conceive, so that women who tried to avoid conception by waiting until mid-month were, according to modern views, actually increasing their chances of becoming pregnant; conversely, women who wanted to conceive might fail to do so. How this would translate into a resultant effect on fertility rates is quite impossible to say.

27. Etkin 1988: 299.

infanticide is also the last, dramatic resort if other more private methods fail.[28]

Musallam, however, makes the important point that to understand a society's fertility patterns we should consider fallible as well as infallible methods. The birth control techniques most frequently referred to in Muslim jurisprudence and in medieval Middle Eastern medical and popular literature (namely, coitus interruptus and vaginal suppositories) were recognized at the time to be possibly rather than infallibly effective.[29] This did not stop people using them with sufficient frequency to have a significant effect on population trends, Musallam believes. I would argue that the same was true of abortion in late imperial China: it worked sometimes but not always, though often enough to have a slightly flattening effect on the famous curve.[30] Indeed it is reasonable to keep an open mind on the efficacy of much wilder-sounding premodern birth control methods, considering that in recent years the number of drugs and techniques scientifically demonstrated to exercise at least a partial control over fertility has expanded considerably. Methods now include oral as well as barrier contraceptives and a whole range of abortifacients; there is currently even a widespread medical interest in how psychological factors might affect

28. Even infanticide is only truly effective in its most drastic form where the infant is actually put to death. Like neglect, exposing or abandoning the newborn is a method that cannot be counted on, as the Egyptian pharoah who ordered Moses to be cast on the waters, and Laius who exposed Oedipus on the mountainside, found out to their cost. Kinney gives the story of a woman in Han China whose child started crying in her belly two months before it was due. When it was born she buried it in a path between the fields, but on the third day some passersby heard the child crying, whereupon the mother dug it up and raised it. Since the third day was the day on which a father publicly acknowledged a newborn child, the timing here is obviously significant (Kinney 1993: 125). Many parents who abandoned an infant did so in the hope that its death could be avoided, and that charitable strangers would care for the child better than they could themselves. This was certainly true in China. It was regarded as an act of virtue, and in later periods also as an act of Buddhist merit, to rescue and care for abandoned children, either as an individual or as a community; see, e.g., Brook 1993; Leung 1987; Waltner 1990 on orphanages and fostering. Fostering was carefully distinguished, however, from adoption, which established a completely different order of claims between the persons involved (Waltner 1990).

29. In the case of paternity suits, for example, Muslim jurisprudence was clear that a man could not deny paternity merely on the grounds of having practiced coitus interruptus (Musallam 1983: 19). Under Muslim law contraception was admissible, but late abortion and infanticide were considered equivalent to murder and were strictly forbidden.

30. For my contribution to Lee and Saito (Bray forthcoming), the editors suggested that I should try to estimate the relative importance of abortion and infanticide. I confess that so far I cannot think of any way of doing so.

conception.[31] There are thus good positivist reasons to look closely at a society's reproductive techniques as a complete repertory, rather than just singling out those that we assume were most likely to have worked.

Musallam's study raises another important methodological point, namely the reconstruction of goals and motives, the "why" of Lavely's "demographic mentalities." The reconstruction of *intentions* is delicate and requires a careful reading of qualitative sources. How, for instance, do we reconstitute a society's understanding of desirable or tolerable ratios between population and resources? Musallam argues strongly that religion and politics cannot be separated from economics in reconstructing the rationale for limiting births in the premodern Middle East. Islamic law permitted birth control during "hard times"; it *required* it under enemy rule.[32] Musallam believes that the reproductive decisions of the city

31. As well as scientifically tested and industrially produced contraceptives, biomedicine has also developed New Reproductive Technologies that aim not to reduce but to enhance fertility. Here both medical and popular understandings of a desired conception and pregnancy emphasize their difficulty and precariousness, and identify innumerable threats to successful childbearing that have reduced the status of pregnant women, or of women attempting to conceive under medical supervision, to a veritable moral and physical enslavement (see, e.g., Bordo 1993: 71–98; Sandelowski 1991). The would-be mother has not only to avoid all potentially harmful material influences—ranging from dioxins in the workplace to cigarette smoke in the home, and from hard drugs to hair colorants—she is also supposed to display motivation and perseverance in following highly intrusive medical regimens, and at the same time to cultivate the serenity that is widely held to contribute to successful fecundation and gestation. One example that particularly took my fancy was a recent series of articles in the French popular media on the NRTs, in which the fertility experts and psychologists interviewed recommended that women who wished to conceive should first undergo therapy to make sure that they were not suffering from unresolved conflicts with their own mothers. If we turn the wisdom concerning successful childbearing on its head, we come up with recipes for controlling fertility. In today's Western culture of reproduction, a woman might well presume that a cocktail every evening and a weekly quarrel with her mother were a guarantee against unwanted pregnancy. Perhaps the most astonishing case of effective premodern birth control I have come across is the system of mandatory abortion practiced by the Siraya in Taiwan, as recorded by seventeenth-century Dutch observers. Married women were not expected to bear children until they were in their late thirties, and until then were likely to undergo numerous abortions obtained through a painful process of violent massage (Shepherd 1990).

32. "The late medieval Hanbalis, strictest of jurists, insisted that birth control was mandatory for a Muslim family under enemy control" (Musallam 1983: 120). It was a fascinating experience to read Musallam's account of classical Islamic jurisprudence and its attitudes toward sexuality, birth control, and men's and women's rights—many of which twentieth-century Westerners would consider extremely liberal—just as the Vatican was forging an alliance with Islamic fundamentalist regimes to repudiate the proposals concerning reproductive rights that

dwellers of Egypt and Syria under Mamluk rule were driven by religious concerns that to us might appear primarily economic. The good Islamic life required a relatively high level of material ease so that children could be educated and religious duties fulfilled properly; it also included the freedom to live a Muslim life in security. That is why Islamic law urged good Muslims to sacrifice the pleasure of children under infidel rule. Reconstructing the "economic" tolerances that helped define the demographic mentality of premodern Egypt and Syria requires a sophisticated consideration of how religion defined parenthood and the rights and duties entailed in reproduction.

Interesting Chinese parallels to the Muslim quest for a "good life" in the face of material difficulties, or of new opportunities to rise in the world, surface in the demographic literature on late Ming and Qing China, especially for the Jiangnan region, which was the most economically advanced of all China. Chinese theories of the state had always been concerned with desirable ratios between population and resources, attempting to redress imbalances by encouraging (or coercing) migration, or by promoting farming methods that increased output or permitted the exploitation of hitherto marginal ecologies. By around 1700 the Qing emperors and many of their civil servants were convinced that a point of no return had been reached, where the population would continue to increase relentlessly without any possibility of a commensurate increase in output. The solutions they advocated were to persuade "unproductive" members of society like urban tradesmen and artisans to return to farming, to promote the cultivation of staple cereals and discourage diversification into commercial crops, and to urge their subjects to economy and moderation in the form of low consumption levels.[33] Nothing is said in the imperial edicts or other official documents to suggest that the ruling elite might have advocated smaller families or sexual restraint as a means of slowing population growth. But if we accept arguments by James Lee, Hsiung Ping-chen and Li Bozhong that a culture of sexual restraint developed in late imperial China, should we consider this as related to official Malthusian forebodings, and if so, how? Can we presume some kind of translation here between the health of the family and the health of the state?[34]

---

formed the agenda of the United Nations Population Conference held in Cairo in 1994.

33. Will 1994.

34. I raise this as a matter for reflection; as I have read them so far, my own sources suggest no connections between macro- and microeconomic concerns.

WHAT IS A BODY?

Barbara Duden claims that demography silences the body, reducing it to a modern stereotype.[35] The historical actors depicted in Chinese demographic history still seem to be equipped with essentially similar bodies to our own, the only difference being that they were rather more ignorant about their workings.[36] The foregoing discussion of efficacy, choices and intentions argued largely in terms of causes, effects, and images of the body that modern science would recognize. But it is necessary to go beyond this view and to examine Chinese ethnobiologies of reproduction— that is to say, "native" understandings of the body and of how babies are brought into this world—the "how" (as well as the "why") of controlling fertility.

I should emphasize that we are dealing here not with a single "Chinese" body, but with a heterogeneous package. The phenomenological body (the physical package of flesh and blood, bones and sinews, vital organs, nerves and senses—perhaps incorporating, perhaps distinct from an immaterial mind, soul or spirit—through which we exist and know ourselves to exist in the world) is differently constituted and organized in different societies, and even within the same society it will be understood and experienced differently by different people.[37]

35. "To social historians of my generation historical demography has become a primary source of statements about body-mediated phenomena [in which] the characteristics of the body within a statistical population are . . . perceived as *probable attributes of an object:* as rates of birth, morbidity, reproduction and mortality" (Duden 1991: 192, emphasis added).

36. Anthropologists have long been aware that the modern Western body, an individual and material body isolated within its own skin and transparent to the scientific gaze, is—as an experience—far from universal (e.g., Worsley 1982; Scheper-Hughes and Lock 1989). The "history of the body" is still in its infancy, and even historians of medicine have only recently begun to break away from the notion that the "objective realities" of the modern Western body inevitably underlie the bodily experiences of other times and places. Foucault's work on epistemic ruptures laid the groundwork for exploring the extent to which the body of scientific biomedicine is a historical and cultural construct; much of the most interesting work in this field has been done by feminists anxious to expose the gendered nature of modern science (e.g., Schiebinger 1987; Martin 1987).

37. Most people work with multiple models of the body, though one will usually predominate at any moment. For example, in our own society we think of our heart as an anatomically fixed organ that pumps the blood around the body, and it is certainly with that model in mind that we might agree to heart surgery. Yet at the same time we are aware of a real physical experience of dislocation when our heart is "in our mouth" or "in our boots." Another simple example of how body image and experience can differ within a common paradigm: all schoolchildren in the advanced economies are taught the same elements of biomedical

Duden's study reveals that the biological ideas of ordinary people in an eighteenth-century German provincial town were vastly different from ours, and their physiological experiences and expectations were correspondingly astonishing. To consider just one bodily function, menstruation, that today we associate purely with female reproduction[38]: for Duden's subjects menstruation was not linked with fertility but was considered necessary for health because it cooled or purged the body; if amenorrhea occurred the sufferer was less likely to think of pregnancy than of a threat to her health; if menstruation failed to resume, some equivalent flux such as a nosebleed or suppuration from sores would allay her fears; though men were so constituted that they needed these regular fluxes less, menses were not always restricted to women, nor was lactation; moreover, it surprised nobody if a woman continued to menstruate well into old age, and indeed her longevity would be attributed to this fact. By comparison the body discussed in late imperial Chinese medicine seems more familiar and predictable, more "true": only women of childbearing age menstruate, and men's nosebleeds do not serve the same function as the menses. But we must take care not to let broad resemblances blind us to real differences.

Duden's study was not specifically concerned with how reproduction

---

anatomy; however, in France the liver looms largest among the bodily organs in patients' perceptions of their afflictions, in the United States it is the heart, and in Japan the *hara* or abdomen. The body models of late imperial classical Chinese medicine and of Chinese popular religions differed enormously (see Schipper 1982 for some examples), and an infertile woman would shift between these models as she sought help from orthodox physicians, wise women or the goddess Guanyin. For different perceptions and experiences of the body in late imperial China beyond the domain of medicine (in ritual, etiquette, clothing, etc.) see the contributions in Zito and Barlow 1994.

38. This said, we can find discrepancies and contradictions in contemporary explanations of exactly how menstruation and reproduction are linked. The prevailing scientific representation of menstruation is that it is the consequence of the body's failure to conceive. The anthropologist Emily Martin argues that in the United States this discourse is most likely to be internalized by well-educated women, while women with less education or less stake in the social hierarchy (the black, Chicana and poor white women in her survey of patients at Johns Hopkins) tend to see menstruation not as a proof of failure but as a positive emblem of fertility (Martin 1987). Meanwhile, in a picturesque reversing of classic pollution imagery, a biologist at Berkeley has achieved instant media fame for publishing a paper in which she argues that menstruation (a phenomenon that is restricted to humans) evolved in response to the peculiar patterns of human sexuality in order to cleanse and protect the womb, eliminating not the impurities generated within her own body, as several Western ethnobiologies have it, but the microbial and other contamination caused by the entry of the (unclean) sperm (Profet 1993).

was understood in her German town, but many of her findings about how women and physicians in Eisenach understood the female body, and how the practitioner and his client reached workable accommodations between high theory and folk belief, would be indispensable to any attempt to reconstruct the people of Eisenach's reproductive cultures, their beliefs about what was possible in the realm of begetting and bearing children, and the reproductive strategies of different persons within that society.

This brings me to the question of how people in China might have experienced their bodies. In a highly influential essay Nancy Scheper-Hughes and Margaret Lock crystallized the theoretical positions of much recent scholarship in medical anthropology and history of medical science, which argues that it is impossible to understand physical bodies or their representations abstracted from their social and political dimensions.[39] Modern scientific thought depends on the process of abstraction; it presents us with an "objective" body apparently unanchored in space, time, or social identity.[40] It is the task of the critical scholar to reconstruct the values inherent in this apparently value-free epistemology, and to imagine subjectivity for the objects of scientific scrutiny.

The phenomenological body, the body that is felt and lived in, is not identical in every society. It cannot be separated from two further levels of embodied experience that Scheper-Hughes and Lock label the "social body" and the "body politic." In *Natural Symbols* the structural anthropologist Mary Douglas observed that bodies are "good to think with," metaphorical embodiments of society; Scheper-Hughes and Lock urge a dialectical application of Douglas's approach, analyzing biological representations and experiences as symbolic systems that are manipulated within a broader framework of contested and hierarchical social relations.[41] As for the "body politic," they remind us that an individual's access to and

39. Scheper-Hughes and Lock 1989. This critical approach is not new. It has its roots in Marx and in the Frankfurt School's critiques of knowledge, but has become more mainstream in recent years under the influence of feminist and post-structuralist theory.

40. The most influential work on the development of the abstract scientific gaze in medicine is Foucault's *Birth of the Clinic* (1973).

41. Metaphors are frequently shared in medicine and in politics. Since the development of anatomy in the Renaissance, the Western body like the Western polity has been successively represented as a system of weights and pulleys, as a machine consuming and producing different forms of energy, and as an information network. Schiebinger (1987) documents the process by which shifting gender and race relations were inscribed in eighteenth- and nineteenth-century European anatomy, and suggests that the increasingly forceful anatomical representations of gender difference, in which women came to be shown as caricaturally large-hipped

experience of health care and medical practice are dependent on means and status, on what Bourdieu calls social and cultural capital as well as on the straightforward economic variety.[42] In the case of late imperial China, medicine produced one set of images of the body that affected what people thought their bodies were and how they experienced them. Religious, magical and cosmological beliefs produced variations on or alternatives to these images. And ideas about kinship, social connection, and the nature of the bonds between living and dead, parent and child, individual and family, generated beliefs about the causes of illness, about what constituted appropriate or "natural" experiences and desires, about where the body began and ended and about who had claims on whose flesh, many of which are strange and unfamiliar to us.

The key issue in the deconstructive approach to the body and its representations is power. Positivist history of science and medicine is concerned with the power of human beings to understand and control the natural world. Poststructuralist history of science and medicine is concerned with the power that people exert over each other, with the representations of such control as facts of nature, and with subordinated people's alternative visions and their struggles to resist domination. Poststructuralists are acutely aware that "the main mechanism of domination operates through the unconscious manipulation of the body,"[43] and in particular through

---

and small-skulled, were at least in part an unconscious reaction against contemporary women's demands for economic and political rights. Martin (1987) and Lock (1993) analyze the sexism inherent in current biomedical descriptions of reproductive processes. And Honig and Hershatter (1988) provide a fascinating account of how biological explanations of gender difference in school texts and the media have shifted as social and economic policies changed in the People's Republic of China.

42. First there is the question of which issues are given prominence in medical practice; for example, it has often been pointed out that a disproportionate amount of the U.S. national health research budget is devoted to the health problems of middle-class, middle-aged white males. Then there is the institutional level of services offered to different sectors of the population. And then there is the question of the respect and active involvement a patient can expect. For instance, the degree to which a hospital patient is treated by a busy specialist as a passive object, a cluster of symptoms, rather than as an active collaborator in the construction and treatment of his or her case may depend on how the physician rates the patient's financial resources, but will also involve assumptions about how much common language they have, and whether this patient can be trusted to contribute reliable information or to contribute positively to the process of treatment (see, e.g., Taussig 1980 on physician-patient relations in a North American hospital setting, or Bray 1995a and Dean-Jones 1995 on Chinese and Greek medical views of the reliability of female knowledge).

43. Pierre Bourdieu, in an interview of 1992, quoted Segal 1994: 263.

intellectual manipulation, through the production of ideas or "discourses" about the body.

In attempting to recapture something of the different modes in which women in late imperial China experienced, were told about, talked about, and acted on their own bodies, I am also attempting to recapture the difference of Chinese understandings of the body. Acknowledging that humans have been almost infinitely inventive in the body images they have created, I nevertheless believe that all these creations are fashioned out of the basic material needs that sustain and reproduce human life: eating and sleeping; pain, illness and death; sex, childbearing, and whatever else goes into making vulnerable little creatures that can be turned into human beings. I find myself at odds with the current trend in feminist theory that dismisses the role of material reality in shaping identity.[44] Contemporary critical theories of gender and of sexuality that deny the relevance of biological reproduction depend on a paradoxically material grounding, namely the separation of sex and procreation that contraceptive advances have recently made possible. The high technology of biomedical diagnostics and therapy allows us to think of the body as a mere surface shaped and filled by words.[45] But we would be wrong to presume that other societies were disembodied in the same way. Of pain, Elaine Scarry says that "whatever [it] achieves, it achieves in part through its unsharability, and it ensures this unsharability through its resistance to language." Pain is not the only bodily experience resistant to language, yet which cannot be ignored. When texts about bodies are what we have to work with, discourse and its political roots will loom larger in shaping *our* understanding of those bodies than it ever did in reality. It is important to remember, as Barbara Duden does, that the woman in the world cannot be detached from the woman beneath the skin. One cannot hope to recapture exactly the body images and feelings of women and men in late imperial China, but I think we may safely accept that procreative preoccupations played a

44. The attitude seems perversely ahistorical. While I agree that "discourse" shapes our understanding and experience of our bodies, I cannot agree that discourse has in effect *invented* the body, or that it encompasses, because it has created, everything we know and feel through our bodies. Lynne Segal may be right to say that "we can only *know* bodies through discourse" (1994: 228), if we accept the dubious modern Western presumption that all knowledge must be expressible in words. But knowledge is only part of what it means to be human, and to imagine that we can only apprehend our bodies through discourse implies a rarified cerebral and hyperliterate mode of life, lapped by the comforts of modern civilization with its attendant discontents.

45. Foucault calls the body "the inscribed surface of events, traced by language and dissolved by ideas" (*Discipline and Punish*, quoted Segal 1994: 227).

central role in shaping their everyday sensibilities, and that these inchoate feelings fed into medical or social discourses, which could shape and direct them but could not invent or disinvent them, or even totally encompass them.[46]

PHYSICIANS, ORTHODOXY AND POWER

Reproductive medicine became increasingly visible over the late imperial period, but its establishment as a group of distinct and related specialisms in the Song did not represent a radical theoretical innovation. The foundational writings on the theory of sexual maturation and fertility to which all late imperial authors refer are the pronouncements of the legendary physician of the Yellow Emperor, Qi Bo, recorded in the *Huangdi neijing* (Yellow Emperor's classic of internal medicine). At the core of late imperial theoretical writings on successful conception lie the recommendations of the sixth-century physician Sun Simiao. The corpus of late imperial writing on reproduction is pretty homogeneous. There are no significant changes in physicians' understanding of reproductive processes, or in their basic attitudes toward reproductive disorders, although diagnostic and therapeutic preferences varied according to time, school or region, and depending on the general theoretical framework within which a physician chose to work.

All Chinese schools of medicine agreed on the fundamental constitution of the human body. Chinese medical theory was primarily interested in the processes of interaction and transformation that nourished and maintained the healthy body and that also determined the transmission and evolution of disorders. The Chinese organs—Heart, Liver, Lungs, Spleen and Kidney—were not the anatomical entities of modern Western medicine. They were functional systems that connected different levels of the same type of physiological activity. Each system corresponded to one of the Five Phases (*wuxing*), the five types of process according to which the energy of the natural world (*qi*) transmuted, producing matter and

46. A good instance is the discourse around menstrual regulation, which I discuss in chapter 8. Several scholars have recently addressed the importance of "surface" and its relation to reality in Chinese conceptions of body and identity (e.g., Elvin 1989; most of the essays in Zito and Barlow 1994; Blake 1994). This literature is suggestive, requiring us to reconsider how we think about skin as a boundary, inside and outside, and nature and ornament (I return to these themes later in my discussion of nature and nurture in China). But many of these essays go too far toward privileging discourse and denying the reality of what lies beneath the skin.

dissolving it, building and transforming. The organ systems interacted with each other in sequences determined by Five Phase theory. *Qi* circulated through the body, maintaining a balance between *yin* and *yang* within the organ systems. Reproductive capacity depended on the Kidney system. The Kidney system represented water-type activities—that is to say, processes of condensing, liquefying and descending; it included the kidneys themselves, but also hair and teeth; it produced male and female vital essences as well as urine.[47] Chinese medical theory did not separate the organic and physiological from the mental or emotional in the way that Western thought has often preferred. The concept of organ systems and of the circulation of vital substances linked the innermost vitals deep within the body to the growth that represented them at the surface, and tied the physiological state of each vital organ to an emotional state that signaled its health or disorder.

Medical schools might differ as to which organ system they saw as predominant. They might disagree as to whether diagnosis and therapy based on theories of cold damage were suitable for treating the fevers prevalent in the semitropical south, or required rethinking in terms of heat factors. One school would prefer to diagnose in terms of how far the disorder had penetrated, another according to which organ was principally affected. Some physicians preferred to rely on drug therapy alone, others also used acupuncture. Some emphasized using gentle drugs to build up the body's natural defenses, others tended to start with strong drugs to eliminate pathogens. One doctor might always include ginseng in his prescriptions, another might be famous for his experiments with aromatics. The Five Phase theory of systematic correspondence between organs was pushed to great lengths during the Song and Yuan dynasties, and many later physicians objected that it was too theoretical, advocating a more empirical approach. But the cosmological models of how the physical and physiological world worked remained essentially unchanged, and so too did the fundamental rationality of learned medicine.[48]

47. I use capitals for the Chinese organs and for the term *Blood* to signal that these terms do not correspond exactly to their meaning in biomedicine. The Chinese term *Blood*, for example, signifies the materialized phase of *qi* energy, and its main function is to nourish the body. As well as the red liquid that circulates through the veins and nourishes the fetus of a pregnant woman, Blood can also take the form of breastmilk. For a concise introduction to the history of Chinese medical theory, see Sivin 1988. Kaptchuk 1983 gives an accessible account of the organs in contemporary practice. On the Kidney system in reproductive thought, see Furth 1986, 1987.

48. Farquhar 1994 is excellent on differences in diagnostics and therapy, again in contemporary practice. On the social factors behind the emergence of the heat

Overall, then, the late imperial period was one of stability in orthodox gynecological theory and practice. Length of time notwithstanding, we are dealing here with a rather homogeneous corpus. We find no significant changes in physicians' understanding of reproduction, or in their attitudes toward or treatment of reproductive disorders. Although scholars became interested in various aspects of European science and technology introduced by the Jesuits in the late Ming and early Qing, Western medicine had no impact on Chinese gynecology—or indeed on any branch of Chinese medicine—during this period.[49] There were no dramatic technical innovations, like the invention of forceps, that upset the balance of control in reproductive medicine or threatened established ethics. No miracle herbs or new acupuncture meridians were discovered, there were no startling improvements in the diagnosis of pregnancy, physicians did not engage in research to improve their knowledge of female anatomy or experiment with new delivery techniques or instruments. Instead they tried to improve the services they offered within the framework of an established medical paradigm. The historically most significant change over the period in which I am interested was the marked increase in orthodox medical activity as wealth spread and towns developed, the demand for medical care grew, and the market for medical publications expanded among specialists and lay readers.

It is difficult to tell how representative recourse to orthodox medicine rather than other forms of healing was and to put any quantitative values on how much it changed say between the Song and the Qing, even among the elite.[50] Nor do we know much about what the alternatives involved.[51] Case histories often mention tantalizing fragments of alternative practices (resort to faith healers, wise women, or self-administered drugs, for exam-

factor school in Jiangnan, see Y. Chao 1995. On differences between medical schools of thought in the premodern period, to cite only Western-language literature, Unschuld 1985 and 1991, and the introduction to 1986, are all suggestive; see also Sivin 1988.

49. The earliest response to Western knowledge in this field comes in the late Qing. Part of the gynecological section from Hobson's treatise on anatomy, written in Chinese in the 1850s, was inserted as an addendum in the 1881 edition of a Chinese gynecological work, Shen Yaofeng's *Nüke jiyao* (Essentials of gynecology). Although Hobson's text conveys a completely different vision of the body, no modifications were made to Shen's text to reconcile the discrepancies.

50. From the nontechnical literature, such as household precepts and novels, we know that elite men frequently criticized their womenfolk for their medical dependence on priests, bonzes and wise women or midwives.

51. One highly bowdlerized account of the healing practices of an eighteenth-century itinerant healer, the *Chuanya*, has survived.

ple), but by the nature of a case history we are only told about alternative treatments when they have failed. Priests' and wise women's successful case histories were not published by their disciples, unfortunately, and we know almost nothing about routine home diagnoses and treatments beyond the corresponding sections in popular encyclopedias and almanacs.

In addition, we cannot be certain of the social scope of orthodox physicians' practice. Case histories almost always tell us the sex and age of a patient; they sometimes provide further social information, such as a patient's name and occupation or title, or in the case of women, the name of their father or husband and their rank (official wife, concubine), or the name of their master if they are serving in a household as a maid. On this basis, a preliminary survey of late imperial Chinese patients by Furth suggests not surprisingly that the wealthy were more likely than poor people to consult a physician, that rich women were likely to consult a sequence of healers even for relatively minor ailments, and that poor women would see an orthodox physician only if they were suffering from a serious complaint.[52] Consequently, the texts written by orthodox physicians, while they do not exclude poor or uneducated patients, are heavily biased toward the well-to-do.

The Chinese medical texts I refer to were all written by what I call orthodox physicians, that is to say, persons whose medical competence was recognized by the educated elite and who shared their social and moral values. They include works by the most famous physicians of the time and others by lesser luminaries, but they demonstrate a general consensus on what constitutes responsibility in the treatment of reproductive problems. Almost all the works I cite were first published between 1550 and 1850, ranging from the later Ming (Xu Chunfu's *Gujin yitong daquan*, an annotated compendium of medical works ancient and modern, published in 1556) to 1846 (Fang Lue's case histories, the *Shangyou tang yi'an*). They include works on general medical theory and practice with gynecological sections (Xiao Jing's *Xuanqi jiuzheng lun*, Xu Chunfu's *Gujin yitong daquan*, Xu Dachun's *Yilue liushu*), works on diagnosis (Lin Zhihan's *Sizhen juewei*), as well as specialized treatises on gynecology (Yan Shunxi's *Taichan xinfa*, Wu Daoyuan's *Nüke qieyao*, Wu Qian's *Fuke xinfa yaojue*), and collections of medical cases (Ye Tianshi's *Linzheng zhinan yi'an*, Cheng Maoxian's *Cheng Maoxian yi'an*, and Fang Lue's *Shangyou tang yi'an*).

The general works on medicine contain, as well as original materials,

52. Furth 1988.

numerous passages from and references to earlier works, commented on by the author in the light of his own theoretical bent and experience. The same is true of specialized gynecological works. Medical publications ran the gamut between highly theoretical works aimed at fellow physicians and popularized works for a general audience. However, a "physician" in late imperial China was not a professional in the modern sense, nor was medical language as impenetrable to nonspecialists as it is in the West today.[53] Most educated people were familiar with the principles of medicine and had at least a nodding acquaintance with foundational works like the *Huangdi neijing.* Works on "increasing descendants" were largely intended for a lay readership to consult at home. Gynecological specialists were likely to include in their preface the hope that their work would help husbands to advise their wives through a healthy pregnancy and recuperation from childbirth (fig. 21).[54] Some authors liked to pen even more accessible medical works on gynecology, pediatrics, or other topics; these were often written in verse for easy memorization, with more technical comments between the verses, as in Wu Qian's *Fuke xinfa yaojue* (Essential esoterics of the new gynecology), written in the eighteenth century.

This brings me to the question of medical knowledge and ideology in late imperial China. The people I have been referring to as "orthodox physicians" were recognized by their contemporaries as trained specialists in a field of expertise known as "medicine" (*yi*) and accorded the title of "physician" (the same word, *yi*). In early China physicians were generally of low social status. Medical theory and philosophical cosmology began to be integrated even before Han times; nevertheless, the knowledge and expertise of healers were still considered distinct from those of philosophers and other educated men, with hints of magical powers and supernatural forces harking back to ancient times when healers were diviners or shamans. Magical, shamanistic and religious healing have never disap-

53. See Bray 1995a on the technical use of everyday terms in late imperial Chinese diagnostics. Today a profession is presumed to be self-regulating and self-certifying: to join the ranks of chartered accountants, lawyers or doctors it is necessary to master the syllabus that the professional group has declared suitable, to pass its examinations and receive its diploma or license; the profession also decides the scope of application of its expertise and the limits of ethical behavior. Although state-organized medical examinations did exist in late imperial China, the candidates were usually low-status people hoping to serve as state medical officers, whose prestige seldom compared to that of either "hereditary" or "Confucian" physicians. Otherwise there was no system of licensing.

54. Leung 1984: 52.

Figure 21. The childbirth chamber (*Qing Customs* A: "Birth" section, 3a). The new mother is sitting on her bed, propped up between piles of quilts. This posture was supposed to keep the mother from sudden movement and prevent hemorrhaging. A maid or perhaps the wet nurse is holding the new baby.

peared in China, but the branch of knowledge called "medicine," *yi*, became progressively more secular, consistent and rationalist over the centuries. Practitioners of "medicine" sought to distance themselves and their expertise from the people they represented as a rabble of quacks, bonzes, and immoral old women—that is to say, their competitors for a fickle clientele.[55]

55. The biographies of doctors, diviners and magicians from the period up to the early Han, written by the Han historian Sima Qian and translated by De-Woskin in 1983, give some idea of how versatile the concept of a healer could be at that period. On the range of healers that a well-off client might consult in the late Ming, see, e.g., Cullen 1993.

One way in which *yi* claimed their authority to heal was through the accumulation of practical expertise. It was common in early dynasties to quote the saying from the *Book of Rites* that one should never consult a physician unless he came from a family that had practiced medicine for three generations. Physicians of this kind, who acquired their expertise through practical apprenticeship as well as more theoretical studies, were often referred to as "hereditary physicians," *shiyi*. Ye Tianshi (Ye Gui, 1667–1746), whose physician father died when he was still young, is said subsequently to have worked under seventeen different specialists before setting up in his own practice, while the famous Ming physicians Wang Ji (1463–1539) and Xue Ji (1487–1559) both learned their craft from their fathers.[56]

Traditionally, one of the Confucian duties of a filial son was to give his elderly parents the medicines they might need,[57] and therefore it was also considered proper that a gentleman or scholar should be acquainted with the works of the medical canon. Often it was filiality, the need to help an ailing parent or relative, that first stimulated a scholar's interest in medicine. In medicine, the cosmological principles and humane values that Chinese political philosophy applied to the regulation of society were applied to the regulation of the human organism; the word for healing is the same as the word for ruling or governing, *zhi*.

The first duty of a gentleman, the primary goal of his scholarship, was to serve the state and to apply his knowledge to regulating society. If for any reason this was impossible or undesirable, for example if the current

56. Ou 1988: 354, 361; Li Jingwei et al. 1988: 97, 281, 668.

57. Sima Guang includes this in his daily rules, saying that the man himself presents his parents with the medicines after his wife has prepared them. (Chinese prescriptions consisted of mixtures of several plant or other drugs, a portion of which was boiled up and infused daily at home in a long-spouted ceramic teapot of the kind that can still be found in any Chinese store or pharmacy. Drugs also came in powder or pill form, and although they could be purchased ready-made at the druggist's, instructions for making some of the most popular of these were included in the health sections of popular encyclopedias.) The most extreme form of filial care for sick parents (and one of the most admired) took the form of self-mutilation, cutting off chunks of one's own flesh to brew up broths that were considered to be particularly effective as a replenishing drug for restoring strength (see Cooper and Sivin 1973). T'ien (1988) traces the history of this practice, and he and Carlitz (1994) both discuss the significance of its popularity over the Ming-Qing transition, when it was a frequent and much-admired expression of female virtue, even though it was legally forbidden. Carlitz also remarks that it was daughters who were the heroines of such tales in earlier dynasties, but that by the Ming and Qing they were replaced by daughters-in-law, showing the extent to which women's kinship loyalties had been forced into the patrilineal mold.

regime was corrupt and unworthy, or if the scholar was unable to obtain a post, then it was considered morally legitimate for him to turn to the practice of healing. "If one does not become a good official, then one should become a good doctor," declared the Song statesman Fan Zhong-yan. In the Yuan dynasty, under alien Mongol rule, many more gentle-men took up medicine as a living than ever before, often justifying this choice on political grounds. But expediency must also have played a role: even then the number of candidates for the state examinations far out-stripped the number of posts available, and the situation became even worse in the later Ming and in the Qing. So it is not surprising that many men who turned to practicing medicine did so after having failed several times to pass the state examinations. Physicians of this background were steeped in the morality of Confucian and neo-Confucian writings, and may be considered as orthodox in their opinions and values as any other scholar.[58]

These physicians were primarily scholars. Their first claim to medical understanding came from deep study of the medical classics and a pro-found grasp of the cosmological principles that governed the workings of heaven, earth, and the human body. They were able to cure not because they were technicians but because they were philosophers. In the Song, Jin and Yuan dynasties medical scholars formalized the application of the Five Phase theory of systematic correspondence to medical etiology and to drug classification and therapy. Although the excessively theoretical bent of these writers was often criticized in Ming and Qing times, philo-sophical learning still provided a solid foundation for claiming medical authority. In Ming and Qing times physicians learned in all the classics, such as Xu Dachun (1693–1771), claimed that one should mistrust those who merely "skipped through" the classical texts.[59] Physicians of this background liked to be known as "Confucian physicians," *ruyi*.

The number of physicians of all kinds increased rapidly during the Ming and Qing. Suzhou on the lower Yangzi, which became the most dazzling of the cultural centers of late imperial China and was very wealthy, attracted physicians and healers of every kind. There are records of 3 physicians practicing in Suzhou in the Tang, 4 in the Song, 5 in the

58. See Hymes 1987 on Yuan physicians and their social status, and Y. Chao 1995 on the educational status of physicians in Jiangnan in the Ming and Qing.

59. See Unschuld's translation of Xu Chunfu: "On those who skip through the classics" (1991). Xu was a noted scholar who published on the Daoist classics, on ancient music and on the earliest medical classics as well as on his own medical practice.

Yuan, 88 in the Ming and 219 in the Qing. Needless to say, they had numerous competitors in the form of folk healers, midwives, bonesetters, priests, herbalists and so on. A battle of labeling ensued: one late Ming physician distinguished between thirteen categories of healer, ranging from illustrious, Confucian, and virtuous physicians, through hereditary physicians, to quacks, devious physicians, immoral physicians, female healers and monks.[60]

People who fell sick were likely to consult as wide a range of healers as they could afford; they might call in several physicians at once, or sack one after another, and that would not stop them also offering prayers and buying magic potions. However, priests, fortune-tellers, female herb-peddlers and midwives offered completely different kinds of worldviews and therapies from educated physicians. Although a distinction was commonly made at the time between "Confucian" and the "hereditary physicians," they all shared a basic cosmological understanding of how the human body worked, used the same diagnostic techniques and methods of treatment, and were all male and educated. It has often been presumed that the competition between Confucian and hereditary physicians played a fundamental role in shaping the debates and new directions of late Ming and early Qing medicine, but Yuan-ling Chao argues that this distinction has been overplayed, and that it was often far from clear whether a physician belonged to one category rather than another.[61]

It does seem that the balance between hereditary and scholarly claims to medical authority shifted in the course of the late imperial period. This means not that hereditary physicians were giving up their activities, but that increasing numbers of outsiders were joining the ranks of physicians, perhaps founding medical lineages of their own,[62] while any physician wishing to build up an urban and wealthy clientele was likely to stress his scholarly claims to authority (which might include publishing learned discussions of the classical literature, collecting prefaces to his work by distinguished scholars, or developing a polished style for the writing up of case histories). Given the increasing emphasis placed on common educational background, shared knowledge and values in determining one's

60. *Xuanji jiuzhenglun* 509, cited Y. Chao 1995: ch. 1.
61. Y. Chao 1995 on the classification of physicians, and on their origins.
62. In his new dictionary of medical biography He Zhixi (1990) collates some twenty thousand names, mostly from the Qing, into medical lineages. These include lineages based on kinship filiation (direct descent and affinal kinship), as well as on adoption and discipleship. The majority of the lineages were based on kinship descent rather than on the intellectual descent traced through master-disciple links.

status as a physician, we might say that medicine was on the way to "professionalization." At the same time as the number of physicians was growing, so too was the volume and range of publications in medicine and the density of communications between physicians, who collected medical books, corresponded, edited each other's cases or essays, and wrote approving prefaces to or attacks on each other's work.[63] Furthermore, there was a growing interest in medicine among the general public. Educated people were able to read medical works in their original form, but now it became quite common for eminent physicians to write medical primers in simple language that commoners could read, like Wu Qian's *Essential Esoterics of the New Gynecology*, written in the seven-character rhymed verse form that was typical of popular songs and ballads. Simplified medical knowledge was also available in sections in household encyclopedias and almanacs. This was yet another way in which elite values were disseminated among the less educated members of late imperial society.[64]

It will have become apparent, though, that however fascinated the late imperial public may have been by medicine, the authority of even the most learned or experienced of physicians in no way compared to that of a medical doctor in the United States today. The knowledge and language of medicine, and even its technical skills, were not esoteric to nearly the same degree. Every educated man could read a medical text and understood the underlying models of the body, greater numbers still had some basic medical knowledge, and many homes had their own medicine chest. Although medical prescription was an admired and sophisticated skill, it was not as removed from everyday experience as brain surgery. The continuities between educated and professional language, knowledge and skills meant that educated clients would often discuss with the physician on more or less equal terms the case for which he had been called in, and they might dispute his understanding of it, dismissing him or modifying the course of treatment he prescribed. Precisely because experience as a claim to medical authority was being replaced by general levels of learning that were shared by patients as well as practitioners, the authority of many physicians in late imperial times must have found itself diminished. Patients were disrespectfully disputatious, and numerous late imperial

63. On the question of professionalization, see the discussion in Y. Chao 1995: 150–203.

64. With the growing and apparently insatiable market for medical works, pirating became a problem. There were complaints that no sooner did a new book come out than unauthorized and cheaper versions appeared everywhere (ibid.: 28).

physicians deplored the unruliness and ignorance of their clients, meaning
that they often refused to do what the doctor told them.[65]

CASE HISTORIES: WHOSE VOICES?

Women were notoriously unreliable patients: emotional and ignorant,
complained the physicians. We may presume that the worldviews of religious or magical healers, or of wise women, were often more appealing to
a sick woman or a mother with a sick child than the Confucian insistence,
embodied in orthodox medicine, on suppressing the emotions.[66] But whoever else they may also have consulted, elite women frequently called in
orthodox physicians, and the flourishing late imperial genre of case histories is a rich source of information on the causes and outcomes of these
encounters.

Diagnosing female patients was acknowledged to be more difficult because social convention severely restricted the direct sensory contacts between physician and patient. The twelfth-century pharmacologist Kou
Zongshi first wrote on the special problems involved in diagnosing female
patients from good families. They would not let their faces be seen, obscured their pulses by draping their wrists, found questioning onerous,
and failed to take medicine as prescribed.[67] In fact, Kou lamented, of the
four normal methods of diagnosis, two were more or less ruled out; looking was impossible and pulse taking was made difficult, so only questioning and listening remained. This complaint became a trope in the late
imperial gynecological literature. Even questioning was considered difficult, since it might well have to proceed through an intermediary, husband, father or servant. In the late imperial cases I have studied, however,
pulse taking was a standard and unquestioned procedure with all women

65. Yuan-ling Chao cites Ye Gui, Lu Maoxiu and Xu Dachun as examples. Ye
writes that the parents of sick children get so desperate that they often cause the
death of the child by constantly interfering with the treatment and by bringing in
spirit mediums. Lu too complains that Suzhou people consult mediums instead of
calling in the physician; he also castigates them for believing that all disorders are
caused by *yin* depletion and demanding prescriptions to replenish *yin*, even
though (he says) they have not the slightest idea of what *yin* and *yang* are (ibid.:
39–40).

66. Emotions like anger, resentment or melancholy were considered very
health-threatening. Orthodox medicine recognized that the social position of
women made them especially prone to these damaging feelings, but the solution
recommended was to control or repress them (Furth 1986, 1987).

67. Quoted in the slightly later *Furen daquan liangfang*: 64–65.

patients, and the other details provided indicate that little information was withheld. Even if the physician himself was not favored with a direct glimpse of the lady's complexion or whiff of her breath, others provided him the necessary descriptions.

Examination procedures in late imperial China were quite different from those with which we are familiar today. The physician did not normally feel the brow for fever, palpate the limbs or torso, or auscultate, let alone poke around inside any orifices. By our standards, the approach was definitely hands off. The purpose was also different. The Chinese concept of disorder, *bing*, does not correspond to our modern notion of disease. A Chinese disorder, though it has similar origins in all patients, will manifest itself differently in individual patients, according to the exact circumstances in which it was contracted and the particular constitution of the patient; it will also evolve over time in ways that vary among patients. Diagnosis must therefore identify a disorder category in its particular manifestation at this moment, *bianzheng*. For this, a complete description and case history was essential.

The most favored examination technique varied according to school or period, but basically diagnosis depended on four essential methods involving all the senses. The Chinese doctor *looked* at the patient's complexion, *listened to* his breathing (and smelled his breath and other bodily odors), *asked* questions to elicit his account of his disorder, and *touched* his wrist during the complex procedure of taking the pulse.

Determining the manifestation type depended not only on the physician's powers of perception, but also on his ability to communicate with the patient and his or her family. The Ten Questions formulated by the master diagnostician Zhang Jiebin (1563–1640)[68] include, in order: feelings of cold and fever; sweating; how the head and body feel; elimination; appetite; how the chest feels; hearing; thirst; pulse and complexion; and finally *qi* and "savor" (matching the medical properties or "savors" of the prescription to the patient's needs). The first eight categories were questions that the physician needed to ask the patient. They would inform him of the superficial phenomena—the exposure to cold, the overindulgence in wine, the aches, the restlessness, the periodicity of fevers, the incidence of diarrhea—that defined the manifestation of the patient's disorder, and

68. Zhang Jiebin's *Shiwen pian* (Treatise on the Ten Questions) was published in the seventeenth century; Lin Zhihan's *Sizhen juewei* (Selection of subtleties in diagnostic technique) of 1723 includes Zhang's work in j.3 with a four-page commentary of Lin's own.

all this information, together with a detailed analysis of the pulse reading and other indicators, provided the basis for diagnosis and the prescription of therapy. Ideally the physician would be called in several times, to investigate how the disorder was responding to treatment, to decide whether his preliminary diagnosis required reformulation, and to prescribe the adjusted therapy appropriate at each stage in the disorder's progress toward health. A full medical case was truly a history, recording the identity of the patient, the events that led to the onset of the disorder (including unorthodox resort to religious healing, charms, herbalists' prescriptions or help from "old women"), the main symptoms at each consultation, and the consequent diagnosis and prescription, through to a cure and often including a follow-up account of the patient's health over several subsequent years.

The earliest medical cases recorded in China date back a couple of thousand years, but until the Song dynasty complete cases are extremely rare, and the genre of collections of case studies did not develop until well into the Ming. From the sixteenth century, however, the genre blossomed. A physician's collected cases might be published by the physician himself during his lifetime, or posthumously by his disciples and admirers. The specialist in febrile diseases Ye Tianshi refused to publish any of his own cases during his lifetime; his disciples edited his case studies and published them thirty years after his death. A physician's collected cases might include only cases he had handled himself (a testimony to his personal expertise) or, if he was a theoretician of a particular medical specialism, they were likely to include cases by previous eminent physicians that struck him as being of particular relevance. Other writers made compendia of outstanding cases over the centuries. Some medical writers held that collections should be pared down so as to include only one or two examples of each syndrome or treatment, or cases of special difficulty; others preferred comprehensiveness to concision. Cases treated by the Qing imperial physicians were systematically recorded in official records, so that it has been possible to compile all the main cases treated in the palace during the course of the dynasty, arranged chronologically and according to the rank of the patient.[69]

In the discussions of how best to write up cases that inevitably began to appear as soon as the genre became important, physicians were advised

69. On the development of collections of medical cases as a genre, see Anon. 1984: 92–98 and Xue 1991. The cases treated by Qing imperial physicians are collected in Chen Keji et al. 1990.

to preface each case by recording the name, age, rank and occupation of the patient and the place from which he or she came.[70] Although it was presumably usual to note this information at the time of the consultation, if only for purposes of making out a bill commensurate with the patient's resources, it does not unfortunately always make it in full into the published cases, but often we have such information at least in partial form. In the case of a woman, her marital status (unwed daughter, legal wife, concubine, servant, widow) was also frequently noted. From the point of view of investigating reproductive behavior, collections of cases of women's complaints (*fuke*) have the advantage that as well as these social indicators they often include information of a kind that is entirely missing from most demographic materials; eventually they might even help us meet the great challenge of retrieving the information on real births and infant mortality obscured by the Chinese registration system. For example, if a woman is seeking help with a pregnancy or with a temporary inability to conceive, we will usually be told how many previous live births she has experienced and how many miscarriages or stillbirths. A woman who wishes to terminate a pregnancy may be described as being exhausted from x pregnancies in y years. A woman anxious about infertility might complain of not having conceived after x years of marriage or within y years of her previous child. This is the kind of qualitative information we need to form a clearer idea both of real conception and birth rates and of what kinds of birth rates women felt were desirable or tolerable.[71]

We have access to the Chinese physician's and patient's experiences only as they appear in the written narrative of the case history, and we have little knowledge of how a physician was likely to select, arrange or rephrase the information provided by the patient, or how his judgment might be affected by the patient's presentation. Both the texts on diagnosis and the case histories, however, give the impression that the physician accepted what the patient told him as reliable and relevant.[72] Zhang

70. The Ming physician Han Mao (fl. early sixteenth century) gives lists of what information should be included in a case history that offer some indication of the conventions of the time (Anon. 1984: 96).

71. Although poor families were less likely than the well-to-do to consult a physician for minor ailments, in desperate circumstances many did resort to orthodox medicine, so we do find a good sprinkling of cases where poor people are treated. Just how representative such treatment seeking was among the poor, urban or rural, or at different periods, is hard to say. But this does not mean, I think, that such cases should be excluded as exceptional.

72. This may be connected to the fact that the majority of cases involve patients of elite or at least middle-class standing, who would often be conversant

Jiebin's Ten Questions seem designed to make sure that no information is omitted, rather than to eliminate categories of irrelevant information that the patient might volunteer.

Chinese medical texts—case histories together with more abstract works of medical theory or diagnostic principle—provide a wonderful opportunity to set prescription against the description of real behavior. The rich body of case histories tells us what real women and the men in their lives did and felt, and provides insights into the complexities of orthodoxy and how it was construed. Medical case histories were constructed by male authors, and the circumstances under which consultations between a physician and a female patient took place certainly affected the mode in which both expressed themselves. Nevertheless, the case histories do not "silence" women but provide valuable insights into their beliefs and actions. They also reveal interesting and unexpected nuances in the orthodox beliefs of elite men.

---

with medicine themselves. Being a physician did not automatically confer social status or prestige as it does in our own society. Except in the case of elite scholars who practiced medicine in their spare time, to cure family members or for charitable reasons, the patient's social rank was often higher than that of the physician.

8 Reproductive Medicine and the Dual Nature of Fertility

In the Greek medical tradition (which still echoes through our own) the explanation of sex differences centers mainly on a contrast in reproductive form and function from which other secondary differences derive. Women's health, constitution and behavior are often explicitly linked to their wombs, a distinct anatomical organ that men do not have; they cannot experience its sensations, though they can examine it. The kind of understanding thus reached by a male medical profession is objective, not subjective. The question arose in Greece whether such knowledge was adequate, or did male physicians need to consult women to reach a truly empathetic understanding of female experience and ailments?[1]

In dealing with women's bodies, Chinese physicians were not faced with this issue of understanding the other, because sex differences were conceived of as a question of degree rather than one of essential nature. The Chinese medical conception of the body was not anatomical, but functional and processual. Differences between male and female were explained in terms of relative predominance of *yin* and *yang*. Chinese medical thought saw the male body as more dominated by male vital energy, *yang qi*, the female body by its female counterpart, *yin qi*. In late imperial texts it is usually said that the processes of the female body are dominated by *yin qi* in its material manifestation, Blood, while the processes of the male body are dominated by nonmaterial *qi* energy. But men also have Blood and women also have *qi*. The difference between male and female is conceived in terms not of two separate essentialized categories, but rather of a continuum of probability. Most women will have more *yin* characteristics than most men; at the same time individuals in the phase

---

1. See Dean-Jones 1995.

of growth and maturation will be more *yang* than those in a phase of aging and decline, so they will occupy different positions along the continuum according to their age and variations in their health.

GENERATION IN MEDICAL THEORY

The process of sexual maturation is described in the canonical *Huangdi neijing* and thereafter as broadly the same in both sexes, though it occurs two years later in males. Puberty marks the ability to procreate, and in both sexes it results from the full development of the Kidney system: "When a girl [reaches the age of] twice seven, her Kidney *qi* is abundant and she acquires her reproductive capacities, *tiangui*. Her *ren* tract goes through, and the greater *chong* tract flourishes,[2] her menses flow regularly and she can bear children. . . . When a boy [reaches] twice eight, his Kidney *qi* is abundant and he acquires his reproductive capacities. His seminal essence overflows and drains, he can unite *yin* and *yang* [have sex] and have children."[3]

The *Huangdi neijing* describes progressive sexual maturation and decline in terms of the Kidney system, the reproductive tracts, and hair and teeth, which are the external features of the Kidney system. Genitalia are not mentioned, nor are certain features that we consider important secondary sexual characteristics such as breasts. The womb is not mentioned in discussions of reproductive characteristics; it comes up only in discussions of pregnancy and childbirth as the organ in which the fetus develops and from which it is born. It is not a synecdoche for woman or a ruling feature of her constitution.

In late imperial Chinese medicine, procreation was not advised until both partners were sufficiently mature. Although young women and youths became fertile at fourteen and sixteen *sui*, respectively, the Song

2. *Qi* circulates through the body along meridians or tracts, *jing*. The *ren* and *chong* tracts are the tracts associated with the reproductive functions.

3. *Huangdi neijing* 4–5, from the *Suwen* chapter, "On Ancient Heavenly Truth." A girl of fourteen *sui* (years) according to Chinese reckoning would be roughly twelve in Western terms, and a boy of sixteen *sui* would be roughly fourteen. The Chinese considered that the child entered its first year at the time of birth, and thereafter each lunar New Year added a year to one's age. The *Huangdi neijing*, the most authoritative source of traditional medical doctrine, was traditionally ascribed to the legendary Yellow Emperor, but recent scholarship suggests that it is the work of several authors compiled in the first century B.C. or early first century A.D. However, the two books that form the core of the canon, the "Basic Questions" (*Suwen*) and the "Divine Pivot" (*Lingshu*) did not exist in their present form before the eighth century.

physician Chen Ziming advised that a woman should not bear children before she was twenty *sui*, while a man should wait until he was thirty *sui*, at which time his *yang* would be firm: the excitability of youth would be past. Chen insisted on the damage to the internal organs that early pregnancy could cause in a woman. Moderation was the key to fertility: moderation in consumption, in emotional behavior, and in frequency of sexual congress. Conception resulted from the joining of male and female essence in the womb; success depended on both partners' general state of health and the quality of their male and female essences, and also on the timing of coition, and on both reaching orgasm simultaneously. Coition was advised at the woman's most fertile period, preferably in the week after her menses ended. There were several incompatible medical theories as to what determined the sex of the conceptus. Some believed that a child conceived on an odd day after the end of the woman's period would be male, one conceived on an even day would be female. Others believed that it depended on the order in which the partners' essence joined: the child would share the sex of the partner whose essence enveloped the other's in its own.[4]

The development of the fetus was understood in broadly similar terms by physicians and lay people alike; the following simplified account can be found in more detailed versions in learned gynecological treatises and in the medical sections of popular almanacs and encyclopedias in late imperial China. The fetus developed over ten lunar months. From the moment of conception it possessed a diffuse living "spirit" (*ling*). During the first month it was the size of a dewdrop, in the second, third and fourth months it gradually grew until by the fifth month it was definitively male or female; by the eighth month the limbs were properly formed and it had hair; by the ninth month the five senses were developed, and by the tenth the child was ready to be born.[5]

In the earliest stages of pregnancy, certain diagnosis was recognized to be difficult. Medical writings indicate that pulse diagnosis was necessary to confirm other possible symptoms. Amenorrhea could signal a wide range of disorders, but the various symptoms we might mention in the West today as possibly signaling early pregnancy in association with missed periods, such as swollen or tender breasts, are not found. Morning sickness was not mentioned in the medical literature as an indication of

4. Chen Ziming, *Furen daquan liangfang* j.9, 286, and see Leung 1984. Wan Quan's formulation of these ideas was also influential; on Wan's advice and on theories of conception in general, see Furth 1994 and Hsiung forthcoming.
5. Furth 1995: 166–72.

possible pregnancy, though it was discussed as a more or less serious prob-lem that many pregnant women experienced.[6]

There are numerous descriptions of the pulses characteristic of the suc-cessive stages of pregnancy, which I shall not give here since pulse termi-nology is highly technical and translates poorly into English. In his critical treatise on diagnostic methods, the eighteenth-century physician Lin Zhi-han cites various opinions, including one that claims to be able to distin-guish between first and second month pregnancies; most authorities ex-pected at best to be able to distinguish between a third and a fifth month pregnancy, and then between a boy, a girl, twins, or "ghost pregnancies." It was recognized that physicians frequently made mistakes, misdiagnos-ing amenorrhea due to other causes, for instance, if the husband was not sufficiently clear in his description of the precise symptoms.[7] Here is one case in which a skilled physician successfully diagnoses pregnancy on the basis of characteristic pulse patterns in the fourth month: "A woman of twenty-seven whose menses had already stopped for three months. Some [doctors] suspected that her menses were blocked. She consulted me and I examined her pulse which was rapid, blending, the foot portion slippery. I said: 'This is no light illness—she is pregnant.' I prescribed *xionggui* syrup and there was a slight movement in her abdomen, indicating that she was pregnant. After several months she did indeed give birth to a child."[8]

There were several pregnancy tests in common use: the *xionggui* syrup just mentioned was one, another popular one was Buddha's hand powder, a third *xiaoyao* powder. These were all mild medications consisting of drugs that nourished and mildly activated the Blood.[9] If the woman who

---

6. Chen Ziming says that the syndrome of nausea, dizziness, lack of appetite, and so on is common in early pregnancy and can be either mild, in which case there is no need for worry or for medical treatment, or heavy, in which case treatment must be given as it seriously threatens the woman's health (*Fujen da-quan liangfang* j.12, 339).

7. On early pulses of pregnancy, *Sizhen juewei* 5/26a; on distinguishing be-tween sexes and real or "ghost" pregnancies, *Nüke qieyao* 3/9a–b; on misdiagno-sis, *Taichan xinfa* 170. It is interesting that Yan Shunxi, the eighteenth-century author of the *Taichan xinfa*, represents the husband as responsible for misunder-standing or misconveying the information. This is one of the paternalistic works addressed to husbands so they can care for their wives better during pregnancy and childbirth.

8. *Yilue liushu* 1858. *Xionggui* syrup is a pregnancy test made of the same ingredients as Buddha's hand powder.

9. *Fushousan*, Buddha's hand powder, consisted of two parts of *chuanxiong* (*Ligusticum wallichii*) to three parts of *danggui* (*Angelica sinensis*), ground to a powder and boiled in water or wine. It was considered effective for treating

used such a test was not pregnant, it would produce a menstrual flow; if nothing happened, or if there was a movement in the abdomen, the chances were that she was pregnant. A physician might prescribe such a test to confirm his diagnosis, or women could easily obtain one of them from an herbalist or a pharmacy and use it themselves.

To prosper, the fetus must remain tranquil and calm. Various factors could trouble the fetus's tranquility: the mother's body might be unable to nourish it sufficiently, or it might react to some physical or emotional indisposition on her part. Agitation of the fetus was always an urgent problem. In extreme cases the fetus might die inside the womb or miscarry. The medical literature distinguished between natural miscarriage at the beginning of pregnancy (which might pass unnoticed), later miscarriage, and premature birth. Two common terms referred to induced abortion, "expulsion of the fetus," *qutai*, or "bringing the fetus down," *xiatai*.

ORTHODOX USES OF ABORTION

Given of the prominence of Confucian or neo-Confucian moral values in the education of late imperial physicians, and the fact that female patients seldom consulted an orthodox physician without their father, husband, or some other male authority figure being present, when I began several years ago to research late imperial Chinese medical attitudes toward abortion and fertility control, I assumed that women who wished to avoid pregnancy or childbirth would have to go underground, to the kind of female counterculture suggested by McLaren.[10] I found something rather

---

stagnant Blood (*Fuke xinfa yaojue* 13–14). *Xionggui* syrup or decoction was made from the same ingredients. *Xiaoyao* powder contains eight ingredients (fully listed in Ou 1988: 610); prominent among them are *danggui* and *baishao* (*Paeonia alba*). Angelica and peony both belong to the category of drug that replenishes Blood. The most common tonic for women's complaints is called the Four Ingredient Decoction, *siwutang*; it was first popularized by the Northern Song Imperial Medical Bureau in the eleventh century and is included in Chen Ziming's *Furen daquan liangfang* (65–66) as an "all-purpose prescription" (*tongfang*) or panacea. It consists of angelica, peony and *chuanxiong* rhizome to replenish Blood, together with *dihuang* (*Radix Rehmannia*) to replenish *qi*. *Siwutang* might be prescribed by a physician, in which case the proportions of the basic formula would be adjusted and other ingredients such as ginseng might be added, but it could also be purchased ready-made at a druggist's. A woman would take them if she felt any weakness or fatigue, or simply as a preventive. This practice continues both in the PRC and in Taiwan today.

10. "In studying abortion beliefs it is possible to glimpse aspects of *a separate female sexual culture that supports the autonomy of women from medical men, moralists and spouses*" (McLaren 1984: 147, emphasis added).

different, namely that despite a distaste for taking life of any form, medical writings invariably put the health of the mother before that of the fetus; moreover, there were sufficient ambiguities in medical theories linking female health and fertility for women to control their immediate fertility while demonstrating their commitment to motherhood.

The medical literature, in particular the collections of medical case studies, indicates that although physicians of good standing might administer an abortifacient if the mother's health was in danger, they preferred to avoid it if they could. They commonly report other physicians, however, as lacking either the necessary skills or the scruples to save both lives. Xu Dachun gives the following example, in which both he and a quack prescribe abortifacients, with dramatically different results:

> The wife [of a junior official]: her fetus was leaking [slight but continuous bleeding]; doctors had treated her but the leaking did not stop. Her husband, given the circumstances, wished to have her abort and consulted me. I prescribed Buddha's hand powder so that if the fetus could be calmed it would, and if not it would abort, but in a natural fashion. She took the dose, but her husband was distressed and feared it would not work. A physician specializing in women's complaints sought out prescriptions to administer and told them to use one ounce of *niuxi* boiled in wine to dose her.[11] The husband believed him and gave her the dose, and indeed the fetus was expelled.
>
> At that time I was visiting my mother's relatives and did not hear about this, but as soon as I knew I rushed back, only to find her chamber overflowing with the smells of cinnamon and musk: since the placenta had not been expelled the women's physician[12] had administered "fragrant cinnamon powder."[13] Thereupon her blood gushed forth like the Yellow River, and it was impossible to stop the flow. I hastily brewed a decoction

11. *Radix Acyranthus bidentatae,* a powerful Blood-moving drug usually prescribed in quantities of two to three grains (*qian*), that is, a thirtieth to a fiftieth of the amount prescribed here.

12. Charlotte Furth has pointed out to me that the term *nüyi* here may signify not a woman's physician but a woman physician, since there were women physicians practicing at the time, whose clientele was of course limited to women patients (Furth, personal communication 1996).

13. "Fragrant cinnamon powder" (*xianggui san*) contains musk and cinnamon bark and was commonly used to expel a dead fetus or the placenta (*Zhong caoyaoxue* 304). Musk was well known in China as an abortifacient. Cinnamon, long recognized in Europe and Latin America too for its emmenagogic effects, in Chinese pharmacopeia belongs to the category of drugs that disperse external pathogens like Cold. It is dangerous to women who are pregnant or suffering from heavy menstrual bleeding because it sets the Blood in motion and damages *yin* (ibid.: 18).

of pure ginseng,[14] but before it was ready she had died. Her husband never recovered from his grief.
I record this as a cautionary lesson.[15]

Note that in this case the husband requests the abortion and Xu provides it without quibbling. Another physician, Cheng Maoxian, documents how he tried to terminate his own wife's pregnancy because he feared for her health. Since it was common for a married woman to communicate with the physician through her husband, I presume that in cases of this kind both spouses had agreed that an abortion was necessary. Many other cases, such as those dealing with the problems caused by a woman taking abortifacients that harmed her, deal too briefly with the fact to give any indication of whether she took the drugs with or without her family's approval.

Except where a woman's health was seriously threatened, skilled physicians were reluctant to prescribe drugs for abortion since, like miscarriage or premature birth, abortion represented the interruption of a natural process. It was therefore by definition, like premature birth, damaging to the health. As the physician Xue Ji (1487–1559) put it: "One should not underestimate premature births; one premature birth may be as exhausting as ten normal births. Premature birth is more serious than normal birth, for a normal birth is comparable to a ripe chestnut which falls from the tree by itself, while a premature birth is like plucking it unripe, rupturing the shell and breaking the stem. Yet most people take it lightly and so many women die."[16] But when the continuation of pregnancy represented an unmistakable and severe danger to the woman's health, abortion was definitely the lesser of two evils. Cheng Maoxian recounts:

My wife's physique was naturally weak; she had been pregnant many times and had had several premature births. Moreover as soon as she became pregnant she would have unbearable morning sickness and would vomit at the smell of rice, so that all she could eat daily was some fruit and other inessentials. Only in the 6th or 7th month would she begin to feel a little better. Therefore each birth meant further depletion, over many years. For these reasons she did not dare to look to become pregnant again. When she was forty years old her menses were one or two days late and she feared she was pregnant, so I used an emmenagogue (*tongjingyao*) to bring on the menses. Two or three doses had absolutely no effect, and so

14. *Dushentang.* This was an extremely strong *yang*-building tonic, not usually suitable for women. But this patient was on the verge of death, that is to say complete depletion of *yang*.
15. *Yilue liushu* 1870.
16. Quoted Huang Shengwu et al. 1983: 12.

she did not dare take any more [assuming she must be pregnant]. She had
no choice but to wait and see what the future would bring—and indeed
she was [pregnant]. When she was three months along, her menstrual
blood suddenly flowed in large quantities. I considered that her weak physique would not allow her to go through another pregnancy and that she
was sure to give birth prematurely. And she feared the difficulty of "sitting on the mat" [giving birth at full term]. If indeed she did give birth prematurely, it would be a fortunate misfortune. Under such circumstances
she could not feel tranquil, and so there was no alternative but to administer a Blood-breaking dose of peach kernels and Tibetan crocus [17] and [other
powerful Blood-moving drugs] to expel the fetus. After one dose of this
medicine, the bleeding stopped. Greatly alarmed, I said: "We used this medicine and contrary to what was intended the bleeding stopped. This child
must be destined for life! It cannot be right to expel its body [from the
womb]." [After a series of difficulties, each treated with mostly tonic and
replenishing drugs, a healthy child was delivered at full term and named
Hanpiao, "Hercules."] [18]

It is interesting that in the case of Cheng Maoxian's wife the fetus is
considered to have shown signs that its fate destined it to survive, and it
is this manifestation of destiny that dictated subsequent treatment. Although there are many cases where physicians admit to having prescribed
abortifacients when the mother's health was endangered, far more common are the cases they relate where their diagnostic and prescriptive vir-
tuosity enables them to save both mother and child, sometimes after
quacks or second-rate doctors, or the pregnant women themselves, have
tried to produce an abortion but failed. While colleagues may be explicitly
criticized for mistreating a case, no blame is apparent in cases where a
woman has tried to terminate her pregnancy herself, often for reasons of
poor health. [19]

17. Peach kernels (*taoren*) and *honghua* (*Carthamus*) were both considered
powerful Blood-breaking drugs and therefore abortifacients (*Zhong caoyaoxue*
379, 381). *Honghua* means "red flower" (*Carthamus* produces a red dye), and the
color red itself seems to have been associated in the popular mind with abortifacient qualities. *Hongyao* (red drugs) and *hongwan* (red pills) were popular terms
for abortifacient drugs into recent times. Stockard records the story of a Cantonese
silk reeler who wished to avoid settling down with her husband, and when she
realized she was pregnant "went to gather herbs in the hills for the purpose of
preparing a medicine, red in color, that would cause her to lose the child" (1989:
24).
18. *Cheng Maoxian yi'an* 2/26b–28a; case and translation generously provided by Charlotte Furth.
19. Xu Dachun gives three cases on the same page: "A woman of almost forty,
weak constitution, induced abortion herself [damaging the Spleen system]. . . .
Wang Huo's concubine, thirty-five, worn out with childbearing, made the mistake
of taking abortifacient drugs and started a violent hemorrhage. . . . A woman five

In the late imperial period distaste for taking life, together with the theory that the interruption of a natural process can be harmful, combined to make many orthodox physicians reluctant to terminate a pregnancy if there was a chance of saving both mother and child.[20] The mother's health, however, had clear priority over the life of the fetus. Furthermore, physicians would not hesitate to prescribe the same Blood-moving drugs that were known to cause abortions if a woman's health was threatened by menstrual irregularity or blockage.

By far the most common method for inducing abortion in late imperial China involved the oral ingestion of drugs.[21] Most studies of induced abortion in the modern world deal exclusively with physically intrusive techniques involving scraping or suctioning the womb.[22] Although both forms of abortion are potentially lethal, there is a phenomenological distinction of some importance. It is difficult to deny the explicit purpose of an abortion technique when a woman has a sharp instrument pushed into her womb until blood and other matter pour out. Far more ambiguity of interpretation is possible with drugs, acupuncture and massage. As long as it is taken early in pregnancy, an oral abortifacient can be labeled—or even believed to be—a "pregnancy test"[23] or an emmenagogue. Such drugs, called *tongjingyao* ("drugs to bring on the menses"), played a central role in Chinese medical treatment of women.

---

months pregnant dosed herself with boiled 'red pills' and aborted her fetus [damaging Spleen and Stomach]" (*Yilue liushu* 1871).

20. There were some physicians who regarded abortion as a sin. Among them was Zhang Gao (1149–1227), who was strongly influenced by Buddhist ideas. He wrote the story of Mme. Bai, who makes a good living from her abortifacient prescriptions, but then contracts a horrible disease and has nightmares of little children sucking at her brain. Before dying she repents and begs her sons to burn all her prescriptions (*Yishuo* j.10/35a–b).

21. Alternatives were acupuncture or massage (Hsiung forthcoming).

22. E.g., Tietze 1983. The dissemination of RU-486 will presumably change this emphasis. In late imperial China the "backstreet abortionist" was usually a druggist like Mme. Bai (see note 20 of this chapter), though as Hsiung says, acupuncture and massage might also be used. Hsiung also quotes texts that describe late imperial midwives killing the fetus in the womb and pulling it out with sharp hooks, but it is not clear how widespread this technique was, or when it began to be practiced (Hsiung forthcoming). Nowadays, however, drug stores in Taiwan, as in Japan, offer services of "menstrual regulation" that are well known to be abortions of the kind with which we are familiar.

23. See Browner 1980 on the concept of "possible pregnancy" and the scope it provides for the use of ambiguous "pregnancy tests" among Catholic women in Cali, Colombia.

MENSTRUAL REGULATION, FERTILITY AND HEALTH:
A DUAL IMAGE OF WOMANHOOD

Chinese medical thought saw the male body as dominated by male vital energy, *yang qi,* and the female body by its female counterpart, *yin qi,* materialized in Blood. One of the most fundamental of natural cycles was the monthly circulation and renewal of female blood. At menstruation, the stale or dirty old blood was flushed away, and new, fresh and fertile blood began to regenerate. The menstrual period signified fertility; the days immediately following its end offered the best chances of conception. It is not surprising, then, to find that the regularity of menstruation is a key diagnostic for female health from the earliest Chinese medical classics to the present day. Menstrual regularity, *tiaojing,* was believed to be the key to female health throughout the reproductive years, and irregularity was cause to consult a physician or healer immediately, for anyone who could afford to do so.

By the late imperial period, almost every work on women's medicine began with an essay on menstrual regularity (fig. 22). Xu Chunfu begins the section of his medical compendium dealing with *fuke* by quoting the passage from the *Huangdi neijing* on reproductive maturation. He continues:

> If sexual intercourse takes place when the menses are regular, there will be a child. If not, it's like trying to lock three fingers into five: this is what is meant by unregulated. If the menses are not regulated then all kinds of disorders will succeed each other, becoming so severe that they cannot be cured. This includes infertility. . . . If a girl has no menses, should it be transmitted as wind-wasting [emaciation due to emotional upsets] or as breathing-anger [a Heart system disorder], then all her life the sufferer cannot be cured. This is even more true of the Heart system, which belongs to the category of *yang* and governs the Blood. The Spleen system enfolds the Blood and thereby activates *qi.* If the menses do not come through, it is invariably because there is an insufficiency of the activities of the Heart system. Worry damages the Spleen system, a cause of exhaustion syndrome: [energy produced by food] is not transmitted, the Metal of the Lung system which nourishes the Water of the Kidney system [which controls the reproductive powers] is lost, and there is nothing to build up the menstrual blood. The bodily secretions dry up day by day. If by the fourth or fifth time [the menses] have not been regulated, they will gradually cease altogether. The depletion will cause damage as an internal Heat syndrome, the symptoms of [the fatal wasting diseases] bone-steaming and consumption will develop, and [the disorder] will suddenly become incurable.[24]

24. *Gujin yitong daquan* 5373–74.

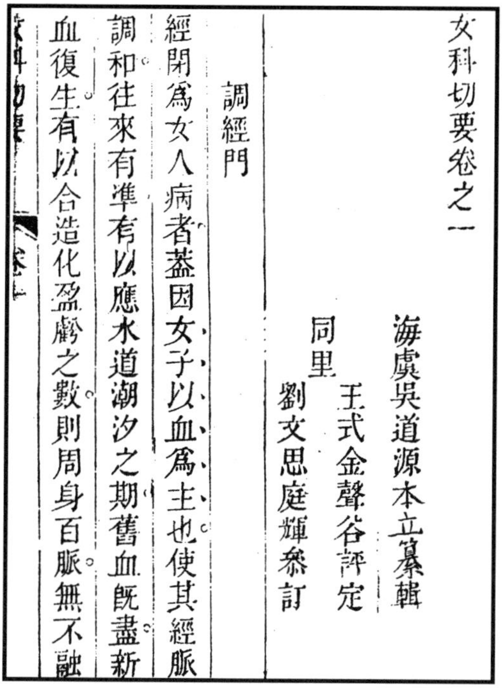

女科切要卷之一

海虞吳道源本立纂輯

同里
王式金聲谷評定
劉文思庭輝參訂

調經門

經閉為女人病者蓋因女子以血為主也使其經脈

調和往來有準有以應水道潮汐之期舊血既盡新

血復生有以合造化盈虧之數則周身百脈無不融

Figure 22. Page 1 of Wu Daoyuan's *Nüke qieyao* (Absolute essentials of gynecology) of 1773. This section on menstrual regulation (*Tiaojing men*) constitutes the first of the seven sections of the book. The first sentence reads: "The reason why menstrual blockage [*jingbi*] causes women's disorders is that women are ruled by Blood."

Menstrual regularity was a sign of mental and bodily health and harmony, a prerequisite for conception certainly, but not separable from a woman's health as a whole. Menstrual irregularity threatened immediate reproductive success, but this was only a secondary consideration in view of the dangers it posed to a woman's overall health and survival. Amenorrhea, like abortion or miscarriage, was a dangerous interruption of a natural process. If a woman wished to be healthy and strong, fruitful but also capable of raising the children she bore, she had to take care that her menses were regular, for once their regularity lapsed she became prey to debilitating and sometimes fatal diseases.[25]

25. This view was not unique to Chinese medicine but is found in many humoral medical systems in which the importance of circulation is stressed, including nineteenth-century Europe.

Menstrual regulation was a dual symbol. On the one hand, it symbolized female fertility, the ability to reproduce life (*sheng*) or to give birth (*chan*); on the other hand, and equally important, it symbolized female health and strength, emotional equilibrium and control, the ability to nurture life and to rear children successfully (*yang*). In the case of an individual pregnancy, the mother's life was more important than that of the fetus. And nonpregnant women were encouraged by medical theory to pay minute attention to every detail of their menstrual cycle, and to seek immediate treatment for any irregularity.[26] Any interruption of natural circulation was viewed as potentially lethal.

There were many causes of menstrual irregularity and many variations in the forms it took, including early and late periods, flow too scanty or too great, unusual consistency or color, and amenorrhea.[27] In one popular Qing work on women's health, written in easily memorized short verses, we find the following variations under amenorrhea or "blocked menses" (*jingbi*) alone: (1) stagnation of Blood, with retention of Blood in the uterus caused by a Cold pathogen (the text says this condition resembles the amenorrhea of early pregnancy); (2) deficiency of Blood, associated with repressed emotions and often resulting in fatal wasting diseases; (3) drying up of Blood from excessive sex or too many pregnancies, likely to produce emaciation, coughing, and "bone-steaming"; (4) amenorrhea caused by chronic coughing or consumption; (5) intermittent amenorrhea associated with menopause[28]; (6) intermittent amenorrhea in young virgins, which was no cause for worry unless it resulted from some fundamental deficiency in Blood or *qi*; (7) amenorrhea of nuns, unmarried women or widows, whose frustrated emotions damaged the Liver and Spleen systems.[29]

26. In 1990 Yuan-ling Chao helped me conduct a series of interviews on menstrual regulation and abortion with Chinese women currently living in Los Angeles. It was clear that, far from being embarrassed to talk about their periods, they found it an engrossing topic. Several claimed to remember details and changes from puberty through successive pregnancies to menopause (if they were that old); all were fonts of wisdom on how menstruation in general related to health and health problems.

27. Furth 1986: 53 gives a table of classification by symptoms.

28. It should be noted here that menopause was not medicalized as a health problem in the texts I have analyzed here; the end of menstruation was seen as a natural and unproblematic passage from one stage of the life cycle to the next, and only abnormalities, such as postmenopausal bleeding, figure in the medical collections (e.g., *Yilue liushi* 1876–78). Because menstrual regularity was so important to the general health of a woman of childbearing age, however, some women of middle age did worry when they first started missing periods.

29. Wu Qian's *Fuke xinfa yaojue* 20–23. In the last case it is clearly the lack of a normal married sex life that is seen as the root of the problem, whereas in the

The amenorrhea itself was just a symptom of a more fundamental imbalance. While ignorant doctors tried to cure such disorders by prescribing simple *tongjingyao*, drugs to make the menstrual blood flow, this could result in long-term damage. Skilled physicians would leave aside the superficial effects to treat the disorder at its source.[30] Given that medical theory interpreted menstrual irregularities as closely linked to fundamental disorders of the visceral systems, resulting in deficiencies of Blood and *qi* energy, and often leading to chronic if not fatal disease, it is hardly surprising that Chinese women paid close attention to their menstrual cycle, and were quick to take medication for any irregularity.

In the case of Cheng Maoxian's wife noted earlier, she starts to worry when her period is only a couple of days late. This is a classic case of "possible pregnancy": she immediately takes a few doses of *tongjingyao;* when a couple of doses fail to work, she reluctantly concludes that she must be pregnant and desists from taking any more. Like the modern Colombians with whom Carole Browner worked, once her pregnancy is confirmed Cheng's wife accepts it, even though she fears—and with reason—for her health.[31]

Although learned physicians discussed the many types of amenorrhea with which women were afflicted at such sophisticated etiological levels as *yin-yang* balance and organ depletion, in general practitioners and patients alike tended to respond primarily to the notion of "blockage" and to resort immediately to "Blood-livening" or "blockage-dispersing" drugs, many of which were recognized to cause miscarriages. The passage by Xu Chunfu quoted earlier is a discussion of the ways in which amenorrhea "is transmitted" (*zhuan*). In the beginning of his analysis Xu quotes the *Huangdi neijing*, writing of menstrual irregularities as basic "disorders of the two *yangs*" with their primary manifestation in the Spleen system. He goes on to illustrate successively severe stages resulting from this original basic problem, suggesting that the course of the disorder can follow different paths, perhaps according to the constitution or emotional predisposition of the patient. Although Xu speaks of amenorrhea "being transmitted" in various forms, he does not go so far as to speak of the phenomenon as causal in its own right. An educated physician was obliged to situate causality at a more profound level even than this dysfunction in a

---

case of the drying up of Blood, sexual excess was the root of the damage. Moderation, physical and emotional, was the key to health.

30. Xu Chunfu explains this point in an essay on the widely used Blood tonic *siwutang*, Four Ingredient Decoction (*Gujin yitong daquan* 5380).

31. Browner 1980.

fundamental natural cycle. He had to place any specific case of amenorrhea as one of a network of symptoms in order to identify the underlying problem and the appropriate treatment.

Xu writes of amenorrhea as a *precursor* of debilitating and sometimes fatal disorders, but we can extend the significance of amenorrhea beyond the level of correlation in Xu's mind to that of instrumentality: amenorrhea not as a *primary* but at any rate as a *secondary cause.* In dealing with amenorrhea, skilled physicians would leave aside the superficial effects to treat the disorder at its source, and yet they were also obliged to deal more immediately with the dangers of impaired Blood circulation that amenorrhea signaled, in other words to treat the amenorrhea as a secondary cause. A woman whose menses stopped would be likely to construe the lack of Blood as a primary cause, and many unskilled or unscrupulous physicians would agree and treat her accordingly. But part of the reason for this therapeutic choice lay in the use of words, namely the conventional grouping of all cases of amenorrhea under the general category of "blocked menses."

Several terms were used in medical writing to describe the category of amenorrhea. Chief among them were *yueshi* (the monthly event) or *jing* (cycle), *bulai* (fails to come) or *butong* (does not come through), and *jingbi* (the cycle is blocked). All of these terms used common lay vocabulary, and writers do not attempt to justify their choice on technical grounds by providing distinctions or precise definitions. The last term, "menstrual blockage," seems to have been the most common and is a category in almost every Chinese medical work on female disorders. It is far more common than the more neutral terms of *bulai* or *wujing* (absence of menses). Learned and experienced physicians clearly took this term as a convenient label covering a far greater complexity of phenomena; "blockage" was in fact their least likely diagnosis. Amenorrhea might reflect a range of deep-seated problems affecting the balance of *yin* and *yang* and the production of Blood, and manifested through the dysfunction of one central organ system which then affected others. However this might be, we may say that Blood was affected in one of two basic ways: either it was depleted and/or dried up, or it was stagnant or blocked. Either of these conditions affected not only menstrual flow but also the circulation of nutrition and energy in the body. The physician's first task was to restore the circulation of a healthy flow of Blood. Once that had been achieved, the deeper levels of the problem could be addressed and treated with a sequence of prescriptions until full health was restored.

And yet at the same time, the very notion of blockage was threatening.

Chinese popular notions of health gave enormous importance to the concept of vital circulation (*tong*). A healthy person, or one affected by a mild but chronic disorder, would be inclined to think in terms of balance, nourishment and replenishment, and to eat and take tonics or other prescriptions accordingly. But any interference with natural circulation would be considered an acute and serious symptom, requiring immediate treatment. Blocked circulation of the vital fluids was particularly dangerous. If *qi* was blocked, then death was imminent; if Blood was blocked, then obstruction of *qi* would soon follow; absence of sweating as well as constipation or retention of urine were also seen as serious symptoms by both physicians and ordinary people. While today Westerners and Chinese alike often contrast the "gentle, gradual" effects of Chinese prescriptions with the drastic and immediate action of biomedical drugs, such a characterization is a modern ideological construct, which has been possible only since Western drugs became available to Chinese for the treatment of acute disease. "Heroic medicine" was as much in demand in late imperial China as it was anywhere else; a physician who made his patient defecate, vomit and sweat could be *seen* to be producing results. While drawing blood European-style was not part of the late imperial Chinese repertory, the prescription of drugs to cause blood to flow was a common response to "female disorders." Elite physicians might rail against quackery and the ignorance of unskilled doctors who treated a fundamental disorder at the level of its most superficial symptom. Nevertheless, categorizing amenorrhea as a "blockage" of vital circulation and treating it accordingly probably corresponded to most patients' understanding of the problem: for them, the blockage was the problem, not a symptom. This level of attributing causality was shared by many healers. Not surprisingly, drugs to bring on the menses and restore this vital circulation were commonly prescribed by physicians of all kinds.

Chinese doctors knew that spontaneous abortion was not unusual in the first trimester. "If a spontaneous abortion takes place in the first months, nobody realizes that it is an abortion—they simply say they are not pregnant; they do not realize that they were already pregnant and have aborted, *anchan*."[32] If a woman was worried about the late onset of her menses, however, and took drugs to restore the regularity, the chances were that several of the ingredients would have been drugs strongly contraindicated for pregnant women. Xu Dachun reports several cases of

32. Ye Tianshi, *Yeshi nüke zhengzhi, anchan xuzhi*, quoted Huang Shengwu 1983: 23.

women worried about amenorrhea being treated by less scrupulous or skilled doctors than himself with extremely strong Blood-vivifying drugs. In one case of a fifteen-year-old, brought in by her mother, whose periods have started and then stopped again, he tells her mother that things will sort themselves out naturally in the course of time, but adds, "If you want to treat it with drugs we can."[33] In another case also noted under the entry for amenorrhea:

> A woman's menses stopped, she alternated between Cold and Heat symptoms, her mouth was dry and her forehead red, she could keep down little food and drink. At evening she would have two or three fits of coughing.[34] The doctors [she consulted] all used such types of drugs as gadfly, leech, dried lacquer,[35] and [a range of purgatives and other drugs]. Only I said we shouldn't do so. "Even if these prescriptions appear in the old collections, if the sick person takes them they will certainly have stomach-ache and be put off their food—and these are drugs that can kill. . . . We should not use gadfly and similar powerful drugs. If we do so then the menses will come, but they will be scanty, and urination on the other hand will stop, with other symptoms arising as a result. When Essence and Blood are insufficient they should always be replenished. These dangerous and powerful drugs are unreliable and violent, and often result in damage."[36]

Physicians as skilled and scrupulous as Xu were probably in a minority, and in any case many women worried about their periods did not choose, or could not afford, to go to a doctor. Instead they procured drugs or ready-made menstrual prescriptions from a druggist.[37]

Many of the drugs used to treat menstrual irregularity belong to the

33. *Yilue liushu* 1846.
34. These are symptoms of a very serious disorder.
35. These are all powerful Blood-breaking drugs that certain physicians even termed "Blood-eating" (like the blood-sucking creatures from which they were obtained), saying that they should only be used where Blood had coagulated into a mass. These drugs were also considered to be intensely cooling, which is perhaps why some other physicians used them to treat amenorrhea, which in certain forms was linked to the drying up of Blood resulting from a strong heat disorder (Furth, personal communication 1996). In any case, because leech and gadfly were so strong they were usually forbidden to pregnant women.
36. *Yilue liushu* 1846.
37. In Taiwan today there are numerous *fuke* or gynecological clinics which advertise their services for regulating menstruation (*tiaojing*), including bringing on the menses (*tongjing*), sometimes stating explicitly that they make no distinction whether the case is early or late. Everybody knows that these are places where one can procure an abortion (Furth and Ch'en 1992). In Singapore the government recently attempted to prohibit certain patent Chinese medicines used to bring on the menses; these medicines were often used by women who were uncertain whether they were pregnant (Ngin 1985: 100–106).

categories that strengthen or nourish Blood or *qi*, or replenish deficiencies; among the most common ingredients are *danggui* (*Angelica sinensis*) and *baishao* (*Paeonia alba*), which nourish Blood, and ginseng and *baishu* (*Atracotylodis macrocephala*), which replenish deficiencies of the *qi*. But it is noticeable that many of the prescriptions for amenorrhea rely much more heavily on drugs to vivify Blood and disperse stagnation, many of which are explicitly recognized as liable to produce miscarriages. These include *taoren* (peach kernels), *honghua* (*Carthamus*), *niuxi* (*Acanthyrus bidentata*), *shuizhi* (leeches), *mangchong* (gadfly), and *ganqi* (dried lacquer); all of these were explicitly recognized as being powerful and requiring very careful use:

> Peach kernels . . . [are among] the most dangerous of all the drugs for breaking up and expelling Blood. When a woman's menses do not flow there are two possible reasons. One is wind, cold, chill and damp, each of which can be transmitted to the *ren* and *chong* tracts [governing menstruation and fertility] to the point that Blood and *qi* congeal and do not flow: in these cases the use of the aforementioned drugs is widely successful. But if the Sea of Blood [*xuehai*] is dry and withered without menses to flow, then one should simply build up the three tracts of the Spleen, Liver and Kidney systems and thus nourish the origins of the transformation [of Blood and *qi*]: this is the way of curing the depletion.[38]

It is interesting that Wu Qian's popular rhymed gynecological text referred to earlier does not include any of the drugs known to cause miscarriage in its prescriptions for amenorrhea, except in the case of nuns, virgins, and widows, where presumably the possibility of pregnancy was not countenanced. Other medical works do include a number of prescriptions for amenorrhea, which include one or several drugs contraindicated in pregnancy. The early twentieth-century *Nüke bijue daquan*, for instance, includes *niuxi* in several prescriptions to cure amenorrhea due to the effects of cold, and *honghua* in most of the prescriptions to counteract stagnation. Furthermore, in a section on testing for pregnancy, it cites one Master Ye who advises the use of a harmless enough prescription consisting of *danggui* and *chauanxiong*, which will cause the abdomen to move if the woman is pregnant but not otherwise; however, if this does not work the first time a decoction of *honghua* should be administered. And a modern collection of popular prescriptions from all over China includes peach kernels, *Carthamus*, leeches, gadflies, and *niuxi* in its prescriptions for amenorrhea due to Blood stasis.[39]

38. *Xuanqi jiuzheng lun* 3/62b–63a.
39. *Nüke mijue daquan* 22–24, 65, 70; Li Wenliang et al. 1982: 186–87, 208–12.

Medical practitioners recognized that the amenorrhea of early pregnancy and of menstrual blockage were easily confused; nevertheless, to obtain powerful emmenagogues a woman would not have to go underground to seek treatment but could consult with the most respectable of physicians, who were quite likely to prescribe drugs contraindicated to pregnant women.

Charlotte Furth remarks that the physiological ambiguity of menstrual regulation meant that "the desire for an abortion could remain inarticulate and so relatively blameless."[40] I would go further: menstrual regularity was a symbol of ideal womanhood, menstrual irregularity was a deviation from this norm, a dangerous interruption of a natural process. Regulation of the menses was not just a means of concealing antisocial behavior, it was taking active steps to regain normality, to conform to the norm and to achieve a feminine ideal that involved active health as well as passive fertility. Menstrual regulation symbolized the ability to reproduce life (*sheng*), and equally important, it symbolized the ability to nurture life and to rear children successfully (*yang*). The medical sources show that orthodox gynecology provided elite women in late imperial China with an approved technology of reproductive control that offered certainly not total reproductive freedom but rather room to maneuver, the possibility of cultivating the role of *mater*, or social mother, maybe at the expense of that of an endlessly fruitful *progenitrix*, or biological mother.

40. Furth 1986: 65.

9 Reproductive Hierarchies

Orthodox medicine in late imperial China unequivocally put a woman's health, short-term and long-term, before the life of a fetus. The same was true of the law: neither procuring nor performing an abortion was a crime in the late imperial code. The law did attribute separate rights of person to a fetus (a pregnant woman could not be executed for a capital crime until she had given birth). However, the legal value of any life was not absolute but determined by hierarchies of age, status and gender. A mother was above her child, born or unborn, in the hierarchy, so her life was more valuable and her right to dispose of her child was legally acknowledged.[1] If we put the tolerance of abortion together with other orthodox inscriptions of female roles that I discuss later, in particular the laws concerning marriage, we find that as a set they provide a web of techniques and strategies for women to play biological motherhood off against social motherhood.

From the generosity and understanding shown toward women in medical theories of fertility and in the laws on abortion, we might be tempted to deduce that the orthodox, elite male reproductive culture of late

---

1. Causing the death of another person's child was another matter: injuring a pregnant woman and thus causing her to miscarry was a punishable crime, the penalty being proportional to the length of the pregnancy. Anyone who sold or administered an abortifacient to a woman that damaged her health or caused her death was liable to punishment. The severity of a crime depended on whether the person who committed it was of superior or inferior rank to the victim. If a son raised his hand against his father, or a wife against her husband or mother-in-law, or a servant against his master, these were all considered much more serious offenses than if the same act had been committed against a stranger. But if a parent killed a child, or a husband his wife, first the crime was judged less serious, and second mitigating circumstances were often found to justify the action (Luk 1977).

imperial China offered reproductive freedoms, dignity and male support
to women in general. But a closer look at institutions such as marriage
laws shows that only in medical theory were women not explicitly differentiated by status. Flexibility of reproductive maneuver was restricted to
high-ranked women and depended on exploiting the inequalities within
female hierarchies; the inequalities among women also underlined inequalities among men. I return to these hierarchies later, but first I want
to look more closely at what a child, or a potential child, signified in late
imperial China. Children were desired, and yet they were disposable. Like
women, they were status symbols. They were pieces in a complex power
game in which each adult player had different stakes and each child a
different value.

CHILDREN: A QUALIFIED BLESSING

Chinese culture is not child-centered, says Sulamith Potter, that is to say,
children are not inherently desirable in themselves; rather "children appear to be the solution to adult problems that the Chinese take very seriously indeed," namely continuation of the family line and assured support
for parents in old age. Decisions about reproduction are not the private
responsibility of the couple; they are a family matter in which the opinion
of the man's father or mother may have more weight than that of either
of the young people.[2] Though Potter is writing about contemporary
China, her description applies to late imperial society, where children also
belonged primarily to families and lineages, not to couples. Since so many
people and so many conflicting considerations were involved, one can
imagine that many decisions about children were extremely painful. We
may often be shocked by what the Chinese expected of a good mother, or
a good parent.

To return to the case of Jiang Yuan, the mother of Prince Millet: Jiang

2. In rural districts of the People's Republic in the 1980s, "the husband's parents are felt to be legitimately concerned in a couple's decisions about birth control" (Potter 1987: 43). In Singapore 53 percent of the couples interviewed by
Salaff reported kin influence on "their decision to contracept, abort, ligate or bear
an additional child" (1985: 178). Today contraception is readily available and star-
vation is seldom a factor in Chinese families' fertility decisions; under these conditions pressures from the kin group are usually to have more rather than fewer
children, as Potter's research on the PRC and Salaff's study of Chinese couples
in Singapore show (though Salaff's study shows that even in affluent Singapore
antinatalist pressures were exerted in some cases). Under the One-Child Family
Policy a woman often finds herself caught between the demands of her family and
those of the state (Potter 1987; Croll 1987; Anagnost 1989).

Yuan abandoned her infant because the mode of his conception led her to believe that he was ill-omened. She was considered a "Maternal Paragon" by the Han writer Liu Xiang precisely because of the fortitude she showed in giving up a child who she believed was a threat to the community. "Infant abandonment [was], on occasion, one among many responsibilities a woman must assume in the sphere of child-care. . . . To dispose of an inauspicious child was not only a reasonable action but a filial duty as well." In ancient Chinese society children were thought of not as individuals with individual rights to existence, but "as one knot in a continuum or mesh of lives connecting ancestors with descendants," and a misplaced knot would weaken the mesh. "How welcome a child was therefore depended upon how much it could contribute to the continuum, specifically the patrilineage. . . . Such decisions were clearly based on the desire to maintain or increase the social standing of the family at large."[3] Although the way in which the boundaries of the patriline were defined and its degree of control over member families changed over the centuries, as did the considerations that made one individual child welcome and another unwelcome, the basic idea that kin-groups could and should distinguish between desirable and undesirable children persisted.

Where family prestige was at issue, presumably the senior men were chiefly involved in laying down the rules, though it was probably up to the senior women (who had direct access to the bedchambers) to police them. The right to procreate in late imperial China depended on both the resources of the household and the couple's status within the kin-group. Where extended families of brothers and cousins lived under the same roof, there is evidence to show that the number of children a couple had depended on how closely they were related to the family head. The eldest son, who would become ritual heir as well as family head in his turn, had the most children and poor cousins might have none at all, at least until they could afford to move out and set up house on their own. Within a lineage group the differences between rich and poor families were also marked; as Stevan Harrell says, "the rich got children," in part because they had the resources to support them, and in part because they could command preferential access to fertile young women.[4] The poor had fewer children and fewer ancestors not just because they could not afford them, but also because children, like ancestors, were carefully husbanded status symbols denoting rank within the patriline and lineage.

3. Kinney 1993: 129, 122–23.
4. Lee and Campbell 1996; Harrell 1985.

Where family honor was not at stake, the mother-in-law—the mistress of the house and the person in charge of food and domestic finances—was a key figure in reproductive decisions. She might consider that the household could not afford to feed another mouth at this point, or conversely she might be anxious for her first grandson. The birth of a daughter-in-law's first child was an ambiguously joyful event for the mistress of the house. She became a grandmother, the most pleasurable of Chinese kinship roles, but the event also marked an irreversible step in the transfer of power from her own hands to those of her son's wife. And sharing a bed and having children together often brought a husband and wife close in a new way, strengthening bonds of affection and respect that developed only gradually in arranged marriages. Previously the chief object of the young man's affections had been his mother, and the severity with which a senior woman controlled her daughters-in-law often smacked of jealousy.[5] However, when Mme. Feng, the mother of the scholar Ye Shaoyuan (1588–1648), refused to allow him to sleep with his bride Shen Yixiu (1590–1635) during his first years of marriage, this was more likely out of consideration for the young woman's health: she was only fourteen *sui* when she was wed, an age at which medically educated people considered childbearing to be dangerous. Shen and his wife did not have their first child for five years, but went on to have twelve children who lived long enough to be named.[6]

5. Although the male-oriented ideology of descent presented the bond between father and son as the main emotional link holding Chinese society together, it has often been remarked that fathers were remote and often fearful figures to their sons, who reserved their warmest and most open emotions for their mothers (Hsiung 1994). Anthropologists like Margery Wolf (1972) have emphasized the quasi-sexual competition between mother and bride for a man's affections; but as far as literary men in late imperial China were concerned, despite the more common occurrence of companionate marriage (Mann 1991; Ko 1994), the mothers usually seem to have won hands down (Hsiung 1994).

6. Ko 1994: 188. A local history of the period records them as having had sixteen children, but Ko was able to identify only eight boys and four girls by name (ibid.: 329). This number of offspring, though by no means unusual by bourgeois standards in Victorian England, seems to me exceptional for a monogamous couple in late imperial China. In the first years of the marriage Mme. Feng also forbade her daughter-in-law to write (Shen Yixiu was already a notable poet, but Mme. Feng feared that she would neglect her household duties and distract her son from his preparation for the examinations). Although it is possible, as Ko implies, that by keeping the young couple apart not only in the bedchamber but also in the study Mme. Feng delayed the transfer of her son's affections, in time great tenderness and intimacy grew up between the couple, and they shared an absolute devotion to their talented but ill-fated daughters, three of whom died young while the fourth was unhappily married.

In late imperial culture the marriage ceremony was conventionally portrayed as the central rite of passage for the new bride. She was ritually carried from her natal home to the groom's house, where she served wine to her new parents, worshiped at the family altar, and spent her first night with her new husband. This was usually spoken of as the point at which her connection to her natal family was severed. A new wife joined her husband in worship at the family altar as soon as she moved to his family's house, and she was now expected to treat his parents as her own. However, her complete incorporation into her husband's lineage depended on her becoming the mother of a son. A wife who did not give birth to a son could be sent back to her family. A son was a key status symbol. A new bride might be treated like a general servant by her in-laws, but once she had a son things would improve: she had the recognized responsibility of caring for an infant within her own quarters and the recognized capacity to continue the family line.

Margery Wolf has interpreted giving birth as a door opening, giving a young bride the means to build up her own power in opposition to her mother-in-law through the formation of a "uterine family."[7] But just as the birth of the first grandchild was an ambivalent event in the life of the mistress of a family, so too was the birth of a first child to the bride. Some young women dreaded it as a gate slamming shut, a definitive loss of autonomy, a final severing of ties to the natal family. Practices in regions as distant as Canton and Shandong confirm that in many places it was not the wedding but the first birth that marked the definitive transfer from one family to another. After marriage the young bride regularly returned to her natal home for longer or shorter periods, and only settled permanently in her husband's home when she was about to give or had given birth. In some regions it was not unusual for her to do all she could to delay this first birth, refusing to have intercourse with her husband or trying to abort if she thought she was pregnant.[8]

Quite apart from whether a particular birth was considered to be materially or socially welcome, magical considerations often played an important role in fertility decisions. In ancient China triplets were unlucky

---

7. M. Wolf 1972. By "uterine family" Wolf means the group formed by the mother and her own children, especially the sons, whose primary affections and loyalty will be given to their mother rather than to the patriline in general. The uterine family therefore offers an in-marrying woman emotional support and security that she cannot find elsewhere.

8. See Judd 1989; Stockard 1989; and Siu 1990 on institutions such as "delayed marriage" and "visits to the natal family."

and were put to death, as were children born with any deformity. A child conceived near the stove would bring misfortune, as would a child born in the same month as a parent; a son born on the fifth day of the fifth month would grow up to murder his family.[9] In late imperial times it was well known that children born or conceived at certain times or in certain places would be unlucky. Though Confucians did their best throughout history to stamp out superstitions of this kind, or at least to rewrite them in such a way as to present them as infractions of the cosmological order with logical consequences, some of these beliefs have persisted up to the present day.[10] Indeed many such beliefs were translated into cosmological prohibitions and integrated into the late imperial medical literature on procreation: rather than a child conceived during a thunderstorm growing up to cause murder and mayhem, it was said that his intelligence or his constitution would be adversely affected.[11]

A woman might act, or be encouraged to act, to control her fertility in the interests of the kin-group, taking all or any of the preceding considerations into account. She might also have her own reasons for wanting or not wanting a child. First there was the social issue of her status within the family. Then there were considerations of health. If she had a weak constitution childbirth could be dangerous, and the medical corpus includes prescriptions for permanently sterilizing married women for whom

9. Kinney 1993: 118 on ancient China. See also the warnings about house layout and how it will affect procreation and family fortune, contained in the last section of the *Lu Ban jing* and reproduced in almanacs as well as popular encyclopedias.

10. Körner records the belief in villages near Beijing in the early twentieth century that if a bride became pregnant in the first month of marriage, her husband's family would be destroyed if the child was a boy, but her husband's, her own, and also the family of the go-between who had arranged the marriage if the child was a girl. In such cases an abortion was procured with drugs from the apothecary during a *yin* month (a month with thirty days) (1959: 29).

11. See the Song physician Chen Ziming on when intercourse should be avoided (*Furen daquan liangfang* j.9, 190). Another object of late imperial Confucian "medicalization" was the blood pollution associated with menstruation and with childbirth. Popular Chinese pollution beliefs held that in the process of childbirth a woman polluted her infant; the pollution had to be removed by ritual bathing of the infant. Such ideas, argues Furth, were mediated by medicine into the theory of "fetal poison," whereby a woman transmitted poisons along with nourishing Blood to the child in her womb. These would then normally be dissipated in early infancy, through rashes and eruptions and in particular through a dose of measles or smallpox. It was considered a cause for anxiety if a small child did *not* catch a case of measles, so that the poison remained trapped inside his or her body (Furth 1987; Ahern 1978).

childbirth might prove fatal. Such prescriptions are not common, however, because the drugs used to sterilize were considered extremely dangerous in their own right.[12] Medical theory represented childbirth as depleting the vital energies, and even without invoking medical authority women knew well that childbirth was dangerous and that repeated pregnancy was exhausting and debilitating, so sometimes in desperation they were willing to take the risk. The essayist Gui Youguang (1506–71) wrote in his memorial for his mother, Mme. Zhou, that by the age of twenty-six *sui* she had given birth, with much suffering, to seven children in ten years, and wanted no more. A close friend eventually found her a permanent remedy consisting of a pair of snails. Unfortunately, on taking the snails Mme. Zhou lost her voice and died not long after.[13] More women wished to prevent a particular pregnancy than to sterilize themselves permanently. On the evidence of medical treatises and general anecdotes, Hsiung Ping-chen believes that a large market for abortifacients grew up in late imperial times, at least in the rapidly expanding towns and cities.[14]

Abortion was not illegal in late imperial China, but it was a sin. In the Buddhist view abortion and infanticide both involved the killing of a living being, and other people had a moral duty to prevent them if possible. In the morality books known as the "Ledgers of Merit and Demerit" (*gong-guo ge*), lists of sins and virtues that became immensely popular in the Ming, stopping a person either from drowning a child or from having an abortion were both worth one hundred merits.[15] But childbirth was also represented in Buddhist scriptures of the period as a karmic sin, a form of

12. They often included mercury compounds as well as fermented wheat products that may have been some form of ergot (Charlotte Furth, personal communication 1996).

13. In the Chinese pharmacopeia snails were intensely cooling (Charlotte Furth, personal communication 1996). The use of snails as a sterilizing drug may have been linked to a prevalent lay belief that prostitutes made themselves sterile by eating tadpoles—a belief that was briefly revived in the People's Republic when new contraceptive methods were being sought in the 1960s.

14. Furth discusses the social significance of medical representations of childbirth as a depleting process (1986, 1987). On the story of Mme. Zhou, on sterilization prescriptions in late imperial China, and on the frequency of induced abortion, see Hsiung forthcoming. When estimating the frequency and availability of abortion, however, we must allow for the fact that our picture draws heavily on condemnations by indignant moralists, whose portrayal of a decadent society where abortion was available openly on every street corner exaggerated the true situation.

15. On the moral accounting that became popular in Ming and Qing times, see Berlin 1985 and especially Brokaw 1991.

cosmic pollution: "By giving birth to children she befouls heaven and earth, and offends the river god by washing bloody skirts."[16]

Buddhist accounts of marriage and reproduction, for instance the scripture translated by Daniel Overmyer, depicted the wife as a necessarily submissive victim of all the sorrows imposed by patriarchy—sorrows that were deserved, because her very existence as a woman was the result of sinning in a previous incarnation. "When a woman is married to a husband for her whole life she is controlled by him. All her joys and sorrows derive from him"; "If she is not in accord with her mother-in-law's wishes, she is never able to return to her mother's home. She thinks of the pain in the hearts of her parents, and of when she will be able to repay their kindness." "After they are married she necessarily suffers the pains of childbirth, and cannot avoid the sin of offending the sun, moon and stars with a flow of blood. Now," says the scripture remorselessly, "I will speak with you in more detail about the sufferings women endure in childbirth." Ten kinds of abnormal birth are described, each of them retribution for past sins; this is followed by a month-by-month account of the discomforts, anxieties and dangers of pregnancy.[17]

The heroine of this particular "precious volume" (*baojuan*) was a young woman named Liu Xiang, or Fragrance Liu, who managed to remain chaste within marriage, as did numerous other Buddhist heroines of the period. Although the explicit conclusion drawn in this and other "precious volumes" was that a son should repay his mother's suffering by procuring her salvation after death,[18] as Overmyer suggests, it seems reasonable to suppose that tracts of this kind might have led some women to question marriage itself, or at any rate childbirth. In the late nineteenth and early twentieth centuries, "precious volumes" of this kind were popular reading in the girls' houses of the Canton region. Delayed marriage was common practice among poor families of the region at the time, and

16. Overmyer 1985: 251–52; see also Seaman 1981 on the Blood-bowl ritual common in recent Buddhist funerals in Taiwan. Seaman says that this virulently misogynistic equation of female fertility with cosmic pollution is not to be found in any Indian precursors of the Chinese Buddhist scriptures, and he believes that it must stem from indigenous Chinese ideas about birth pollution.

17. Overmyer 1985: 251–52.

18. The Blood-bowl ritual described in Seaman 1981 involves a woman's soul being saved from Hell during her funeral ceremony by her eldest son publicly draining a bowl of red liquid that represents the blood she shed in giving him birth. It is, as Seaman remarks, a shattering experience and a powerful test of a man's filial devotion. Ebrey mentions the existence of several Daoist scriptures of Song date that contain similar themes (1993: 175).

in some villages it was even customary for one daughter in a family to be given permission not to marry at all.[19] Many of these young women were silk reelers earning good wages, and Marjorie Topley reports one case of a young woman who entered into a delayed marriage but managed to postpone it permanently, using her savings to buy a concubine to keep house for her husband and to bear children for him and for herself.[20] Only in these recent cases is it possible to establish a firm connection between women's adherence to Buddhism and celibacy. But as early as the Song women were noted for their particular devotion to Buddhism, and "historical accounts emphasize the presence and equality of women in popular sects from the thirteenth century on."[21] One wonders whether the Buddhist emphasis on the dangerous nature of carnal desires, and on the pollution and sin associated with childbirth, might have influenced some women in their attitudes toward sex and childbirth through the imperial period.[22]

NATURE, NURTURE AND THE BOND
BETWEEN MOTHER AND CHILD

Pregnancy and childbirth promised a woman the joys and fulfillment of motherhood, but at the price of depletion, pollution, pain, sickness and sin. Could one perhaps become a mother without paying this price, and if so, how did this affect the nature of the bonds between mother and child?

The most explicit discussions of nature versus nurture are found in the large body of writing on adoption. As Ann Waltner's study of adoption and the construction of kinship makes clear, many of the chief points at issue arose from the patrilineal organization of society. Would the ancestors accept sacrifices from a man who did not share his adoptive father's

19. Topley 1978; Stockard 1989.

20. Topley 1978: 264. Many of the women who remained celibate under this system adopted a daughter to worship their tablet after death, thus establishing a female descent line that paralleled the male orthodoxy except that it required no male participation at all, no marriage and no procreation. This arrangement is still common in the female vegetarian halls in Hong Kong, whose occupants are mostly women who came to the colony to work as maids and never married.

21. Overmyer 1985: 228.

22. It was usual for women to devote themselves more fully to Buddhism once they reached their middle years, becoming vegetarians, studying sutras, and praying to Guanyin. By that time it would be relatively easy to justify ceasing sexual relations on the grounds that carnal desires were spiritually harmful. During her childbearing years the common belief that conception only occurred if both partners reached orgasm would presumably have required even a pious woman to refrain from total suppression of her carnal desires.

qi? Could one count on the loyalty of a child adopted from outside the lineage when it came to the management of patrimonial property?[23] Although these debates about human nature and human relatedness are all written from the male perspective, they also tell us a great deal about how the bonds between mother and child were construed in late imperial China.

Let us start with theories of natural kinship. Ideas about physical heredity varied in late imperial China.[24] Medical theories of generation agreed that the embryo grew out of male and female essence, and that it was nourished through pregnancy by the mother's Blood. Blood is the *yin*, materialized form of physiological *qi* energy. Some applied classic *yin-yang* reasoning to deduce that the father contributed *qi* in its energetic forms to the infant's make-up, and the mother offered *qi* in its materialized forms: the mother contributed the child's flesh and bones, while the father contributed the spirit and the intelligence. Others thought that bones were essentially male while flesh was female.[25] Some believed the father's seed determined what the child would look like, so that the children of the same father by different mothers would all look alike, while the children of the same mother by different fathers would not. Some held that the paternal *qi* was passed on only through the male line, others that it was transmitted through daughters as well as sons.[26]

Qi is the natural link among kinsmen and among descendants and ancestors—remember that the goal of grave-siting *fengshui* is to channel ancestral *qi* productively toward the living descendants. One important reason why it was not legal to adopt heirs of another lineage or surname in late imperial China was that only members of the same patriline shared the same *qi*. People who believed that *qi* was also passed down through daughters, however, could find good reasons for adopting a sister's son if a brother's son was not available.[27]

23. Among the central themes in Waltner 1990 are the discrepancies between adoption laws and actual practice, and the justifications that people offered for rejecting the theories of filiation on which the laws were founded.

24. See Leung 1984; Furth 1987; Waltner 1990; Hsiung forthcoming.

25. See J. Watson 1982 and 1988 on burial rituals and the importance of bones in rural South China. This seems to be a deep-rooted popular belief distinct from medical theory. The belief that the true line of descent is transmitted through the bones is also found in Korea, and it plays a role analogous to the European belief that blood is what really counts in reckoning kinship and descent.

26. Waltner 1990: 30.

27. Adoption practices varied enormously and seldom adhered precisely to the legal and ritual recommendations (see Wolf and Huang 1980 as well as Waltner 1990). For some families they seem to have served a dual function like marriage,

The natural bond between father and child, then, was the *qi* transmitted through the father's semen in the single moment of coition.[28] The mother's natural bond (not discussed in the debates on adoption, which were concerned only with patrilineal descent) was more complicated and took longer to construct. First she contributed female essence, at the moment of coition. Then there was a period of ten lunar months during which her Blood nourished and developed the fetus; if she breastfed the child herself that also contributed to the child's constitution (fig. 23).[29] This slowly forged bond of flesh, of food, of maternal responsibility and of infant dependence was quite different from the instantaneous transfer of *qi* energy that tied a son to his father.

Despite the fact that the *qi* transmitted at the moment of conception was the essential element in natural kinship between father and son, and through them between ancestors and descendants, the majority of orthodox thinkers believed that upbringing and education could supplant nature and create true bonds of filiation between biologically unrelated people. Zhu Xi believed that sincerity was more important than inherited *qi*, and that anyone who *acted* as a proper son *was* a proper son, even in the eyes of the ancestors. This transformation was produced through proper treatment. As Mencius had said, to treat a person as a son made him a son. In this context a poem in the *Book of Odes* was frequently quoted:

> The mulberry insect has young ones.
> The sphex [wasp] carries them away.

---

both providing heirs and expanding or reinforcing the network of social connections. In a genealogy compiled in the 1590s for the Cheng lineage of Anhui Xin'an, over 280 adoptions are recorded, of which 89 were sons of brothers; many of the other couple of hundred were not of agnatic relatives, but of maternal, sororal or affinal connections, and families connected by adoption were also frequently connected by marriage (Waltner 1990: 90–99).

28. The instantaneity of the paternal contribution seems natural and accurate to us, since it coincides with our own biological understanding. But the Chinese view of paternity, like our own, requires scrutiny. There are other societies where the biological construction of paternity is quite different, where it is held that the father must contribute biologically to the child's formation right through pregnancy, perhaps through repeated intercourse in order to "fix" the fetus, as among the Melanesian Melpa, perhaps by undergoing a parallel pregnancy as in the couvade of certain North American societies. See Ingold 1991 on "becoming persons."

29. Gynecological texts contain copious advice about behavior in pregnancy. A pregnant or lactating woman was not supposed to contaminate her Blood or breastmilk (a transformation of Blood) by eating rich or spicy foods, or by drinking too much wine. Equally important, she was not to indulge in excessive emotions that would trouble the fetus; anger and melancholy were especially to be avoided.

Figure 23.   "The first sleep of the silkworms": a woman is breastfeeding a child in the silkworm shed while another sits by sewing; the trays of dormant silkworms are on stands at the back of the picture (*Gengzhi tu*, Ming version of 1462 [Franke 1913, fig. 60]).

> Teach and train your young ones
> And they will become as good as you are.

The wasp entreats the young mulberry insects to become like itself, and they grow up into wasps. This was certainly the principle that led emperors or generals to adopt grown men in order to ensure their loyalty. The only problem was that upbringing might engender misplaced feelings of sincerity and closeness. For example, a foster child, especially one who had received a bequest, might expect to participate in his foster family's sacrifices even though he did not share the family's surname.[30]

How does this apply to the bonds between mother and child? A birth mother contributed to her child's constitution through the transfer of ma-

---

30. Waltner 1990: 74, 4. Adoption was a transaction that benefited the adopting family, who needed an heir. Fostering was an act of kindness or charity, taking care of a child in need. The distinction between adopted sons and foster sons was clearly marked in law; a foster son did not adopt the foster family's surname, he was not supposed to inherit, and he was forbidden to worship the family's ancestors (ibid.: 4, 60).

terial substances during pregnancy and lactation.[31] But how essential, how insuperable was this? In the elite reproductive cultures of late imperial China, the belief is clearly expressed that a mother's most important contribution was *educating* the child, turning it into a social being by inculcating moral values. This was what forged the truest bonds of tenderness and respect. "The true measure of a woman's greatness, many [Song] writers seemed to imply, was how well they brought up their children," and in the Ming and Qing debates on female education, the touchstone is always whether it will help them to be better mothers.[32] A good mother instructed her children how to behave properly and perform rituals correctly; she not only taught them to read the simple classics at home before they went to school but also expounded the moral messages the texts contained, and, most important of all, she instilled them with a sense of moral purpose and determination and encouraged them to pursue honorable ambitions.

The importance accorded to a mother's role as formal educator increased during the late imperial period. Stories about the mother of the great Confucian philosopher Mencius celebrate her moral rectitude but not her erudition; by the Song and Yuan dynasties, however, biographies of famous men often credit mothers with teaching the Confucian classics

---

31. It was usual throughout the late imperial period for well-off families to hire wet nurses. (In the Song, if a woman nursed her child herself, "men thought it a beautiful sign of motherly devotion" [Ebrey 1993: 179].) Moralists sometimes argued against this practice because it was felt that it led poor women to neglect their own infant, sometimes even to the point of death (Waltner 1990: 44); a woman who had lost her infant was therefore ideal as a wet nurse. The *Qing Customs* says a wet nurse received a salary of thirty to forty silver coins a month, and had to provide her own clothes and linen; but if she came from outside the town and had to take care of her family, she would be given seventy-five to eighty coins, and the family who hired her would also provide her clothes. The nurse usually stayed with the child until it was five or six *sui* (three or four by our reckoning) and then was sent home. However, if her nursling grew up to become rich and successful, and she had no son or other source of support, he would often invite her to join his household and take care of her for the rest of his life (*Qing Customs* A: 327). Medical texts, conscious of the direct effect of the quality of the nurse's milk on the health and constitution of the child, gave advice on how to choose a good nurse: she should be healthy and of kind and moderate disposition, said Wan Quan, while Xu Chunfu emphasized that she should be of good disposition and conduct (Leung 1984: 63–65). Physicians recommended close supervision of the nurse to make sure she had a suitable diet and did not give way to excessive emotions. Long lists of different milk disorders and how to cure them appear as early as Chen Ziming's *Furen daquan liangfang* (j.23).

32. Ebrey 1993: 183; Ko 1994; Mann 1991, 1994.

to their sons, and the Ming state "formally recognized women's contribution to men's education by conferring honorary titles on wives and mothers of scholar-officials."[33] It became conventional for successful men to
attribute their achievements to their mother's devotion, intelligence and
moral influence.[34] Their father played little direct role in their upbringing
or education, and it was their mother who played the role of the wasp.

Yet it would be wrong to think of the "natural" and the "cultural"
elements in the maternal role as separate and distinct. The medical theory
of menstrual regulation connected fertility and motherly aptitude through
the concept of organ systems and the circulation of vital substances: *qi*,
Blood, and essence (*jing*). Body and psyche were not distinct in this theory, which linked the innermost vitals deep within the body to the hair
and nails, eyes and ears that represented them at the surface, and tied the
physiological state of each vital organ to an emotional state that signaled
its health or disorder. A biological mother's fertility depended on her natural endowments but also on her behavior; the vigor, fortitude and equanimity required of a good social mother were achieved in part through
her conscious control of natural emotions whose roots lay in the equilibrium of the internal organs.

Similarly, in Chinese thought the physical processes of nourishing the
infant were one end of a spectrum of proper maternal care, a scale of
cumulative, attentive contributions that shaded gradually from the material to the moral. Men loved their mothers for having nursed them
through sickness as well as for teaching them to distinguish right from
wrong. And in effect the bond created by education is just as physical as
that created by conception, pregnancy and lactation: the latter involve a
transfer of material substances, but upbringing and teaching require the
transfer of "bodily [as well as intellectual] structures of perception and
action"; they too are "organically embodied" contributions to the child's

33. Ko 1994: 158–59. There seems to have been a general concensus among
elite males that women should be literate, although men did not always agree
what forms of literature women should study or learn to write. However, not
all women, even among the elite, thought education and maternity were com-
patible. Ko cites a poem by the poet-matriarch Gu Ruopu, in which she defends
herself against an old woman who criticized her bringing in a teacher for the girls
in her family; far from neglecting proper womanly work, says Gu, the girls are
studying so they can distinguish right and wrong, and rely on their moral training
to make the right decisions for themselves when difficult situations arise (1994:
163–64).
34. Hsiung Ping-chen gives numerous examples from over eight hundred biographies and letters she has studied from the Ming and Qing (1994).

development into a mature adult.[35] Chinese thought recognized how closely the two were connected. Du You (735–812) wrote in his encyclopedia *Tongdian* that although an adopted child receives his four limbs from his biological mother, he grows his hair and skin under the care of his adoptive mother. In his *Household Instructions* Yan Zhitui (531–c. 591) declared: "Confucius was right in saying: 'What is acquired in babyhood is like original nature; what has been formed in habit is equal to instinct.' "[36]

In late imperial China education and moral and intellectual cultivation were the key to male social success; physical strength and prowess were of no account. Is it surprising that elite males construed the ideal mother as an educator, and the quintessence of motherhood as symbolized not by giving birth, not by suckling or changing diapers, but by giving the child a proper moral upbringing?

Here I would like to give a beautiful literary illustration of the physical and social duality of motherhood in late imperial China, from an eighteenth-century novel analyzed by Lucie Borotová. There is a long tradition in Chinese thought and aesthetic expression of "doubles" or "parallels," paired objects or forms of expression whose full character or meaning emerges through the echoings, complementarities and contrasts between the pair.[37] In a study of the novelistic device of paired characters, Borotová points out that, unlike the Western postromantic tradition of doubling where "one person is to be perceived as two" (Dr. Jekyll and Mr. Hyde being perhaps the most famous example), in Chinese novels "two persons are to be perceived as one."[38] In illustration she discusses a pair of doubles from the novel *A Lantern at the Crossroads (Qilu deng)*. Its author, Li Yuyuan, makes frequent use of doubled characters; in each case one is a member of the gentry, the other is a commoner.

One prominent pair consists of the antihero Tan Shaowen's wife, Kong Huiniang, and his concubine, Bingmei. Kong is "tall, with an oval face," Bingmei is "plump, with a round face." Bingmei was brought into the household as a slave girl and seduced by Tan, giving birth to a son. Tan

35. Ingold 1991: 363. The bodily element is readily apparent when teaching skills like cooking or sewing, where experience and knack are more important than verbalized logic. But it is also present in the transmission even of highly formalized skills. It is almost impossible to learn to use a computer from written instructions.

36. Both cited Waltner 1990: 47.

37. The most obvious example is the ubiquitous pair of scrolls, *duilian*, each bearing one line of a couplet and hung on either side of a doorway or recess, whether in a temple, in a scholar's study, or in a busy restaurant.

38. Borotová 1992: 1.

then marries his childhood fiancée, Kong, whose distress at his debauchery leads her to fall ill and lose her ability to conceive. She has great affection for Bingmei's baby, however, who likes her even better than his birth mother, and on her deathbed Kong urges the grieving Bingmei to make sure that the boy is educated to study for the examinations. As Borotová points out, this division of maternal labor allows the social mother, whose chief concern is represented as giving the child a good upbringing and education, to remain pure from the taint of sexuality and the pollution associated in popular Chinese culture with childbirth; these negative burdens, along with the other material tasks of motherhood, are assumed by the biological mother.

The doubling of Kong Huiniang and Bingmei is not simply a literary conceit. I would argue that the ambiguities inherent in the medical concept of menstrual regulation and the way in which it presented the relationship between health and fertility opened the way for the doubling of maternal roles, and that social techniques of reproduction such as adoption or concubinage made possible the completion of the maternal pair.

In late imperial times medical texts on gynecology, which dealt primarily with the health problems of the well-off, not only provided a dual understanding of female fertility and how it should be expressed but also explicitly distinguished between the childbearing capacities of women of different classes. Women of gentle birth were represented as frail and inherently less fertile, likely to suffer terribly in childbirth; peasant women were naturally fertile and gave birth without trouble—the babies just popped out like "ripe melons."[39] The elite ideal of feminine beauty in late imperial China was one of almost unhealthy slenderness and delicacy suggestive of sexual immaturity.[40] This was a fitting physical frame for a social mother whose desirable characteristics were moral purity, sensitivity and refinement, but for a biological mother another physical type was required, robust and untroubled by the delicate emotions that threatened

39. Furth 1987: 16. Any real differences should perhaps be assessed in terms of, on the one hand, exposure to venereal infection and a predisposition toward rickets caused by strict seclusion (I presume these would be more likely to have affected women in elite households) and, on the other hand, lowered fertility, increased miscarriage rates and/or skeletal deformation caused by poor nutrition and overwork (presumably more common among peasant and working-class women, though the idealization of slenderness in late imperial elite culture might well have affected elite women's attitudes toward food; compare Bordo 1993).

40. Ebrey 1993: 41–42.

successful pregnancy. The maids and concubines in well-off households came from the supposedly robust and fertile lower classes.

MATERNAL DOUBLES: WIVES, CONCUBINES AND MAIDS

The duality of motherhood portrayed in literature and medical texts found concrete expression in the institutions of polygyny and adoption, which gave rights to elite women to appropriate the offspring of women lower down the social scale, underpinning female hierarchies as well as male. The flexibility of norms of motherhood among the elite of late imperial China depended both on class differences between families and on female hierarchies within a polygynous household. If we read Chinese records and discussions of kinship with the assumption that women were all equally subordinate within a male-dominated hierarchy, and if we presume that individual women had no control over their own reproductive patterns apart from infanticide, then these sources can be read as substantiating the stereotype of "woman as womb." But if we reread the materials on marriage forms and adoption from the perspective of female hierarchies, another picture emerges.[41]

Legally, late imperial China was a monogamous society: whatever his rank, a man was entitled to only one official wife (*qi*). Legal marriages usually took place between families of similar social status. A legal wife brought a dowry with her and went through a formal marriage ceremony in which she joined her new husband in making offerings to his ancestors. She occupied the main bedroom or wing in the couple's quarters. She acted as her husband's partner in all the rituals of ancestral worship and was in charge of running his household. She was the legal or formal mother (*dimu*) of all her husband's recognized offspring, born or adopted; they mourned her and worshiped her as their full parent. A wife was legally incorporated into her husband's lineage, and on marriage she assumed full mourning obligations for his kin while her obligations toward her own family were reduced by one degree. Her husband also assumed the obligation to mourn her relatives (though at a lower degree). A wife retained her family name after marriage; her relatives were integrated into the

41. Dennerline 1986 makes a powerful case that late imperial kinship practices can be properly understood only if women's interests are taken into account. This operates at two levels. First, men might act to protect the interests of women for whom they were responsible, most usually through the natal tie (i.e., their daughters or sisters). Second, women might exert pressure or take action on their own account.

network of her husband's affinal connections, and they retained an interest in and responsibility for her welfare.[42]

If a wife was barren, this could (but need not) be grounds for divorce,
in which case most men would hope to take a second wife.[43] Rather than
divorcing his wife and severing the ties that the marriage had created, a
man who still had no heir at the age of forty was encouraged by the laws
to take a concubine (qie). Strictly speaking it was illegal to take a concubine except if one had no heir, and then only one was permitted. In practice, a well-off man might take several young and attractive concubines in
the course of his life. Sometimes these young women came from poor
families who needed money or could not afford to give them a proper
dowry, and sometimes they were girls who had been sold in youth to be
trained as a prostitute or singing girl; sometimes a man would present one
of his own maids or singing girls to another man as a concubine.[44] In the
first case, the man made gifts of suitable value to the family (or baldly
gave them money), in the second, he made a payment to redeem the
young woman from her employer, and usually gave some fine cloth and
jewels to the young woman as well. But this arrangement was a quite
different transaction from the exchange of gifts between families that
marked a legal betrothal. The concubine entered her master's house without ceremony; she was not presented to his ancestors, nor did she partici-

42. On mourning obligations and how they were affected by marriage, see
Ebrey 1993: 50. If a woman was mistreated by her in-laws, her father or brothers
would usually be the people to take the case to court.

43. A wife who had nursed her husband's parents through sickness or gone
through mourning for them, or one who had no home to return to, could not
legally be divorced.

44. Li Yu was twice presented with concubines by wealthy friends or patrons.
See Ebrey 1993: 219 on acquiring a concubine in Song times; Ko 1994: 252 on
concubines in the Ming and Qing; R. Watson 1991 on concubinage during the last
century. By the late Ming the Jiangnan city of Yangzhou was famous for having
the most numerous, elegant and accomplished prostitutes. The Yangzhou merchants bought pretty young girls all over China and trained them to dress well,
practice calligraphy, play music and write verse. This was where anyone who could
afford it went to look for a concubine (Ko 1994: 261). The economic and political
uncertainties of the later imperial period sometimes reduced even educated families to selling their daughters. Ko cites the case of Huang Yuanjie (c. 1620–c. 1669),
born into a poor branch of a scholarly Jiangnan family, who distinguished herself
early as a poet, painter and calligrapher—indeed she helped support her parents
and brothers with her earnings. The family was so poor that her sister had to
become a concubine. Huang herself was solicited as a concubine by a high official
but she managed to hold out and eventually made a respectable if unsatisfactory
marriage to a failed scholar. She became a famous teacher in Jiangnan and in the
capital (Ko 1994: 118).

pate in the ancestral rituals. She was accommodated in separate quarters at the side or to the rear of the compound, and she was expected to obey the legal wife in all matters. Once the initial transaction of exchange had been concluded, the concubine's family no longer existed as far as her master was concerned, and he had the right to rename her as he wished. She assumed minor obligations of mourning for her master's kin only if she bore him a son. Her master and mistress did not mourn her even if she had given birth to sons.[45]

Maids were usually purchased for an outright sum, from their family, an employer, or a house of entertainment or brothel. How the contract was construed varied enormously, but the purchase price was often like an indenture, entitling the purchaser to a certain period of service after which time he was supposed to find a husband for the maid. At the bottom of the scale were scullery maids, at the top body servants who provided personal care either to a woman or to a man. There were no legal restrictions on how many maids a family could keep, and although it was considered better for a gentleman to avoid sleeping with the maids—indeed the quasi-paternal obligation to arrange their marriage meant that such intercourse smacked of incest—it was not illegal, and men often did.

A man's children by his concubines were legally his; they made offerings to him after his death, and a man's sons by a concubine shared the inheritance with his wife's sons. If a man fathered any children on his maids, the legal choice of recognition was up to him. If a maid gave birth to a boy and her master decided to recognize him, she would be raised to the status of concubine. But all the children recognized by the husband also became the legal children of his wife. For a concubine, giving birth to a son was no guarantee of social motherhood. On the contrary: her biological motherhood imparted neither the ritual nor the legal status of mother, and one wonders how many concubines watched their mistress steal their son's affections with the equanimity and approval shown by the fictional Bingmei. Giving birth to a son gave a concubine a more secure position within the family. She could no longer be sent away or sold, because she was now a (very lowly) member of the kin-group, tied to them by mourning obligations. She did now have someone to make offerings for her after her death.[46] But however many sons she gave birth to, she could never make the transition to a proper wife. The legal code most strictly forbade

45. See, e.g., Ebrey 1993: 228, 230.
46. Concubines who did not have a son might adopt one, but the child did not become a member of her master's lineage.

making a concubine a wife, or a wife a concubine. Concubines like maids were considered menials, persons of a different class from legal wives, notes Rubie Watson.[47]

Although concubines' sons did also make offerings to their deceased birth mothers, their *real* mother in this sense was their father's wife, their "formal mother." While both women were living, the son's behavior toward each of them had to be ranked in consequence. Once he was beyond the toddling stage, he would spend a lot of time in his formal mother's company. Family instructions of late imperial times stressed that it was important for a wife to take the education of concubine's sons in hand herself, lest their birth mother's lowly origins taint their characters.[48] The emotional strength of these formal bonds should not be underestimated. "The woman who made a vehement loyalist of Gu Yanwu (1613–82), the woman after whom Wang Huizu (1730–1807) wanted to name his collected writings, and the woman who pressed Liang Qi (1859–1918) to reward her with his success [were all] their 'formal mothers.'"[49]

Medical theories of heredity and conventions of family morality both supported the institution of polygyny and argued that a wife had natural reasons to treat all her husband's children with equal affection. In reality, many women strongly favored the children to whom they had given birth. A wife with sons of her own often bitterly resented any children born to her rivals and had no interest at all in educating them or propelling their careers, though this neglect was strongly condemned by moralists. Many children did retain strong affections for their birth mother despite all the pressures to the contrary. However, there was no socially sanctioned way to express such feelings. The late nineteenth-century governor general of Fujian, Xu Yingkui, was the son of a concubine. When his mother died he requested that her coffin be taken out through the main gate of the house, as if she were a legal wife. All his relatives thought this both unorthodox and unreasonable; his father's principal wife pointed out that Xu's own eminence did not affect his biological mother's status: "You were an embryonic dragon, nurtured temporarily in a dog's belly."[50]

---

47. R. Watson 1991: 250; see also Ebrey 1993: 230; Waltner 1990: 22. Watson argues that the distinction between free and servile status was not so clearly defined legally in the case of women as it was for men, because since even free women were not full members of patrilines the distinctions were less urgent. To this we need to add that a woman's status was more fluid than a man's: it could be inflected, if not transformed, by her connection to a man and by bearing him children.

48. Waltner 1990: 30.

49. Hsiung 1994: 88.

50. T'ien 1988: 9.

I would not go so far in my revisionist interpretation of polygyny as to suggest that wives welcomed it unequivocally or felt completely mistress of the situation. As far as a wife was concerned, concubines and maids represented a triple threat. First, they competed for her husband's attentions in general and his sexual favors in particular. Second, they could disrupt her control over the inner quarters: a favored concubine might fail to treat her with due respect, or persuade her husband to squander family resources. Finally, they presented a threat to her biological children, for when the family property was divided her own sons would have to share with the concubines'.

The jealousy of wives was a favorite subject with male writers through the late imperial period, starting in the Song, when concubinage first spread beyond the aristocracy as the number of men who could afford to take a concubine increased dramatically. Since a wife stood in relation to her husband's concubines as mistress to servant, jealousy was often expressed violently. "Biographies of [Song] wives regularly state that the woman was even-tempered and patient and rarely if ever beat the concubines or maids—suggesting that such forbearance was rare." There are numerous cases or stories of wives beating concubines or maids to death, especially if they were pregnant, or selling them before they gave birth, sending their infants away or killing them.[51] As Ebrey points out, strict gender segregation had the effect of rendering husbands powerless to protect the junior women they were fond of. A Ming medical case records an attempt to poison a pregnant maid: "Dr. Lü was called in [to treat a sick maid]. He said she had a case of poisoning which had agitated the Blood and reached her fetus, killing but not expelling it. . . . [After the physician had successfully treated her and expelled the fetus] the master of the house took him aside to say: 'So my sick concubine really was pregnant. My wife was jealous and so she gave her drugs to abort, but none of the other doctors realized this.' "[52]

A true gentleman remained monogamous unless his wife was barren—yet concubines were a mark of status. Whether for reasons of concupiscence or social ambition, many educated men failed to follow the injunction to sexual moderation and indulged in women just like the parvenus they affected to despise.[53] In cases like these polygyny was a guilty pleasure, not

51. Ebrey 1993: 167, 230.
52. *Yilue liushu* 1864.
53. The late Ming novel *Jinpingmei* is the classic tongue-in-cheek example of a kind of voyeurism whereby we are regaled with all the indulgences, misdemeanors and faux pas of a rich and pretentious wastrel, supposedly so we can draw the

a filial duty, and to compensate men stigmatized and mocked jealous wives mercilessly. No doubt the naked display of female passion made them feel uncomfortable and helpless, partly because it was their own deplorable lack of emotional and sexual moderation that gave rise to such rivalry between women in the first place, and partly because their attempts to control the consequences often failed. Dorothy Ko draws our attention to the enormous sympathy that late imperial male literati showed for Xiaoqing, a talented poetess taken as concubine by the feckless son of a high official. She was banished by his jealous wife to an island on West Lake where she lived neglected, visited only by one faithful woman friend, and devoting her short and tragic life to writing poems on the theme of *The Peony Pavilion*. Men found Xiaoqing an infinitely touching and noble figure. The women writers whom Ko has studied showed little sympathy for Xiaoqing and her sufferings, preferring instead to devote their eloquence to the life and character of the heroine of *The Peony Pavilion*, Du Liniang, also a talented woman, but a wife, not a concubine. Since the elite women Ko studied were wives or marriageable daughters, it is not surprising that they had little sympathy to waste on a concubine.[54]

Polygyny and adoption in China have usually been interpreted from a male perspective as ways of ensuring heirs for the lineage and for its individual male members, and they were highly effective practices at this level. A patriline could employ these techniques to enhance its overall prestige—for instance, a large lineage might organize adoptions to ensure that no male member was left without a real or assigned heir. But these practices also served to underline social difference. Female infanticide together with polygyny ensured that there were not enough women for all men to get married; by moving women and children up the social scale, polygyny and adoption further enhanced the prestige of elite families.[55] What has been less remarked is that they also moved children up the female hierarchy, enhancing the prestige of legal wives.

Evidence is now beginning to emerge that some wives in late imperial China played an active role in securing heirs for their husbands and for

---

correct moral conclusion that lust is not only vulgar but ultimately fatal. Li Yu's *Carnal Prayer Mat* takes a sardonic step further, casting an erudite scholar familiar with all the subtleties of Confucian morality as his lustful villain.

54. On jealousy as a male literary trope in the Ming and Qing, see Ko 1994: 106; on the male cult of Xiaoqing, see ibid.: 92–110.

55. Harrell demonstrates how differentiation between lineage branches could progress historically, as "members of wealthier branches married earlier, married younger women, and married or brought in more fertile women" (1985: 108).

themselves. A wife who had not borne any sons might urge her husband to take a concubine, or go so far as to choose one for him herself.[56] Such occurrences were much praised by men as examples of true wifely virtue, and it appears to us that these women were simply acquiescing in their own oppression. Yet we should not neglect the fact that such actions also offered to a childless woman the promise of a child who was formally hers. For a wife without sons of her own, adoption and polygyny were both preferable to divorce or childlessness. Adoption clearly benefited childless wives as well as husbands,[57] but concubinage too could benefit a wife who had been unable to bear a son of her own.

Such transactions not only occurred if a woman had no son, but also served other levels of personal fulfillment or family advantage. A woman might adopt the daughter of a dear friend as a way of keeping close, just as the two might exchange children in betrothal.[58] Since concubinage was only considered legitimate by moralists as a means of acquiring an heir, the examples they give of good wives urging their husband to take a concubine all concern childless women. But a wife might already have one or two children and not want to give birth to more, perhaps because childbirth was difficult for her, or because she fell ill in pregnancy, or because she wanted to devote her full energies to running the household. Or she might wish to avoid sex, whether for religious reasons or simply because she found it distasteful.[59] Under such circumstances she might well have

56. Ebrey gives some examples from the Song literature, including the case of Sima Guang: because he had no sons, his wife and her sister acquired a concubine for him, but failed to persuade him to take any interest in her (1993: 220).

57. Dennerline cites the case of a lineage in the late Qing where 20 percent of married males died without sons, but all were assigned heirs after death (1986: 202). Dennerline underlines that this practice was also in the interests of the widows and suggests that they may have been active proponents of this strategy. Waltner's investigation of adoptions recorded in the 1590 genealogy of a large Anhui lineage also shows that widows were often active in adoptions (1990: 90–99).

58. Shen Yixiu, the well-known poetess whose fruitful marriage to Ye Shaoyuan I have already referred to, was brought up with her cousin Zhang Qianqian: when Yixiu's mother died, her father's sister came to look after the children and brought her daughter Qianqian with her. Qianqian married Yixiu's brother. Four of her children died in infancy and she longed for a daughter, so she adopted Yixiu's third daughter when the baby was six months old. The adoption "was primarily a means whereby a pair of best friends commemorated their intimacy" (Ko 1994: 209).

59. This was certainly true of some men. One Song writer records that two of his male relatives could not bear sex. One gave it up completely as soon as he had a son. The other, although he had a wife and a concubine, was sent into fits of uncontrollable vomiting by the smell of women's hair oil; he remained a virgin all

suggested to her husband that a concubine would be a good idea. It would be interesting to search through biographies, occasional writings and medical works for evidence of this kind. Because in our eyes polygyny appears a humiliating and oppressive situation for all the women involved, we have tended to accept the literature on female jealousy as the true image of the polygynous condition and to dismiss the pictures that moralists drew of a team of women working contentedly under a wise mistress. But a wife who saw the core of her role not as a lover, but as a matriarch ruling the inner quarters, may have felt that concubinage helped serve her own purposes as well as those of her husband.

THE WIFELY ROLE

According to the *Book of Rites* and the moral works that quoted it down the centuries, a wife should be "the fitting partner of her husband." The ritual purpose of marriage was to produce heirs for the lineage and to continue the ancestral cult. The more mundane purpose of marriage was to keep the household running in good order, with the husband responsible for outside matters, the wife for the inner domain. I now consider where motherhood fitted into the wifely role and how these different feminine duties contributed to social hierarchies on the one hand, and to gender roles on the other.

Let us break down the wife's responsibilities into two main categories: the reproduction of family members and the management of the household economy. As these were construed in Chinese understanding, the first category included reproducing both the past, by performing the ancestral cult and taking care of parents (fig. 24), and the future, by forming the next generation. The latter task included giving birth to children, rearing and instructing them, and also making outsiders who came into the household into proper family members. The wife trained her daughters as future wives; she trained her sons as heirs to the line, the persons who would represent its honor in the male world. When a son married she trained her daughter-in-law as a new member of the household team, as she did the maids, and also the concubines if her husband took any. The quality of the persons she "produced" was evaluated not only in the seclusion of the inner quarters but also in the outer world; others would be the final judges of how well a woman had trained her sons and daughters.

his life (Ebrey 1993: 164). The literature on Buddhism in late imperial China indicates that women of all classes often insisted on maintaining celibacy once they reached middle age, and that this was generally recognized as their right.

Figure 24.   Caring for the parents (from the series of sericultural illustrations in the *Bianyong xuehai junyu* of 1607, modeled on the *Gengzhi tu;* copy in the Sinological Institute of Leiden, first published by Kuhn [1976: 367]). The younger women of the household present the fancy silks they have woven to the grandfather and grandmother, who will choose what to have made up into warm winter clothes. The mistress, namely the wife of the eldest son, is in charge of tending to the old couple's needs and also organizes the household production of silk yarn and cloth.

What is interesting is that the only purely biological element in all these reproductive tasks, namely the generation of children, could be circumvented by the wife. If she belonged to a wealthy family, adoption or polygyny would allow her to substitute the fertility of lower-status women for her own without forfeiting her status either as wife or as mother. She could also expect concubines, maids and wet nurses to undertake most of the physical care of the infants. But she was in charge of their instruction and education. She was the model of deportment for her daughters, she supervised the binding of their feet and their learning of "womanly work" such as sewing and embroidery (fig. 25), and if she was herself literate (as became increasingly probable in the course of the late

Figure 25.   Young ladies at their embroidery (*Qing Customs* A: 338–39). The illustration on the preceding two pages of *Qing Customs* shows the family tutor supervising the boys as they practice writing Confucian texts.

imperial period) she would teach them to read and write as well. Her sons learned their first lessons in morals and in letters from their mother before they went to school or acquired a private tutor at age seven or eight. These were tasks that required breeding, education and character; as such they were beyond the capacities of maids and of most concubines.

Nor could any of the menial women substitute for the wife in the ancestral cult or the proper running of a family. The wife was her husband's

繡
花
之
圖

social and ritual equal, but none of his other sexual partners was. Wives participated with husbands, and daughters with sons, in the complex liturgy of the ancestral sacrifices; wives like husbands performed the daily greetings and offerings at the domestic altar. Concubines and maids had no role in these performances—they had gone through no formal marriage ceremony and had not been presented to the ancestors. Explaining why a maid who bore a son could be made a concubine but never a wife, the commentary to the Song legal code remarks: "A wife transmits the family affairs and carries on the ancestral sacrifices. . . . How could a maid-servant, even if freed, be qualified to perform the important responsibili-ties of a legal wife?" If a man lost his wife, the moral consensus in late imperial times was that he should remarry, despite the problems that could arise between stepmother and stepchildren. A concubine could not step in to take the wife's place. "If one analyzes the situation according to degrees of importance, [a wife] is essential to care for parents, manage the family, perform sacrifices, and continue [the descent line]. Therefore there is the principle of taking a second wife." [60]

In the management of the household economy too, the role of a wife in an elite family was more moral and intellectual than physical, though in times of difficulty she would be expected to roll up her sleeves and set to work. In a well-off family maids and concubines swept and cleaned, cooked and served, tended the silkworms or sat at the loom. A good wife organized and supervised all these activities, calculating resources against expenditure, keeping the accounts, and making economic choices of all kinds. She would often invest in a business, sell land, or deal with tenants. This may seem an infringement of female segregation, but only if we think of seclusion as intended simply to confine women within a physical boundary rather than to structure the differences between male and fe-male. A wife had many legitimate duties connecting her to the world be-yond her walls, for the feminine role covered all that the masculine role did not.

An educated gentleman was concerned with learning and with the ad-ministration of the public domain. A civil servant was posted away from home, and a scholar living at home concerned himself with his books, not with petty money matters of the kind that merchants or tradesmen dealt in. As his fitting partner, his wife dealt with such matters, leaving him free for the work that marked his class and status. The husband of Miss Li (1104–77) was able to concentrate entirely on his responsibilities in government " 'never having asked about family supplies.' Miss Li took on management of their property as her responsibility, buying fertile fields

---

60. The commentary on the Song code and the rationale for remarriage by Zhang Zai (1020–77) are translated by Ebrey (1993: 47, 213). Wang Huizu, men-tioned earlier as the man who wished to name his collected writings after his *dimu*, was the son of a concubine who served two mistresses: his father was widowed and remarried. Both his stepmother and his birth mother were influential in shaping his views on family, expressed in a set of family instructions dedicated to his children (Mann 1991: 216).

and building a house by a stream. Once a peasant came into the courtyard carrying a sack of rice on his back, to the amazement of Miss Li's husband, who had no idea who he was or what he carried. She just laughed and said, 'That is our rent.' " In the marriage between Ye Shaoyuan and Shen Yixiu, Ye spent long periods away from home in pursuit of a degree. Nevertheless, he found the time to deal with lineage disputes over land that threatened to bankrupt his branch of the family. But he knew nothing of the household finances; Shen Yixiu was in charge of the bursar's chest, and Ye wrote in his diary that "all monetary transactions were handled by my wife."[61]

A wife was expected to be a wise and humane mistress, guiding her charges so that they lived together harmoniously and productively. While her husband represented the family position within the hierarchy of the lineage, she was expected to maintain the correct order of hierarchical distinctions between the heterogeneous group of household women that included high-status family members (daughters and wives of sons) as well as different degrees of menials (concubines and maids). The tensions could be severe: quite apart from any jealousy the wife herself might feel, polygyny meant, for example, that a young gentlewoman might find herself required to serve an illiterate peasant as her mother-in-law. No wonder late Ming and Qing writers insisted that the roots of good government were planted in the inner quarters. The analogy between state and household was apt, for in effect the mistress was expected to rule peacefully over an explosive microcosm of male class society.[62]

Distinctions among men—between menial and free status, among scholar, merchant and peasant, rich and poor—became increasingly blurred and impermanent as the economy commercialized. Ever greater numbers of families aspired to gentle status, educating their sons and entering them for the examinations, investing in land and establishing lineage organizations, collecting objets d'art and accumulating women. The ideal male of

61. Ebrey 1993: 118; Ko 1994: 191. Ebrey gives several examples of how Song wives might build up family property or business, and McDermott 1990 gives examples from the Qing.

62. Not surprisingly, discord and violence were common, especially across class boundaries. "Wives took out their frustrations, their boredom, and their jealousies on their servants because propriety forbade striking relatives or even children. In fact, physical abuse of servants was so common among women of the upper classes [in the mid-Qing] that one text . . . supplies detailed descriptions of types of abuse as a warning to readers. Servants, by their conduct and appearance, offered a living testimony to the faults of an abusive mistress: 'One may enter her home, observe her servants, and know whether she is a good wife or not' " (Mann 1991: 220).

the elite possessed qualities that could not be purchased. He was a person of erudition and firm moral purpose, distinguished by his refinement and self-control.[63] The marks of the gentleman were achieved through *wen* (education and the acquisition of culture)—and yet although this may seem a rarefied and disembodied ideal compared to that of, say, the European warrior-nobleman, it would be a mistake to think of *wen* as an adornment or a mental attribute hung on the neutral frame of a somehow irrelevant body. Bodily practices—how to stand, and how to feel while standing thus, when to move and in relation to whom—were fundamental to the acquisition both of ritual competence and of ritual understanding, and the same was true of morality, of learning, and of every other mark of the gentleman in late imperial China.

Beneath his skin, his vital organic constitution also played a role in defining the gentleman. The patrilineal organization of Chinese society compelled all gentlemen to be concerned with their fertility, for it was their filial duty to have children. The medical literature defined the fertile man as one who had learned to limit his desires and passions, and the fertile couple as partners: conception depended on both achieving orgasm simultaneously, and throughout pregnancy the husband was advised to care solicitously for his partner's health. The stress on sexual moderation and on the active cooperation of the couple in producing a healthy child might lead one to expect that the ideal elite union was monogamous. The corresponding female ideal, however, was interestingly split. Its dual image of motherhood provided an implicit rationale for polygynous marriage, a medical justification for reinforcing social distinctions by shifting women as well as children up the social scale.

If we piece together the ideal of the elite woman as expressed in medical literature, marriage laws and other forms of inscription, we see that she too was distinguished primarily by her *wen*, cultivated qualities that made her a fitting partner of her husband. Because of their need for heirs, men were deeply concerned with female fertility, too, and with maternal qualities. Yet for an elite wife, giving birth was the least important part of motherhood: the heart of the emotional bond between mother and son was the process of upbringing. For this role her intellectual and moral

63. Restricted opportunities for state service and political upheavals made it difficult for many men to fulfill this role completely in late imperial times. T'ien (1988), Mann (1991) and Carlitz (1994) have all suggested that this led men to project their ideals of honor onto women, for example transmuting the political loyalty that they were unable to express into the idealization of widow chastity.

qualities were all-important, but again these qualities were acquired through the exercise of body as well as mind; they were not superficial accomplishments, but qualities that became physically rooted deep inside her body. Her self-control and tranquility not only allowed her to deal successfully with domestic problems, but also reached down into her internal organs and enhanced her fertility. An elite woman's role as wife in a polygynous household encompassed and expanded her role as mother. She was not at the mercy of her own fertility, for she disposed of a range of techniques that permitted her to manipulate her maternal role. And yet she was obsessed with the workings of her womb, constantly preoccupied with the regularity of her menses, which signaled her capacity to fulfill all aspects of her maternal and wifely role.

The ideal of elite womanhood stands in contrast to the elite image of the lower-class woman, constitutionally fertile and unconscious of any need to control her emotions. One of the signs of elite women's inferiority to men was their relative lack of emotional control—a control that was tried to the utmost, moreover, by the demands of polygyny. Lack of self-control was a mark of inferior class as well as gender, but in the lower classes it was allied not to the elegant neurasthenia of gentlewomen, but to a robust physique and solid nerves. Peasant children grew up strong and healthy; direct exposure to sun, wind, and the *qi* of the soil strengthened their muscles and protected them from the nervous ailments to which well-born children were prey. But it was the duty of gentle parents to put their children's moral education (and the bodily delicacy that this implied) before sturdiness.[64] Peasants were enviably fecund because of the strength of their desires, and their desires were strong in part because they were illiterate and uncultivated. This was the medical image of the young women who were brought into polygynous households as concubines and maids: their fecund constitutions fitted them to give birth, but not to act as social mothers or wives. For such women their natural fertility was indeed a matter of enormous concern, for their position within the household depended on their ability to conceive.

Since the rich took for themselves so many women from poor families, one might argue that poor men had relatively little chance to indulge their strong, earthy desires. In the present state of knowledge it is hard to tell how the incidence of concubinage in rich families, or of male celibacy among the poor, might have varied historically. Ebrey speaks of the Song as a time when concubinage first become commonplace in literati as well

64. Leung 1984: 66–68, citing Wan Quan and Xu Chunfu.

as aristocratic families.[65] Ko says that in seventeenth-century Jiangnan it was rampant in scholar-official and merchant families. In the first half of the twentieth century taking a concubine was accepted in the Canton Delta, where even poor peasants might do so, although generally it was a mark of wealth or local status; but in rural North China taking a concubine was considered unacceptable even if the principal wife was barren.[66] I suspect that concubinage was slightly less common than the writings of the late imperial period might imply, if only because there were so few girls to go round. But polygyny was a status symbol that could be purchased (unlike educational polish or distinguished ancestors). This presumably made it popular among upwardly mobile families, and at the same time it must have increased the ambivalence and unease with which established literati men regarded it, not least because they knew that if their fortunes changed, their own daughters might end up as concubines.

Meanwhile many poor men were never able to marry at all, and those who did could seldom afford maids or concubines. A poor man's wife had no alternative to her own fertility. If she bore no sons, her life was likely to be ruined, however well she performed the other wifely roles. Social identity was unstable in the increasingly competitive world of late imperial China. "The more commoditized the economy, the more active the market, the easier it was to lose or gain land, animals, and other means of production. Its labor power was a poor family's last resort, its only hope of retaining or gaining property, and the production of that labor—for use or for sale—was a woman's job." [67] Since the productive role of wives was largely masked in the course of the late imperial period, their success in their role as mothers became increasingly the criterion by which they

65. She suggests that wives in good families may have started routinely binding their daughters' feet in the Song precisely because of the threat that concubinage posed to legitimate wives. The practice is first noted for the Tang; it seems that only dancers and courtesans bound their feet at first, but the practice started to spread among gentlefolk in Song times and had become common among all classes by the Ming. It was considered that foot binding increased fertility by redirecting *qi* and Blood from the lower extremities into the loins. Chinese men found the tiny golden-lotus feet irresistibly erotic, and as Ebrey and others have remarked, the concealed promise of bound feet hidden beneath the petticoats was a delicate and private erotic attraction that was not unbecoming in a refined lady (Ebrey 1993: 37–43; see also Blake 1994 and Ko 1994: 147–51).
66. R. Watson 1991: 237; see Ebrey 1993: 217–34 on the Song, and Ko 1994: 106–20 on Ming-Qing Jiangnan.
67. Gates 1989: 817.

were judged. In a poor family with no aspirations to education, material concerns loomed far larger in the understanding of motherhood than in elite families. A scholar might attribute his early understanding of Mencius and his success in the examinations to his mother's instruction and encouragement. But although a skilled farmer or an expert lacquer carver might love his mother dearly and honor her for giving him a decent upbringing, she was not the person who had taught him the rudiments of his craft. At this level of society men's work and women's work were distinct rather than continuous, and a woman's fertility did play the central role in determining her success or failure.

In this section I have discussed a set of reproductive technologies that allowed women in late imperial China to control or negotiate their own fertility. Reproductive medicine was a specialism that expanded enormously during the late imperial period, both in the number of practitioners and publications and in the social range of clientele and readership. Physicians instructed men and women in medical techniques to enhance fertility; they also provided socially acceptable solutions to unwanted or suspected pregnancy. The theories of natural fecundity and of menstrual regulation which form the core of late imperial gynecology are particularly interesting because their dual image of motherhood implicitly justifies the appropriation of children of low-ranking women through polygyny. The reproductive techniques I have described did not benefit all women or all families. They enabled women at the top to stay at the top, but they did not help women move up the social scale. They permitted rich families to exploit poor families, and high-status women to exploit their inferiors within the polygynous household. In a world where children were status symbols, these techniques reproduced social inequalities in macrocosm and in microcosm.

It is clear that the role of "mother" in late imperial China was not unique and indivisible. The marked emphasis on the maternal phase in images of late imperial femininity was a natural response in a world where the patriline was increasingly represented as the fundamental social and moral building block. However, motherhood was an identity that individual women experienced in quite different ways, depending on their social status as well as their natural fertility. A woman's social status also affected her experience as daughter, and as wife or menial, as well as her access to the roles of mother-in-law or grandmother, and although here I have only addressed the question of how motherhood was modulated by wifehood, to understand maternal identity in late imperial China fully we need to take into account that it was experienced as one crucial phase in a whole life cycle.[68]

I have also explored how motherhood, female fertility and feminine ideals were constructed in relation to paternity, male fertility and male ideals, as formulated by the male elite. First we should note that late imperial gender theories placed elite men at the topmost of the social pyramid, but elite women were placed above both the men and the women of the lower orders. The control of emotion and desire that was the criterion in this scale depended on moral and intellectual education. The mental, moral and physical processes of upbringing and education rendered elite men and women cultivated, *wen*. These acquired characteristics became part of nature, so education could naturalize the bond of kinship formed with children born lower down the social scale whom the elite might wish to integrate into their families. Although elite men restricted access to the ultimate refinements of *wen* to themselves, they recognized that their wives must also be educated so that they could play their roles properly, as participants in the ancestral cult, as household managers, and as the social mothers of their sons. Elite women played a more important part than anyone else in imparting the fundamentals of *wen* to their sons, and the sons were duly grateful. Elite women were not passive objects of the patrilineal drive for sons: late imperial reproductive ideals and reproductive technologies gave them an honorable role as "good wives and wise mothers" (a role in which biological fertility played a rather minor part) and a stake in the system of class and gender hierarchies that was quite different from that of the menial women in their own households, or of the wives of poor men.

68. Hsiung Ping-chen shows that the women themselves played a central role in creating the "suffering and sacrificing mother" stories that men in the Ming and Qing loved to include in their accounts of their lives and that tied sons to their mothers in relations of perpetual obligation and grateful affection. "In this historical literature, glimpses of a cheerful and innocent girlhood, or of an accomplished, comfortable and powerful older-motherhood, grandmotherhood, or mother-in-lawhood had to be deliberately expunged, due to their counter-effects on the portrait intended [of a hard-working and suffering provider]" (Hsiung 1994: 106). It is in women's writings about their own largely homosocial lives that we find descriptions of pleasure, confidence and fun experienced by groups consisting of daughters and grandmothers, wives and daughters-in-law (Widmer 1989; M. Robertson 1992; Ko 1994).

Conclusion
Gynotechnics and Civilization

Two arguments are at the core of this book. The first is that technology is a form of cultural expression, and as such plays a key role in the creation and transmission of ideology. The second is that the technologies that define women's place and roles are not marginal but integral to these historical processes.

From this perspective it is not helpful to think of technology as a distinct material and intellectual domain with its own transcultural dynamics, an autonomous transformative force that "culture" or social institutions may either impede or encourage. Instead I have followed Elias, Mumford, and of course Marx in presuming that technology *is* culture, that its work is as much the making of subjects and the production of meaning as the making of objects and the mastery of nature.

Like any other cultural expression, technology both divides and unites; the forms it takes seldom hold the same meaning for all, and struggles over the forms and meanings of technology are as significant for cultural as for economic history. Since a technology embeds material techniques in social practices, how it is represented and argued about reveals meanings of the maker's identity as well as of the objects made. Technologies give material form to dimensions of difference: men plow, women weave; men work outside, women inside; those who work with their minds govern, those who work with their hands are governed; farming is the fundamental occupation, crafts lure people to waste. Changes in technology create social tension, requiring a reconfiguration or renegotiation of these complex, interlocking patterns of difference. At the same time technology is a powerful force for cultural stability, since it creates material forms that embody shared values and beliefs, tying people into orthodoxy through their everyday practices.

369

Technology is not interesting or successful only when it produces social or epistemological ruptures; though the energy generated by changes in technology is by nature disruptive, it may be successfully contained and channeled. No less energy goes into continuity and cohesion than into revolution, and no less careful explanation is required.

The educated elite who by the Song had displaced the hereditary aristocracy as the governing class of China developed a new form of civility that endured for several centuries. The population growth, economic transformation, wars and invasions that one might have expected to shear late imperial China apart failed to do so. Despite the recurring fears of many Chinese that their civilization was threatened, it proved strong and flexible enough to absorb the energies released, although in the process many important relationships were significantly reconfigured—including the ties between state and subject, as well as significant aspects of gender roles. Technologies played both a disruptive and a cohesive role in these processes: relations of production, for example, were transformed, but the dissemination of such vehicles of integration as orthodox living space helped contain the tensions generated by changes in the nature of work. The success of neo-Confucianism in drawing an increasingly broad group of Chinese subjects, women as well as men, into sharing the values and practices of its particular brand of civility depended in large part on its capacity to translate its moral and social principles into material form and bodily practices. Such embodied forms of knowledge are by their nature polysemic and flexible, and may therefore be even more powerful than words or texts.

To readers acquainted only with stereotypical images of "traditional" Chinese women as dependent victims of patriarchy cut off from the significant male stage, it may seem paradoxical to claim that "female technologies" could illuminate the complex processes by which Chinese society met the challenges of the late imperial period. This, however, is to misunderstand the nature of Chinese domesticity and how inner and outer worlds related in Chinese thought. Gender was a fundamental organizing principle in the social structure of late imperial China, as of any other society. The core social bond was that between husband and wife, ideally represented as an active partnership in which the wife, through her work in the inner quarters, contributed material, social and moral goods to the world outside as well as to her family. Taking material activities and experiences as my point of departure, I have analyzed a set of technologies that defined women's place and roles—a *gynotechnics* that includes technologies of space, of work and of reproduction—to show not only how the real nature and extent of wifely contributions shifted in the course of the late imperial period, but also how perceptions and representations of the wifely role changed. These changes served to reformulate gender and status relations within particular social groups as well as to mark or mediate new forms of distinction among groups.

Chinese social theory did not distinguish between private and public spheres, but held explicitly that the household was at one end of a political and moral continuum, at the other end of which was the state. Women were thus closely tied into the polity, by the goods they contributed and by their own behavior: the roots of a well-ordered state were planted in the inner chambers. It is therefore easy to see why the set of three technologies examined here not only defined women's lives, but also were bases for a distinctively Chinese civility.

Civilization and civility are concepts that both correspond to the Chinese term *wen*, which also signifies cultivation, refinement, literary competence and written texts. The term *wen* has figured prominently in every section of this book: in part 1 in connection with the man's study as an attainable symbol of elite male status, and with women's increasing encroachments into the literate domain; in part 2 in connection with the refinement of womanly work, and the parallels between male literary accomplishment and female skills in embroidery; and in part 3 in connection with the physical constitution and moral endowments of ideal parents of both sexes, as compared to the rude health and manners of the naturally fertile peasant. As I discussed in chapter 9, late imperial China was a society which held that upbringing overrode birth in determining to which social group a person belonged. Just as an individual could improve himself and achieve *wen* characteristics of moral and intellectual refinement through study and self-cultivation, *xiu*, so outsiders could acquire the necessary cultural qualities to become insiders through education, *jiao*.

Self-cultivation and education did not just mean learning or teaching from books; both were more akin to the concept of apprenticeship, representing a process in which mental, physical and moral instruction were inextricably entwined and a new identity was achieved. One dominant Chinese view of human nature held that through *jiao* barbarians could be assimilated and become Chinese, brides from another village could become loyal members of their husband's lineage, adopted infants could become true sons, and peasant boys could acquire the knowledge and the social poise to serve as a successful minister of state. There were other strands of neo-Confucian orthodoxy that accorded greater importance to birth in determining nature, or held that irreducible biological differences between the sexes determined moral worth. But as we might expect of a regime where the elite rooted its claims to authority in learning rather than birth, the "hegemonic" forms of neo-Confucian ideology in late imperial China were notable for their meritocratic trust in education, *jiao*.

The openness of this social philosophy was an important key to the success both of the state and of gentry elites in coopting widespread support. By our Western progress-oriented criteria we might say that in the very success of the Chinese civilizing processes lay their failure. The attractions of *wen* gentility were as great as its material trappings were accessible, so for example merchants did not seek to establish themselves as an independent political interest group but instead built studies for themselves, constructed lavish inner quarters for their wives and daughters, and hired tutors to give their sons a classical education. The social flexibility of the inclusion strategies developed by the new Song meritocratic elite was so encompassing that for the most part all classes of society gladly embraced them: even a poor man now had ancestors, his wife shared the same spatial practices of female dignity as the wife of the local landlord, and in theory even a plowman's child, if he studied hard, could become a minister of state. The internalization of values was so powerful that emperors felt confident they could propagate their policies by instruction rather than coercion, while the empire was able to run (not always efficiently, it is true) with a civil service whose size steadily dwindled in proportion to the population.

Chinese civility, *wen*, and its processes of acquisition were thoroughly rooted in material objects and bodily experience, so that our Western category of "technology" is an important perspective for apprehending them. In the introduction I pointed out that the Chinese have left a particularly rich legacy not only of artifacts, but also of written and illustrated materials on technical matters. This reflects classical views of the importance of proper forms of work, and the closely connected belief that there is an intimate relation between morality and physical habit. I have stressed the interdependence of written and material "texts," demonstrating a variety of ways in which hegemonic ideas translated into material expressions such as spatial forms and practices, work patterns, or understandings of the menstrual cycle. I have also demonstrated the importance of analyzing *sets* of technologies and the interplay between them, just as one would with other forms of discourse, since the messages they convey may diverge, reinforce, qualify or even contradict each other, creating space for the flexibilities of "practice." In other words, I have used the concept of gynotechnics as a way of organizing materials from more varied sources into new patterns, providing a new perspective on gender and its place in the social order as well as a way of getting beyond what written texts alone can tell us.

Approaching ideology through its material forms adds appreciably to our understanding of historical shifts in gender and social difference. The changes that occurred in the three technologies discussed here were complex and in many cases mutually or even internally contradictory—they do not tell a clear *linear* story about how women's status changed in late imperial China, which is as we would expect. The differing views of gender that have emerged in the course of this study of gynotechnics point to divergences between social groups and to interplay between different strands of orthodoxy within groups. I have described how the various strands of Chinese orthodoxy interwove like the threads of a patterned cloth—here one color predominated, there another.

One strand of neo-Confucian orthodoxy can be considered "hegemonic," since it represented the beliefs underlying the meritocratic system of access to power, as well as many state policies for educating the masses. This school of thought stressed that status and merit depended on a range of diffuse manifestations of respectability or refinement, *wen*, theoretically available to all through learning, self-cultivation, and proper behavior. These activities and attributes were not confined to men— women were also defined by degrees of *wen*. Indeed not only could they attain such virtues for themselves but by doing so they could also confer respectability on their families, even if they were poor and humble. Material practices could play an important part in this kind of achievement, for example, women could obtain respect in the community by carefully observing all the principles of seclusion.

This "hegemonic" ideology represented the relationship between husband and wife as a moral and material partnership, harking back to the classical gender images of the *Liji*. As I have argued in relation to "womanly work" as well as to the hegemonic representations of ritual responsibility and of parental qualifications, this strand of orthodoxy shows *wen* women as actively contributing to the state from within the seclusion of their quarters, and as partners whose duties are not supplementary but complementary to their husbands'. In the course of the late imperial period, as the *nature* of women's participation in productive work changed, so the *location* of wifely duties shifted, deemphasizing the productive role symbolized by the weaving of cloth and highlighting the complex range of reproductive tasks that fell to the duties of a wife.

Although this strand of orthodoxy asserted that moral refinement was available to all, in fact it justified social institutions and practices that reinforced social hierarchies of refinement, *wen*, not by separating classes, but by building them into organic structures of complementarity. To take the example of raising children: a child is the product of biological processes that produce a material object, a baby, and of cultural processes that turn it into a social person, a son or a daughter. It is possible to be a mother without giving birth, and to give birth without being a mother. In late imperial China the social practices of polygyny and adoption allowed high-status families to appropriate the fertility of families lower down the social scale. Meanwhile, medical theories of reproduction and theories about character formation that related to adoption justified such forms of exploitation in terms of a fruitful collaboration between the morally and physically refined gentlewoman and the strong and fertile but morally undeveloped peasant girl.

Wen characteristics could be acquired, but only within certain limits; the joint production of children did not blur the boundaries between classes but reinforced the social distinctions. Families lower in the social scale were coopted not by the promise of real social advancement for their daughters or for themselves, since a concubine, however much polish she might acquire in her new home, could never become a legal wife as she would if she married within her own class, nor did her natal family gain affinal status. The social advancement would be for the concubine's children. They would belong to a superior class thanks to the endowment of *qi* from their father, and thanks to the inculcation with *wen* that they received first from the care of the wife, their social mother, and later from formal education. But this offered no benefit to the concubine's family, since these grandchildren did not belong to that lineage, and little benefit even to the woman herself, since her claims to these children were tenuous. The rewards this exchange offered to the concubine's parents were immediate and material: they were relieved of the burden of providing for their daughter and finding her a dowry, and they also received a cash reward when they handed her over.

In an earlier epoch and a different material domain, we can see parallels in the case of a manorial family hiring local peasant girls to work at its looms. The girls brought some income to their family and improved their skills under the guidance of the mistress. Her cultural superiority gave her the authority to work with her mind rather than with her hands, organizing the labors of her junior women. Elite refinement and peasant strength were brought together in this case to produce fine cloth and virtuous weavers. From this ideological perspective the inner quarters were a well-ordered, harmonious realm of a specifically female *wen*, in which fine cloths or embroideries, like healthy and well-taught children, were material symbols of the fruitful collaboration between women of different ranks and attributes that provided essential goods to the outside world.

In this strand of orthodoxy, where status was marked by *wen* character-istics of intellectual and moral cultivation, differences between rank and class were in many respects more salient than those between sex. Male and female ideals of the superior person shared physical, intellectual and moral characteristics that enabled them to act as partners in their separate spheres; the striking contrast was not between male and female, but be-tween cultivated and uncultivated. I have suggested that this philogynistic philosophy, according to which a wife was far more than a childbearer, represented one strand of neo-Confucian belief and practice that was espe-cially prevalent at the level of statesmanship, and also among certain elite and aspirant families. The growing market in the late Ming and early Qing for women's primers and for tutors for girls, the proud delight with which the merchants of the *Qing Customs* described the refinement of their wives and the accomplishments of their daughters, suggest that for not a few socially aspiring families educating their women and treating them respectfully was a claim to gentility that paralleled giving sons a classical education.

Wen refinement was by nature complex and diffuse, and its social ide-ologies *were* ideals, at best an intermittent or partial experience of real life. Even in families that acknowledged women's potential for virtue, there was frequently occasion for more misogynistic values to operate. The late imperial period saw the steady spread of patrilineal practices and values to all social classes. I have described how even commoners' houses came to embody a space of neo-Confucian decorum, with its strong sense of hierarchy and order reflected in the very heights of the roofs. The se-clusion of women, and the spatial reflection of female hierarchies in the allocation of sleeping quarters, did not in itself imply any moral inferior-ity. This sense was supplied, however, by the beliefs of another strand of neo-Confucian morality, a strongly patriarchal form which held that disorder, profligacy and vice threatened on every side, so that the patriarch must exercise constant control and vigilance to ward off disaster.

This school saw women as moral inferiors and social dependents, a view that was accentuated, I have argued, by the veiling of the value of their work at textiles and other productive activities. Because this strand of so-cial thought paid little heed to the notion of partnership between husband and wife, the ability to bear sons, among the many possible reproductive contributions, became most prominent in the definition of the wifely role. Furthermore, belief in the moral weakness of women implied that while strict seclusion was necessary to protect the family honor, by the same token the inner quarters housed a moral threat. Brides were represented as disloyal outsiders, a view that projected onto women the real threat to family solidarity, namely the rivalries between brothers, and between father and sons, that inevitably arose under a system of patriarchy and partible inheritance. In this strand of neo-Confucianism, the internal female hierarchies of a polygynous household were represented not as a harmonious ordered contribution to overall family gain but as a destructive force. After the reorganization of formerly all-female tasks like weaving, where women could clearly be seen to collaborate for the benefit of the family, it became even easier to represent the inner quarters as a battlefield riven by jealousy and rivalries over children, threatening to engulf the whole family in destruction. This is a slightly caricatured version of what was undoubtedly an important strand of thought in shaping views of gender, one that was probably shared by greater numbers of families than the more generous and egalitarian views of neo-Confucian orthodoxy, though again, seldom in completely undiluted form.

Among elite or aspiring families male and female superiority was associated with the often intangible qualities associated with *wen*—refinement, self-control, moral purity, a thorough knowledge of proper behavior. This was contrasted with the unrefined morals and behavior of the lower orders. And in reality as well as in representation, among poor people the late imperial trend toward commercialization and competition tended to highlight the importance of visible, *material* factors like work or boy babies, not only in deciding a particular woman's status but also in defining the more general meanings attributed to gender. In the case of poor commoner households with few members or resources, by the late Ming women no longer produced half the family's tax goods, while the prevailing commercial competition meant that in such families material contributions to competitive survival loomed large. Here the changes in textile production that I have documented contributed to isolating the inner quarters from the world outside, emphasizing female separation and dependence. Discounting women's work was not, however, a universal feature of a late imperial "culture of poverty," for where wives were still recognized as making significant contributions to the family income they might be described as the family's "chief ministers."

More generally, however, women's contributions to the family economy became marginalized, and as a consequence the wife's role shifted emphatically toward reproduction. A good wife gave her husband sons: heirs for the lineage, extra hands for the farm or business, and supports in old age. A "son" is both a biological and a social product, but in poor families a mother could make fewer useful contributions to her son's practical education than in gentle families; furthermore, polygyny being an expensive business, the resources available to an elite wife for supplementing her own natural fertility were seldom available to a poor man's wife. In poor families, then, the role of wife was frequently reduced to the role of childbearer; here we see emerging the "traditional" Chinese stereotype of a woman whose worth lay beyond her own control, in her ability to bear sons.

We cannot presume, however, that a single strand of thought determined values among the poor any more than among the rich. There were peasant communities in China that refused to recognize a wife's sterility as reasonable grounds for divorce or concubinage. And the materialist disposition has to be set in the context of the overarching view that women, like men, could attain *wen* and confer status on their families. Social mobility, both upward and downward, was high in the late Ming and Qing, and competition was not confined to the level of economics. Educating sons was beyond the means of most poor families, but women were able to contribute actively to family status at the level of low-cost claims to respectability such as ritual competence, diligence in filial observance and mourning, and the strict upbringing of daughters so they made good daughters-in-law. Careful observance of the separation of the women's quarters, even if they were marked only by a curtain, was an inexpensive sign of respectability that must often have been appreciated by women as well as men—indeed, one form of public recognition of moral refinement, the imperial honors granted to chaste widows, was specifically reserved for women from poor families.

In this study I have used texts to explore the polysemic nature of material activities and experiences. This materialist approach has located and clarified various contradictions between different strands of orthodoxy and between representations and experience. We might ask at this stage whether it has thrown any light on issues of contemporary feminist concern such as resistance or counterculture, particularly since it is clear that even the most benevolent theories of gender in late imperial China were essentially patriarchal. My method, however, is particularly suited to revealing the mechanisms whereby women were integrated into the social order not simply as objects of ideology but as its active producers—it is more illuminating about female versions of dominant culture than about subversion. I have shown some instances of what might be considered female resistance to, or subversion of, male institutions—the marriage laments mentioned in chapter 2, for example, and certain cases of abortion—though I have argued that for some classes of women Chinese theories of health and fertility, and constructions of maternity, provided hegemonic justification for "regulating the menses" or even for an explicit abortion. And I have discussed certain material objects, such as dowry chests, Buddhist altars, and embroideries, that could be taken as symbols of female resistance to patriarchal values. However, even the bride's wish to retain control over her dowry goods, symbolized by her keeping her chests under lock and key in her own room, was only an act of resistance to one level of patriarchy. Rejecting the claims of the patriline that all family wealth should be pooled in the patrimony and controlled by the patriarch, the bride affirmed the hegemonically approved responsibility of the wife to manage the family finances on behalf of her husband and children. In the other cases I have just cited, it seems useful to think of the objects as material signs or instruments of a female culture that was not an alternative or challenge to male culture, but rather a complementary form, without which male-centered culture could not function. For instance, the female networks of kinship marked and sustained by the exchange of embroidered items constituted the weft threads, all but unmentioned in orthodox discourse, that wove the warp lines of male descent into a coherent fabric. My intention has been to emphasize the light that is thrown on such "muted" expressions of culture by focusing on the material world.

In late imperial China the intermeshing of different hierarchies, like the meritocratic ideology of status, gave most women as well as most men some stake in the system, even if it was long-term rather than immediate. A desperate daughter-in-law would one day be a mother-in-law herself; a son chafing at his father's strictness would eventually become a patriarch. While a new bride might ritually curse her parents for sending her to the hell of her groom's house, by the time she was a grandmother she would be a practiced purveyor of traditional family values. Historians are now beginning to investigate how different stages of the life cycle in China were experienced and portrayed, and this will certainly require still more nuanced interpretations of gender and status. But there were certain members of late imperial society whose lives could never become truly fulfilled and who always remained marginal, namely those who had no descendants of their own: men who could not afford to marry and concubines. Marriage set women as well as men on the path toward fulfillment and power.

One technological domain alone, however significant, cannot reveal all the complexities and nuances, the divergent representations, and the different dimensions of experience that make up gender roles. In the case of late imperial China, common stereotypes portray "traditional" Chinese women as cut off from the rest of society by their seclusion, as economic dependents largely uninvolved in production and unable to control their own reproduction. From this perspective, since there were no significant female technologies of production or reproduction, the production of secluded domestic space would appear to be the key technology that defined women's roles and place. An analysis of domestic space does indeed clarify the complex family hierarchies as well as the ritual responsibilities that shaped life in the inner quarters. We are obliged to qualify our interpretations of spatial seclusion significantly, however, as soon as we take into consideration other domains of material experience. Looking at the history of women's work in China, we see that economic dependency and isolation were not immemorial traditions. Once we take into account the fact that man and wife were classically viewed as filling complementary productive roles, then it becomes clear that the spatial dimensions of gender can be understood only if we take into account the flow of women-produced goods between inner and outer worlds. The focus on textiles shows that women's work originally tied women not only into the community but also into the state. The organization of female work and its evaluation changed, as did the meanings and importance of men's work, in response to the expansion and diversification of the economy. Though work did retain its importance in certain elite expressions of femininity, reproduction became increasingly important in the definition of the wifely role. If we then look closely at Chinese reproductive technologies and the forms of collaboration they involved, we find that far more than childbearing was involved. In the reproductive technologies available to elite women we see writ large expressions of class and status hierarchies that were already hinted at in the allocation of domestic space and the organization of womanly work. Each domain completes and qualifies the others, giving new density and definition to the complex historical negotiations of gender and other social hierarchies that underpinned the ideological continuities of late imperial China.

To understand how technologies shape a society's characteristic identity, we need to study significant *sets* of technological domains. And if we want to identify and analyze the technological domains that were most significant in characterizing a past society, we must often look beyond our modern notions of what constitute key sectors and technical desiderata. I have argued here for the study of gynotechnics, sets of technologies that produce ideas about women and about gender, as a creative new way of looking at how societies give material form to their ideas. Most conventional history of technology treats women as marginal players, as consumers rather than creators. But I have shown that gynotechnics was in no way marginal: the historical shaping and interplay of the three dimensions of material existence discussed here were central to the elaboration of a distinctively Chinese civilization. In producing ideas about women these technologies produced ideas about social relations and identities in general, requiring us to reconsider what concepts like domesticity, motherhood, femininity or masculinity might mean as applied to China. We are also obliged to rethink the meanings of "productive" activities and the applicability of terms like *commodities* or *efficiency* in a society where economic and moral values were related in ways quite different from in our own. And we are led to consider the nature of knowledge and action in a society that rooted intellectual and moral activity in the physical body and in its material environment.

I have shown the key role that Chinese gynotechnics played in what Norbert Elias would have called the Chinese "civilizing process," and I believe this is an approach that could be applied fruitfully elsewhere—by not only looking at gynotechnics in other societies, but also, for example, developing an androtechnics to analyze the role of technologies in the construction of masculinities. As feminist historians have shown, the study of gender is essential to understanding social organization and the production of knowledge in any society. The concept of gynotechnics requires us to study the bodily experiences of gender as a system. Its attention to the material base can elucidate apparent contradictions between different stands of representation or discourse. It roots social ideas in material experience, connects the production of culture to the production of objects, and in the process integrates women into what is too often still considered to be a male world.

Glossary of Technical Terms

anchan 暗產	spontaneous abortion
baishao 白芍	*Paeonia alba*
baishu 白朮	*Atracotylodis macrocephala*
baojuan 寶卷	precious scroll (Buddhist text)
baxian zhuo 八仙卓	Eight Immortals Table
ben 本	root; fundamental occupations
bianzheng 辨證	distinguishing a disorder manifestation (medical diagnosis)
bing 病	disorder
bulai 不來	[the menses] do not come (amenorrhea)
butong 不通	[the menses] do not come through (amenorrhea)
buyu 不育	infertility
ceshi 側室	side chamber; concubine
chan 產	to give birth
chanke 產科	obstetrics
chong 衝, 冲	name of acupuncture tract
chuanxiong 川芎	*Ligusticum wallichii*
citang 祠堂	ancestral hall
danggui 當歸	*Angelica sinensis*
dihuang 地黃	*Radix Rehmannia*
dili 地歷	geomancy (learned term; also *fengshui*)
dimu 嫡母	formal mother
duan 段	a length of hemp or ramie cloth (roughly twenty feet)

duilian 對聯	parallel scrolls
dushentang 獨參湯	pure ginseng decoction
erke 兒科	children's medicine, pediatrics
fang 房	wing of a building; branch of a family
fengshui 風水	geomancy (vulgar usage; also *dili*)
fuke 婦科	women's medicine
fushousan 佛毛散	Buddha's hand powder (pregnancy test)
ganqi 幹漆	dried lacquer
gongjiang 工匠	male artisans
guangsi 廣嗣	multiplying descendants
hangtu 坑土	tamped earth
honghua 紅花	*Carthamus tinctoria*
hongwan 紅丸	red pills (abortifacients)
hongyao 紅藥	red drugs (abortifacients)
houshi 後室	rear chambers; concubine
hu 戶	door; household
hutou 戶頭	foreman
jia 家	house; family
jiamiao 家廟	family shrine
jian 間	bays of a house (the space between pillars)
jiao 教	teaching, education
jiaxun 家訓	household instructions
jiejing 借景	borrowing views
jin 斤	pound (Chinese weight)
jing 精	essence; semen
jing 經	warp threads; canonical texts; natural cycles; acupuncture tracts or meridians; menses
jingbi 經閉	blocked menses
juan 卷	scroll; section of a book
kang 炕	heated platform
kun 困	trouble
li 禮	ritual; etiquette
liang 兩	ounce (Chinese weight)
ling 靈	living spirit
liu po 六婆	the six old women
luan 亂	to ravel a skein; civil disorder
lun 綸, 論	silk yarn; philosophical discourse, treatise

lutai 露臺	dew platform (veranda of ladies' quarters)
manchong 虻蟲	gadfly
mei 美	beautiful (in description of good geomantic sites)
min 民	the people
mo 末	branch; secondary occupations
mu 畝	unit of land (about one-sixth of an acre, one-fifteenth of a hectare)
nangeng nüzhi 男耕女織	men till, women weave
neiren 內人	the person inside (wife)
nie 鑷	patterning devices (loom)
niuxi 牛膝	*Acanthyrus bidentata*
nügong 女工, 功, 紅	women's work, womanly work, 女工 female workers
pi 匹	a bolt of silk cloth
pipa 琵琶	type of lute
qi 氣	cosmic energy
qi 妻	legal wife
qiao 巧	craft, cunning, skill
qie 妾	concubine
qin 琴	type of lute
qutai 去胎	to eliminate the fetus (abort)
ren 任	name of an acupuncture tract
ruyi 儒醫	Confucian physician
shanshui 山水	mountains and streams (landscape painting)
shanze 山澤	mountains and marshes
sheng 生	to generate, to give birth; raw, immature
shengcai 生財	to produce wealth
shi 石	bushel (Chinese measure)
shi 室	house, room
shiren 室人	unmarried girl; virgin
shiyi 世醫	hereditary physician
shu 熟	cooked, mature
shufang 書房	study
shuizhi 水蛭	leeches
siming 司命	Overseer of Fates
siwutang 四物湯	Four Ingredient Decoction

sui 歲	year
ta 榻	couch
tang 堂	rear hall
taoren 桃仁	peach kernels
tian 天	from heaven (a natural endowment)
tiangui 天癸	reproductive capacities
tianhuan 天宦	natural eunuch
tianjing 天井	heaven-well (common northern term for courtyard)
tiaojing 調經	menstrual regulation
ting 廳	front hall
tong 通	vital circulation
tongfang 通方	all-purpose prescription, panacea
tongjing yao 通經藥	emmenagogue
wanwu 萬物	the myriad phenomena (Nature)
wen 文	pattern; written word; cultivation, refinement
wenren 文人	a literary man
wujing 無經	absence of menses (amenorrhea)
wulun 五倫	the Five Relationships
wuxing 五行	the Five Phases
xi 席	mat
xiang 廂	wing of a building
xianggui san 香桂散	fragrant cinnamon powder
xiansheng 先生	master
xiao 孝	filial piety
xiaoyao san 曉曜散	xiaoyao powder (pregnancy test)
xiatai 下胎	to bring down the fetus (abort)
xionggui tang 芎桂湯	xionggui decoction (pregnancy test)
xiu 繡	embroidery
xiu 修	self-cultivation
xiu 秀	graceful (in description of good geomantic sites)
xuehai 血海	the Sea of Blood
yang 養	to nourish, to rear
yangsheng 養生	longevity practices
yangzhai 陽宅	yang sites (houses of the living)
yi 醫	medicine; physician

yinzhai 陰宅   yin sites (graves)
yueshi 月事   the monthly event (menses)
zhai 宅   geomantic site
zhangfang 帳房   credit houses
zhi 治   to reel silk; to bring order, govern; to heal
zhongzi 種子   sowing seed (begetting sons)
zhu 主   host, owner; to rule, to preside
zhuan 傳   to transmit
ziran 自然   spontaneous (natural)
zuofang 作房   family workshops
zuoxi 坐席   to sit on the mat (to give birth)

References Cited

PRIMARY CHINESE SOURCES

Bencao gangmu [Systematic pharmacopeia]. 1597. Li Shizhen. Modern edition in 4 vols., Beijing, Renmin Weisheng Press, 1981.

Bianmin tuzuan [Collection of pictures for ordinary people]. 1593. Possibly by Guang Fan. Modern edition by Shi Shenghan and Kang Chengyi. 1959. Repr. Beijing, Nongye Press, 1982.

Bianyong xuehai junyu [Seas of knowledge and mines of jade: encyclopedia for convenient use]. 1607. Compiler unknown, ed. Wu Wei zi. Illustrations on sericulture reproduced Kuhn 1976.

Binfeng guangyi [Enlarged explanation of the sericultural crafts of Bin]. 1740–42. Yang Shen. Repr. Taibei, Yiwen yinshuguan, *Guanzhong Zongshu*, 1970, vol. 18.

Bu nongshu [Supplemented treatise on agriculture]. 1658. Zhang Lüxiang. Incorporating *Shenshi nongshu*, a treatise on agriculture by an anonymous Mr. Shen, probably written just before 1640; the edition used here is the critical one incorporating a translation into modern Chinese by Chen Huanli and Wang Dacan, *Bu nongshu jiaoshi*, Beijing, Nongye Press, 1983.

Cheng Maoxian yi'an [Medical cases of Cheng Maoxian]. Preface 1632. Repr. Shanghai, Rare Books Press, c. 1982.

Fuke xinfa yaojue [Essential esoterics of the new gynecology]. 18th century. Wu Qian. Repr. Taibei, Xuanfang Press, 1981.

Furen daquan liangfang [Good prescriptions from the compendia of gynecology]. Preface 1237. Chen Ziming. Repr. Beijing, Renmin Weisheng Press, 1985.

Gengzhi tu [Agriculture and sericulture illustrated]. 1145. Lou Shou. The pictures were first presented to the emperor in 1145, but were not made into woodblocks and published probably until the early thirteenth century. On the complex history of this extremely influential work, see Kuhn 1976. The versions used here are the Ming version of 1462 and the Qianlong version of 1742 (both illustrated in Franke 1913), as well as the Kangxi imperial edition (*Yuzhi gengzhi tu*) of 1696.

Gujin tushu jicheng [Imperial encyclopedia]. 1726. Ed. Chen Menglei. Repr. Taibei, Wenxing Editions, 1964.

Gujin yitong daquan [Complete ancient and modern medical compendium]. Preface 1556. Xu Chunfu. Repr. Taibei, Xinwenfeng Press, 1978.

Huangdi neijing: Su wen [Yellow Emperor's classic of internal medicine: basic questions]. Compiled first century B.C. or A.D. Edition cited: Shanghai, Kexue Jishu Press, 1983.

Huitu Lu Ban jing [Illustrated canon of Lu Ban]. 1808. A late Qing edition of the Ming text of the *Lu Ban jing* (q.v.), in the collection of the Needham Research Institute, Cambridge.

Jujia biyong shilei quanji [Householder's vademecum]. 1301. Probably by Xiong Zongli. I refer here to the revised edition of 1560 by Tian Rucheng, n.p.

Linzheng zhinan yi'an [Medical records as a guide to diagnosis]. Preface 1776. Ye Tianshi. Repr. Taibei, Chongde Bookshop, 1984.

Lu Ban jing [Canon of Lu Ban, patron saint of carpenters, or Carpenter's Canon]. The earliest extant edition of this text dates from the Ming, the *Xinjuan jingban gongshi diaozhuo zhengshi Lu Ban jing jiangjia jing*, compiler Wu Rong (Director of the Superintending Office of Imperial Artisans of the Board of Works in Beijing), assistant compiler Zhang Yan (Commandant of the Office of Service Artisans), corrector Zhou Yan (Aide to the Office for the Assignment of Artisans in Nanjing). See Ruitenbeek 1993: 117 for the history of this work. The edition used here is the *Huitu Lu Ban jing* (q.v.).

Mianhua tu [Illustrations of cotton planting and manufacture]. C. 1765. Fan Guangcheng. Original album of paintings and explanations, reprinted with added poems by the Jiaqing emperor and with woodblock versions of the illustrations as *Shouyi guangxun* (q.v.).

Nong shu [Agricultural treatise]. 1149. Chen Fu. Repr. Beijing, Zhonghua Editions, 1956.

Nong shu [Agricultural treatise]. 1313. Wang Zhen. Ed. Wang Yuhu, Beijing, Nongye Press, 1981.

Nongzheng quanshu [Complete treatise of agricultural administration]. 1639. Xu Guangqi. Ed. Shih Shenghan. 3 vols. Shanghai, Guji Press, 1979.

Nüke mijue daquan [Compendium of secrets of gynecology]. Preface 1908. Chen Lianfang. Repr. Beijing, Beijing Ribao Press, 1989.

Nüke qieyao [Absolute essentials of gynecology]. Preface 1773. Wu Daoyuan. Repr. Beijing, Zhongguo Shudian, Foundations of Chinese Medicine Series, 1987.

Shangyou tang yi'an [Medical case histories from the Hall of Honored Friendship]. Preface 1846. Fang Lüe. Repr. Shanghai, Rare Books Press, c. 1983.

Shenshi nongshu. See *Bu nongshu*.

Shinzoku kibun [Recorded accounts of Qing customs]. 1800. Compiled by Nakagawa Tadahide. The two editions I refer to are A: facsimile of 1800 edition, Taipei, Tali Press, 1983; B: Sun Boshun and Muramatsu Kazuya, annotated translation into modern Japanese, 2 vols., Tokyo, Heibonsha, 1966.

Shouyi guangxun [Expanded instructions on procuring clothing]. 1808. A revised edition of the *Mianhua tu* (q.v.) by Fan Guangcheng. Repr. as vol. 4 of *Zhongguo gudai banhua congkan*, Beijing, Zhonghua Press, 1960.

Sizhen juewei [Selected subtleties of the four methods of diagnosis]. Preface 1723. Lin Zhihan. Repr. Beijing, Zhongguo Shudian, Foundations of Chinese Medicine Series, 1987.

Taichan xinfa [New methods for pregnancy and childbirth]. Preface 1739. Yan Shunxi. Repr. Beijing, Renmin Weisheng Press, 1988.

Tiangong kaiwu [Exploitation of the works of nature]. 1637. Song Yingxing. References are to the 1771 edition as reproduced in *Jiaozheng tiangong kaiwu*, ed. Yang Jialuo, Taibei, Shijie Editions, 1962. For an English annotated translation see Sung 1966.

Xianqing ouji [Casual expressions of idle feeling]. 1671. Li Yu. Facsimile edition, Taipei, Guangwen Press, 1977.

Xuanqi jiuzheng lun [Discourse on rectification according to the Yellow Emperor's treatise]. Preface 1644. Xiao Jing. Repr. Beijing, Rare Books Press, 1983.

Yilue liushu, nüke zhiyan [Medical compendium in six books, experiences in gynecology]. 18th century. Xu Dachun. The edition cited here is the *Xu Dachun yishu quanji*, ed. Beijingshi Weisheng Ganbu Jinxiuyuan Zhongyibu, 2 vols., Beijing, Renmin Weisheng Press, 1988.

Yishuo [Talking about medicine]. Zhang Gao [1149–1227]. Repr. 2 vols., Shanghai, Kexue Zhishu Press, 1984.

OTHER REFERENCES CITED

Abdel Nour, Antoine. 1979. Types architecturaux et vocabulaire de l'habitat en Syrie aux XIVe et XVIIe siècles. In Chevalier: 59–93.

Adas, Michael. 1989. *Machines as the measure of men: science, technology, and ideologies of western dominance.* Ithaca, Cornell University Press.

Ahern, Emily M. 1973. *The cult of the dead in a Chinese village.* Stanford, Stanford University Press.

———. 1978. The power and pollution of Chinese women. In A. Wolf, ed.: 269–90.

Ahern, Emily M., and Hill Gates, eds. 1981. *The anthropology of Taiwanese society.* Stanford, Stanford University Press.

Alleton, Viviane. 1993. *Les Chinois et la passion des noms.* Paris, Aubier.

Anagnost, Ann. 1989. Family violence and magical violence: the woman as victim in China's one-child family policy. *Women and Language* 11, 2: 16–22.

Anon. 1984. *Zhongguo yiyao shihua* [Historical account of medicine and pharmaceutics in China]. Hong Kong, Mingwen shuju.

Appadurai, Arjun, ed. 1986. *The social life of things: commodities in cultural perspective.* Cambridge, Cambridge University Press.

Ardener, Shirley. 1981a. Ground rules and social maps for women: an introduction. In Ardener, ed.: 1–30.

———, ed. 1981b. *Women and space: ground rules and social maps.* 2d ed. 1993. Oxford, Berg.

Arendt, Hannah. 1958. *The human condition.* Chicago, University of Chicago Press.

Ariès, Philippe, and Georges Duby, general eds. 1985–87. *Histoire de la vie privée.* 5 vols. Paris, Seuil.

Baker, Hugh. 1979. *Chinese family and kinship*. London, Macmillan.

Banister, Judith. 1987. *China's changing population*. Stanford, Stanford University Press.

Bao Jialin, ed. 1988. *Zhongguo funü shi lun ji* [Collected essays on the history of Chinese women]. Beijing, Daoxiang Press.

Barlow, Tani E. 1994. Theorizing woman: *funü, guojia, jiating*. In Zito and Barlow: 253–89.

Bates, Donald, ed. 1995. *Knowledge and the scholarly medical traditions*. Cambridge, Cambridge University Press.

Bayly, C. A. 1986. The origins of swadeshi (home industry): cloth and Indian society. In Appadurai: 285–321.

Bean, Susan S. 1989. Gandhi and *khadi*, the cloth of Indian independence. In Weiner and Schneider: 355–75.

Bennett, Steven J. 1978. Patterns of the sky and earth: a Chinese science of applied cosmology. *Chinese Science* 3: 1–26.

Berardi, Roberto. 1979. Espace et ville en pays d'Islam. In Chevalier: 99–124.

Berlin, Judith A. 1985. Religion and popular culture: the management of moral capital in *The Romance of the Three Teachings*. In D. Johnson et al.: 188–218.

Birge, Bettine. 1992. Women and property in Sung dynasty China (960–1279): neo-Confucianism and social change in Chien-chou, Fukien. Ph.D. dissertation, Columbia University.

Blake, C. Fred. 1994. Foot-binding in neo-Confucian China and the appropriation of female labor. *Signs* 19, 3: 676–712.

Blue, Gregory, Timothy Brook, Immanuel Wallerstein and Bin Wong. Forthcoming. *China and capitalism: interrogating "the rise of the West."* Cambridge, Cambridge University Press.

Bordo, Susan. 1993. *Unbearable weight: feminism, Western culture, and the body*. Berkeley, University of California Press.

Borotová, Lucie. 1992. A making of the *doubles* of character-types in an eighteenth-century novel. Paper presented at the European Association of Chinese Studies Conference, Paris, 14–17 September.

Bourdieu, Pierre. 1973. The Berber house. In Mary Douglas, ed., *Rules and meanings*, Harmondsworth, Penguin: 98–110.

———. 1977. *Outline of a theory of practice*. Cambridge, Cambridge University Press.

———. 1990. *The logic of practice*. Stanford, Stanford University Press.

Boyd, Andrew. 1962. *Chinese architecture and town planning: 1500 B.C.–A.D. 1911*. Chicago, University of Chicago Press.

Braudel, Fernand. 1992. *Civilization and capitalism, 15th–18th century*. Vol. 1, *The structures of everyday life*. Tr. Sian Reynolds. Berkeley, University of California Press. Originally published as *Civilisation matérielle, économie et capitalisme*, Paris, Armand Colin, 1979.

Bray, Francesca. 1984. *Science and civilisation in China*. Vol. 6, part 2, *Agriculture*. Cambridge, Cambridge University Press.

———. 1986. *The rice economies: technology and development in Asian societies*. Oxford, Basil Blackwell. Repr. Berkeley, University of California Press, 1994.

———. 1994. Le travail féminin dans la Chine impériale: sur l'élaboration de nouveaux motifs dans le tissu social. Tr. P. E. Will. *Annales, Histoire, Sciences Sociales* 49, 4 (July–Aug.): 783–816.

———. 1995a. A deathly disorder: understanding women's health in late imperial China. In Bates: 235–50.

———. 1995b. Textile production and gender roles in China, 1000–1700. *Chinese Science* 12: 113–35.

———. Forthcoming. Meanings of motherhood: reproductive technologies and their uses in late imperial China. In Lee and Saito.

Brokaw, Cynthia. 1991. *The ledgers of merit and demerit: social change and moral order in late imperial China.* Princeton, Princeton University Press.

Brook, Timothy. 1993. *Praying for power: Buddhism and the formation of gentry society in late-Ming China.* Cambridge, Mass., Harvard University Press.

———. Forthcoming. Capitalism, modern history, and the Chinese premodern. In Blue et al.

Browner, Carole. 1980. The management of early pregnancy: Colombian folk concepts of fertility control. *Social Sciences and Medicine* 148: 25–32.

Buck, John Lossing. 1937. *Land utilization in China.* Shanghai, University of Nanking.

Burnham, Dorothy K. 1981. *A textile terminology: warp and weft.* London, Routledge and Kegan Paul.

Cahill, Suzanne. 1993. *Transcendence and divine passion: the queen mother of the West in medieval China.* Stanford, Stanford University Press.

Carlitz, Katherine. 1994. Desire, danger, and the body: stories of women's virtue in late Ming China. In Gilmartin et al.: 101–24.

Cartier, Michel. 1984. Travail et idéologie dans la Chine antique. In Cartier, ed., *Le travail et ses représentations,* Paris, Editions des archives contemporaines: 275–304.

Casault, André. 1987. The Beijing courtyard house. *Open House International* 12, 1: 30–41.

Casual Expressions. See *Xianqing ouji.*

Chang, Kwang-chih. 1977. *The archaeology of ancient China.* 3d rev. and enlarged ed. New Haven, Yale University Press.

———. 1980. *Shang civilization.* New Haven, Yale University Press.

Chao Kang. 1977. *The development of cotton textile production in China.* Cambridge, Mass., Harvard University Press.

Chao, Yuan-ling. 1995. Medicine and society in late imperial China: a study of physicians in Suzhou. Ph.D. dissertation, Department of History, University of California, Los Angeles.

Chard, Robert L. 1990. Folktales on the God of the Stove. *Chinese Studies* 8: 149–82.

———. 1993. "The Stove God and the Overseer of Fate." In *Minjian xinyang yu zhongguo wenhua: guoji yantaohui lunwenji,* Taipei, Research Center for Chinese Studies (Hanxue yanjiu zhongxin): 655–82.

Chen Keji, Zhou Wenquan, Hong Yaoli, Dan Shikui and Xu Yipu, comp. 1990. *Qinggong yi'an yanjiu* [Study of the medical cases of the Qing palace]. Beijing, Zhongyi Guji Press.

Chen Shiqi. 1958. *Mingdai guanshougongye de yanjiu* [Study of official handicraft production during the Ming dynasty]. Wuhan, Renmin Press.

Chen Weiji, ed. in chief. 1984. *Zhongguo fangzhi kexue jishu shi.* Beijing, Science Press. Citations are from the English ed., *History of textile technology of ancient China,* tr. Gao Guopei, New York, Science Press, 1992.

Chevalier, Dominique, ed. 1979. *L'espace social de la ville arabe.* Paris, Maisonneuve et Larose.

Clément, Sophie, Pierre Clément and Shin Yong-hak. 1987. *Architecture du paysage en Extrême-Orient.* Paris, Ecole nationale supérieure des Beaux-Arts.

Clifford, James. 1988. *The predicament of culture: twentieth-century ethnography, literature, and art.* Cambridge, Mass., Harvard University Press.

Clunas, Craig. 1988. *Chinese furniture.* London, Victoria and Albert Museum/ Bamboo.

———. 1991. *Superfluous things: material culture and social status in early modern China.* Oxford, Polity Press.

———. Forthcoming. Luxury knowledge: the *Xiushilu* [Records of lacquering] of 1625. *Techniques et culture.*

Cohen, Myron. 1976. *House united, house divided: the Chinese family in Taiwan.* Stanford, Stanford University Press.

Collins, Jane L., and Martha Gimenez, eds. 1990. *Work without wages: domestic labor and self-employment within capitalism.* Albany, SUNY Press.

Connerton, Paul. 1989. *How societies remember.* Cambridge, Cambridge University Press.

Cooper, William C., and Nathan Sivin. 1973. Man as medicine: pharmacological and ritual aspects of traditional therapy using drugs derived from the human body. In Shigeru Nakayama and Nathan Sivin, eds., *Chinese science: explorations of an ancient tradition,* Cambridge, Mass., MIT Press: 203–72.

Cornell, Laurel. Forthcoming. Infanticide and the origin of low fertility in early modern Japan: a sociological perspective. In Lee and Saito.

Cowan, Ruth Schwartz. 1983. *More work for Mother: the ironies of household technology from the open hearth to the microwave.* New York, Basic Books.

Croll, Elisabeth. 1987. New peasant family forms in rural China. *Journal of Peasant Studies* 14, 4: 469–99.

Crow, John Armstrong. 1985. *Spain, the root and the flower.* 3d ed. Berkeley, University of California Press.

Cullen, Christopher. 1993. Patients and healers in late imperial China: evidence from the *Jinpingmei. History of Science* 31: 99–150.

Dardess, John W. 1989. A Ming landscape: settlement, land use, labor, and estheticism in T'ai-ho County, Kiangsi. *Harvard Journal of Asiatic Studes* 49 (Dec. 1989): 295–364.

de Bary, William Theodore, ed. 1960. *Sources of Chinese tradition.* New York, Columbia University Press.

De Groot, J. J. M. 1892–1910. *The religious system of China.* 6 vols. Leiden, E. J. Brill.

Dean-Jones, Lesley. 1995. Autopsia, historia and what women know: the authority of women in Hippocratic gynaecology. In Bates: 41–59.

Dennerline, Jerry. 1986. Marriage, adoption, and charity in the development of lineages in Wu-hsi from Sung to Ch'ing. In Ebrey and Watson: 170–209.

Desrosiers, Sophie. 1988. Les techniques de tissage ont-elles un sens? Un mode de lecture des tissus andins. *Techniques et culture* 12: 21–56.

———. 1994. La soierie méditerranéenne. *La revue du Musée des Arts et Métiers* 7: 51–58.

Devereux, George. 1976. *A study of abortion in primitive societies.* Rev. ed.; original ed. 1955. New York, International Universities Press.

DeWoskin, Kenneth J., tr. 1983. *Doctors, diviners and magicians of ancient China.* New York, Columbia University Press.

Diamond, Norma. 1988. The Miao and poison: interactions on China's southwest frontier. *Ethnology* 27, 1 (Jan. 1988): 1–25.

Douglas, Mary. 1982. *Natural symbols.* New York, Pantheon.

Du Zhengsheng. 1994. Neiwai yu bafang: Zhongguo chuantong jushi kongjian di lunliguan he yuzhouguan [Inner and outer and the eight directions: social and cosmological aspects of traditional Chinese dwellings]. Paper presented at the conference "Space, House and Society," Academia Sinica Institute of Ethnography, Taipei, 22–26 February 1994.

Duby, Georges. 1984. *The age of the cathedrals: art and society, 980–1420.* Tr. E. Levieux and B. Thompson. Chicago, University of Chicago Press.

Dudbridge, Glen. 1992. Women pilgrims to T'ai-shan: some passages from a seventeenth-century novel. In Naquin and Yü: 39–64.

Duden, Barbara. 1991. *The woman beneath the skin: a doctor's patients in eighteenth-century Germany.* Cambridge, Mass., Harvard University Press.

Ebrey, Patricia Buckley. 1984. *Family and property in Sung China: Yuan Ts'ai's precepts for social life.* Princeton, Princeton University Press.

———. 1986. The early stages in the development of descent group organization. In Ebrey and Watson: 16–61.

———. 1991a. *Chu Hsi's family rituals: a twelfth-century Chinese manual for the performance of cappings, weddings, funerals, and ancestral rites.* Princeton, Princeton University Press.

———. 1991b. *Confucianism and family rituals in imperial China.* Princeton, Princeton University Press.

———. 1991c. Introduction. In Watson and Ebrey: 1–24.

———. 1991d. Shifts in marriage finance from the sixth to the thirteenth century. In Watson and Ebrey: 97–132.

———. 1993. *The inner quarters: marriage and the lives of Chinese women in the Sung period.* Berkeley, University of California Press.

Ebrey, Patricia, B., and James L. Watson, eds. 1986. *Kinship organization in late imperial China, 1000–1940.* Berkeley, University of California Press.

Ecke, Gustav. 1962. *Chinese domestic furniture.* Rutland, Vt., and Tokyo, Charles E. Tuttle. Originally published Beiping (Beijing), n.p., 1944, in a limited edition of 200 copies.

Eichhorn, Werner. 1955. Zur Vorgeschichte des Aufstandes von Wang Hsiao-po und Li Shun in Szuchuan (993–995). *Zeitschrift der deutschen morgenländischen Gesellschaft* 105: 192–209.

Elias, Norbert. [1933] 1985. *La société de cour* [Die höfische Gesellschaft]. Tr. Pierre Kamnitzer and Jeanne Etoré. Preface Roger Chartier. Paris, Calmann-Lévy.

——. [1939] 1982. *The civilizing process* [*Über den Prozess der Zivilisation: Soziogenetische und Psychogenetische Untersuchungen*]. Tr. Edmund Jephcott. 2 vols. Oxford, Basil Blackwell.

Elman, Benjamin. 1984. *From philosophy to philology: intellectual and social aspects of change in late imperial China.* Cambridge, Mass., Harvard University Press.

Elman, Benjamin, and Alexander Woodside, eds. 1994. *Education and society in late imperial China, 1600–1900.* Berkeley, University of California Press.

Elvin, Mark. 1973. *The pattern of the Chinese past.* Stanford, Stanford University Press.

——. 1989. Tales of *shen* and *xin:* body-person and heart-mind in China during the last 150 years. In Michel Feher, ed., *Fragments for a history of the human body,* part 2, New York, Zone Books: 266–350.

Engels, Friedrich. [1884] 1972. *The origin of the family, private property and the state.* New York, International Publishers.

Etkin, Nina L. 1988. Cultural constructions of efficacy. In S. van der Geest and S. R. Whyte, eds., *The context of medicine in developing countries: studies in pharmaceutical anthropology,* Dordrecht, Kluwer Academic Publishers: 299–326.

Fan Jinmin and Jin Wen. 1993. *Jiangnan sichou shi yanjiu* [Historical studies of silk spinning and weaving in Jiangnan]. Beijing, Nongye Press.

Farquhar, Judith. 1994. *Knowing practice: the clinical encounter of Chinese medicine.* Boulder, Colo., Westview Press.

Feen, Richard Harrow. 1983. Abortion and exposure in ancient Greece: assessing the status of the fetus and "newborn" from classical sources. In W. B. Bondeson, H. T. Engelhardt, S. F. Spicker and D. H. Winship, eds., *Abortion and the status of the fetus,* Dordrecht, Reidel: 283–300.

Feng Xianming. 1982. *Zhongguo taoci shi* [History of Chinese pottery]. Beijing, Zhonghua Press.

Feuchtwang, Stephen D. R. 1974. *An anthropological analysis of Chinese geomancy.* Vientiane, Laos, Vithagna.

Finley, M. I. 1973. *The ancient economy.* 2d ed., 1985. Berkeley, University of California Press.

Foucault, Michel. 1973. *The birth of the clinic.* New York, Vintage.

——. 1979. *Discipline and punish: the birth of the prison.* New York, Vintage.

Franke, Otto. 1913. *Keng Tschi T'u: Ackerbau und Seidengewinnung in China.* Hamburg, L. Friederichsen and Co.

Franklin, Ursula. 1990. *The real world of technology.* Montreal, CBC Enterprises.

Freedman, Maurice. 1969. Geomancy. *Proceedings of the Royal Anthropological Institute 1968.* London, Royal Anthropological Institute.

——. 1970. Ritual aspects of Chinese kinship and marriage. In Freedman, ed.: 153–88.

——, ed. 1970. *Family and kinship in Chinese society.* Stanford, Stanford University Press.

Friedland, Roger, and A. F. Robertson. 1990. Beyond the marketplace. In Friedland

and Robertson, eds., *Beyond the marketplace: rethinking economy and society,* New York, Aldine de Gruyter: 3–49.

Furth, Charlotte. 1986. Blood, body and gender: medical images of the female condition in China 1600–1850. *Chinese Science* 7: 43–66.

———. 1987. Pregnancy, childbirth and infancy in Ch'ing dynasty China. *Journal of Asian Studies* 46, 1: 7–35.

———. 1988. A social analysis of medical practice in late imperial China. Paper presented at the 6th International Conference on the History of Chinese Science, University of California at San Diego.

———. 1990. The patriarch's legacy: household instructions and the transmission of orthodox values. In K. C. Liu, ed., *Orthodoxy in late imperial China,* Berkeley, University of California Press: 187–211.

———. 1994. Rethinking Van Gulik: sexuality and reproduction in traditional Chinese medicine. In Gilmartin et al.: 125–46.

———. 1995. From birth to birth: the growing body in Chinese medicine. In Kinney 1995: 157–91.

Furth, Charlotte, and Ch'en Shu-yueh. 1992. Chinese medicine and the anthropology of menstruation in contemporary Taiwan. *Medical Anthropology Quarterly* 6, 1 (n.s.): 27–48.

Gao Hanyu. 1986. *Zhongguo lidai zhi ran xiu tulu.* Hong Kong, Commercial Press. Citations are from the English ed., *Chinese textile designs,* tr. Rosemary Scott and Susan Whitfield, London, Viking/Penguin, 1992.

Gao Yinxian and Yi Nianhua. 1991. *Nüshu—shijie weiyi di nüxing wenzi* [Women's script: the world's only female script]. Ed. Gong Zhebing. Taipei: Funü xinzhiji jinhui Press.

Gates, Hill. 1989. The commoditization of Chinese women. *Signs* 14, 4: 799–832.

Geertz, Clifford. 1963. *Agricultural involution: the processes of ecological change in Indonesia.* Berkeley, University of California Press.

———. 1973. *The interpretation of cultures.* New York, Basic Books.

Giddens, Anthony. 1984. *The constitution of society: outline of the theory of structuration.* Berkeley, University of California Press.

Gille, Bertrand. 1978a. Les systèmes bloqués. In Gille, ed.: 441–507.

———, ed. 1978b. *Histoire des techniques.* Paris, Encyclopédie de la Pléiade.

Gilmartin, Christina K., Gail Hershatter, Lisa Rofel and Tyrene White, eds. 1994. *Engendering China: women, culture, and the state.* Cambridge, Mass., Harvard University Press.

Glahn, Else. 1982. The tradition of Chinese building. In K. G. Izikowitz and P. Sorensen, eds., *The house in East and Southeast Asia: anthropological and architectural aspects,* London, Curzon Press: 25–34.

Goodman, Jordan. 1993. Cloth, gender and industrial organization: towards an anthropology of silkworkers in early modern Europe. In S. Cavaciocchi, *La seta in Europa sec. XIII–XX,* Florence, Le Monnier: 229–45.

Goody, Esther N. 1982. Introduction. In Esther N. Goody, ed., *From craft to industry: the ethnography of proto-industrial cloth production,* Cambridge, Cambridge University Press: 1–37.

Goody, Jack. 1971. *Technology, tradition and the state in Africa.* London, Oxford University Press.

———. 1986. *The logic of writing and the organization of society.* Cambridge, Cambridge University Press.

———. 1987. *The interface between the written and the oral.* Cambridge, Cambridge University Press.

———. 1990. *The oriental, the ancient and the primitive: systems of marriage and the family in the pre-industrial societies of Eurasia.* Cambridge, Cambridge University Press.

Goto, Junko, and Naraomi Imamura. 1993. Japanese agriculture: characteristics, institutions, and policies. In Tweeten et al.: 11–29.

Greenhalgh, Susan, and Jiali Li. 1995. Engendering reproduction policy and practice in peasant China: for a feminist demography of reproduction. *Signs* 20, 3: 601–41.

Guo Aichun. 1984–87. *Zhongguo fensheng yijikao* [Chinese medical books classified by province]. Tianjin, Kexue Jishi Press.

Hanan, Patrick. 1988. *The invention of Li Yu.* Cambridge, Mass., Harvard University Press.

———. 1990. Introduction. In Li Yu: v–xiv.

Handlin, Joanna F. 1975. Lü Kun's new audience: the influence of women's literacy on sixteenth-century thought. In Wolf and Witke: 13–38.

Harrell, Stevan. 1985. The rich get children: segmentation, stratification, and population in three Chekiang lineages, 1550–1850. In Susan B. Hanley and Arthur P. Wolf, eds., *Family and population in east Asian history,* Stanford, Stanford University Press: 81–109.

Hartwell, Robert M. 1982. Demographic, political and social transformations of China, 750–1550. *Harvard Journal of Asiatic Studies* 42, 2: 365–442.

Haudricourt, André-Georges. 1987. *La technologie, science humaine: recherches d'histoire et d'ethnologie des techniques.* Paris, Editions Maison des Sciences de l'Homme.

Hayden, Dolores. 1986. *Redesigning the American dream: the future of housing, work, and family life.* New York, Norton.

Hayes, James. 1985. Specialists and written materials in the village world. In D. Johnson et al.: 75–111.

He Zhixi. 1990. *Zhongguo lidai yijia chuanlu* [Historical dictionary of Chinese medical biographies]. 3 vols. Beijing, Renmin Weisheng Press.

Herlihy, David. 1985. *Medieval households.* Cambridge, Mass., Harvard University Press.

Himes, Norman E. [1936] 1970. *Medical history of contraception.* New York, Schocken.

Hirschon, Renée. 1981. Essential objects and the sacred: interior and exterior space in an urban Greek locality. In Ardener, ed.: 70–86.

Ho, Ping-ti. 1959. *Studies on the population of China, 1368–1953.* Cambridge, Mass., Harvard University Press.

———. 1975. *The cradle of the East: an inquiry into the indigenous origins of techniques and ideas of neolithic and early historic China.* Hong Kong, Chinese University Press.

Hommel, Rudolf P. 1937. *China at work: an illustrated record of the primitive industries of China's masses, whose life is toil, and thus an account of Chinese civilization.* New York, John Day Co. Repr. Cambridge, Mass., MIT Press, 1969.

Honig, Emily. 1986. *Sisters and strangers: women in the Shanghai cotton mills, 1919–1949.* Stanford, Stanford University Press.

Honig, Emily, and Gail Hershatter. 1988. *Personal voices: Chinese women in the 1980s.* Stanford, Stanford University Press.

Hsiung Ping-chen. 1994. Constructed emotions: the bond between mothers and sons in late imperial China. *Late Imperial China* 15, 1: 87–119.

———. Forthcoming. More or less: Chinese medical and cultural traditions of fertility control. In Lee and Saito.

Hsu, Francis L. K. 1948. *Under the ancestors' shadow: Chinese culture and personality.* New York, Columbia University Press.

Huang, Philip C. C. 1985. *The peasant economy and social change in North China.* Stanford, Stanford University Press.

———. 1990. *The peasant family and rural development in the Yangzi Delta, 1350–1988.* Stanford, Stanford University Press.

Huang, Ray. 1974. *Taxation and governmental finance in sixteenth-century Ming China.* Cambridge, Cambridge University Press.

Huang Shengwu, ed. 1983. *Zhongguo yixue baike quanshu. Zhongyi fukexue* [Chinese medical encyclopedia. Traditional Chinese gynecology]. Shanghai, Xinhua Press.

Hymes, Robert. 1987. Not quite gentlemen? Doctors in Sung and Yuan. *Chinese Science* 8: 9–76.

Hymes, Robert P., and Conrad Schirokauer. 1993. Introduction. In Hymes and Schirokauer, eds., *Ordering the world: approaches to state and society in Sung dynasty China,* Berkeley, University of California Press: 1–58.

Ingold, Tim. 1988. *The appropriation of nature: essays on human ecology and social relations.* Manchester, Manchester University Press.

———. 1991. Becoming persons: consciousness and sociality in human evolution. *Cultural Dynamics* 4, 3: 355–78.

Janelli, Roger L., and Dawnhee Yim Janelli. 1982. *Ancestor worship and Korean society.* Stanford, Stanford University Press.

Jin Hansheng. 1988. Songdai nüzi zhiye yu shengji [Female occupations and livelihoods in the Song]. In Bao: 193–204.

Johnson, David, Andrew J. Nathan and Evelyn S. Rawski, eds. 1985. *Popular culture in late imperial China.* Berkeley, University of California Press.

Johnson, Elizabeth. 1977. Patterned bands in the New Territories of Hong Kong. *Journal of the Royal Asiatic Society, Hong Kong Branch* 17: 81–91.

———. 1988. Grieving for the dead, grieving for the living: funeral laments of Hakka women. In Watson and Rawski: 135–63.

Johnson, Kay Ann. 1983. *Women, the family, and peasant revolution in China.* Chicago, University of Chicago Press.

Johnston, R. Stewart. 1983. The ancient Chinese city of Suzhou: town planning in the Sung dynasty. *Town Planning Review* 54, 2: 194–222.

Judd, Ellen R. 1989. *Niangjia:* Chinese women and their natal families. *Journal of Asian Studies* 3 (Aug. 1989): 525–44.

Kaptchuk, Ted. 1983. *The web that has no weaver: understanding Chinese medicine.* New York, Congdon and Weed.

Kates, George N. 1948. *Chinese household furniture.* New York, Dover.
Keightley, David N. 1987. Archaeology and mentality: the making of China. *Representations* 18 (spring 1987): 91–128.
———. 1989. Craft and culture: metaphors of governance in early China. *Proceedings of the Second International Conference on Sinology.* Taipei, Academia Sinica.
———, ed. 1983. *The origins of Chinese civilization.* Berkeley, University of California Press.
Kendall, Laurel. 1985. *Shamans, housewives, and other restless spirits: women in Korean ritual life.* Honolulu, University of Hawaii Press.
Khalib-Chahidi, Jane. 1981. Sexual prohibitions, shared spaces and "fictive marriages" in Shi'ite Iran. In Ardener, ed.: 112–34.
Kidd, Alan. 1993. *Manchester.* Keele, Ryburn Publishing/Keele University Press.
Kinney, Anne Behnke. 1993. Infant abandonment in early China. *Early China* 18: 107–38.
———, ed. 1995. *Chinese views of childhood.* Honolulu, University of Hawaii Press.
Knapp, Ronald. 1986. *China's traditional rural architecture: a cultural geography of the Chinese house.* Honolulu, University of Hawaii Press.
Ko, Dorothy. 1992a. Crossing boundaries: public women as surrogate men in seventeenth-century China. Paper given at the Workshop on Chinese Women's History, University of California, Los Angeles, December 1992.
———. 1992b. Pursuing talent and virtue: education and women's culture in seventeenth and eighteenth century China. *Late Imperial China* 13, 1:9–39.
———. 1994. *Teachers of the inner chambers: women and culture in seventeenth-century China.* Stanford, Stanford University Press.
Koechlin, Bernard, François Sigaut, Jacqueline M. C. Thomas and Gerard Toffin, eds. 1987. *De la voûte céleste au terroir, du jardin au foyer: mosaïque sociographique.* Textes offerts à Lucien Bernot. Paris, Editions EHESS.
Kong, Yun Cheung, Shiu Ying Hu, Fung Kut Lau, Chun Tao Che, Hin Wing Yeung, Siu Cheng and Joseph Chi Chiu Hwang. 1976. Potential anti-fertility plants from Chinese medicine. *American Journal of Chinese Medicine* 4, 2: 105–28.
Körner, Brunhild. 1959. *Die religiöse Welt der Baüerin in Nordchina.* Reports from the Scientific Expedition to the North-Western Provinces of China under the Leadership of Sven Hedin, 8: *Ethnography.* Stockholm, State Ethnographic Museum.
Kuhn, Dieter. 1976. Die Darstellung des *Keng-chih-t'u. Zeitschrift der deutschen morgenländischen Gesellschaft* 126, 2: 336–67.
———. 1977. *Die Webstühle des Tzu-jen i-chih aus der Yuan-Zeit.* Wiesbaden, Steiner.
———. 1987. *Die Song-Dynastie (960 bis 1279): eine neue Gesellschaft im Spiegel ihrer Kultur.* Weinheim, Germany, Acta Humaniorum VCH.
———. 1988. *Science and civilisation in China.* Vol. 9, *Textile technology part I: spinning.* Cambridge, Cambridge University Press.
———. 1992. Family rituals. *Monumenta Serica* 40: 369–85.

————. 1993. Review of Smith 1991. *Journal of the American Oriental Society* 113, 1: 93–97.

————. 1995. Silk weaving in ancient China: from geometric figures to patterns of pictorial likeness. *Chinese Science* 12: 75–112.

————. Forthcoming. *Science and civilisation in China.* Vol. 5, part 10, *Textile technology part II: weaving.* Cambridge, Cambridge University Press.

Kulp, Daniel H. II. 1925. *Country life in South China: the sociology of familism.* New York, Columbia University Press.

LaFleur, William R. 1992. *Liquid life: abortion and Buddhism in Japan.* Princeton, Princeton University Press.

Lamouroux, Christian. 1995. Crise politique et développement rizicole en Chine: la région du Jiang-Huai (VIIIe–XIe siècles). *Bulletin de l'Ecole Française d'Extreme-Orient* 85: 145–84.

Latour, Bruno. 1993. Ethnography of a "high-tech" case: about Aramis. In Lemonnier, ed.: 372–98.

Lavely, William, James Lee and Wang Feng. 1990. Chinese demography: the state of the field. *Journal of Asian Studies* 49, 4: 807–34.

Lawrence, Denise L., and Setha M. Low. 1990. The built environment and spatial form. *Annual Review of Anthropology* 19: 453–505.

Lee, James. 1994. Historical demography of late imperial China: recent research results and implications. In F. Wakeman, ed., *China's quest for modernization,* Shanghai, Fudan University Press: 289–312.

Lee, James, and Cameron Campbell. 1996. *Fate and fortune in rural China: social structure and population behavior in Liaoning, 1774–1873.* Cambridge, Cambridge University Press.

Lee, James, Cameron Campbell and Guofu Tan. 1992. Infanticide and family planning in late imperial China: the price and population history of rural Liaoning, 1774–1873. In Rawski and Li: 145–76.

Lee, James, and Osamu Saito, eds. Forthcoming. *Abortion and infanticide in East Asia.* Oxford, Oxford University Press.

Lefebvre, Henri. 1974. *La production de l'espace.* Paris, éditions anthropos.

Legge, James, tr. 1885. *Li Chi, book of rites.* 2 vols. Oxford University Press. Repr. New York, University Books, 1967.

Lemonnier, Pierre. 1992. *Elements for an anthropology of technology.* Anthropological Papers, Museum of Anthropology, University of Michigan, no. 88, Ann Arbor.

————. 1993a. Introduction. In Lemonnier, ed.: 1–35.

————, ed. 1993b. *Technological choices: transformation in material cultures since the neolithic.* London, Routledge.

Leroi-Gourhan, André. 1964–65. *Le geste et la parole.* Vol. 1, *Technique et langage.* Vol. 2, *La mémoire et les rythmes.* Paris, Albin Michel.

Leung, Angela K. C. 1983. L'amour en Chine: relations et pratiques sociales aux XIIIe et XIVe siècles. *Archives des sciences sociales des religions* 56, 1: 59–76.

————. 1984. Autour de la naissance: la mère et l'enfant en Chine aux XVIe et XVIIe siècles. *Cahiers internationaux de sociologie* 76: 51–69.

———. 1987. Organized medicine in Ming-Qing China: state and private medical institutions in the Lower Yangzi region. *Late Imperial China* 8, 1: 134–66.

Li Bozhong. 1990. *Tangdai Jiangnan nongyedi fazhan* [Agricultural development in Tang Jiangnan]. Beijing, Nongye Press.

———. 1994. Kongzhi zengzhang, yi bao fuyu—Qingdai qianzhongqi Jiangnan di renkou xingwei [Preserving prosperity by controlling population growth—demographic behavior in Kiangnan during the mid-Ch'ing]. *Xin shixue* [New History] 5, 3: 25–71.

Li Chien-lang. 1980. *Taiwan jiangong shi* [History of architecture in Taiwan]. Taipei, Beiwu Press.

Li, Chu-tsing, and James C. Y. Watt, eds. 1989. *The Chinese scholar's studio: artistic life in the late Ming period: an exhibition from the Shanghai Museum.* New York/London, Asia Society Galleries/Thames and Hudson.

Li Jingwei, ed. in chief. 1988. *Zhongyi renwu cidian* [Dictionary of Chinese physicians]. Shanghai, Shanghai Zishu Press.

Li, Lillian M. 1981. *China's silk trade: traditional industry in the modern world 1842–1937.* Cambridge, Mass., Harvard University Press.

Li Wenliang, Qi Qiang, Wang Tianming, Liang Jirong, Peng Shuxian, Ma Yindu and Cui Hongfu, comps. 1982. *Qianjia miaofang* [Fine prescriptions of the thousand families]. Beijing, Liberation Army Press.

Li Yu. [1657] 1990. *The Carnal Prayer Mat.* Tr. Patrick Hanan. New York, Ballantine Books.

Li Zhende (Jen-der Lee). 1995. Han Sui zhi jian di "shengzi buju" wenti [Infanticide and child abandonment from Han to Sui]. *Bulletin of the Institute of History and Philology* (Academia Sinica, Taipei) 66, 3: 747–812.

Liang Fangzhong. 1980. *Zhongguo lidai hukou, tiandi, tianfu tongji* [Historical statistics of China's population, arable land, and land-tax]. Shanghai, Renmin Press.

Liang, Ssu-ch'eng. 1984. *A pictorial history of Chinese architecture: a study of the development of its structural system and the evolution of its types.* Ed. Wilma Fairbanks. Cambridge, Mass., MIT Press.

Liu Dunzhen. 1980. *La maison chinoise.* Tr. and introduced by Georges and Marie-Hélène Métailié, Sophie Clément-Charpentier and Pierre Clément. Paris, Berger-Levrault. Originally published as *Zhongguo zhuzhai gaishuo*, Beijing, Architectural Press, 1957.

Liu, K. C., ed. 1990. *Orthodoxy in late imperial China.* Berkeley, University of California Press.

Liu, Ts'ui-jung. 1994. Demographic constraint and family structure in traditional Chinese lineages. In Stevan Harrell, ed., *Chinese historical micro-demography,* Berkeley, University of California Press: 121–40.

Lock, Margaret. 1988. Japanese mythologies: faltering discipline and the ailing housewife. *American Ethnologist* 15, 1: 43–60.

———. 1993. *Encounters with aging: mythologies of menopause in Japan and North America.* Berkeley, University of California Press.

Luk, Bernard H. K. 1977. Abortion in Chinese law. *American Journal of Comparative Law* 25: 372–92.

Mahias, Marie-Claude. 1989. Réflexions pour une ethnologie des techniques en Inde. *Techniques et culture* 14: 1–22.

Mair, Victor H. 1985. Language and ideology in the written popularizations of the *Sacred Edict*. In D. Johnson et al.: 325–59.

Mann, Susan. 1991. Grooming a daughter for marriage: brides and wives in the mid-Ch'ing period. In Watson and Ebrey: 204–30.

———. 1992a. Household handicrafts and state policy in Qing times. In Jane Kate Leonard and John R. Watt, eds.: *To achieve security and wealth: the Qing imperial state and the economy 1644–1911*, Ithaca, Cornell University East Asia Program: 75–95.

———. 1992b. Women's work in the Ningbo area, 1900–1936. In Rawski and Li: 243–70.

———. 1994. The education of daughters in the mid-Ch'ing period. In Elman and Woodside: 19–49.

Mao Dun. 1956. *Spring silkworms and other stories.* Tr. Sidney Shapiro. Beijing, Foreign Languages Press.

Martin, Emily. 1987. *The woman in the body.* Boston, Beacon Press.

———. 1988. Gender and ideological differences in representations of life and death. In Watson and Rawski: 203–26.

Mauss, Marcel. [1935] 1979. Les techniques du corps. In M. Mauss, *Sociology and psychology,* tr. Ben Brewster, London, Routledge and Kegan Paul: 97–123.

McDermott, Joseph P. 1990. The Chinese domestic bursar. *Ajia bunka kenkyu* 2: 15–32.

McLaren, Angus. 1984. *Reproductive rituals: the perception of fertility in England from the sixteenth to the nineteenth century.* London, Methuen.

———. 1990. *A history of contraception from antiquity to the present day.* Oxford, Basil Blackwell.

Medick, Hans. 1976. The proto-industrial family economy. *Social History* 3: 291–315.

Meskill, Joanna. 1970. The Chinese genealogy as a research source. In Freedman, ed.: 139–62.

Métailié, Georges. 1995. Some hints about the "scholar garden" in ancient China. Unpublished manuscript.

Métailié, Georges, Marie-Hélène Métailié, Sophie Clément-Charpentier and Pierre Clément. 1980. Préface. In Liu Dunzhen: 7–23.

Mokyr, Joel. 1990. *The lever of riches: technological creativity and economic progress.* New York, Oxford University Press.

Moore, Henrietta L. 1986. *Space, text and gender: an anthropological study of the Marakwet of Kenya.* Cambridge, Cambridge University Press.

———. 1988. *Feminism and anthropology.* Oxford, Polity Press and Basil Blackwell.

Mumford, Lewis. 1934. *Technics and civilization.* 2d ed., 1963. New York, Harcourt Brace.

Musallam, B. F. 1983. *Sex and society in Islam.* Cambridge, Cambridge University Press.

Naquin, Susan. 1988. Funerals in North China: uniformity and variation. In Watson and Rawski: 37–70.

———. 1992. The Peking pilgrimage to Miao-Feng Shan. In Naquin and Yü: 333–77.

Naquin, Susan, and Chün-fang Yü, eds. 1992. *Pilgrims and sacred sites in China.* Berkeley, University of California Press.

Needham, Joseph, et al. 1954– . *Science and civilisation in China.* Cambridge, Cambridge University Press.

Needham, Joseph, with Wang Ling. 1959. *Science and civilisation in China.* Vol. 3, *Mathematics and the sciences of the heavens and earth.* Cambridge, Cambridge University Press.

Needham, Joseph, with Wang Ling. 1966. *Science and civilisation in China.* Vol. 4, part 2, *Mechanical engineering.* Cambridge, Cambridge University Press.

Needham, Joseph, with Wang Ling and Lu Gwei-Djen. 1971. *Science and civilisation in China.* Vol. 4, part 3, *Civil engineering and nautics.* Cambridge, Cambridge University Press.

Needham, Joseph, with Ho Ping-Yü and Lu Gwei-Djen. 1976. *Science and civilisation in China.* Vol. 6, part 3, *Spagyrical discovery and invention: historical survey, from cinnabar elixirs to synthetic insulin.* Cambridge, Cambridge University Press.

Needham, Joseph, with Lu Gwei-Djen and Huang Hsing-tsung. 1986. *Science and civilisation in China.* Vol. 6, *Biology and biological technology,* part 1, *Botany.* Cambridge, Cambridge University Press.

Ngin, Chor-Swang. 1985. Reproductive decisions and contraceptive use in a Chinese New Village in Malaysia. Ph.D. dissertation, University of California at Davis.

Nishijima, Sadao. [1949] 1984. The formation of the early Chinese cotton industry. In Linda Grove and Christian Daniels, eds., *State and society in China: Japanese perspectives on Ming-Qing social and economic history,* Tokyo, University of Tokyo Press: 17–79.

Ohnuki-Tierney, Emiko. 1993. *Rice as self: Japanese identities through time.* Princeton, Princeton University Press.

Ohta Motoko and Sawayama Mikako. Forthcoming. An analysis of the motivation for *mabiki* and abortion as related to child rearing customs in early modern Japan. In Lee and Saito.

Ong, Aihwa. 1987. *Spirits of resistance and capitalist discipline: factory women in Malaysia.* Albany, SUNY Press.

Ortner, Sherry, and Harriet Whitehead. 1981. Introduction: accounting for sexual meanings. In Ortner and Whitehead, eds., *Sexual meanings: the cultural construction of gender and sexuality,* Cambridge, Cambridge University Press: 1–27.

Ou Ming, ed. 1988. *Chinese-English dictionary of traditional medicine.* Hong Kong, Joint Publishing.

Overmyer, Daniel L. 1985. Values in Chinese sectarian literature: Ming and Ch'ing *pao-chüan.* In D. Johnson et al.: 219–54.

Ozawa, Kenji. 1993. A new phase for rice in Japan: production, marketing, and policy issues. In Tweeten et al.: 367–75.

Palmer, Martin, ed. 1986. *T'ung Shu: the ancient Chinese almanac.* London, Rider and Co.

Pan Jixing. 1989. *Tiangong kaiwu jiaozhu ji yanjiu* [Critical edition and researches on the *Tiangong kaiwu*]. Chengdu, Bashu Press.

Perdue, Peter C. 1987. *Exhausting the earth: state and peasant in Hunan, 1500–1850.* Cambridge, Mass., Harvard University Press.

Perkins, Dwight H. 1969. *Agricultural development in China, 1368–1968.* Chicago, Aldine.

Peterson, Willard. 1979. *Bitter gourd: Fang I-chih and the impetus for intellectual change.* New Haven, Yale University Press.

Pinch, Trevor J., and Wiebe E. Bijker. 1987. The social construction of facts and artifacts. In Wiebe E. Bijker, Thomas P. Hughes and Trevor J. Pinch, eds., *The social construction of technological systems,* Cambridge, Mass., MIT Press: 17–51.

Plaks, Andrew H. 1976. *Archetype and allegory in the Dream of the Red Chamber.* Princeton, Princeton University Press.

Potter, Sulamith Heins. 1987. Birth planning in China: a cultural account. In Nancy Scheper-Hughes, ed., *Child survival: anthropological perspectives on the treatment and maltreatment of children,* Dordrecht/Boston, D. Reidel: 33–58.

Profet, Margie. 1993. Menstruation as a defense against pathogens transported by sperm. *Quarterly Review of Biology* 68, 3: 335–86.

Rawski, Evelyn S. 1972. *Agricultural change and the peasant economy of South China.* Cambridge, Mass., Harvard University Press.

———. 1979. *Education and popular literacy in Ch'ing China.* Ann Arbor, University of Michigan Press.

———. 1985. Economic and social foundations. In D. Johnson et al.: 3–33.

Rawski, Thomas G., and Lillian M. Li, eds. 1992. *Chinese history in economic perspective.* Berkeley, University of California Press.

Reddy, William M. 1986. The structure of a cultural crisis: thinking about cloth in France before and after the revolution. In Appadurai: 261–84.

Reynolds, B., and M. A. Scott. 1987. *Material anthropology: contemporary approaches to material culture.* New York, University Press of America.

Richardson, M. 1982. Being-in-the-market versus being-in-the-plaza: material culture and the construction of social reality in Spanish America. *American Ethnologist* 9, 2: 421–36.

Robertson, Jennifer. 1991. *Native and newcomer: making and remaking a Japanese city.* Berkeley, University of California Press.

Robertson, Maureen. 1992. Voicing the feminine: constructions of the gendered subject in lyric poetry by women of medieval and late imperial China. *Late Imperial China* 13, 1: 63–110.

Robinet, Isabelle, tr. 1993. Discours sur les incertitudes. In Claude Larre, Isabelle Robinet and Elisabeth Rochat de la Vallée, trs., *Les grands traités du Huainan zi,* Paris: Institut Ricci/Editions du Cerf: 157–93.

Rosaldo, Michelle Z., and Louise Lamphere, eds. 1974. *Woman, culture and society.* Stanford, Stanford University Press.

Ruitenbeek, Klaas. 1986. Craft and ritual in traditional Chinese carpentry. *Chinese Science* 7: 1–24.

———. 1993. *Carpentry and building in late imperial China: a study of the fifteenth-century carpenter's manual Lu Ban jing.* Leiden, E. J. Brill.

Sacks, Karen. 1974. Engels revisited: women, the organization of production, and private property. In Rosaldo and Lamphere: 207–22.

———. 1979. *Sisters and wives: the past and future of social equality.* Westport, Conn., Greenwood Press.

Saito, Osamu. 1992a. Gender, workload and agricultural progress: Japan's historical experience in perspective. Discussion Paper Series A, no. 268, Institute of Economic Research, Hitotsubashi University, Tokyo.

———. 1992b. Infant mortality in pre-transition Japan: levels and trends. Discussion Paper Series A, no. 273, Institute of Economic Research, Hitotsubashi University, Tokyo.

Salaff, Janet W. 1985. The state and fertility motivation in Singapore and China. In Elisabeth Croll, Delia Davin and Penny Kane, eds., *China's one-child family policy,* New York, St. Martin's Press: 162–89.

Sandelowski, Margarete. 1991. Compelled to try: the never-enough quality of conceptive technology. *Medical Anthropology Quarterly* 5, 1: 29–47.

Scarry, Elaine. 1985. *The body in pain: the making and unmaking of the world.* New York, Oxford University Press.

Scheper-Hughes, Nancy. 1992. *Death without weeping: the violence of everyday life in Brazil.* Berkeley, University of California Press.

Scheper-Hughes, Nancy, and Margaret M. Lock. 1989. The mindful body: a prolegomenon to future work in medical anthropology. *Medical Anthropology Quarterly* 3: 6–41.

Schiebinger, Londa. 1987. Skeletons in the closet: the first illustrations of the female skeleton in eighteenth-century anatomy. In Catherine Gallagher and Thomas Laqueur, eds., *The making of the modern body,* Berkeley, University of California Press: 42–82.

Schipper, Kristofer. 1982. *Le corps taoïste.* Paris, Fayard.

Schneider, Jane. 1987. The anthropology of cloth. *Annual Review of Anthropology* 16: 409–48.

Schneider, Jane, and Annette B. Weiner. 1989. Introduction. In Weiner and Schneider: 1–29.

Sciama, Lidia. 1981. The problem of privacy in Mediterranean anthropology. In Ardener, ed.: 87–111.

Scott, Joan Wallach. 1989. History in crisis? The others' side of the story. *American Historical Review* 94: 690.

Seaman, Gary. 1981. The sexual politics of karmic retribution. In Ahern and Gates: 381–96.

———. 1992. Winds, waters, seeds and souls: folk concepts of physiology and etiology in Chinese geomancy. In Charles Leslie and Allan Young, eds., *Paths to Asian medical knowledge,* Berkeley, University of California Press: 74–97.

Segal, Lynne. 1994. *Straight sex: the politics of pleasure.* London, Virago Press.

Sen, Amartya. 1990. More than 100 million women are missing. *New York Review of Books,* 20 Dec. 1990: 61–66.

Sheng, Angela Yu-yun. 1990. Textile use, technology, and change in rural textile production in Song China (960–1279). Ph.D. dissertation, University of Pennsylvania.

————. 1995. The disappearance of silk weaves with weft effects in early China. *Chinese Science* 12: 39–74.

Shepherd, John R. 1990. Marriage and mandatory abortion among the seventeenth century Siraya. Unpublished manuscript, California Institute of Technology, Pasadena.

Shuttleworth, Sally. 1990. Female circulation: medical discourse and popular advertising in the mid-Victorian era. In Mary Jacobus, Evelyn Fox Keller and Sally Shuttleworth, eds., *Body/politics: women and the discourses of science,* London, Routledge: 47–68.

Sigaut, François. 1985. More (and enough) on technology! *History and Technology* 2, 2: 115–32.

————. 1987. Préface. In Haudricourt: 9–34.

Silber, Cathy. 1994. From daughter to daughter-in-law in the women's script of southern Hunan. In Gilmartin et al.: 47–68.

Sillitoe, P. 1988. *Made in Niugini: technology in the highlands of Papua New Guinea.* London, British Museum Publications.

Simmons, Jack. 1978. Technology in history. *History of Technology* 3: 1–12.

Singer, C., E. J. Holmyard, A. R. Hall and T. I. Williams, eds. 1954–78. *A history of technology.* Oxford, Clarendon Press.

Siu, Helen. 1990. Where were the women? Rethinking marriage resistance and regional culture in South China. *Late Imperial China* 11, 2: 32–62.

Sivin, Nathan. 1988. *Traditional medicine in contemporary China.* Ann Arbor, University of Michigan Press.

Skinner, G. William. 1977. *The city in late imperial China.* Stanford, Stanford University Press.

————. 1985. The structure of Chinese history. *Journal of Asian Studies* 44, 2: 271–92.

Smith, Paul J. 1991. *Taxing heaven's storehouse: horses, bureaucrats and the destruction of the Sichuan tea industry.* Cambridge, Mass., Harvard-Yenching Institute Monograph Series.

So, Alvin Y. 1986. *The South China silk district: local historical transformation and world-system theory.* Albany, SUNY Press.

Sontag, Susan. 1989. *"Illness as metaphor" and "AIDS and its metaphors."* New York, Doubleday.

Stacey, Judith. 1983. *Patriarchy and socialist revolution in China.* Berkeley, University of California Press.

Staudenmaier, John M. 1990. Recent trends in the history of technology. *American Historical Review* 95: 715–25.

Stockard, Janice E. 1989. *Daughters of the Canton Delta: marriage patterns and economic strategies in South China, 1860–1930.* Stanford, Stanford University Press.

Stone-Ferrier, Linda. 1989. Spun virtue, the lacework of folly, and the world wound upside-down: seventeenth-century Dutch depictions of female handwork. In Weiner and Schneider: 215–42.

Strathern, Marilyn. 1992. *Reproducing the future: anthropology, kinship and the new reproductive technologies.* New York, Routledge.

Sung, Lung-sheng. 1981. Property and family division. In Ahern and Gates: 361–80.

Sung Ying-Hsing. 1966. *T'ien-kung K'ai-wu: Chinese technology in the seventeenth century.* Tr. E-Tu Zen Sun and Shiou-Chuan Sun. University Park, Pennsylvania State University Press.

Tamanoi, Mariko Asano. 1990. Body as a vehicle of resistance: women in the silk industry in modern Japan. Paper presented at the 42nd Annual Meeting of the Association of Asian Studies, Chicago.

———. 1991. Songs as weapons: the culture and history of *komori* (nursemaids) in modern Japan. *Journal of Asia Studies* 50, 4: 793–817.

Tanaka Issei. 1985. The social and historical context of Ming-Ch'ing local drama. In D. Johnson et al.: 143–60.

Taussig, Michael. 1980. Reification and the consciousness of the patient. *Social Science and Medicine* 14: 3–13.

Telford, Ted A. 1990. Patching the holes in Chinese genealogies: mortality in the lineage population of Tongcheng County, 1300–1880. *Late Imperial China* 11, 2: 116–37.

Thilo, Thomas. 1977. *Klassische chinesische Baukunst: Strukturprinzipen und soziale Funktion.* Berlin, Edition Tusch.

Thompson, Stuart E. 1988. Death, food, and fertility. In Watson and Rawski: 71–108.

T'ien, Ju-k'ang. 1988. *Male anxiety and female chastity: a comparative study of ethical values in Ming-Ch'ing times.* Leiden, E. J. Brill.

Tietze, Christopher. 1983. *Induced Abortion: A World Review,* 1983. 5th ed. New York, The Population Council.

Tong Shuye. 1981. *Zhongguo shougongye shangye fazhan shi* [History of the development of handicrafts and commerce in China]. Jinan, Jilu Press.

Topley, Marjorie. 1978. Marriage resistance in rural Kwangtung. In A. Wolf, ed.: 247–68.

Tsing Yuan. 1979. Urban riots and disturbances. In Jonathan D. Spence and John E. Wills, Jr., eds., *From Ming to Ch'ing: conquest, region, and continuity in seventeenth-century China,* New Haven, Yale University Press.

Tsur, Nyok-Ching. [1907] 1983. Forms of business in the city of Ningpo in China. Tr. Peter Schran. *Chinese Sociology and Anthropology* 15, 4.

Tweeten, Luther, Cynthia L. Dishon, Wen S. Chern, Naraomi Imamura and Masaru Morishima, eds. 1993. *Japanese and American agriculture: tradition and progress in conflict.* Boulder, Colo., Westview Press.

Twitchett, Denis. 1959. The Fan clan's charitable estate. In David Nivison and Arthur Wright, eds., *Confucianism in action,* Stanford, Stanford University Press.

Übelhör, Monika. 1989. The community compact of the Sung. In William Theodore de Bary and John Chaffee, eds., *Neo-Confucian education: the formative stage,* Berkeley, University of California Press: 371–88.

Unschuld, Paul. 1979. *Medical ethics in imperial China: a study in historical anthropology.* Berkeley, University of California Press.

———. 1985. *Medicine in China: a history of ideas.* Berkeley, University of California Press.

———. 1986. *Medicine in China: Nan-Ching, the classic of difficult issues.* Berkeley, University of California Press.

———. 1991. *Forgotten traditions of Chinese medicine.* Dordrecht, Kluwer.

van der Leeuw, Sander. 1993. Giving the potter a choice: conceptual aspects of pottery techniques. In Lemonnier, ed.: 238–88.

Van Gulik, R. H. 1961. *Sexual life in ancient China: a preliminary survey of Chinese sex and society from ca. 1500 BC till 1644 AD.* Leiden, E. J. Brill.

Veith, Ilsa, tr. 1987. *The Yellow Emperor's classic of internal medicine.* Berkeley, University of California Press.

Wagner, Donald B. 1995. The traditional Chinese iron industry and its modern fate. *Chinese Science* 12: 136–59.

Wakefield, David. N.d. Draft Ph.D. dissertation on family divisions. Department of History, University of California, Los Angeles.

Wallerstein, Immanuel. Forthcoming. The West, capitalism, and the modern world system. In Blue et al.

Waltner, Ann. 1990. *Getting an heir: adoption and the construction of kinship in late imperial China.* Honolulu, University of Hawaii Press.

Wang Feng, James Lee and Cameron Campbell. Forthcoming. Marital fertility control among the Qing nobility: implications for two types of preventive check. In Lee and Saito.

Wang Shixiang. 1991. *Classic Chinese furniture—Ming and early Qing dynasties.* Tr. Sarah Handler and Wang Shixiang. Hong Kong/Chicago, Joint Publishing/Art Media Resources Ltd. Tr. from *Ming shi jiaju zhen shang,* Beijing/Hong Kong, Cultural Relics Press/Joint Publishing, 1988.

Watson, James L. 1982. Of flesh and bones: the management of death pollution in Cantonese society. In Maurice Bloch and Jonathan Parry, eds., *Death and the regeneration of life,* Cambridge, Cambridge University Press.

———. 1985. Standardizing the gods: the promotion of T'ien Hou ("Empress of Heaven") along the South China coast, 960–1960. In D. Johnson et al.: 292–324.

———. 1988. The structure of Chinese funerary rites: elementary forms, ritual sequence, and the primacy of performance. In Watson and Rawski: 3–19.

Watson, James L., and Evelyn S. Rawski, eds. 1988. *Death ritual in late imperial and modern China.* Berkeley, University of California Press.

Watson, Rubie S. 1985. *Inequality among brothers: class and kinship in South China.* Cambridge, Cambridge University Press.

———. 1986. The named and the nameless: gender and person in Chinese society. *American Ethnologist* 13, 4: 619–31.

———. 1988. Remembering the dead: graves and politics in southeastern China. In Watson and Rawski: 203–26.

———. 1991. Wives, concubines, and maids: servitude and kinship in the Hong Kong regions, 1900–1940. In Watson and Ebrey: 231–55.

Watson, Rubie S., and Patricia B. Ebrey, eds. 1991. *Marriage and inequality in Chinese society.* Berkeley, University of California Press.

Weiner, Annette B. 1992. *Inalienable possessions: the paradox of keeping-while-giving.* Berkeley, University of California Press.

Weiner, Annette B., and Jane Schneider, eds. 1989. *Cloth and human experience.* Washington, D.C., Smithsonian Institution Press.

Weixian Museum. 1984. *Shandong Weixian Shizihang yizhi fajue jianbao* [Preliminary report of the Shizihang site in Weixian, Shandong]. *Kaogu* 8: 678–79.

Wheatley, Paul. 1971. *The pivot of the four quarters: a preliminary inquiry into the origins and character of the ancient Chinese city.* Chicago, Aldine.

Widmer, Ellen. 1989. The epistolary world of female talent in seventeenth-century China. *Late Imperial China* 10, 2: 1–43.

Will, Pierre-Etienne. 1991. Of silk and potatoes: efforts at improving agriculture in eighteenth-century China. Paper given at Cornell University, East Asia Program, Ithaca.

———. 1994. Développement quantitatif et développement qualitatif en Chine à la fin de l'époque impériale. *Annales Histoire, Sciences Sociales* 49, 4 (July–Aug.): 863–902.

Wilson, Verity. 1986. *Chinese dress.* London, Victoria and Albert Museum.

Wolf, Arthur. 1974. Gods, ghosts and ancestors. In Arthur Wolf, ed., *Religion and ritual in Chinese society,* Stanford, Stanford University Press: 131–82.

———, ed. 1978. *Studies in Chinese society.* Stanford, Stanford University Press.

Wolf, Arthur P., and C. S. Huang. 1980. *Marriage and adoption in China, 1845–1945.* Stanford, Stanford University press.

Wolf, Margery. 1968. *The house of Lim.* New York, Appleton-Century-Crofts.

———. 1972. *Women and the family in rural Taiwan.* Stanford, Stanford University Press.

———. 1985. *Revolution postponed: women in contemporary China.* Stanford, Stanford University Press.

Wolf, Margery, and Roxane Witke, eds. 1975. *Women in Chinese society.* Stanford, Stanford University Press.

Wong, R. Bin. Forthcoming. The political economy of agrarian empire and its modern legacy. In Blue et al.

Worsley, Peter. 1982. Non-Western medical systems. *Annual Review of Anthropology* 11: 315–48.

Wright, Susan. 1981. Place and face: of women in Doshman Ziari, Iran. In Ardener, ed.: 135–55.

Wu, Pei-Yi. 1992. An ambivalent pilgrim to T'ai-shan in the seventeenth century. In Naquin and Yü: 65–88.

Xu Wen, ed. 1991. *Zhongguo gu jiaju tu'an* [Chinese traditional furniture patterns]. Taipei, Nantian Press.

Xu Zhongjie. 1985. *Nanjing yunjin shi* [History of Nanjing brocades]. Jiangsu, Science Press.

Xue Qinglu, ed. 1991. *Quanguo zhongyi tushu lianhe mulu* [Cumulative catalogue of national library holdings in Chinese medicine (arranged by genre)]. Beijing, Zhongyi Guji Press.

Yamaji, Susumu, and Shoichi Ito. 1993. The political economy of rice in Japan. In Tweeten et al.: 349–65.

Yanagisako, Sylvia J. 1979. Family and household: the analysis of domestic groups. *Annual Review of Anthropology* 8: 161–205.

Yin Dengguo. 1984. *Guiyin* [Beauties of the inner quarters]. Taipei, Xitai Press.

Zhang Zhongyi. 1957. *Huizhou Mingdai zhuzhai* [Ming houses of Huizhou]. Beijing, Architecture Press.

Zhong caoyaoxue [Chinese materia medica]. 1987. Shanghai, Shanghai Institute of Traditional Medicine/Commercial Press.

Zhu Xinyu, ed. 1992. *Zhongguo sichou shi* [History of silk spinning and weaving in China]. Beijing, Fangzhi Gongye Press.

Zito, Angela, and Tani E. Barlow, eds. 1994. *Body, subject and power in China.* Chicago, University of Chicago Press.

Index

abortion, 290, 293, 295n, 355; Buddhist opposition to, 325, 341; induced by medical means, 321–26; orthodox acceptance of, 321–26; self-induced, 324; spontaneous, 331–32. *See also* drugs; menstrual regulation

adoption, 98n, 106, 343–46, 349; distinct from fostering, 346; serving interests of women, 356–57. *See also* "nature"

agriculture: agricultural treatises, 25, 44, 185n, 213; diversification of rural economy, 34, 37n, 213–14, 221, 247; male work, 5, 245; patterns of technological development, 25, 26; northern dryland farming, 33–34; southern wet-rice farming, 34–36; state policies, 25–37; symbolic value of, 24, 31–32; women's participation in, 5, 132, 218–19 (fig. 16). *See also* individual authors and titles; rice

Ahern, Emily, 115n, 121n. *See also* Martin, Emily

ancestors: ancestral altar, 75, 96–105, 127; ancestral hall or temple (*citang*), 74, 97 (fig. 5); informed of events, 102, 114; offerings to, 102, 104–5 (fig. 6), 106–7; presentation of bride to, 116, 351

Ardener, Shirley, 53

Ban Zhao, 140, 184

body: Chinese religious and popular understandings of, 286n, 300; demographic epistemologies of, 297; eighteenth-century German constructions of, 298; phenomenological, 297n, 299–302; "politic," 299–301

Borotová, Lucie, 349

bound feet, 90n, 271, 359, 366n; enhancing fertility, 366n

Bourdieu, Pierre, 2, 38, 57, 300

Braudel, Fernand, 13–14

breast-feeding, 345, 346 (fig. 23), 347. *See also* maternal roles; wet nurses

brides: delayed marriage, 260n, 269n, 339n, 342; ill-treatment of, 117, 147; incorporation into lineage, 91, 116; presentation to ancestors, 116, 351. *See also* dowries; marriage

Bu nongshu [supplemented treatise on agriculture]. *See* Shen, Master; Zhang Lüxiang

Buddhism: chastity and, 342–43, 358n; neo-Confucian campaigns against, 100, 103n, 135n, 157; "precious volumes," 342–43; spiritual perils of sex and procreation, 341–43; stigmatization of women as inferior, 129, 133; women as adherents of, 105, 133–36, 342–43. *See also* pollution

Can shu [book of sericulture], 211, 240, 251

Carlitz, Katherine, 308n, 364n

Compositor   Maple-Vail Composition Service
Text: 10/13 Aldus
Display: Aldus
Printer and binder: Maple-Vail Book Manufacturing Group